TH NAPOLEONIC WARS

THE RISE AND FALL OF AN EMPIRE

THE NAPOLEONIC WARS

THE RISE AND FALL OF AN EMPIRE

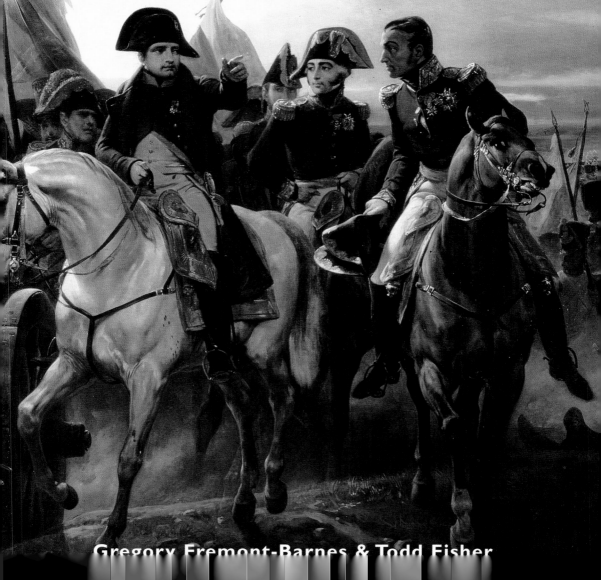

Gregory Fremont-Barnes & Todd Fisher

First published in Great Britain in 2004 by Osprey Publishing,
Elms Court, Chapel Way, Botley, Oxford OX2 9LP, UK
Email: info@ospreypublishing.com

Previously published as Essential Histories 3: *The Napoleonic
Wars (1) The rise of the Emperor 1805–1807*, Essential Histories
9: *The Napoleonic Wars (2) The empires fight back 1808–1812*,
Essential Histories 17: *The Napoleonic Wars (3) The Peninsular
War 1807–1814*, Essential Histories 39: *The Napoleonic Wars (4)
The fall of the French empire 1813–1815*

ISBN 1 84176 831 6

Editor: Alexander Stilwell
Design: Ken Vail Graphic Design, Cambridge, UK
Cartography by The Map Studio
Index by Alan Thatcher
Picture research by Image Select International
Origination by Grasmere Digital Imaging, Leeds, UK
Printed and bound in China by L. Rex Printing Company Ltd.

04 05 06 07 08   10 9 8 7 6 5 4 3 2 1

For a complete list of titles available from Osprey Publishing
please contact:

Osprey Direct UK, PO Box 140,
Wellingborough, Northants, NN8 2FA, UK.
Email: info@ospreydirect.co.uk

Osprey Direct USA, c/o MBI Publishing,
PO Box 1, 729 Prospect Ave,
Osceola, WI 54020, USA.
Email: info@ospreydirectusa.com

www.ospreypublishing.com

Contents

Part IV: The fall of the French empire 1813–1815

Foreword
by Bernard Cornwell

At around half past seven on the smoke-shrouded evening of 18 June 1815, Napoleon's Imperial Guard marched to their last attack. These were the Emperor's shock troops, battle-hardened veterans going to deliver the killing blow against an enemy desperately weakened by an afternoon's fighting. The sinking sun was hidden by cloud and further obscured by powder smoke that thickened as the artillery on the low hill began to drive round shot, shells and canister into the Guard's ranks. But cannon alone would never stop elite troops like the Guard who were marching in columns, each a thick mass of men driven by the sound of drums, and watched by their Emperor as their Eagle-topped banners advanced across sodden ground obstructed by hundreds of dead horses and men. Napoleon's finest troops, supported by the survivors of the afternoon's attacks, advanced across flattened rye that had been scorched black by cannon fire, and so up the gentle slope to where the enemy, they were assured, needed just one blow to collapse.

The majority of the Imperial Guard had never met that enemy. It was British infantry, many of them veterans of the Peninsular War and trained to one deadly skill; the delivery of musket volleys. And on the ridge of Waterloo, under the foul-smelling gun smoke, the irresistible Imperial Guard met the immovable redcoats. It was the climax of the Napoleonic Wars and a moment when history trembled in the balance. The Guard could not know it, but they were about to be defeated and with them ended the Eagles, the Empire and twenty-two years of warfare.

That warfare had started in 1793, and the Napoleonic Wars are the second half of the long struggle that was sparked by the French Revolution. During those years capitals as far apart as Moscow and Washington were put to the torch, and battles were fought in India, Egypt, the Caribbean and South America. It was, truly, a World War, yet at the heart of it was Europe, and at the heart of Europe was France, and at France's heart was Napoleon Bonaparte, the man who has given his name to the titanic struggles that ended on Waterloo's ridge.

The story of the Napoleonic Wars begins in 1802 with the Peace of Amiens, known to some in Britain as 'the peace which passeth all understanding', an ironic quotation from the Bible. The peace treaty, signed between Britain and France, was, at best, cynical, for both countries must have known the wars would begin again since their competing ambitions were utterly unresolved, and at stake was nothing less than the domination of the planet. The mighty British war fleets already controlled the world's oceans, but there had to be some purpose to that domination, and it was trade. The English, Napoleon sneered, are a nation of shopkeepers, but the shopkeepers had to be beaten if France's ambitions were to be realised, and the chief of those ambitions was to become the world's super-power. If Britain fell then France could take her growing empire and all the vast trade of the world, the spices and sugar and cotton and metals, would flow through Paris and from their profits France would become ever richer, more powerful and glorious.

This, then, is the story of a power struggle, and the odds, at the tale's beginning, seem to favour the French. Britain, it is true, has those great battle fleets, but her army is small, and the armies of her European allies have mostly suffered defeat at the hands of the resurgent French. The Revolution thrust France into turmoil, but out of the wreckage emerges a conscript army which has astonished Europe with its victories, many of them gained by a young Corsican officer who was christened Nabulion Buonaparte. He was born in 1769, also the year of the birth of Arthur Wellesley, later the Duke of Wellington. Wellesley was born to aristocratic privilege, but Napoleon's family, even though they claimed noble lineage, was impoverished. Corsica was a wild place on Europe's edge, and then, as now, there was a struggle in the island against French domination, but Napoleon, after flirting with the cause of Corsican independence, moved to France and trained as an artillery officer. His rise, from that moment, was extraordinary. In 1792 he was a Lieutenant, and a year later, aged 24, he was a Brigadier-General thanks to his brilliance in evicting the British fleet from Toulon harbour. Two years later he used his artillery to suppress a revolt in Paris and was rewarded with command of the French armies fighting the Austrians in northern Italy. The war there was going badly for the French, but the young general, still in his mid-twenties, showed that he had a supreme talent for battle. The Austrians were humiliated.

That campaign made Napoleon famous and it did not hurt that, as a young man, he had rock star good looks. He became corpulent later, but he never lost his youthful appetite for military conquest. After the Italian success he conceived an ambitious plan to take Egypt which, he declared, would offer a stepping stone to India where France's native allies were fighting the British. He captured Egypt, but when his fleet was destroyed at Aboukir Bay by Horatio Nelson, he was effectively stranded in the desert. The campaign was a failure, but Napoleon evaded the British naval blockade and, leaving his army behind, sailed to France and spun the Egyptian adventure as a success. He arrived in Paris when France was again in turmoil as yet another post-revolutionary government collapsed and, from its wreckage, Napoleon seized power. He became First Consul, one of three men who led the French government,

but being one of three would never satisfy Napoleon and once again he used warfare to establish his supremacy. Austria was still France's most dangerous enemy on the European mainland and Napoleon, in his second Italian campaign, defeated them utterly and secured a peace treaty which ceded vast areas to France. It was another spectacular victory and Napoleon was rewarded by being made Emperor. He was 35 now, the sole ruler of France, and the most feared soldier in Europe.

That is where the story of the Napoleonic Wars begins. The Peace of Amiens, which Britain and France signed after Austria's defeat, lasted little more than a year. Napoleon had been trying to extend the French empire overseas, specifically in the sugar-rich West Indies, and Britain, seeing its trade supremacy threatened and, as ever, fearing an over-mighty power on mainland Europe, went back to war, and there would be little peace now for the next twelve years. That is the story you are about to read and it is a magnificent tale, shot through with horror and blood and heroism, and with an ending so dramatic and unlikely that no Hollywood screenwriter or historical novelist would dare to contrive it. It is, at times, a complicated tale. It begins simply enough with Napoleon devising a plan to invade Britain and thus end the wars at a single stroke, but Nelson's victory at Trafalgar sealed the doom of that endeavour, and from then on Britain followed a twofold strategy. She encouraged her European allies to attack France on land while she attempted to strangle French trade with her sea-power, but, when Napoleon's invasion of Spain and Portugal turned sour, Britain saw an opportunity to intervene with her small army. That resulted in what we know as the Peninsular War, the chief contribution of the British army to Napoleon's defeat and the arena in which my fictional hero, Richard Sharpe, has his adventures. It was, in truth, a sideshow, but one that drained French strength and out of it emerged a re-invigorated British army, led by a man who proved himself to be the pre-eminent soldier of the day, the Duke of Wellington. The Duke had never fought Napoleon himself, but on that rain-soaked ridge, south of Brussels, in June 1815, the two finally met in the horrendous clash of Waterloo, and from that carnage emerged a world dominated by one super-power, Britain, that would last until, a century later, new armies and new ambitions again tore Europe apart.

Thousands of books have been written about the wars. I have at least two thousand on my shelves, but whenever I am plotting new mischief for Sharpe I invariably start with an Osprey book because I know it will provide a well-written and comprehensible account of whatever campaign I am describing. Then, when I need to know the colour of a French hussar's uniform or the exact weapon carried by a Spanish grenadier, it is back to the shelves for another Osprey book. Now, in one volume, Osprey Publishing is gathering its narratives of the Napoleonic Wars and in this book you will find all of the Osprey virtues; a concise and clear story presented with superb illustrations. It is, indeed, essential history, and its authors, Todd Fisher and Gregory Fremont-Barnes, bring it to vivid life. So, imagine yourself at the beginning of the nineteenth century, with an overmighty Emperor about to indulge his passion for war . . . and read on.

Introduction

Background

When Napoleon Bonaparte became First Consul by coup d'etat on 9 November 1799 he issued an ominous proclamation to the soldiers of France: 'It is no longer a question of defending your frontiers, but of invading enemy states.' The gauntlet was thus laid down before the world, and England in particular. No longer was France fighting to defend the French Revolution but to expand her frontiers for larger and less definable aims.

In 1793, Austria, Prussia, Spain, the United Provinces and England had formed the First Coalition and in the same year the young Napoleon Bonaparte had shown his potential by freeing Toulon from a Royal Navy siege. He showed his star quality once again the same year when he took command of the French Army fighting Austrian and Sardinian forces.

In May 1798 Napoleon sailed from Toulon to Egypt with plans to conquer the Ottoman Empire. The French fleet was destroyed by Admiral Nelson at Aboukir Bay, the French Army failed to take Acre and Napoleon returned to Paris in advance of the army.

In 1800 Napoleon launched an attack over the Alps to take on a larger Austrian force at Marengo on 14 June and snatched victory from the jaws of defeat. This was followed by the Treaty of Luneville in February 1801.

By 1802, Napoleon had not only signed the Peace of Amiens, which brought peace with England, but he also had a Concordat with the Vatican and had declared Consulship for life.

The peace with England constituted a period of consolidation before war broke out with even greater ferocity in May 1803. The pattern from now to 1806 was to be one of domination on land by the French and domination at sea by the British, culminating in the epic victory of Trafalgar in October 1805.

Following the Berlin Decrees of December 1806, which had established the Continental System, Napoleon sought ways to use this mainland European blockade against the British. The real hole in his net was the Iberian peninsula.

Spain, under a weak King Charles and a wicked first minister, Godoy, had been France's official ally since 1795. Spain's participation in the war had often been half-hearted, and its major contribution, its navy, had been smashed by the British at Trafalgar. Godoy had flirted with the idea of joining Prussia in 1806 and attacking France from the south. At the time, Napoleon had been embroiled in his campaign in Germany, but he had learned of the scheme and had bullied Spain into fulfilling her role as ally.

He had demanded they send the cream of their army to northern Germany as Imperial support troops. Deprived of her main strike force, Spain had then had to sit out the war.

Napoleon's aim was to close off the Portuguese ports and on 21 October 1807 Godoy signed the Treaty of Fontainebleau allowing French troops access to Portugal via Spain. An army, under Junot, took Lisbon that November and more French troops followed into Spain.

By this time, Spain was on the verge of civil war. Two opposing camps were forming, one around the king, the other around Ferdinand, the king's son. When Ferdinand overthrew his father and arrested Godoy, both camps appealed to Napoleon for support. A conference with all parties was called in Bayonne in May 1808. Napoleon made the mistake of assuming that after the corrupt Bourbon family, the former rulers of France, the Spanish people would welcome a more liberal, efficient government. He installed his brother Joseph upon the throne.

In fact the opposite was true. Joseph was crowned in Burgos on 7 July 1808 and entered

Madrid only after a Spanish revolt had been suppressed in the city. He was not to stay long. The French suffered several reverses in the field and Joseph had to evacuate Madrid soon after his arrival. By August, little of Spain was left in French hands.

Napoleon planned his counter-attack. His first step was to call a meeting in Erfurt with his new ally, Tsar Alexander of Russia. Following the French victories of 1805–07, the Tsar had signed an alliance with Napoleon at Tilsit. Austria had had first chance to play this role of French ally, but had spurned the opportunity, preferring instead another attempt to regain its losses of the last 15 years' conflict. She now stood alone on the continent among the great powers, wishing to renew the war against Napoleon.

The meeting at Erfurt, from September through October of 1808, was intended to secure the French peace while Napoleon moved into Spain to re-establish his brother Joseph on the throne. Although Alexander agreed to hold up his end of the alliance and keep an eye on Austria, he was not being sincere. Talleyrand, Napoleon's special envoy, had been plotting against Napoleon and France. Throughout the Erfurt conference he had held meetings with Alexander, urging him to feign compliance and divulging Napoleon's state secrets.

When the conference ended, Napoleon hurried south to join the army assembling along the Spanish border. France's honor was on the line, and with an eye to restoring it Napoleon began his campaign at the beginning of November. Madrid fell once again into French hands, but the effort meant that much of Napoleon's main army was now committed to the Spanish enterprise. Not only were they fighting the Spanish armies and the guerrillas, but they now had to deal with the British, who had landed an army in Portugal, under Sir Arthur Wellesley, the future Duke of Wellington.

While Napoleon was embroiled in Spain, Austria was considering her options.

Still smarting from the defeats by Napoleon in 1796, 1800, and 1805, she looked for a chance of revenge. With wildly exaggerated reports of French defeats in Spain reaching the Austrians, they saw an opportunity to strike.

Napoleon could not have foreseen in 1807 the significance of the Peninsular War, however wise we have become with the benefit of hindsight. Napoleon's lightning campaigns of 1805–1807 were based on a system that relied on rapid march and concentration of force. The army lived off the land rather than being dependent on lengthy supply lines, cumbersome commissariat wagons and static depots. In short, his armies fed themselves on the move, and maximum force could thus be concentrated at a desired point. However, Napoleon's experiences in east Prussia and Poland in the first half of 1807 had shown how difficult it was to conduct operations when laboring under the twin disadvantages of poor land and roads. The Iberian Peninsula had both these disadvantages. The Grande Armée could sustain itself under such conditions for a limited period – but not for years on end. Extreme poverty, primitive communications by road – in many cases merely a shabby dirt track – unnavigable rivers, and forbidding mountain ranges created formidable obstacles to large bodies of men and horses.

The problems experienced by the French were greatly exacerbated by the fact that they faced not only the regular armed forces of the Allies, but also the ordinary peoples of the Iberian peninsula themselves. As Clausewitz put it a few years later: 'In Spain the war became of itself an affair of the people ...' Ordinary French soldiers like Albert de Rocca, a veteran of many campaigns, captured the essence of the kind of fanatical resistance that he and his comrades faced:

We were not called to fight against [professional] troops ... but against a people insulated from all the other continental nations by its manners, its prejudices, and even the nature of its country. The Spaniards were to oppose to us a resistance so much more the obstinate, as they believed it to be the object of the French government to make the Peninsula a secondary state, irrevocably subject to the dominion of France.

Indeed, the French soon discovered that neither the geography nor the population were at all hospitable. No conflict prior to the twentieth century posed such a daunting combination of native resistance and natural obstacles. Topographical features in Iberia ranged from the snow-capped Pyrenees to the burning wastes of the Sierra Morena. If geography and climate were not extreme enough, combatants were constantly subject to virulent diseases including typhus, dysentery, and malaria.

Napoleon's decision to occupy Spain proved a great miscalculation. Past experiences of occupation in western and central Europe were characterized, with some notable exceptions, by passive populations who submitted to French authority in general and in some cases to Bonapartist rule specifically. Spain was the only country occupied by France that Napoleon had not entirely conquered. For the Emperor, waging war against regular armies was the stuff that had made his armies legendary in their own time. However, in the Peninsula a national cause, very different from that which had so animated the French during the 1790s, but just as potent, rapidly and inexorably spread the spirit of revolt across the provinces. All across Spain's vast rural expanse, with its conspicuous absence of a large middle class, which might have acted as a moderate force, a virulent form of nationalism took firm hold. Far from embracing any liberal notions of political or social reform on the model of the French Revolution, this movement championed a cause diametrically opposed to change, with an anachronistic and almost blind faith in Crown and Church. In a society that was overwhelmingly rural, the mass of simple, ignorant peasantry held up the Bourbon monarchy as the defenders of the true faith, descendants of their forebears who had liberated medieval Spain from the hated Moors.

In short, the war became something of a crusade, but of liberation rather than conquest, and the clergy enthusiastically invoked divine help in ridding the land of occupiers whom they portrayed as agents of the Devil. Such bitter sentiments had not been seen in Europe since the dreadful days of the wars of religion in the sixteenth and seventeenth centuries. So great was the depth of feeling that even Protestant British troops were considered heretics: the Spanish even sometimes objected to the burial of those troops – their own allies – in consecrated Catholic ground. The atheistic, liberal principles of the French Revolution were seen by many reactionary Spanish nobles and clergymen as grave threats to their authority and property, to social harmony and the spiritual righteousness of the one true religion. The French became a convenient focus of attention for all Spanish society's problems, not least its grinding poverty.

The contrast between the conduct of the regular, professional forces and those of the guerrillas was remarkable. Two distinct types of war, one conventional and the other unconventional, were quickly to emerge. The British and French met in set-piece battles and skirmishes and generally treated each other with courtesy off the battlefield. In fact, fraternization was commonplace, despite Wellington's strict orders to the contrary. Provided they were observed in advance, foraging parties were generally left in peace and sentries at outposts frequently bartered goods, smoked together and chatted. Informal truces between pickets enabled each side to exchange small numbers of badly injured prisoners.

The guerrilla war, however, marked a low point in barbarity for both sides. Partisans, whose proliferation proved unstoppable, ruthlessly cut down small groups of soldiers at isolated posts, stragglers, and the wounded. French troops regularly committed atrocities in the countryside, including pillage, murder, and arson. Atrocities committed by both sides rapidly assumed an enormous scale and a horrendous nature, with reprisal feeding bloody reprisal, thus continuing the cycle of bitterness and swelling the partisan ranks. The conflict in the Peninsula, therefore, being both a clash of professional armies and a struggle involving entire peoples, contained elements of both conventional and unconventional warfare, making it a precursor in many ways to the conflicts of the twentieth century.

The Peninsular War spanned most of the years of the Napoleonic Empire. When it began the Emperor of France stood triumphant over nearly the whole of the European continent. The reputation of the British Army had not yet recovered from its defeat in the War of American Independence and from its poor showing in the French Revolutionary Wars, and Sir Arthur Wellesley, the future Duke of Wellington, was only a minor general whose destiny was not yet clear. Yet in the course of the war Wellington heaped victory upon victory. By the time the war had ended, in 1814, the British Army had, despite many retreats, marched from the shores of Portugal to southern France, emerging as one of the most professional, well-motivated, and efficient fighting forces ever to have left British shores, led by the nation's greatest soldier. That the French were doomed from the start is certainly open to question; but that the Peninsular War ultimately played a critical role in the defeat of France is incontestable.

Napoleon himself acknowledged the fact years later during his exile on St. Helena when he admitted that

… that miserable Spanish affair turned opinion against me and rehabilitated England. It enabled them to continue the war. The markets of South America were opened to them; they put an army on the Peninsula … [which] became the agent of victory, the terrible node of all the intrigues that formed on the Continent … [the Spanish affair] is what killed me.

By 1810 Napoleon had established an empire in Europe that surpassed that of Charlemagne a millennium before. Yet within the space of a few years it would collapse and the battles that were fought during the climactic years 1813–15, included two of the most decisive in history.

The seeds of destruction were sown during the Russian campaign in 1812, after which,

despite having lost over half a million men, Napoleon prepared for a new campaign in the coming spring. The Russians, emboldened by Napoleon's retreat, were prepared to carry the war, which was to become the War of the Sixth Coalition, into Germany, with Prussia as a junior partner in a new alliance.

That this alliance had been preceded by five others provides a good indication of the Great Powers' failure to curb French expansion since the start of the wars two decades earlier. Yet for Prussia and for a number of other German states, this new struggle was to have an ideological component which had been absent from her war of 1806–1807: the campaign of 1813 was to become known by its patriotic title: the 'War of German Liberation'. The moral forces which had once given impetus to the armies of revolutionary France were now coming back to haunt them, though with some adaptations. The Prussians had no desire for a republic, but their nationalism had been awakened, and the war was to be for the liberation of 'Germany', more than half a century before an actual nation state by that name emerged.

At this stage, the coalition did not contain all the Great Powers, yet unity was essential for success. Some nations, such as Austria and Sweden, wished to wait and see how the tide of fortune moved, but ultimately they and most of the former members of the Confederation of the Rhine, including Bavaria and Saxony, would side with the Allies in numbers which Napoleon could never hope to match. Britain, too, would play a vital diplomatic and financial role in the war, ensuring Allied unity and providing millions of pounds in subsidies to nations that could supply the manpower required. Britain had committed tens of thousands of men to the ongoing struggle in Spain, and continued to man the fleets which blockaded French ports and starved Napoleon's empire of seaborne trade.

Yet Napoleon was not to be daunted by circumstances that lesser commanders might have deemed hopeless. Quickly raising new armies composed of young, inexperienced conscripts and invalided veterans, but seriously deficient in competent non-commissioned officers (NCOs) and trained officers, and with a critical shortage of cavalry, Napoleon resolved to preserve his empire in Germany, despite the rapidly spawning forces of nationalism. The Emperor's organizational genius resurrected a new army with which he achieved hard-fought victories at Lützen and Bautzen before, in late summer, Austria finally threw in her lot with the Allies, thereby creating the most formidable military alliance Europe had ever seen and the combination of Great Powers that was absolutely essential if Europe was to free itself of Napoleon's control.

Further epic struggles were to follow in the autumn campaign, including the battles of Dresden and Leipzig. When operations shifted to French soil in 1814, the beleaguered Emperor found himself outnumbered by more than three to one, yet in a series of brilliant actions he managed to hold the Allies at bay, displaying a military genius reminiscent of his earlier years. Nevertheless, with Paris threatened, his army overwhelmed by vastly superior numbers, and his marshals refusing to fight on, Napoleon was ultimately forced to abdicate, only to return the following year to fight his last, and history's greatest, battle.

Waterloo was more than a battle with far-reaching political effects: it was a human drama perhaps unparalleled in military history, and it is no accident that far more has been written about this eight-hour period of time than any other in history. The defense of La Haye Sainte and Hougoumont, the charge of the Scots Greys, Wellington's steadfast infantry defying the onslaught of the cuirassiers, the struggle for Plancenoit, and the repulse of the Imperial Guard – all became distinct and compelling episodes in a battle on which hinged nothing less than the future of European security. When it was all over, the Allies could at last implement their extensive and historic plans for the reconstruction of Europe. Though these plans did not guarantee peace for the Continent, they offered a remarkable degree of stability for the next 40 years. Indeed, the Vienna Settlement, in marked contrast to those before it and since – especially that achieved at Versailles in 1919 – stands as the most effective and long-lasting political settlement up to 1945.

For both the ordinary ranks of Napoleon's army and for senior commanders, campaigning had always been accompanied by a degree of hardship, particularly after nearly 20 years of unremitting war. Yet the immediate wake of the Russian campaign was to render the campaigns of 1813 and 1814 especially hard, with march, countermarch, bivouac, hunger, thirst, rain, mud, cold, and privation. It would also be a time when commanders would be tested to the limit and the flaws in Napoleon's command structure would become glaringly apparent.

In the past, field commanders had seldom been allowed to coordinate their operations except with the express orders of Napoleon and little was done to encourage them to develop independent thought or initiative. Without adequate understanding of the Emperor's grand strategy or their own roles in it, Napoleon's subordinates could do little but follow orders unquestioningly at a time when armies had grown so much larger than in past campaigns that Napoleon simply could not oversee everything, and needed commanders capable of independent decision-making. By 1813 some of these had been killed in action (Desaix, Lannes, Lasalle), others would die in the coming campaign (Bessières and Poniatowski), and still more were simply tired of fighting or were busy in Spain. Some were excellent as leaders of men in combat, but were not themselves strategists and were reluctant to take independent decisions lest they fail.

With marshals constantly shifted from command of one corps to another and corps changing in composition as circumstances seemed to require, no viable command structure could be created. Proper control of increasingly poorer-quality soldiers became all the more difficult. Under such circumstances, with Napoleon unable to be everywhere and monitor everything, errors were inevitable, and at no time in his military career were these errors so glaring as in 1813–15.

Chronology

1803   **20 May** War breaks out between France and Britain.

1804   **2 December** Napoleon's coronation as Emperor of the French.

1805   **9 October** Ney forces the Danube at Gunzburg.

14 October Ney closes the door on the Austrian army at Elchingen.

19 October Mack and the Austrian army capitulate at Ulm.

21 October Battle of Trafalgar.

30 October Massena fights Archduke Charles at Caldiero.

10 November Mortier escapes destruction at Durenstein.

2 December Battle of Austerlitz.

26 December Austria makes peace in the Treaty of Pressburg.

1806   **23 January** Pitt dies.

14 February Massena leads the invasion of Naples.

30 March Napoleon's brother Joseph is proclaimed King of Naples.

5 June Napoleon's brother Louis is proclaimed King of Holland.

12 July Creation of the Confederation of the Rhine.

6 August Holy Roman Empire is dissolved.

9 August Prussia begins to mobilize for war.

7 October Napoleon receives the Prussian ultimatum; he crosses the border the next day.

10 October Battle of Saalfield.

14 October Twin battles of Jena and Auerstädt.

27 October Napoleon enters Berlin

21 November Napoleon institutes the Continental Blockade.

28 November French troops enter Warsaw.

26 December Battles of Pultusk and Golymin.

1807   **8 February** Battle of Eylau.

21 March A British adventure in Egypt ends in defeat at Damietta.

27 May Selim III dethroned in Turkey.

10 June Battle of Heilsberg.

14 June Battle of Friedland.

7 July Treaties of Tilsit between France, Russia and Prussia.

7 September Copenhagen surrenders to a British army.

18 October French troops cross into Spain en route to Portugal.

27 October France and Spain conclude the Treaty of Fontainebleau.

30 November Junot occupies Lisbon.

1808   **16 February** French troops enter Spain.

17 March Charles IV of Spain abdicates.

23 March French troops occupy Madrid.

16 April Conference at Bayonne opens.

2 May Dos de Mayo: Madrid uprising.

6 June Joseph Bonaparte proclaimed King of Spain.

8 June Asturian junta appeals for aid from Britain.

15 June–13 August First siege of Saragossa.

14 July Bessières defeats the Spanish under Cuesta, and under Blake at Medina del Rio Seco.

21 July General Dupont surrenders his corps at Bailén.

1 August Wellesley's army lands in Portugal; Joseph evacuates Madrid.

17 August Wellesley defeats the French at Roliça.

21 August Wellesley defeats Junot at Vimeiro.

27 September The start of the Congress of Erfurt.

30 October French evacuate Portugal.

4 November Napoleon arrives in Spain to attack the Spanish armies on the line of the Ebro.

10 November Battles of Espinosa and Gamonal.

23 November Battle of Tudela. French defeat the Spanish.

29–30 November Battle of Somosierra.

4 December Napoleon enters Madrid.

10 December Sir John Moore advances from Salamanca.

20 December Second siege of Saragossa begins.

25 December–14 January Retreat to Corunna.

1809 **13 January** Victor defeats Venegas at Ucles.

16 January Battle of Corunna.

20 February Fall of Saragossa.

22 March French take Oporto.

28 March Battle of Medellín. Victor defeats Cuesta.

9 April The Fifth Coalition against France is proclaimed; the Austrian army attacks Bavaria.

16 April Battle of Sacile.

19 April Battle of Raszyn.

20 April Napoleon victorious at the Battle of Abensberg.

22 April Napoleon victorious at the Battle of Eckmuhl.

22 April Wellesley returns toPortugal.

3 May Battle of Ebelsberg.

8 May Battle of the Piave.

12 May Wellesley defeats Soult at Oporto.

13 May Napoleon enters Vienna.

21/22 May Battle of Aspern-Essling.

24 May Siege of Gerona begins.

27–28 July Wellesley defeats the French at Talavera.

14 June Battle of Raab.

5/6 July Napoleon victorious at the Battle of Wagram.

12 July The 1809 campaign ends with the Armistice of Znaim.

29 July The British land in Walcheren.

17 September Peace of Frederikshamm confirms Russia's conquest of Finland from Sweden.

18 October Spanish victory at Tamames.

20 October Construction of the Lines of Torres Vedras begins.

19 November Mortier defeats the Spanish at Ocaña and Alba de Tormes.

11 December Fall of Gerona.

1810 **January** French conquer Andalusia. A coup ousts the Central Junta.

5 February French troops invest Cadiz.

10 July Masséna captures Ciudad Rodrigo.

24 July Ney defeats Craufurd at the River Coa.

28 July Almeida surrenders.

21 August Bernadotte becomes Crown Prince of Sweden.

16 September Revolt in Mexico.

24 September The new Cortes convenes near Cadiz.

27 September Battle of Busaco. Wellington defeats Masséna.

10 October Wellesley occupies the Lines of Torres Vedras.

14 October Masséna encounters the Lines and halts.

16 November French troops retreat from the Lines of Torres Vedras.

1811 **26 January** French lay siege to Badajoz.

19 February Soult defeats the Spanish at the Gebora River.

5 March Graham victorious at Barrosa; French leave Portugal.

9 March Badajoz falls to the French.

15 March Masséna withdraws to Spain.

1 May Wellington occupies Almeida.

3–5 May Battle of Fuentes de Oñoro. Wellington defeats Masséna.

6–15 May First British siege of Badajoz.

16 May Battle of Albuera.

19 May–17 June Second British siege of Badajoz. They fail.

5 July Venezuela declares independence from Spain.

25 September Battle of El Bodón.

1 December Tsar Alexander publicly repudiates the Continental System.

1812 **8 January** Siege of Ciudad Rodrigo.

19 January British storm and capture Ciudad Rodrigo.

16 March Wellington begins the third siege of Badajoz.

24 March Secret Russo-Swedish pact.

6–7 April Wellington takes Badajoz.

28 May Treaty of Bucharest between Russia and Turkey.

18 June US declares war on Britain.

24 June The French army crosses the Niemen River.

23 July Battle of Salamanca

12 August Wellington enters Madrid.

17–19 August Battles of Smolensk and Valutino.

24 August French abandon siege of Cadiz.

7 September Napoleon victorious at the Battle of Borodino.

14 September French enter Moscow.

19 September–22 October Wellington besieges Burgos.

2 October Wellington appointed C-in-C of the Spanish armies.

19 October French leave Moscow.

22 October–19 November Allies retreat from Burgos to Ciudad Rodrigo.

23 October Conspiracy of General Malet in Paris.

24–25 October Napoleon blocked at the Battle of Maloyaroslavets.

2 November French reoccupy Madrid.

27–29 November Napoleon escapes the trap at the River Beresina.

5 December Napoleon leaves the Grande Armée to return to Paris.

14 December French rearguard reaches the Niemen; end of the 1812 campaign.

28 December General Yorck signs the Convention of Tauroggen.

30 December 1813 campaign starts.

1813 **16 January** Russians cross the Vistula.

7 February Russian troops enter Warsaw unopposed.

28 February Prussia ratifies the preliminary agreement of Kalisch with Russia.

3 March Britain and Sweden conclude the Treaty of Stockholm.

12 March French garrison evacuates Hamburg.

13 March Prussia declares war on France.

27 March Allied troops occupy Dresden, capital of Saxony.

3 April Battle of Möckern.

1 May French open their offensive in Germany.

2 May Battle of Lützen.

8 May French reoccupy Dresden.

20–21 May Battle of Bautzen.

22 May Wellington opens his offensive.

27 May French evacuate Madrid.

28 May French reoccupy Hamburg.

1 June French troops reach Breslau.

2 June Allies besiege Tarragona.

3 June Allies cross the Douro.

4 June Napoleon and the Allies sign an armistice.

13 June French abandon Burgos; Allies abandon siege of Tarragona.

17 June Wellington crosses the Ebro.

21 June Battle of Vitoria. Wellington defeats King Joseph.

28 June Siege of San Sebastian begins.

30 June Siege of Pamplona.

7 July Sweden joins Allied coalition.

11 July Soult takes command of French troops at the Pyrenees.

19 July Austria concludes the Convention of Reichenbach.

25 July Soult counterattacks in the Pyrenees at Maya and Roncesvalles.

28–30 July Wellington defeats Soult at Sorauren.

12 August Austria declares war on France.

13 August Prussian troops advance, terminating the armistice early.

23 August Battle of Grossbeeren.

26–27 August Battle of Dresden.

30 August Battle of Kulm.

31 August Graham captures San Sebastian; Battle of Vera; Wellington repulses Soult at San Marcial.

6 September Battle of Dennewitz.

8 September Citadel at San Sebastian capitulates.

24 September French troops withdraw behind the Elbe.

6 October Treaty of Ried.

7 October Allied troops cross the Bidassoa and enter French territory.

9 October Battle of Düben.
14 October Battle of Liebertwolkwitz.
16–18 October Battle of Leipzig. Napoleon retreats to the Rhine, abandoning control of Germany.
18 October Württemberg and Saxony join the Allies.
30 October Battle of Hanau.
31 October French surrender Pamplona.
10 November Wellington defeats Soult at the River Nivelle.
9–12 December Wellington defeats Soult at the River Nive.
11 December Treaty of Valençay.
13 December Action at St. Pierre.
22 December Some Allied forces cross the Rhine into France.

1814 11 January King Murat of Naples joins the Allies.
14 January Denmark concludes peace with the Allies at Kiel.
22 January Prussian forces cross the river Meuse in France.
27 January Battle of St Dizier.
29 January Battle of Brienne.
1 February Battle of La Rothière.
3 February Negotiations for peace begin at Châtillon-sur-Seine.
10 February Battle of Champaubert; start of the Six Days' Campaign.
11 February Battle of Montmirail.
12 February Battle of Château-Thierry.
14 February Battle of Vauchamps.
17 February Battle of Valjouan.
18 February Battle of Montereau.
25 February Allies establish a war council at Bar-sur-Aube.
7 March Battle of Craonne.
9 March Treaty of Chaumont.
9–10 March Battle of Laon.
13 March Battle of Rheims.
20 March Battle of Arcis-sur-Aube.
24 March Allies hold war council at Sommagices.
25 March Battle of La-Fère-Champenoise.
31 March French troops at Montmartre and in Paris surrender.
6 April Napoleon abdicates.

16 April Treaty of Fontainebleau gives Napoleon sovereignty over Elba.
17 April Marshal Soult surrenders to Wellington in southern France, ending the Peninsular War.
28 April Napoleon departs for Elba.
30 April Treaty of Paris concluded, bringing a formal end to the war.
1 November Proceedings of the Congress of Vienna begin.

1815 26 February Allies besiege Bayonne.
27 February Wellington defeats Soult at Orthez.
1 March Napoleon escapes from Elba and lands in France.
14 March Ney defects, with his troops, to Napoleon at Auxerre.
15 March King Murat of Naples, declares war on Austria.
20 March Action at Tarbes.
20 March Napoleon enters Paris; beginning of the 'Hundred Days'.
24 March Ferdinand VII returns to Spain.
25 March Allied representatives, still conferring at Vienna, agree to form a Seventh Coalition.
6 April Napoleon abdicates in Paris.
10 April Wellington defeats Soult at Toulouse.
14 April French sortie from Bayonne.
17 April Soult surrenders.
27 April Bayonne surrenders.
30 April Treaty of Paris.
2–3 May Neapolitans defeated by the Austrians at Tolentino.
9 June Congress of Vienna terminates.
15 June Napoleon crosses the river Sambre into Belgium.
16 June Battles of Quatre Bras and Ligny are fought simultaneously.
18 June Battles of Waterloo and Wavre.
22 June Napoleon abdicates. Later he surrenders to British authorities.
8 August Napoleon exiled to St Helena.
26 September Holy Alliance concluded at Vienna.
20 November Second Treaty of Paris.

Part I
The rise of the Emperor 1805–1807

Napoleon in the Battle of Jena (by Vernet).
(AKG London)

A temporary peace

When Napoleon Bonaparte signed the Peace of Amiens on 25 March 1802, he became the most popular man in France. Not only had the crown of victory constantly sat upon his brow as he had defeated one enemy army after another – the Piedmontese, the Austrians, the Mamelukes, the Turks and the Austrians again – but now he gave France what she really wanted: peace.

Peace allowed First Consul Bonaparte to put France's domestic house in order. He reorganized the laws of the land, the economy and the education system. Earlier in the year he had established freedom of religion, and his treaty, or Concordat, with the Pope had finally brought religious peace.

The Treaty of Amiens, 1802

The Treaty of Amiens between France and Britain ended the last of the wars of the French Revolution. It represented a defeat for William Pitt the Younger, but he was more than happy to see the blame for it fall on his successor as Tory Prime Minister, Henry Addington. Pitt never regarded the peace as anything other than a pause in a continuing power struggle with France. But Great Britain needed time. She had lost or alienated many of her potential and traditional allies. Austria had been badly mauled by France in the last war as a result of the battles of Marengo and Hohenlinden. Russia appeared on the verge of an alliance with France. Denmark had been thrown into France's arms by the unprovoked British attack on the Danish fleet at Copenhagen in 1801. Prussia coveted Hanover, a British crown possession and home of the royal house, and had also been offended by Britain's behavior in the Baltic. Britain was somewhat isolated as a result. More vexing to Pitt and his friends was their perception that France had violated the spirit of the Peace of Amiens by absorbing

Signing of the Louisiana Purchase. This vast sale of land to the United States put much-needed money in the hands of France in return for a territory that Napoleon saw as indefensible. (Hulton Getty)

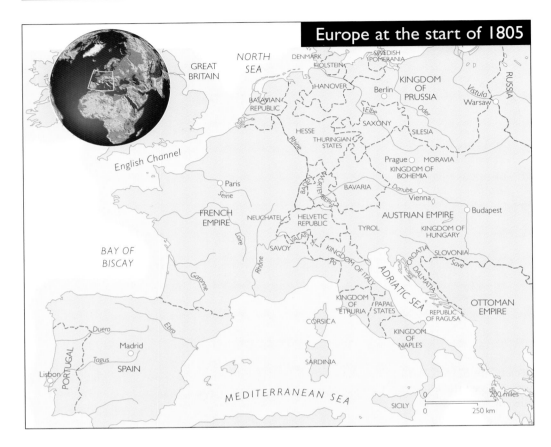

Europe at the start of 1805

NORTH SEA

GREAT BRITAIN

DENMARK

HOLSTEIN

SWEDISH POMERANIA

RUSSIA

HANOVER

Berlin

KINGDOM OF PRUSSIA

Vistula

Warsaw

Oder

BATAVIAN REPUBLIC

Elbe

SAXONY

SILESIA

English Channel

HESSE

THURINGIAN STATES

Rhine

Prague

MORAVIA

KINGDOM OF BOHEMIA

Paris

Seine

BAVARIA

Danube

Vienna

Budapest

FRENCH EMPIRE

NEUCHATEL

HELVETIC REPUBLIC

BADEN

WÜRTEMBERG

AUSTRIAN EMPIRE

BAY OF BISCAY

Loire

Rhône

SAVOY

VALAIS

TYROL

KINGDOM OF HUNGARY

CROATIA

SLOVONIA

Save

DALMATIA

Garonne

KINGDOM OF ITALY

Po

ADRIATIC SEA

PORTUGAL

Duero

Ebro

Madrid

Tagus

SPAIN

Lisbon

KINGDOM OF ETRURIA

PAPAL STATES

CORSICA

REPUBLIC OF RAGUSA

OTTOMAN EMPIRE

KINGDOM OF NAPLES

SARDINIA

MEDITERRANEAN SEA

SICILY

0   200 miles

0   250 km

parts of Italy and interfering in the internal affairs of Switzerland.

Following the treaty, France quickly made peace with the Turks. Britain viewed this with alarm as a possible threat to India or Egypt. She countered by refusing to withdraw from Malta, a specific violation of the peace accord. Addington even went so far as to say that every gain made by France should be countered by a concession given to Britain. Bonaparte stirred up discontent among the British merchants by charging a higher tariff on British goods than French. French trade rose by 50 percent in the year following the treaty and the British middle class saw little advantage in continuing a military peace that was coupled to a trade war.

No more a believer that peace would last than Pitt, Bonaparte took advantage of the respite to expand the French fleet, further threatening recent British naval dominance. The sale of Louisiana to the Americans in

1803 brought 80 million francs into the French treasury. Bonaparte also made largely unsuccessful and somewhat shameful efforts to reestablish the French colonies in the Caribbean. While these attempts would ultimately prove a failure, they caused great alarm in the British Parliament.

Seeing no advantage in maintaining the peace, the British ambassador to France, Sir Charles Whitworth, gave an ultimatum to Bonaparte to evacuate Holland and Switzerland. This was refused as being outside of the treaty's terms. France then countered by offering to have the Tsar, Alexander of Russia, who had plans for the islands himself, mediate the question of Malta; this was refused in turn, further alienating the Russians. But the tide would soon turn in Britain's favor. Following the withdrawal of the British ambassador in May 1803, Addington broke the Peace of Amiens by seizing French ships without giving a

Napoleon Bonaparte as First Consul. First Consul was his office after he seized power in the Brumaire coup. In 1800 he won the Battle of Marengo, which led to the establishment of his Imperial reign. (Hulton Getty)

This led the Bourbon reactionaries to take extreme measures. The Bourbons felt that since they were God's appointed, any measures to reestablish themselves on the throne of France were justified, including assassination. No fewer than 11 plots or attempts on Bonaparte's life were made and failed, and considerable controversy remains as to whether he ultimately died of natural causes.

Bonaparte recognized that if he intended to live long enough to achieve his goals, he would have to put a stop to the Bourbons' assassination bureau. He established a police department to spy on his enemies under the supervision of the notorious Joseph Fouché, who was a former priest, a terrorist and a man well known for his corrupt nature, but

declaration of war. This infuriated Bonaparte, who ordered the arrest of all British citizens currently in France. While he had been provoked, the monarchs of Europe, biased against Republican France anyway, viewed Bonaparte's act as criminal.

Napoleon the Emperor

Bonaparte's popularity in France had one potential drawback. As the prospects of a popular revolt against him faded, the former ruling family of France, the Bourbons, became more desperate. At several points during the period of the Directory (1795–99), France had seemed on the verge of restoring the monarchy. But now all hope was fading, for the First Consul's government shone in comparison to the Directory that it replaced.

William Pitt the Younger. Although early in his career he espoused liberal ideas, as head of the government 1784–1801 and 1804–06 he increasingly employed repressive measures. As an implacable enemy of Napoleon and the Revolution, it was said that the news of Austerlitz led to his death. (Ann Ronan Picture Library)

who was highly qualified for the job. He pressured neutral states into evicting the troublesome émigrés who had been operating with near impunity along France's borders. Finally, he learned that the young Duc d'Enghien was in Baden planning to lead an insurrection against him. Bonaparte's Foreign Minister, Charles Maurice Talleyrand, convinced him to send out a raiding party to capture Enghien as a way to strike against the Bourbons. As a result, on 10 March 1804, a group of dragoons rode into Ettenheim, abducted the young duke and quickly brought him back to the château of Vincennes outside Paris. A quick

The Duc d'Enghien, kidnapped on Napoleon's orders at Baden, which was neutral territory, and executed in the moat of the château of Vincennes. (Ann Ronan Picture Library)

court-martial found Enghien guilty of being in English pay and planning an invasion, and he was executed in the early morning of 21 March 1804.

This act was a turning point of Bonaparte's career. The execution of a prince galvanized the monarchies of Europe against him. It can be argued that Bonaparte had little choice but to send the message to the Bourbons that two could play at the game of murder. In fact, the assassination plots against Bonaparte dwindled considerably after this event.

At this juncture the First Consul for Life decided that his best security lay in having a hereditary title. At the urging of many of his closest advisers, Bonaparte introduced a bill into the Senate declaring the French Empire. This was passed in May 1804 and overwhelmingly approved by a plebiscite

put to the French people. So it was that First Consul Bonaparte became Napoleon I, Emperor of the French. His coronation ceremony took place at Notre Dame on 2 December 1804, with the Pope presiding. The symbolic height of the ceremony occurred when Napoleon placed the crown upon his own head, further antagonizing the European dynasties, who regarded him as 'the usurper'.

A death in St Petersburg

The Russian nobility had been shifting towards the British camp for some time. The previous Tsar, Paul, had been on the verge of allying Russia with Napoleon's Republic, alarming both the Russian aristocracy and the British, so the British envoy extraordinary to Russia, Sir Charles Whitworth, helped hatch a plot for the removal of the francophile Tsar. A number of disgruntled nobles and generals fell in with the plot and assassinated Tsar Paul on 11 March 1801. The new Tsar, Paul's son Alexander, was aware of the plot and became beholden to the conspirators. From the complex feelings of guilt regarding his father's murder, Alexander would develop something of a messianic complex

Tsar Alexander. After the murder of his father, Alexander took over the vast Russian Empire. While he was a most eccentric ruler, he expanded its holdings until after the end of the Napoleonic Wars, when he went mad and abdicated to follow the life of a monk. (Ann Ronan Picture Library)

wherein he played the role of savior of Christian Europe.

Over the next few years, relations between Russia and France deteriorated. Alexander saw every move on the part of the French as a threat to the areas of the Mediterranean over which he claimed a protectorate. Despite some false moves by the British, Alexander gradually drew closer to a British alliance. The execution of the Duc d'Enghien was the telling event. After this, Alexander joined with Britain in forming the Third Coalition in April 1805, and was rewarded with a lavish British subsidy.

Efforts were now made to get Austria to join the coalition. While Austria had met Napoleon twice before in war and been humiliated, Napoleon's consolidation of northern Italy was a direct threat to Austrian interests. Austria had been building up her armies for several years. When Napoleon crowned himself the King of Northern Italy in March 1805, this was too much. Austria joined the Third Coalition in August of that year, and received a generous subsidy too. The stage was now set for one of history's greatest campaigns.

Napoleon's coronation, 2 December 1804. In a
ceremony presided over by the Pope, Napoleon
placed the crown on both Josephine's and his
own head. (AKG London)

The armies prepare

With Britain renewing the war in the late spring of 1803, Napoleon went about reorganizing his army for the possible invasion of England. He sent orders to his Chief of Staff, Alexander Berthier, to prepare camps for his Army Corps at Bolougne. Here they would train and prepare for the time that the English Channel was clear of British ships and invasion could take place.

France

Napoleon organized his army incorporating the ideas of French military theorists of the previous generation. He was the first to attempt to use a permanent corps structure. Prior to the French Revolution, any organization above the brigade was temporary. The French had established permanent divisions to great effect during the wars of the French Revolution (1792–1801). Now Napoleon decided to create permanent corps that were in effect miniature armies, each with its own cavalry and artillery complements attached to two or three infantry divisions. The success of this structure can be shown by the fact that modern armies use the same organization in a largely unaltered form.

The French corps had a permanent staff attached. Commanders would learn to know their subordinates. Divisions would become accustomed to maneuvering in conjunction with their sister divisions. The Light Cavalry, attached to the corps, went through exercises that brought a higher degree of cooperation than any other army in the world enjoyed.

European armies consisted of a series of building blocks. Infantry regiments were made up of battalions, which in turn were comprised of companies. A brigade consisted of regiments, and divisions were composed

Alexander Berthier. As Napoleon's Chief of Staff, he stayed by the Emperor's side until his first abdication in 1814. He was said to be the only man in the Empire who could keep up with and understand Napoleon's mind. (Photo Musee de l'armée, Paris)

of two or more brigades. On top of this, Napoleon added infantry corps of two or more infantry divisions with one or two cavalry brigades attached.

Napoleon had infantry of two types, line (*ligne*) and light (*légère*). The light infantry, more than the line, tended to be used for skirmishing, reconnaissance and rearguard protection. Infantry battalions at this time were made up of nine companies: seven center companies and two elite companies;

the latter were a *voltigeur* (light) company and a grenadier or carabinier company, depending on whether it was a line or light battalion. In 1805, Napoleon stripped the elite companies from a number of regiments left in garrison to form an elite division under General Oudinot. This formation became known as Oudinot's grenadiers.

The light cavalry attached to the infantry corps was one of two types, either hussars or chasseurs. These were functionally the same outside of their dress, although the hussars generally had the better reputation, due in part to their dashing appearance.

Napoleon then created the Cavalry Reserve Corps from the line cavalry (dragoons) and the heavy cavalry regiments (cuirassiers and carabiniers). Their intent was to act as the 'arm of rupture', to be committed to break an enemy that had been worn down by the infantry. To a lesser extent they could be used to stabilize a situation that was getting out of hand. To accompany these heavy cavalry were batteries of horse artillery, whose 8pdr guns could be brought quickly into position and deliver tremendous hitting power. The combination of these two arms was extremely hard to resist.

Napoleon, having trained as an artillerist himself, aided by fine gunners like Marmont, had implemented many improvements that greatly increased the power of the French artillery. Better, lighter and more mobile guns, better gunpowder, better training and better tactics gave France a major superiority in this field.

One problem for the French in the 1805 campaign was that they did not have enough mounts for their dragoons. Therefore, one division of dragoons had to fight dismounted as infantry. They would not prove to be effective as infantry, but they eventually received their horses from captured stocks.

Finally there was the Imperial Guard Corps. These elite men combined the two Guard infantry regiments (the grenadiers and chasseurs of foot), the Guard cavalry (the grenadiers, carabiniers and chasseurs of horse) and the flying horse artillery batteries. The Guard acted as a final reserve and as the force that would deliver the *coup de grâce*.

In 1803, as this army formed in its various camps, Napoleon was making preparations for an invasion of England. He had barges built and began to stockpile large quantities of supplies for the anticipated campaign. While the invasion would never occur, the intensive training that the men received over a two-year period would hone this army into a superb fighting machine.

When France was declared an Empire, Napoleon quickly adapted many of his creations into Imperial ones. As First Consul he had created the Legion of Honor. This now became a method of rewarding people who had excelled in their field – a sort of minor nobility, but one based on merit. Along the same lines, Napoleon now created the Marshalate. Originally, 18 generals became marshals. They were chosen for their ability and either for their personal loyalty or because they represented a political or military faction that Napoleon wished to win over. The military factions were made up of members of the army who had served in an army not commanded by Napoleon. These were many of the men who would lead Napoleon's Corps in the following years. With these titles came a large salary. To become a marshal was the aspiration of every French soldier. The phrase 'There is a marshal's baton in every knapsack' was more than just propaganda, for some of Napoleon's marshals had indeed come up through the ranks.

The life of a French soldier was very hard by modern standards. The soldiers on campaign slept on the ground, wrapped in their bedroll. The French had learned that to carry tents and other camp baggage slowed the army down considerably. Unless the army went into winter quarters, it was generally frowned upon to billet inside a house, although this rule was violated frequently and did not apply to higher-grade officers.

The soldier received 24 ounces (680g) of bread each day and 8 ounces (227g) of meat. In addition, there were vegetables and wine. The meat and legumes were pooled and most often turned into a soup or stew. These were the official rations, and the soldiers were free to buy other items from the locals, *vivandières* or *cantinières*. There was also pillage or loot from the surrounding countryside, although this was discouraged in varying degrees by the different marshals, Davout being the strictest, and Massena perhaps the most slack.

If required, the infantry could march 20 miles (32km) a day or more. The soldiers of this French army could achieve this rate with astoundingly low rates of attrition. It was in no small part a result of their training, for later less-trained armies of Napoleon would not come close to this standard.

While Napoleon had his headquarters and two of his corps near Boulogne – the 4th Corps under Marshal Soult, the largest in the army, and the 5th Corps under Marshal Lannes – the remainder of the army was spread along the coastline. Marshal Bernadotte's 1st Corps was in Hanover. General and future Marshal Marmont's 2nd Corps was in Utrecht. Marshal Davout's 3rd Corps was in Bruges. Marshal Ney's 6th Corps was in Montreuil. Marshal Augereau's 7th Corps was at Bayonne. Finally, there were cavalry camps in which Marshal Murat oversaw the formation of his cavalry reserve. These were located in Amiens, Bayonne, Bruges, Compiègne, Montreuil, and Nijmegen.

Let us view Napoleon's corps commanders. Marshal Bernadotte, in command of the 1st Corps, was a veteran of the Revolutionary Wars, where he had distinguished himself as much for his political intrigues as for his fighting ability. He was personally brave, while often hesitant to commit his command to battle. He had been in opposition to Napoleon's seizure of power in 1799, and had plotted against him with General Moreau in the Affair of the Placards in 1802. Bernadotte's erratic behavior under the Empire, in which he was entrusted with commands after repeated failures, was initially protected by a strong following among the Republicans, but

was ultimately saved by his marriage to Desirée Clary, Napoleon's former fiancée and sister to Joseph Bonaparte's wife, Julie. As a brother-in-law by marriage, Bernadotte would be spared the wrath that he would so often deserve – and he would ultimately reward Napoleon with betrayal.

General Marmont of the 2nd Corps was one of Napoleon's few friends. He had shown great organizational skills. He showed a particular talent for the artillery. It would be under him that the artillery reforms of 'Year 11' or 1804 would take place. It shows Napoleon's high opinion of him that he was the only non-marshal to command a corps in the *Grande Armée*.

Marshal Davout was to earn himself renown in the years 1805–07. He was the youngest of the original marshals. Totally devoted to Napoleon and France, he was a shrewd tactician and a harsh disciplinarian and did not suffer fools gladly. The result was that, although respected by his men and immediate subordinates, he was unpopular with his equals.

Marshal Soult was considered the best organizer in the army. He would make his 4th Corps the envy of the world. It was significantly larger than any other corps and was made up of some of the best fighting units in Europe. Soult had been a hero during the Revolution. He had fought determinedly in actions on the Rhine, in Flanders and in Italy. He always led from the front. In 1800 he was attempting a breakout from encircled Genoa when he received a near fatal wound. This would change him for ever. Never again would he be so cavalier in exposing himself to enemy fire. This meant that at times he was too far from the action to react quickly to opportunities at the front. In 1805, however, this was not yet known.

Marshal Lannes of the 5th Corps is considered in detail on pp. 82–85. Marshal Ney had a deserved reputation as a fiery leader. He had been in the thick of the fighting during the Revolutionary campaigns on the Rhine and in Flanders. He had never served under Bonaparte, and worse had been a friend of the 'traitor' Moreau, but his fortune was assured when he married one of the Empress Josephine's favorite ladies-in-waiting. He had the confidence to project victory in everything he did, and that attitude played well with the Emperor. When the marshals' batons were being handed out, Ney was considered the most trustworthy among the former Army of the Rhine generals. For these reasons, he received command of the 6th Corps and became a marshal.

Marshal Augereau had served with Bonaparte in Italy and had played a critical role in holding off one wing of the Austrian army, while Napoleon had crushed the other at the Battle of Castiglione. This, coupled with his avowed Republican sentiments, was sufficient to earn Augereau his marshalate and the 7th Corps command. Augereau was a braggart and somewhat of a bully. He had floated from one soldier-of-fortune job to the next until the French Revolution had given him the opportunity to rise. He was a rapacious looter and scoundrel, but he knew how to fight when cornered.

Marshal Murat was now Napoleon's brother-in-law after marrying his sister Caroline. He was the *Beau Idéal* of the cavalry; dashing, daring, leading from the front, and dressed in the most flamboyant uniforms of the army. He had limited intelligence, but had a killer eye for the timing of a cavalry charge. Vain and frivolous, he always seized the day and had been instrumental in Bonaparte's successes in the Vendémiaire uprising and the coup of Brumaire. He had been with Bonaparte throughout all of his campaigns and had served him well.

Several other commanders deserve our attention. The most important of them is Marshal Massena. He had been an army commander before Bonaparte and resented being forced to take a subservient role to him in 1796. He soon came to appreciate the 'Little Corporal's' talents. He fought by his side in 1796–97 and remained in Europe while the expedition to Egypt took place. He won great fame at the Battle of Zurich in 1799, when he destroyed a Russian–Austrian army under Rimsky-Korsakov. This caused

the Russians to withdraw from the Second Coalition and set the table for Bonaparte's return, the *coup d'état* of Brumaire, and victorious Marengo campaign. While Napoleon was descending on the rear of the Austrian army under Melas in 1800, Massena was doggedly holding Genoa. Here he made superhuman efforts to hold out until Bonaparte could make the winning maneuver. In 1805, Massena may have been the best man in France to command an army apart from the Emperor. He would square off in northern Italy against Austria's best commander, Archduke Charles. While highly skilled as an army leader, Massena had a deserved reputation for being the worst looter in the French army, for his libertine lifestyle required constant sustenance. It seems his attitudes never changed after his early life as a smuggler.

Marshals Mortier and Lefevbre were both daunting fellows; no thinkers but possessed with a determination to forge ahead into the thickest of the fighting. They were admired by their men and competent only under the direct eye of the Emperor. Both men would command corps during the campaigns of 1805–07.

Marshal Bessières had been by Napoleon's side for much of his time as a commander. He was a noble of the *ancien régime* and brought an air of class to the Imperial entourage. A stickler for detail and dress, Bessières would lead the Guard for many of the campaigns, where his renown for courage was coupled with a reputation for being priggish.

Marshal Brune had been one of the most devoted Republicans. He was given his marshalate to help mollify that faction. He commanded the army that defeated a Russo-British army under the Duke of York in 1799 in Holland. He had a Reserve Corps created around him to protect the coast against a British invasion once the *Grande Armée* moved inland.

As 1805 wore on and France's navy had not the slightest prospect of clearing the English Channel, Napoleon recognized that he would have to deal with the continental threats of Russia and Austria before he could once more turn his attention to the British. When Austria declared war, Napoleon made his move. The 'Army of the Ocean Coast' became the *Grande Armée*. He issued orders and on 31 August the well-oiled military machine turned its back on the Channel and marched towards the Austrian and Russian threat.

Austria

The Austrian army that awaited Napoleon was in a state of confusion, still reeling from the debacles of the First and the Second Coalitions. In these wars, the armies of the French Revolution and Consulate continually outperformed their Habsburg counterparts. The problems that confronted the armies of the Holy Roman Emperor, Francis II, were broad: logistically, tactically, strategically, and politically, the armies suffered handicaps compared to the rapidly modernizing French. The army of the Empress Maria Theresa of Austria had held off the greatest general of his day, Frederick the Great of Prussia. Her artillery was the envy of the world, and the infantry and cavalry accounted well for themselves. Following the Seven Years War (1756–63), a number of 'reforms' were attempted. The worst of these was an overhaul of the artillery arm. The result was a disaster, with several humiliating defeats at the hands of the Turks. Attempts to redress this situation succeeded only partially. Austria had the best artillery of the continental allies, but it could not compare to that of the French.

Throughout the reigns of the Emperors Joseph and Leopold, a number of changes were attempted in the infantry. Light infantry regiments were raised in 1798, but disbanded in 1801. The Habsburg commanders had no faith in the average troops performing well when not under the direct supervision of their officers. There were *Jäger* battalions (elite rifle-armed light troops) and the *Grenz* troops (hardy frontiersmen from the Balkans with a

traditional duty of military service), but there were never enough to counter the French swarm of skirmishers. To compound the problem, the Austrians were introducing greater discipline into the *Grenzer* to ensure their political reliability and make them more compatible with the rest of their army, but suppressing their old flair for irregular warfare.

The problems faced by the Austrian Emperor were in large part due to past Habsburg successes. Primarily through marriages they had acquired many provinces with varied ethnic and racial populations. Therefore, no universal language existed in the army. Further, many of these provinces owed no loyalty to the Austrians, just to the Emperor personally. This meant that the Hungarians, for example, believed they could decide among themselves how much they would support the war effort. As the Empire was teetering on bankruptcy in 1805, the regiments were dispersed to minimize the costs of upkeep and to aid recruitment. Whatever its economic advantages, such dispersal meant that mobilization was a long process.

The Emperor's brother, the Archduke Charles, had set about reforming the army in 1801. He had taken power from the Hofkriegsrat, a military/civilian assembly, and had streamlined the logistical procedures. He was unquestionably Austria's best field commander, but he had a knack of alienating the court personalities and the ossified high command. He had close favorites whom he allowed to dictate to others considered above their station. Charles was constantly at odds with a series of foreign ministers and a combination of his enemies worked to remove him from his position of power. They launched a two-front attack, playing on Francis's paranoia regarding his brother's popularity, while urging him to join the alliance against Napoleon. Charles was adamant that the army was in no shape to fight the French and that Austria needed further peace to get her financial house in order. To that end he even advocated recognizing Napoleon's

General Mack. Despite defeat and capture while on loan to the Neapolitan army in 1805, Mack still appeared to the Austrians as the model of a modern scientific soldier and much was expected of him. (Roger-Viollet)

imperial status, humiliating as that might be for the oldest ruling family in Europe.

Charles, by advocating peace, gave his opposition an opening. Pitt, succeeding Addington as British Prime Minister in May 1804, offered subsidies and lavished bribes around the Viennese court, and Charles's enemies pounced. First they persuaded Francis to reinstate the Hofkriegsrat, then they stripped Charles's allies of their offices and commands. Finally, they advocated General Mack von Leiberich as a counterweight to Charles on military matters. Mack advocated joining the alliance and going to war. While Charles said the army was not ready, Mack's soothing words to Francis dismissed such worries. When Britain provided the required subsidies, the die was cast. Francis joined the alliance and Charles was assigned to the nominal 'main

theater' of Italy, while Mack took the largest army and in the late summer of 1805 prepared to invade Bavaria.

Mack chose this ill-suited time to reorganize the infantry regiments. He changed their existing structure, three battalions of six companies each, into four battalions of four companies. To complete the confusion, Mack did not provide for properly trained higher commanders for the extra battalions. That Mack attempted this change on the eve of war shows how unrealistic he could be.

The Austrian cavalry had started the French Revolutionary Wars as completely dominant over their French counterparts. As the war continued, their advantage waned. By 1801, they still believed themselves to be the best horsemen in Europe, but they were in for a shock four years later. While the Austrians' tactics and training remained stagnant, their French counterparts were creating cavalry that could function *en masse*. The majority of the Austrian cavalry was parceled out in 'penny packets' to the various infantry formations, which led to occasion after occasion where they would be thrown over by superior enemy numbers at the point of attack. Individually their cuirassiers, dragoons, *chevau-légers* and uhlans (lancers) were still good, but coordination was all but nonexistent.

While major efforts were being made to meet the supply and tactical needs of the Austrian army, scant attention had been given to its strategic doctrines. Austria still fought her wars by trying to maneuver her opponent out of theoretically vital geographic objectives. The concept of annihilation was foreign to the expensive armies that Austria fielded. However, the French Revolution and its levies had changed the way that war would be waged. Austria was not ready to adapt, adhering to a belief in a cordon style of defense, with fortresses holding key points. These would act as rocks against which the enemy would dash himself, while the field army massed to strike a decisive blow. Austria would in turn take the enemy's strong points and achieve 'checkmate'. The problem with this thinking was that it had failed against Napoleon in the past. But Mack would not tolerate the cautious thinking coming out of Charles's camp.

One final consideration hampered the Austrians: in order to place their troops under an Austrian commander, the Russians insisted that the commander be of the appropriate royal stature. The Protestant Mack would never do, therefore Mack's army was nominally placed under Francis's younger brother Ferdinand. Ferdinand failed to grasp that he was a figurehead until late in the campaign, causing no small amount of friction between the two leaders.

Russia

The Russian army during the Napoleonic Wars owed its origins to Peter the Great. It had grown and matured under the Tsarina Elizabeth and had nearly wrecked Frederick the Great's army during the Seven Years War. Under Catherine the Great and her son Paul, there had been a number of reforms and counter-reforms, depending on the political winds. But throughout there was a history of almost unbroken successes. Only during the last stages of the wars of the French Revolution did the Russians suffer any serious reverses. These the Tsar and his nobility blamed on their allies, the British and Austrians, and by and large it was a fair assessment.

The army was a typical *ancien régime* army, organized upon the regimental basis. There was no standing formation above the regiment and regiments were switched from one brigade to another on a moment's notice. The *inhaber* or commanding officer rarely took to the field. The drudgery of command was left to his subordinate.

The life of the typical Russian soldier was brutal even by the standards of the time. He was beaten on a regular basis, and while this was not unusual in *ancien régime* armies, the capricious nature of it was. The junior officers were of the mind that the majority of the men were animals. The food of the day was vegetable soup, most often made with barley and cabbage. The dark bread was baked to a rock-like consistency. This was either ground up into a mush or those brave souls that still had most of their teeth could attempt to bite it.

The Russian army was conscripted. Notice was given to landowners to provide a certain number of men, and he would pick the required number of his serfs (slaves) to send to the army. The term of enlistment was so long that villagers often held funerals for the departing men. With this attitude, it is easy to see that a high degree of fatalism consumed the vitality of the army. The men complained little, compared to their French counterparts, and had a reputation for withstanding high casualties stoically. While Russian soldiers were brave, numerous chroniclers have said that this was more from a sheep-like willingness to follow their leaders than from *élan*.

The Russian artillery arm was greatly admired throughout Europe. Their guns were plentiful and packed a good punch. The artillerists would doggedly defend their pieces, in many cases to the death, rather then abandon them to the enemy. While fierce, the gunners lacked the skill needed to get the most out of their guns. On many occasions the French out-dueled the Russians even though they were often outnumbered by more then two to one.

Poor training caused a chronic problem. The senior officer corps was made up of the upper nobility from St Petersburg and Moscow. The line officers, however, were often ill-educated, under-trained men who were beyond their depth at command level. Only the best-trained troops could perform the maneuvers required to keep up with the French. This meant that the best units saw continual service in battle. The command of Bagration would see more combat than the standard line division. They always responded well, but it meant that it was always the pick of the army that was taking casualties. It was with this brave but flawed army that Kutusov took the field.

Prussia

The Prussian army of the Napoleonic Wars was the direct descendant of Frederick the Great's. Perhaps no army has been so undeservedly maligned throughout history. One is required to examine the motives and perspectives of the authors of these attacks.

It has been said that the army generals were extremely antiquated. While the senior commanders and staff were old, this also meant that they had a great deal of experience. The commander, after the King, was the Duke of Brunswick. He was a veteran of the Seven Years War, where he had won a number of spectacular victories over the French. He had commanded the army during Prussia's participation in the wars of the French Revolution, 1792–95, and had performed well, with the exception of the Valmy campaign. His failure to perform at Valmy was just possibly a result of a well-placed bribe, rather then a lack of

The Duke of Brunswick. Nominal commander of the Prussian army in 1806, he was forced to fight a war he opposed. Mortally wounded at Auerstädt, he died at Ottensen on 10 November 1806. (Hulton Getty)

military acumen, for when the Duke's estate was catalogued following his death, a number of the former crown jewels of France were found. The Duke's biggest problem was that he stood between the King and a number of 'War Party' generals, who resented his more prudent policies.

The army itself started the campaign dispersed throughout Prussia. They gathered slowly and were still assembling in 1806 when the French thunderclap fell on them. The 200,000 men were well trained and efficient. Such was their level of training that only the French of the *Grande Armée* were better. The structure of the army was similar to every other *ancien régime* army. There was no permanent structure above the regiment. Units were brigaded together as befitted the wishes of the wing commander.

The Prussian cavalry was considered by many to be the best in Europe. Certainly their mounts were of the highest quality, and the troopers were brave and skilled in personal combat. If they lacked anything, it was the ability to coordinate multiple squadron charges efficiently.

The infantry, which had won such high renown during Frederick's early campaigns, retained the impressive level of fire discipline of their forebears. These battalions could pour out a devastating level of fire, and maintain this pace until their ammunition ran out. This meant that when the French met the Prussians in a stand-up firefight, as history would verify, huge casualties could be expected for both sides.

The Prussians, however, had a significant disadvantage in their inability to match up well against the French skirmishers. This failure of tactical doctrine became a decisive factor when Prussian line battalions exposed in the open tried to exchange volleys with skirmishers who were able to take advantage of cover. When the Prussian fusiliers had cover, such as in the woods around Closwitz and Isserstadt, they gave the French *tirailleurs* all they could handle. But Prussian commanders did not exploit villages or woods as defensive strongpoints, instead preferring open ground to use the

musketry machines that their infantry
battalions had become.

Another problem was Prussia's artillery
arm, the majority of which used obsolete
guns. They lacked much of the hitting power
of the French pieces, weighed more, and
therefore suffered in maneuverability. The
French gunners were able time and again to
outduel the Prussians and deprive the stolid
Prussian infantry of critical artillery support.

Finally, we come to the much-maligned
Prussian General Staff. While it is true that the
Prussians lacked a modern General Staff, they
were no different from any other *ancien régime*
country such as Russia, Austria or Britain.

Prince Louis Ferdinand. The pride of the
Prussian aristocracy, he commanded at Saalfeld
and did not survive the experience. (Roger-Viollet)

Only the French command and control
system had evolved its capabilities
significantly since the Seven Years War. It is no
coincidence that the other countries would
basically adopt the Napoleonic model as the
wars continued. The much-vaunted Prussian
staff system of the nineteenth and twentieth
centuries grew directly out of the failures of
1806, such that the later armies of Bismarck
and the Kaiser could be said to trace a more
direct lineage to Napoleon than to Frederick.

From Ulm to the Treaty of Tilsit

General Mack of Austria believed that the security of the Rhine front depended on closing off the gaps that led through the mountainous Black Forest area of southern Germany, where much of the 1796–97, 1799, and 1800 campaigns had been fought. He assumed that central Germany was out of play – in effect, neutral ground. The linchpin to his plan was the city of Ulm on the borders of Bavaria and Württemberg. By seizing and holding Ulm, he would maintain the position until General Kutusov arrived with the Russian reinforcements, whereupon the combined army would crush the upstart Corsican. At Ulm, the fortified position of the Michelsberg rose above the town, and Mack believed that this position was virtually impregnable. In this way, Mack predicated his defense upon a chimerical view of the situation.

The Ulm campaign

The first part of Mack's plan was to cross into Bavaria and, with the combined Austrian–Bavarian army, occupy the Ulm position. Francis sent his emissary to the Bavarian Elector to win him over by a combination of promises and threats. While the Elector's wife actively lobbied on the Habsburgs' behalf, a combination of Austrian blunders, popular sentiment, and Napoleon's offers of succor led to the Bavarians retreating to Würzburg and allying themselves to the French cause.

At almost the same moment that the Austrians were crossing into Bavaria, Napoleon was setting his army into motion. He correctly judged Mack's strategy and played up to Mack's preconceptions. While Mack took up a position at Ulm, the *Grande Armée* would feint at his front while making a large wheeling motion and descending on his northern flank. That would interpose part of the French army between the Austrians and their supply line running through Munich.

On 25 September 1805, the 3rd and 6th Corps crossed the Rhine and moved on Stuttgart. Mack's army was strung out between Ulm and Augsburg as the trap began to close on the unsuspecting Austrians. Mack finally realized that he was

being outflanked on 3 October. Ordering garrison forces to deploy along the Danube, he waited with his main army in Ulm.

The first of Napoleon's hammer blows fell on 8 October. After crossing the Danube the day before, elements of the 5th Corps and Murat's cavalry reserve met a column under General Auffenberg hurrying to stop the French crossing to the right bank. As was to happen time and time again in this campaign, the Austrians were too late, and were in turn caught wrong-footed. In a running battle, Auffenberg's column was crushed at the Battle of Wertingen.

The following day, elements of Ney's corps forced the bridge at Gunzburg against determined opposition. The Austrians fought well, but again were defeated. Napoleon assumed that Mack would attempt to escape. In his mind the most logical route was for them to head south and meet up with a small force in the Tyrol under Archduke John. Therefore, Napoleon had most of his army swing south to head them off. He left Marshal Murat in charge of sweeping up the rearguard around Ulm. All forces were ordered south of the Danube. But Ney was still getting reports of significant activity north of the river. One of his divisions under General Dupont was up there, having been

The Battle of Elchingen. The abbey high on the hill was stormed while the battle raged on the flats below. (Roger-Viollet)

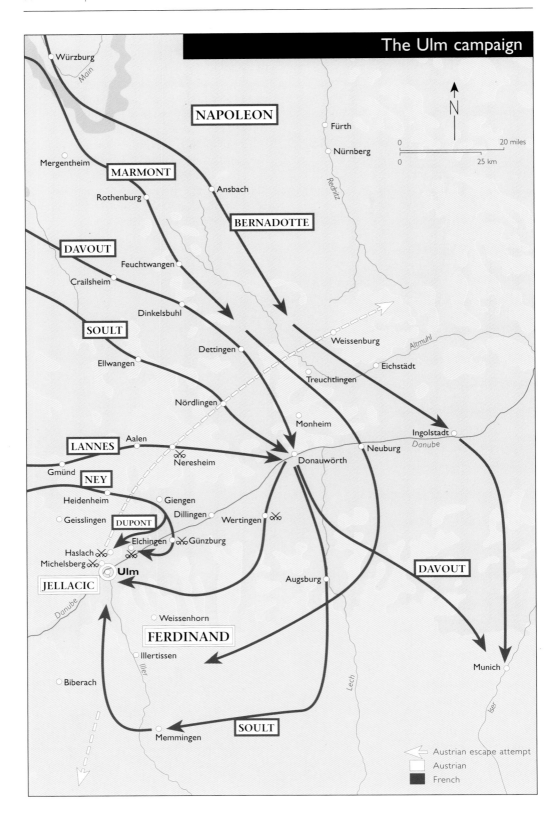

The Ulm campaign

Würzburg

Main

NAPOLEON

Fürth

Nürnberg

Rednitz

0 _____ 20 miles

0 _____ 25 km

Mergentheim

MARMONT

Rothenburg

Ansbach

BERNADOTTE

DAVOUT

Feuchtwangen

Crailsheim

Dinkelsbuhl

Weissenburg

Altmuhl

SOULT

Dettingen

Eichstädt

Ellwangen

Treuchtlingen

Nördlingen

Monheim

Ingolstadt

Danube

LANNES   Aalen

Neresheim

Neuburg

Donauwörth

Gmünd

NEY

Heidenheim

Giengen

Geisslingen

Dillingen

DUPONT

Wertingen

Elchingen   Günzburg

DAVOUT

Haslach

Michelsberg

Ulm

Augsburg

JELLACIC

Danube

Weissenhorn

FERDINAND

Illertissen

Iller

Biberach

Lech

Munich

Iser

SOULT

Memmingen

⟵ Austrian escape attempt

☐ Austrian

■ French

General Dupont. Superb and aggressive performances at Jungingen and Friedland suggested Dupont was a coming man in the French army, but a craven defeat at Bailen in 1808 led to the greatest disgrace of any French general in the Napoleonic Wars. (Roger-Viollet)

from overwhelming the French right flank, diverting them into a wasteful attack on the French baggage. In all, not only did Dupont hold out against four-to-one odds, but he also inflicted five times the casualties, almost the equal of his entire force. The French were spent, no doubt, but they had put on an amazing performance. In the face of such Austrian numbers, with yet more Austrians that could be committed, Dupont beat a hasty retreat on the night of the battle. He had no desire to tempt fate twice, no matter how gallant his men.

On 12 October, the proverbial veil had fallen from Napoleon's eyes. Mack was still in Ulm and still in the trap. Mack, for his part, believing that his position was invulnerable, saw an opportunity to destroy the exposed French line of supply north of the Danube. After dithering and repeatedly changing his mind, he sent two columns out of Ulm on the afternoon of the 13th. One under General Riesch went towards Elchingen to secure the bridge there

Marshal Michael Ney. Although keen to display his worth before the Emperor, Ney's ill fortune was to shine outside his sight at Elchingen, but to be a scapegoat for failures at Jena and Eylau. Finally, at Friedland he was victorious while Napoleon was present. (Ann Ronan Picture Library)

ordered to move along the right bank to sweep up isolated units. Ney argued with Murat all day on the 10th that it was urgent to move his entire 6th Corps to the north of the river to support this increasingly isolated division. Nothing was resolved, and Dupont marched on.

Early on the morning of the following day, as he reached the suburbs of Ulm, Dupont discovered a horrifying sight: Mack and his army were still at Ulm and issuing forth to meet him. What transpired marked a clear demonstration of the superiority of the troops of the *Grande Armée* over their Habsburg opponents. In this desperate day-long battle, Dupont used the French superiority in street fighting to hold the village of Jungingen, counterattacking skillfully when the Austrians broke themselves on this strongpoint. The rest of Dupont's infantry barely managed to hold their left flank against the sluggish Austrians. His cavalry were defeated by their Austrian counterparts, but gallantly prevented them

Surrender at Ulm, by Thevenin. Although many of the uniforms are anachronistic, this painting gives a good idea of the scale of the surrender. (AKG London)

and prevent the French doubling back over the river. The other column, under Werneck, headed north with most of the heavy artillery. After Riesch chased a small detachment out of the town, he prepared his defenses. According to Mack's calculations, no French should have been in the Elchingen area. What were they doing there?

Napoleon and Ney had hurried to reestablish contact with the isolated Dupont. The quickest route to this goal lay over the bridges at Elchingen. On the morning of 14 October 1805, Ney led his men to a position south of the Danube opposite Elchingen. Having assaulted south over the river at Gunzburg, Ney had to storm back over it at Elchingen. The field was a partially wooded flood plain, rising suddenly and steeply to a hill town overlooking all. After clearing the Austrian pickets with

This last defeat was too much for Archduke Ferdinand. He took most of the remaining Austrian cavalry and headed north, following after Werneck. He was going to escape, even if the foolish Mack would not. He rode through much of the night and out of this phase of the campaign to report to Vienna.

Following the victory at Elchingen, Napoleon released Murat to chase down Werneck. He finally caught up with him on the 16th at Neresheim and destroyed him in a running battle over the next two days. Meanwhile, Napoleon ordered the *coup de grâce*. As Ney, followed by part of Lannes' corps, approached the Austrian position on the Michelsberg on the afternoon of the 15th, Napoleon ordered an assault following a 30-minute bombardment. Stripped of their heavy guns a day earlier, the Austrians had no adequate response, and it turned out that the fortifications had yet to be completed because of sloth and the rains. Ney's 3rd Division under General Malher trudged up the muddy slopes. About 45 yards (40m) from the fortified lines they broke into a run. Amazingly, the 'unassailable position' of the Michelsberg was taken in the first try. Vicious hand-to-hand fighting left hundreds of dead strewn around the fortifications. By nightfall, the remainder of Mack's army was completely surrounded in the walled town of Ulm. With the loss of the Michelsberg their position was hopelessly compromised. Napoleon could shell them at his leisure from the heights.

Negotiations were opened on 17 October. Assured that the Russians could not come in time to his aid, and informed of Werneck's fate, Mack agreed to surrender on the morning of the 20th. As the remains of his army marched out of the city on that October morning, history witnessed one of Napoleon's most complete triumphs. Mack had lost over 60,000 of the 72,000 men with whom he had entered Bavaria. He had been no match for Napoleon's speed, and learned too late that no position is unassailable. Now Napoleon could face the Russians.

artillery, the corps advanced across the bridge. One regiment fought up through the town and took the abbey at the top with the bayonet. The rest of the division moved right across the low ground. They faced down the Austrian cavalry and scattered Riesch's infantry. Ney won the title of Duke of Elchingen for annihilating the enemy despite the imposing terrain. By evening on the 14th, communications had reopened and Ney was advancing towards Ulm, 6 miles (10km) away.

The Austerlitz campaign

After the capitulation of Mack's army on
20 October 1805, Napoleon took several days
to gather the spoils of war and reorganize his
army to head for the Russians under
Kutusov. The latter's army had marched as
far as the Inn river, on the borders of Austria
and Bavaria, and then stopped. The march
had been a terrible ordeal. Straggling and
disease had cost the Russians about one-third
of their men. In the past, much has been
made of the scheduling problems caused by
the Russian and Austrian use of the Julian
and Gregorian calendars respectively,
accounting for an 11-day difference.
However, it appears that most of their
difficulties arose from the false assumption
that Napoleon could not bring his army to
bear before the two armies of his opponents
were able to combine.

When word reached Kutusov of the
disaster at Ulm, he knew that the nature of
the war had changed. He devised the

Prince Mikhail Kutusov. Immortalized as the ideal
Russian commander in Tolstoy's *War and Peace*,
in reality he was a very different man. Blind in one
eye from a battle wound, well educated and a
libertine, he conducted retreats with great skill, but
seemed at a loss to do much else. (Hulton Getty)

obvious plan of falling back upon his supply
lines and support. As he withdrew from the
Inn river, Kutusov barely kept ahead of the
rapidly marching French. He left rearguards
who fought the French in a succession of
skirmishes. At Amstetten, Murat rode too far
ahead of his support and almost got himself
killed. At Mariazell, Davout destroyed one of
the last contingents of Austrians under
General Merveldt.

The Russians faced the problem that their
line of supply ran south from Brünn. This
meant that to secure their retreat they had to
move north of the Danube river. To do this,
however, would expose the Austrian capital
of Vienna. Understandably, the Habsburgs
preferred that a defense of their capital be
made, but after a show of making a stand,
Kutusov slipped his army north of the river
and positioned himself around Krems.

While this happened, Murat pushed
ahead and found that the way to Vienna was
open. With his cavalry he entered the city
on 11 November. As Murat rode for the glory
of capturing the enemy's palaces, to the
north of the Danube dramatic events were
unfolding. Napoleon had hoped to prevent
the Russians from crossing the river and had
sent a newly formed corps under Marshal
Mortier over the river by a pontoon bridge
to cut them off. The first division, led by
General Gazan and Mortier himself, moved
along the left bank. Following behind was
another division under Dupont. Without
any cavalry screen, Mortier did not know
he was walking into a trap. As he spent
the night encamped around the town of
Dürrenstein, Kutusov had complete
knowledge of his position and sent several
columns around to the north to come into
the rear of the Marshal while attacking at
the same time to the front.

This plan worked, but the march through
the freezing night took much longer than
anticipated. Gazan's men fought fiercely
most of the day against heavy odds. They
were able to exploit the vineyards on the
hillsides to their best advantage and were on
the point of preparing a final push to break
the troops to their front when the tardy

The Austerlitz campaign

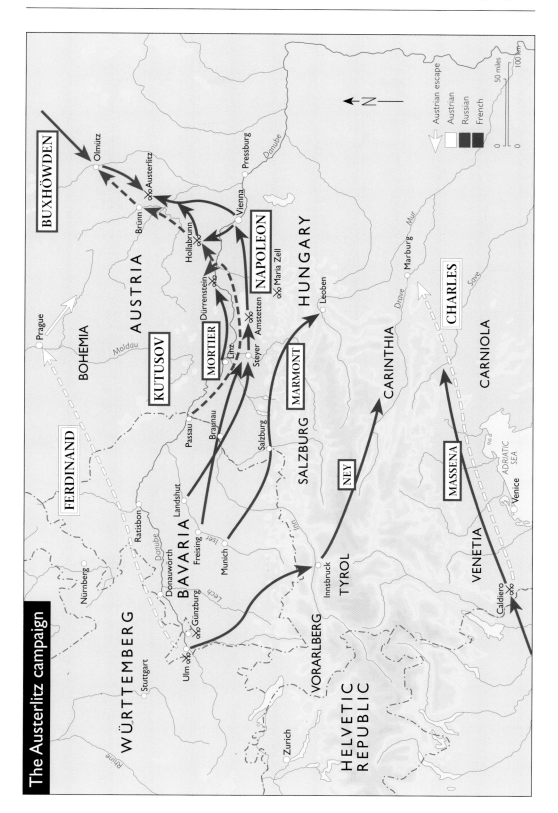

Russian columns appeared in their rear. Mortier turned his men around and tried to punch his way out. Much of the fighting occurred in the streets of Dürrenstein. The men were running out of ammunition and were completely exhausted. Surrender seemed inevitable when the report of cannon coming from the west was heard. Dupont's men had force-marched and were launching bayonet attacks in the evening gloom. The Russians, now fearing they were the ones who were in danger of being surrounded, broke off the action and retreated into the hills. The French had barely avoided a disaster that would have wiped out the propaganda benefits of Ulm. Only the tenacity of the French soldiers, outnumbered five to one, had saved the day.

Breathing a sigh of relief, Napoleon looked for a way to transport his army to the north of the Danube. He had dispatched the 2nd and 6th Corps of Marmont and Ney to cover the Tyrol and the approaches to Vienna from the south, for both Archdukes Charles and John with armies from Italy and Hungary could have threatened his rear had he not done so. This still left him with the 1st, 3rd, 4th and 5th, most of the cavalry,

Joachim Murat. The dashing cavalry leader became a Prince of the Empire because of his marriage to Napoleon's sister Caroline. While extremely skilled in leading cavalry, his performance in independent command left something to be desired. (Ann Ronan Picture Library)

Prince Peter Bagration. As the fearless leader of the Russian avant-garde, he caused more problems for the French than any other Russian. (Roger-Viollet)

and Mortier's *ad hoc* corps to face the Russians. Napoleon found the answer to his problem when Lannes and Murat bluffed the guards of the Vienna bridges into believing that an armistice had been signed. While the Austrian guards were distracted by the glittering French marshals, some French grenadiers swiftly seized the bridge. This act of daring allowed the quick pursuit of the now fleeing Russians. Murat caught up with them at Hollabrünn.

It was here that the Russians turned the tables, for Bagration now bluffed Murat into signing a temporary armistice in preparation for a permanent peace. While Lannes fumed, both sides agreed to a four-hour warning before resuming combat. A message was sent to Napoleon, who was enraged and ordered a resumption of the war. The respite had given the cunning Kutusov time to get most of his army away. After the required four hours the

Napoleon at the chapel of St Anthony. He is viewing the progress of the annihilation of the allied left, sending in his reserves as needed from this position. (Roger-Viollet)

French attacked into the night's gloom. Only the light provided by the burning town of Schöngraben allowed the men to work their way through the vines of the fields in front of the Russian position. Receiving canister fire from the Russian guns that overlooked their approach, they pressed on despite the huge swaths cut through their ranks. As they reached the Russian position it gave way, yielding many prisoners. However, Prince Bagration, the rearguard commander, had done his job. He broke off the fight and saved most of his command while allowing the main army to escape against overwhelming odds.

Kutusov was able to retreat through Brünn and continue on to Olmütz, where he

Lieutenant General Buxhöwden. A man much more interested in his drink and prostitutes than in military tactics, he spent much of the Battle of Austerlitz drunk while presiding over a monumental disaster. (Roger-Viollet)

exhaustion, and cold. The allies also had the chance to catch Napoleon with his army spread out. Desire for a victory prevailed at allied headquarters – ultimately, the Tsar wanted to gain the glory of commanding the army that would destroy this champion of the French Revolution.

met up with the reinforcing army of General Buxhöwden, including the Tsar, on 24 November. The combined army, which included about 15,000 Austrians, would number around 72,000 men.

An allied conference was held to decide what was to be done. Kutusov argued for a continued retreat to draw the French further from their supply sources, and this, in retrospect, was exactly the strategy Napoleon feared. It had the obvious advantage for the allies that they would not have to face the French immediately in battle. Further, there was an increasing chance that the Prussians would throw in their lot with the allies. The alternative was to bring on battle. This had the attraction of avoiding a prolonged retreat in winter, which could produce terrible losses from hunger,

The Mamelukes were part of the Imperial Guard Cavalry that Napoleon unleashed on the Staré Vinohrady. Many of them had followed Napoleon from Egypt, but over the years they were often recruited from Paris 'toughs'. (Musee de l'armée, Paris)

Napoleon wished to lure the allies into a decisive battle. His supply line was stretched and, in addition, his intelligence sources told him that Prussia was preparing to enter the war. Finally, and most importantly, the news of the naval defeat at Trafalgar, combined with the rumors floating around Paris about the situation of the army, had caused another financial panic. The Emperor was always aware that he was only one defeat away from a coup that could topple his throne. Napoleon therefore decided to bait the allies into bringing on a battle. He made the appearance of weakness by asking for an

armistice and being unusually polite to emissaries. While doing this, he sent orders to Bernadotte to march on Brünn and he recalled Davout from Vienna.

By 1 December the trap was set. In a further sign of weakness, Napoleon withdrew from the powerful position of the Pratzen Heights and deliberately weakened his right flank to tempt the Russians to attack there. The allies gladly occupied the heights and made plans to turn the French right flank and place their army between Napoleon's army and his line of communication. What the Tsar and his advisers did not know was that Davout had marched his two divisions the 92 miles (150km) from Vienna and was falling into place on the French right. Davout's men brought Napoleon's army up to about the same strength as that of the allies.

The allies were not the only ones who thought the French were in a bad way. On the night of 28 November, a group of marshals were meeting in the Imperial Headquarters waiting for the return of the Emperor. Soult and Murat were convinced that they were in for a drubbing and wished to convince Napoleon to retreat. Knowing that they did not hold the ear of the Emperor like Lannes, they cajoled him into finally putting forward the idea. When Napoleon returned, Lannes pulled him aside and suggested a retreat. Napoleon had never before heard such words out of the fighting Marshal and asked him where he had got such an idea. 'It was the idea of all of us,' responded Lannes nobly. 'I will place my corps at your service sire, and it will perform as double its number,' said Soult, trying to squirm out of the responsibility, whereupon Lannes drew his sword at Soult and demanded a duel. Lannes vainly tried to obtain satisfaction over the next few days. When challenged on the morning of the battle, Soult responded that they had enough warm work ahead of them that day without a duel. This incident would be the cause of a feud between the two marshals for the rest of Lannes's life.

Napoleon's battle plan was to tempt most of the allies off the Pratzen Heights in an effort to turn his weak right flank. He would then launch an attack up the center and break the enemy in two, after which he would roll up both flanks from the middle. The allied plan fell right into Napoleon's trap. Three columns were to descend from the heights and crush the French right and then turn to drive Napoleon against the Moravian hills.

On the night before the Battle of Austerlitz, Napoleon went on an inspection of the troops. As his soldiers recognized him, they lit his way by burning their bedstraw, which they bundled into torches. Soon the entire camp area was illuminated by the men coming to see their Emperor. Napoleon would call it the finest night of his life.

By 6 am the Russian and Austrian columns were on the march. The Austrian Weyrother, Tsar Alexander's Chief of Staff, had drawn up a detailed general plan the night before while Kutusov slept. Weyrother's timetable exceeded the capabilities of the army, and had not accounted for various columns crossing paths and becoming confused. Count Langeron had to stop his column to allow for the cavalry of General Liechtenstein to pass through to their assigned place. Ironically, this delay nearly upset Napoleon's plans.

As the allies came into the fields opposite the towns of Telnitz and Sokolnitz, Vandamme's and St Hilaire's divisions were massing at the foot of the Pratzen Heights, waiting for the signal to advance. Their position was hidden from above by thick fog which hung in the low ground.

At around 8 am the first allied column attacked the village of Telnitz. Defending the village was the 3rd Line regiment. After several assaults on the town, the French were expelled and retreated to the west of the Goldbach stream. Moments later a French brigade came up, as Davout arrived on the scene and immediately poured his men into battle. They launched a counterattack and once more regained Telnitz. They in turn were routed when coming out the other side of the village, attacked by Austrian hussars. The allies once more regained the village, but were prevented from advancing further

Nicolas-Jean de Dieu Soult. Called the greatest maneuverer in Europe, he was a master in training and bringing his corps to the battlefield. Once there he took a less active role. (Ann Ronan Picture Library)

by French artillery, which raked the exits from the town.

Slightly to the north was the village of Sokolnitz. A little time after the battle began at Telnitz, the allied second column made its first assault against the village of Sokolnitz with its castle and walled pheasantry. Defending here was the 26th Light, the Tirailleurs du Po and the Tirailleurs Corses. These were some of the best troops in the *Grande Armée*. The fire from these battalions battered the advancing column. General Langeron, the column commander, decided to blast them out of the village. He unlimbered his guns and began a deadly barrage. While this was going on, the third column arrived and began an assault upon the castle. Though they were taking withering fire, the allies' superiority in numbers told and the French light infantry was expelled. They fell back, rallied and

counterattacked. This time it was the Russians who were driven back. They in turn rallied and once more threw out the French. Then Friant's division came forward and once more expelled the Russians.

For most of the rest of the battle, control of Sokolnitz passed to and fro. After Friant's attack, the French never completely lost control of Sokolnitz. All was going according to Napoleon's plan, for the more in the balance the issue appeared upon the Goldbach, the more reserves the allied commanders would commit to that fight and the less they would have elsewhere.

The last two weeks of the campaign had been fought under overcast skies. On the morning of 2 December 1805, the sun broke through the clouds and began to burn off the haze that covered the battlefield. At 8.30 am, Napoleon turned to Soult and asked how long it would take for his men to reach the top of the Pratzen Heights. 'Twenty minutes, Sire.' 'Good,' replied the Emperor. 'Start your men off in a quarter of an hour.'

So it was that the 'Sun of Austerlitz' shone down on St Hilaire's division as it began its ascent. The Tsar spotted this movement and asked what it could be. This wasn't supposed to happen! Kutusov was ordered to send men over to stop the French from seizing the Pratzen and splitting the allied army in two. The fourth allied column was on the march, but could only feed in several battalions at a time. They were no match for the finest line division in the *Grande Armée*, but their numbers were almost twice those of St Hilaire. In some of the most desperate fighting of the Napoleonic Wars, both sides blasted away at each other. As one Russian battalion gave way, another took its place. Charge and countercharge led to melees in which no prisoners were taken and the wounded were bayoneted. After an hour of the most savage fighting, the allied fourth column effectively ceased to exist.

As all appeared lost for the allies, the delayed portion of the second column arrived on the scene. These were the troops who had been separated from their main body by errors in the marching order. They

were Austrians and inexperienced, but still they weighed in and attacked the tired French. Finally, the weight of numbers drove the French back off the heights. With ammunition getting scarce, retreat seemed the only way out. Instead the men fixed bayonets and charged. The battle had hung in the balance, but French *élan* carried the day. The Austrians fled down the back slope of the hill, and the French had broken the center.

Further to the north, Vandamme, with Soult's second division, launched an assault against the Staré Vinohrady, the summit of the northern portion of the Pratzen Heights. Two pockets of troops held out here. The first was dispatched when hit by three times their number after receiving point-blank

canister fire from guns that had been unlimbered in their face.

The second group was five battalions holding the Staré Vinohrady proper. These men were first tormented by the French light infantry tactics, then treated to a crushing series of short-range volleys from Vandamme's veteran soldiers. The Austrians were routed. The entirety of the Pratzen was in French hands. The Tsar had no reserves left to commit except his precious Imperial Guard. When it became clear to Napoleon that both ends of the Pratzen were in the hands of his men, he came forward from his headquarters of the morning, and advanced with his Guard to the top of the recently captured ridge. At the same time, he ordered Bernadotte's

Austerlitz (by Gerard). The prisoners of the Russian guard are presented to Napoleon. (AKG London)

battle, the first battalion of the 4th Line was crushed and its standard taken.

As Napoleon watched this from his new vantage point, he committed his Guard cavalry to counter the enemy's Guard. The field squadrons of his mounted Guard chasseurs and grenadiers slammed into the magnificent Russian cavalry. The French impetus was too much and the Russians were driven back on to their own Guard fusiliers, who had just re-formed. As they were on the verge of breaking, Constantine committed the last of his available reserve, the Guard Cossacks and the Chevalier Guard. These men swung the balance back in the Russian favor. Napoleon countered by sending in his personal guard of the service squadrons of Guard cavalry. They flew into the swirling melee, but the Russians still held a large numerical advantage.

As the fight hung in the balance, Bernadotte's 2nd Division under General Drouet finally made its appearance. Advancing on the flank of the Russians, they came forward in serried ranks, their battalions deployed in a chessboard fashion. This new support allowed the outnumbered French cavalry to fall behind the cover of their infantry in order to catch their breath, while maintaining pressure on the Russians with a galling fire. On the occasions where the Russians tried to follow, they met with a devastating crossfire and fell back. Given this development, the battle shifted in the French favor. When the Guard horse artillery rode up, unlimbered and poured canisters into the Russian Guard cavalry, the day was won. Falling back through the ranks of the Russian infantry, they disordered the Guard fusiliers just as the combined French Guard cavalry bore down on them. The result was a massacre. Sabering the fleeing Russians, the French Guard cavalry followed up for 0.25 mile (0.4km) until they called off the pursuit because of the exhaustion of their mounts. The victory was won – the only

1st Corps to advance and support the left of Vandamme's men.

With the loss of the Pratzen, the Grand Duke Constantine, the Tsar's brother and commander of the Russian Imperial Guard, launched a counterattack in an attempt to restore the situation. Vandamme's men had taken up a position in a vineyard just below the Staré Vinohrady. Sending forward his Guard fusiliers, Constantine saw these men push back the first battalion of bicorned soldiers, only to have the second French battalion drive back his men with a withering volley. As his men came back down the hill, the Grand Duke sent in several squadrons of his heavy Guard horse. They rode down the rows of vines and slammed into the weary infantry. In a brief question remaining was the escape of the allied army.

As Vandamme made his assault on the Staré Vinohrady, the action on the north side of the battlefield was heating up. The Russian cavalry column, under Prince Liechtenstein, was making its way towards the right flank of the French 5th Corps. Opposing them was General Kellerman and his division of light cavalry. Kellerman's command made up part of the cavalry reserve under Murat. Behind them was the infantry division under General Caffarelli. For an hour and a half, Kellerman fought a series of battles with the much more numerous enemy cavalry, besting them initially, then falling behind the infantry to regroup as their infantry comrades fired volley after volley into the increasingly disordered enemy ranks. Finally, Murat sent two cuirassier divisions to finish the job. These heavy cavalry, tremendously impressive in their polished steel breastplates and helmets, crashed into the remaining enemy cavalry, and sent it packing.

With the defeat of the Russian cavalry, Lannes could turn his attention to the defeat of the Russian avant-garde under Prince Bagration. All morning the brave and aggressive Russian Prince had been eager to make his attack, but no orders had come. Finally, as the situation in the center began to deteriorate, Bagration sent his men forward to seize the Santon, a small but prominent hill that jutted forth from the heights to the north. In an attempt to overlap Lannes's line to the north, Bagration sent a Jäger regiment around to the flank. There they met a murderous fire from the elite 17th Light and a large battery of former Austrian light guns that were placed upon the Santon. Reeling back, they fell behind their own artillery.

Lannes advanced in a counterattack only to be stopped by Russian artillery fire. Directing his guns to suppress the Russian artillery, the French corps artillery drove off the Russian guns after sustaining high losses. Once this was accomplished, Lannes could advance again, and with the help of his supporting cavalry he eventually drove Bagration's men off the field. Lannes wanted to pursue the Russians but was held up by Murat, who held command on this part of the field. The failure to follow up aggressively would leave the Russians the nucleus of an army when it mustered a few days later.

The greatest spoils of the battle were won on the southern front. Napoleon now directed the unengaged units of his army to wheel to the south and crush the first three columns of the allied army. The brunt of the fighting fell once more on Soult's two divisions, St Hilaire's and Vandamme's. Descending the slope of the Pratzen, they crashed into the remains of the 3rd column. At the same time, Davout sent in his last reserves to take the two villages of Sokolnitz and Telnitz. The Russians who now held the castle at Sokolnitz were hit on two sides, by Davout's men from the west and St Hilaire's men from the north. Fighting heroically, most of the Russians perished rather than yield.

Count Langeron, commander of the 2nd column, could now see all was lost and made provision to get out with what he could. The commander of the avant-garde of the 1st column, General Kienmayer, did the same. The commander of the front, Buxhöwden, was evidently so drunk that he made a run for it, leaving little direction for his men.

To cover the withdrawal, Kienmayer deployed his best cavalry regiment, the O'Reilly chevau-légers. To counter, the dragoon division of General Beaumont, with six regiments, advanced. In a dramatic charge, the O'Reillys broke through five of the regiments. Only the sixth was able to force them to withdraw. Re-forming, the O'Reillys came on again against a line of stationary dragoons. The French cavalry peeled away, exposing a line of French Guard artillery, which belched fire and shot at the surprised Austrians. The gallant cavalry had had enough and broke. This now fed the panic that was spreading among the allies. Many dropped their weapons and ran for their lives. The path that many took was across frozen ponds that blocked their way to the south. As the men fled across the ponds, a combination of their weight and French artillery fire broke the ice and many men plunged into the freezing water. While these ponds were shallow, undoubtedly the shock killed many. With the ice breaking, those troops who were still north of the ponds threw down their weapons and, pleading for mercy, surrendered.

The allies had lost 25,000 men, 182 guns and 45 standards. The French had lost 8,500 men and one standard. While the numbers engaged had been about equal,

it is worth pointing out that Napoleon fought most of the battle with only two-thirds of his troops. The entire 1st Corps, Oudinot's grenadier division, Legrand's division of Soult's 4th Corps, and the Guard infantry had seen very little action, while the allies had left almost nothing uncommitted. Napoleon had many

Napoleon meets Francis I following Austerlitz. Francis was relieved to get off so lightly after such a defeat, but Napoleon had other foes in mind. (Hulton Getty)

options left to him at the end of the day; Alexander had none. The battle had been won when Napoleon had lured the allies into the battle he had wanted.

Napoleon, in his address to the troops the following day, said that he was well pleased with them. Their hard work on the plains above Boulogne had paid off. They were superior in skill and training to their counterparts. Added to this, there was Napoleon himself – seldom has a general not only predicted the enemy's moves, but actually provoked them. Perhaps Tsar Alexander summed it up best: lamenting the defeat, he declared, 'We are babies in the hands of a giant.'

On 4 December 1805, the Austrians signed an armistice, and on the 27th, by the Treaty of Pressburg, they exited the war. The Russian army was allowed to withdraw to its homeland and the French army began to disengage from Moravia. Eventually they would set up in cantonments throughout southern Germany. Napoleon returned to Paris amid the triumph afforded a conquering hero.

With the formation of the Confederation of the Rhine, the role for the Holy Roman Emperor ceased to exist. Facing a *fait accompli*, the Emperor Francis II gave up his title and became Emperor Francis I of Austria-Hungary. The news of Austerlitz was said to have killed the British Prime Minister, William Pitt the Younger, Napoleon's arch-antagonist. The Sun of Austerlitz was shining on all Napoleon's realm.

Prussia joins the war, 1806

As 1806 arrived, there was little thought in the court of France of a war with Prussia. On the contrary, negotiations were continuing for a formal Franco-Prussian alliance. Napoleon had offered the much-prized Hanover to Prussia in exchange for the small provinces of Cleves, Berg, and Neufchatel. Additionally, Bavaria would swap Ansbach for part of Bayreuth. All these territorial changes would serve two purposes for France. They would consolidate the holdings of the two spheres of influence as well as alienate Great Britain from a potential ally. In fact, once Prussia occupied Hanover, Britain declared war on Prussia, although it can hardly be said that the conflict was prosecuted in any serious manner.

Napoleon continued to pursue the war against Britain and her allies, the greatest success coming with the removal of the

Queen Louisa of Mecklenburg. As Prussia's Queen, she became the focal point of those wishing war with France. She used every weapon at her disposal to defeat Napoleon. Her death in 1810 came before her country's resurrection. (Ann Ronan Picture Library)

Officers of the elite Prussian gendarmes cavalry regiment show their contempt by sharpening their swords on the steps of the French embassy (by Myrbach).

Bourbons in Naples and the installation of his brother Joseph on the vacated throne. While this was happening, however, more storm clouds were gathering. Prior to Austerlitz, Tsar Alexander had visited the court of Prussia and had fallen under the spell of the beautiful francophobe Queen Louisa. Making a pledge of mutual support in a melodramatic ceremony in the crypt of Frederick the Great, Russia and Prussia made plans to work in concert. The first result had been Prussia's tardy decision to exploit her position and enter the war on the side of the allies, just as Napoleon had reached his most extended point of the 1805 Austerlitz campaign.

Arriving at the Imperial headquarters just prior to the great battle, Haugwitz, the Prussian Foreign Minister, had been prepared to deliver the ultimatum that would bring Prussia into the war. Napoleon berated Haugwitz for hours and sent him away before the message could be officially delivered. When Napoleon next met Haugwitz on 15 December, the situation had changed significantly. Haugwitz meekly offered congratulations from the Prussian court to the recent victor. Napoleon quipped, 'It seems that there has been a change of address since the letter was penned.'

Prussia was caught between a rock and a hard place. Napoleon exploited her position by demanding the alliance and a break with Britain. While Prussia was handsomely compensated for the action, Queen Louisa and the 'War Party' were in a state of near apoplexy. Napoleon had triumphantly outmaneuvered them.

He was helped in no small measure by the 'Peace Party', which was led by the King, Haugwitz, and the Duke of Brunswick. They sought to obtain the best deal for Prussia while not risking her army. This prudent course had the disadvantage of having no appeal to the brash character of the Prussian nobility, who still regarded their army as the finest in the world. Louisa loathed the French Revolution and its minions and had been busy trying to gather allies for a renewed war effort against 'the Usurper'. The 'War Party' was made up of most of the General Staff, including Hohenlohe and Blücher, plus the young, dashing Prince Louis. They all relished the opportunity to attack and destroy the French.

Napoleon had been busy consolidating the gains of the last year and had formed the Confederation of the Rhine, which was an assembly of German states under the protection of France. This move threatened the Prussians, even though Napoleon had encouraged Prussia to take similar measures for the northern German states. Napoleon genuinely wanted peace at this stage of his career, and in the spring of 1806 he made strong overtures to Britain and Russia. The Russian ambassador had worked out a treaty that offered Russian withdrawal from the Ionian Isles in exchange for the withdrawal of French troops from Germany. This had every prospect of bringing about peace, but Queen Louisa had been haranguing her husband into opening negotiations with Russia for a renewal of hostilities.

The Prussians vacillated between committing for war or peace until word reached Berlin from the Russians that Napoleon had offered Hanover back to Britain. This was only partially true, for Napoleon had indeed floated the idea, but with the stipulation that suitable compensation be given Prussia in exchange. It is doubtful that this latter stipulation was passed on to the Prussians, but whatever the truth, the news tipped the balance in favor of the War Party. Russia and Prussia signed an agreement and prepared for war. The treaty Napoleon had signed with the Russian ambassador was repudiated and Russia began once more to mobilize.

As the summer wore on, Napoleon remained convinced that the peace would be maintained. He delayed call-up of the reserves until 6 September 1806. He believed that the Prussians would never commit the 'folly' of going to war against him, but took measures to secure himself against all eventualities. As late as 10 September, a full

month after Russia and Prussia had determined to go to war against the French, he wrote to Berthier that he expected peace.

After the Russians rejected the treaty, Napoleon began to take measures that would allow him to gather his army together quickly. The implications of the rejection of such a generous treaty could only mean one thing. Letters were sent to Prussia saying that Saxony must not be forced to join any confederation against her will. As this letter was going out, Prussia was doing just that to the reluctant Elector. Under threat of invasion, Saxony was instructed to ready its army to march with the Prussians against France.

The problem the Prussians faced during their one-month head start on Napoleon was the lack of any consensus on how to prosecute the war. For over a month the General Staff argued, and ultimately came to no final opinion. This weakness has to be placed squarely at the feet of the King, for had he taken charge and decided on any one of the alternatives presented, even the worst of them would have trumped indecision and turmoil.

By 18 September, Napoleon, after receiving many reports from his diplomats and spies, decided that war was inevitable. He dispatched orders to his various corps that were spread out all over southern Germany. Within days his army was on the march. He headed toward Würzburg where, headquartered in the Bishop's residence, he made his final plans for his campaign. After receiving the reports as to where the enemy was located, he initiated his plan to move through the Thuringerwald area of forest and hills and descend off the plateau into the valley of the Saale, thereby placing his army between the main Prussian force and Berlin. Furthermore, he wished to move with his usual speed, for he hoped to defeat the Prussians before the Russians could march to their support.

The Prussians assumed that the Russians under General Bennigsen would join up with their army by the beginning of November. Totally misjudging the speed with which Napoleon could react, the Prussians issued an ultimatum to Napoleon intended to

King Frederick William of Prussia. Crowned in 1797, he preferred a neutral policy with France until his Queen and the army's militants dragged him into war. (Ann Ronan Picture Library)

provoke war. He was given until 8 October to respond. Napoleon had arranged for signalling stations to be set on commanding ground throughout the territories he controlled, where flags or lights were used to pass messages. Because of this semaphore system he knew of the ultimatum's contents at once, but no official delivery could be made to the Emperor in Paris as he was already in the field preparing for his lightning stroke against the Prussians. The messenger finally caught up with him on 7 October after going by way of Paris. Napoleon's answer was to send the lead corps of his army over the border into Prussia on the morning of the 8th.

The opening moves

As the *Grande Armée* advanced, it moved in three parallel columns, each within one day's march of the other. The left column was made up of Lannes' 5th Corps and Augereau's 7th Corps. The middle column was headed up by Bernadotte's 1st Corps followed by Davout's 3rd Corps, both supported by cavalry. The right column consisted of Soult's 4th Corps, Ney's 6th Corps, and the Bavarians.

The first contacts occurred at Hof and Saalburg; at both places the French cavalry pushed back the Prussian screen. The following day, 9 October, Murat, heading up Bernadotte's light cavalry and the lead division of his infantry, attacked the Prussian rearguard at the town of Schleiz. With Napoleon on the field, Murat led a number of impetuous charges that required the infantry to extricate him. In the end, reserves arrived and drove the Prussians from the field. On the next day, Marshal Lannes came down the slope leading towards the town of Saalfeld. There waiting for him was a sizable force under the command of Prince Louis. The battle that followed demonstrated all the French tactical advantages in this campaign.

The contest opened with the 17th Light Infantry breaking out into skirmish formation opposite stiff combined arms opposition. While the French lights could not press the Prussians, their ability to use the terrain to the best advantage worked in their favor. It bought time for Lannes to send a column through dense woods to emerge half a mile (0.8km) away, thereby expanding the front. As more of his corps came up, Lannes was able to mass his troops in preparation for a coordinated assault. Using the ground to their advantage and massing quickly to assault key positions, Lannes's men were able to drive back the now outnumbered Prussians and Saxons. In a sharp battle the French overwhelmed their opponents, killing the Prince in the process. The French had taken 34 guns and four flags, and inflicted 1,700 casualties for a loss of fewer than 200. The victory would send shock waves through the Prussian royal household. Not only had the pride of Prussia, Prince Louis, fallen, but the French were obviously able to deal with the Prussian army as they had the Austrians and Russians.

Napoleon's army swept up the right bank of the Saale, and the towns of Jena and Gera fell into their hands. On 13 October, the lead element of Davout's 3rd Corps entered Naumburg and captured a number of pontoon bridges over the Saale. The Prussians were hurriedly concentrating on the left bank of the river with the center of their forces around Weimar. Having

been beaten in two piecemeal engagements, Brunswick wished to meet the French threat massed.

Lannes's 5th Corps entered Jena on the morning of the 13th and soon crossed the river, climbed to the heights above the town and assembled on a sheltered plateau below

the village of Cospeda. Here his scouts reported that he was faced by 40,000–50,000 Prussians. Lannes sent a report to the Emperor and deployed his men to face any attack. Retreat doesn't seem to have entered his mind, for Lannes had total confidence in his men. On the evening of the 13th, Prussian Prince Hohenlohe began to move troops forward to the attack, but he canceled the assault, probably after being reminded of his role as a rearguard and not an attack wing.

Napoleon assumed that the Prussians had gathered an army on the heights above Jena for the purpose of cutting across his lines of communication should he advance upon Berlin. This was an entirely logical assumption and reflected what he would have done in the same situation. Napoleon felt the need to bring the Prussians to battle soon, for if too much of a delay occurred, the Russians under Bennigsen might arrive in the theater of war. He told Lannes to hold in place and quickly ordered Soult, Ney, the Guard infantry, and two divisions of heavy cavalry to force-march to Lannes's assistance. Once assembled, he would bring on a battle.

The orders to Marshal Bernadotte were to work in conjunction with Marshal Davout and move upon Dornburg and, from there, Apolda. The two marshals detested each other and Bernadotte chose to follow one part of the order, while deliberately ignoring the other. He did not feel he should act in a subordinate role to a junior officer, no matter what the Emperor's intentions were. His behavior would place Davout's corps in the greatest of peril, yet ironically bring eternal credit to the man he loathed.

Throughout the night Napoleon pushed his men as they passed through Jena, over the Saale and up the steep slope to the bridgehead on the Landgrafenberg plateau above. To get his cannon up the slope, caissons were double and even triple teamed. The Guard chopped down trees to widen the road where possible.

The death of Prince Louis (by Knotel). Separated from any escort, trying to rally his troops, Prince Louis was run through by a bold French cavalryman who did not even recognize him. (AKG London)

Even the Emperor dismounted and directed operations to get as many men as possible into position. As the men arrived, they took their place on the increasingly crowded field, some literally sleeping shoulder to shoulder. Tomorrow Napoleon would have enough men to fight a battle, for the danger of a desperately outnumbered Lannes being crushed had passed.

The Prussians had sprung to life after Saalfeld, and Brunswick had decided to restore equilibrium to the war by stealing a march on Napoleon in order to get his army between Berlin and the French. He decided to force-march towards Magdeburg, where he would be able to join up with the command of the Duke of Württemberg, which was at Halle. His plan was to leave a blocking force under General Hohenlohe, swing behind that force,

Prince Hohenlohe-Ingelfingen. Drubbed at Jena, he later surrendered humiliatingly at Prenzlau. (Roger-Viollet)

and make an end run through Auerstädt and up the river towards Halle and Magdeburg. The plan might have worked but for two things: the aggression of Hohenlohe and the heroics of Davout and the 3rd Corps.

Jena

The dawn of 14 October 1806 was very foggy; men claimed that they could not see 30 feet (10m) in front of them. While Napoleon was aware of the Prussians' position from the previous evening's reconnaissance, their exact alignment remained a mystery. What was needed was room to deploy his army as it hurried up throughout the day. This could be achieved only by driving the enemy out of their positions around Lutzeroda and Closewitz. Napoleon's main battle plan seems to have been to separate the Prussians from their

anchored position on the cliffs above the Saale river. Once the Prussians had been unhinged from this position, the French could use their superior ability to exploit the terrain.

Towards that end, at about 7.30 am, Napoleon ordered the 17th Light of Lannes's 5th Corps to the advance. They moved through the fog and opened fire blindly on the position in front of them. As they had advanced, they had approached slightly at an oblique, which exposed their left flank to deadly fire from part of von Zezschwitz's Saxon division. Fortunately for the light infantry, their supporting light cannon had been wheeled up to short-range canister position and poured in devastating salvoes. The Saxons fell back, which relieved the pressure.

As it became clear that this was quickly developing into a serious battle, General Tauentzien sent reports to his commander, General Hohenlohe. After initially dismissing Tauentzien's fears, Hohenlohe was convinced by the increasing level of noise of the battle that this was much more than a French reconnaissance in force. He now made the critical decision of the day. Rather then attempting to break off the action and withdrawing in accordance with his rearguard orders, Hohenlohe decided to counterattack and throw the French off the Landgrafenberg plateau.

It was now about 8.30 am and the fog, while still thick, had lessened to the extent that the Prussian army's position was coming into view. The advanced guard under Tauentzien held this area of the battlefield. These were the best light troops in the Prussian army. Lannes launched an attack that slowly cleared the Closwitz woods and unhinged the Prussian line. Several counterattacks were made by the troops Hohenlohe fed forward, but these were repelled by the fresh troops Lannes was also placing into the line. Not believing in a strongpoint doctrine that would have allowed them to anchor in a village, the Prussians were left with no other option but to fall back and realign their battle front

in a north–south axis, so as not to be outflanked.

As soon as the first shots had been fired, a message was sent to General Holtzendorff to support the Prussian effort by marching to the battlefield from his position above Dornburg. This he did, and arrived almost to upset the French day. As the Prussians and Saxons fell back to their new position beyond Vierzehnheiligen and Krippendorf, Marshal Soult was able to send his lead division around Lannes's right flank. It swung into the open ground beyond the woods above Closwitz. Here Holtzendorff appeared. His column consisted of a combined-arms force that included some of the finest cavalry in the world.

As the fog lifted, Holtzendorff launched his attack to break through to the main army. He had the misfortune to have run into perhaps the finest line division in the world, St Hilaire's. The cavalry made their charge and instead of following the standard infantry tactical procedure of forming square to meet cavalry attacks, St Hilaire, with both of his flanks protected by two villages, kept his infantry in line to deliver a volley. With no way to envelop the French line, the cavalry attack fell apart. The Saxons and Prussians formed up and tried again, but with similar results. Soult now released his cavalry against the disordered and blown enemy cavalry and put it to rout. The French infantry subsequently advanced and put the Prussian supporting infantry to flight. This work done, the division formed up and turned to march back into the main battle some time after 11.30 am.

At about 10 am, the situation had stabilized around Vierzehnheiligen. The French were waiting for reserves to come up and the Prussians were recovering their breath, covered by fresh reserves of cavalry. All night Marshal Ney had been pushing the lead element of his corps to arrive at the battlefield in good time. Ney had missed Austerlitz and had never performed in front of Napoleon. He was anxious to correct this shortcoming and make a dramatic difference in the battle. The lead element of the

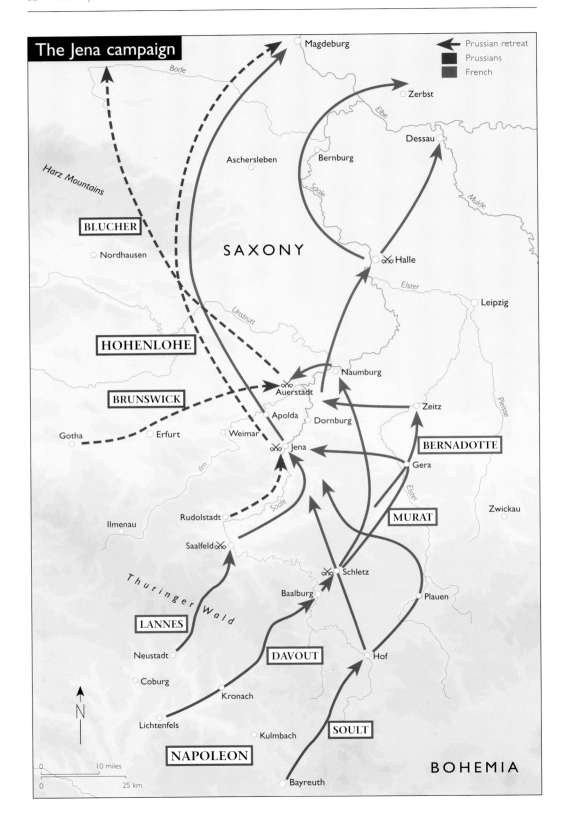

The Jena campaign

Prussian retreat
Prussians
French

Bode

Magdeburg

Zerbst

Dessau

Aschersleben

Bernburg

Elbe

Harz Mountains

Saale

Mulde

BLUCHER

Nordhausen

SAXONY

Halle

Elster

Leipzig

Unstrutt

HOHENLOHE

Naumburg

BRUNSWICK

Auerstädt

Zeitz

Pleisse

Apolda

Dornburg

Gotha

Erfurt

Weimar

BERNADOTTE

Ilm

Jena

Gera

Zwickau

Elster

Ilmenau

Rudolstadt

Saale

MURAT

Saalfeld

Thuringer Wald

Schletz

LANNES

Baalburg

Plauen

Neustadt

DAVOUT

Hof

Coburg

SOULT

Kronach

Lichtenfels

NAPOLEON

Kulmbach

BOHEMIA

N

0   10 miles

0   25 km

Bayreuth

Napoleon in the Battle of Jena (by Vernet). Eager for battle, the Guard asked Napoleon to be committed, but he did not need them that day. (AKG London)

6th Corps pushed its way through a gap in the line, led personally by the red-haired Marshal. He launched an impetuous attack with just his lead infantry regiment supported by his two light cavalry regiments. The first cavalry regiment, the 10th Chasseurs, moved out of the woods and into the open, and overran a 30-gun battery. They were soon under attack from two Prussian cavalry regiments, one cuirassier and one dragoon.

Ney's second cavalry unit, the 3rd Hussars, fell upon the flank of the Prussians. A swirling melee ensued with the French having the worst of it. It was when several squadrons of Saxon dragoons joined

in that the French broke and fled to the rear. The German allies in turn charged and quickly overthrew the hapless infantry. A gap developed in the center of Napoleon's line and the crisis of the battle from the French viewpoint had arrived. Napoleon was much annoyed by Ney's rash decision, but reacted calmly to the situation. The Prussian cavalry had broken through the center and were threatening to roll up the line by wheeling to their left. Ney's remaining cavalry rallied and were still having the worse of it when the corps cavalry of Lannes charged into the fray, slowly driving back the Prussians.

While French quick thinking had averted a disaster, Napoleon had little fresh cavalry on the field. This meant that the Prussians could not be pushed until either more cavalry came up or artillery blew open a hole. Napoleon therefore began to assemble a massed battery of his Guard artillery and some of Lannes's guns in order to blast his way through Hohenlohe's line.

Around 11 am, Hohenlohe ordered an attack to retake Vierzehnheiligen. General Grawert sent forward the infantry of his column to assault the village. The French skirmishers of the 21st Light poured deadly fire into the massed infantry formations, but had to give way when Grawert brought up cavalry to outflank and surround the town. The Prussians seized the village, and were preparing to come out into the open on the other side when they spotted the massed guns of Napoleon. Seeing that they could not go forward and having no desire to defend the town, they set it ablaze and fell back.

The French countered by sending Gazan's brigade of Lannes's 5th Corps around the north of the village. They were met by Prussian and Saxon cavalry and driven back in confusion. Again the Prussian follow-up was stopped, this time by the battery supported by the newly arrived heavy cavalry under d'Hautpoul.

To the south of Vierzehnheiligen lay the village of Isserstadt, and there was a large wood just to the east. Since 10 am the French of Desjardin's division of Augereau's 7th Corps had been attempting to seize the village. Three times it had changed hands. Each time the French were able to keep a toehold in the woods because of their superior ability to skirmish. Any attempt to push the attack, however, was stopped by the two Saxon brigades and supporting cavalry arrayed to the south and west of Isserstadt.

A stalemate ensued, but by 12.30 pm the situation was looking grim for the Prussians. Fresh French units were pouring on to the battlefield. Heudelet's division of the 7th Corps was coming up from the south. The 2nd and 3rd Divisions of Soult's 4th Corps were moving to a reserve position behind the French center, and perhaps more telling, St Hilaire's division had swung into a position extending the French line further to the north, threatening to envelop the Prussian left. Napoleon had concentrated his artillery fire against the center of the Prussian line opposite Vierzehnheiligen.

Hohenlohe had few options left. His line was fully committed, with the exception of Tauentzien, who had rallied his men to take up a reserve position behind the center-left of the main line. He had sent word for General Ruchel to march from Weimar that morning, but as yet there was no sign of him. Napoleon kept up pressure everywhere along the line, while pounding the center. Finally, the pressure was too much and the decimated battalions began an orderly withdrawal. It was now that Napoleon gave the order to Marshal Murat to unleash his reserve cavalry. Eleven regiments passed through the gap between Vierzehnheiligen and the Isserstadt woods and plunged into the retreating enemy. This was too much for the Prussians and the center snapped like a dry twig.

The order passed down the French battle line to advance all along the front, and the result was repeated everywhere except on the right flank, where the Saxons were mostly unaware of the disaster befalling their allies. The remaining cavalry of the center and left tried to slow down the French, but they were swept back in the tide of retreating infantry. Only Tauentzien remained steady. His troops acted as a breakwater that their routed compatriots could rally behind. Although gallant, they did not last long, however. Hopelessly outnumbered and receiving a terrific pounding by the French artillery, they too gave way. What remained of the organized cavalry fell back trying to cover the retreat.

In the south, the two Saxon brigades held on grimly. They had lost almost all of their cavalry support and were now being assaulted by the entirety of Augereau's corps. To make matters worse, several regiments of French dragoons had peeled off the pursuit in the north and had come to harass these helpless heroes. Having no option but to form squares in the face of the enemy cavalry, they were systematically pounded by the 7th Corps batteries. For almost an hour they had huge holes ploughed through their ranks until sanity prevailed and the formations surrendered. Several of the battalions had taken advantage of the terrain to make an escape, only to be captured later that night.

While this was taking place, Ruchel had at last arrived at Kappelendorf. Here he formed up his 15,000 men and began an advance. Kappelendorf had a fortified château that would have been a formidable obstacle in the path of the French pursuit, but again Prussian doctrine prevented them from occupying it. As Ruchel moved up the slope past his fleeing comrades, he was first assaulted by the pursuing French cavalry. These charges his men were able to fend off, but it gave time for more of the French army to close in. As the cavalry withdrew, six French batteries bombarded Ruchel's men. Spearheaded by Lannes's and Ney's men, the French infantry came on. In their opening volley, Ruchel went down with a grievous wound. Napoleon's men would not be denied. The massed bands struck up 'Victory is Ours' and with a shout the French charged. It was over in the blink of an eye. The Prussians had had enough and broke and ran. Once more Murat launched his cavalry into a pitiless chase.

As the sun set on this gloomy October day, the French advanced guard rounded up the last of any organized opposition. Of the 54,000 men with whom Hohenlohe and Ruchel started the day, over 20,000 were lost,

in addition to 30 standards and 300 guns. These losses compared to about 6,000 of the French. While this disparity shows the magnitude of the victory, almost 14,000 of the Prussians lost were captured, making the killed and wounded almost equal on both sides. This was a testament to the firepower of the Prussians. Napoleon was triumphant, for he had crushed the main Prussian army, or so he thought. It was only late in the evening that he received his report from Marshal Davout. Looking up from the message, he told his assembled generals and marshals, 'Davout has had a rough time of it and Bernadotte has behaved badly.'

Auerstädt

On the night of 13 October 1806, Marshal Davout received his orders for the next day at his headquarters in Naumburg. He was to move on Apolda by the road of his choice. Similar orders were given to Marshal Bernadotte. This, Napoleon conjectured,

Prince-Field Marshal Blücher. A general at the time of Auerstädt, he heroically but foolishly led his cavalry against the French during the battle. A staunch member of the 'War Party', he surrendered near Lübeck – a stinging memory that fed his francophobia. He obtained his revenge in the 1814 and 1815 campaigns. (Hulton Getty)

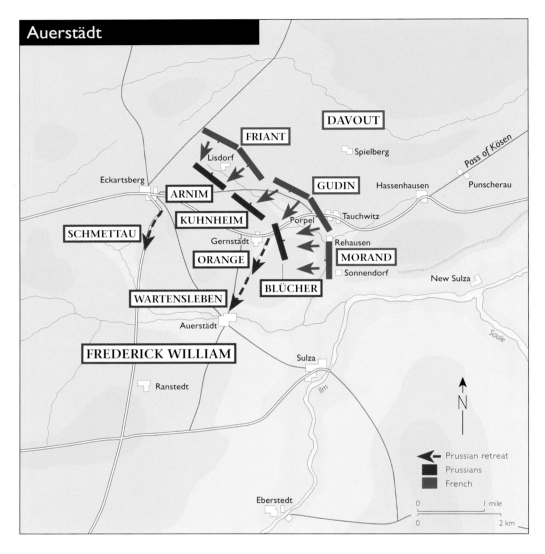

Auerstädt

would allow both corps to fall on the Prussian rear. Davout dispatched orders for Morand's division to come up through the night so as to be able to support his other two 3rd Corps divisions under Friant and Gudin. Bernadotte chose to ignore the second part of the order to support Davout and marched his corps out of the action towards Dornburg. Bernadotte had hated Davout ever since 1799, when Napoleon asked Davout to spy on him and Davout had helped expose a conspiracy to overthrow Bonaparte. Lacking absolute proof, Napoleon pardoned Bernadotte, but the Gascon had never forgiven Davout. And now Bernadotte

saw no reason to subordinate himself to a younger man whom he outranked.

At 4 am on the 14th, the 3rd Corps scouting party ran into a large Prussian cavalry force in the village of Poppel. They scurried back to the protection of the leading infantry elements of Gudin's division, who quickly formed into a square. They had just come up the steep slope rising from the Saale river. They were approaching the village of Hassenhausen when the cavalry under General Blücher deployed between them and the village. Some French skirmishers had got into Hassenhausen just before Blücher's troops arrived and now came out and chased off Blücher's supporting cavalry battery, taking half the guns in the process. Stripped of this artillery support, Blücher launched several furious attacks upon the French squares. The heavy fog added to the confusion, but the crack French troops held firm and delivered deadly salvoes, both from their muskets and from the cannon that had been deployed at the corners of the squares. Blücher brought up more cavalry and another battery, which he deployed near the town of Speilburg.

Marshal Davout, who had been on the field since the opening moments of the action, rode from square to square to encourage his troops. After repeated attacks, the Prussian cavalry had had enough and broke fleeing from the battle. Blücher had a

The Prussian command decapitated (by Knotel). The mortally wounded Duke of Brunswick is led from the field. (AKG London)

horse shot out from under him, which in addition to the fog made rallying any of his cavalry problematic. The lull in the action allowed the rest of Gudin's division to arrive and deploy. Coming right behind them were the lead elements of Friant's *fantassins* (infantry).

As the fog lifted, Davout was able to see that it was much more than an isolated contingent that had attacked him. There spread before him was the main Prussian army. The largest contingents were deploying on the plain on either side of the village of Poppel. The King and the Duke of Brunswick had come up with Schmettau's division and had deployed it to the north of Poppel, but had waited to bring the division of Wartensleben into position south of the town to make a coordinated attack. This attack aimed to sweep aside the isolated force and allow the army to continue its retreat to Magdeburg.

This delay gave Friant a chance to arrive on the field, and after deploying he moved towards Spielburg in an attempt to outflank the Prussian line from the north. They overran the battery that had been dealing out death to Gudin's squares and swung their line to face south. At this same time, Davout broke Gudin's infantry out of square and formed a line extending north from Hassenhausen to meet the threat of Schmettau. Both sides closed and began a deadly firefight. Schmettau went down with two wounds and his line faltered.

To the south, things were going much better for the Prussians, directly under the command of Brunswick. They had maneuvered to a position south of the village of Hassenhausen and were on the verge of turning the flank. All that stood between them and the capture of the key town was the 85th Line. A withering fire was poured into the outnumbered Frenchmen and, when a cavalry charge came crashing upon them, the line gave way.

Davout had anticipated that the 85th could not hold out much longer and sent another regiment over to succor them. The 12th Line pulled up alongside the

retreating 85th and released a volley into the pursuing cavalry. The effect was to send them reeling back. The 85th rallied and formed square. The French position could have given way at any moment, and Brunswick was hurrying up two elite grenadier battalions to overturn the French. It was at this moment that a musket ball passed through both of his eyes, making him *hors de combat*. Ultimately, Brunswick succumbed to this wound on 10 November.

French marksmanship had decapitated the Prussian army. Schmettau was down, Brunswick was mortally wounded and Wartensleben had just been knocked senseless when his horse had been shot out from under him. The King was in charge, but seemed incapable of giving orders. The army command fell to the aged General Mollendorf, who proceeded to get himself captured. As a result, with no central command, the Prussians were incapable of getting off another coordinated attack, while the French under Davout were able to respond rapidly to each slow-developing threat.

Despite the dramatic change of fortune, the Prussians were able to exert tremendous pressure on the French holding Hassenhausen. Friant was attacking aggressively in the north, but just as Schmettau's right flank gave way, a new division under the Prince of Orange came rolling up to counterattack. Once more the two sides leveled crushing volleys against each other. It was now 10 am and Morand arrived on the field with his division. It fell into line, extending the left flank from Hassenhausen to the steep slopes falling down to the Saale.

By 10.30 am the Prussian cavalry of the reserve, along with the few remains of Blücher's command, deployed opposite Morand's infantry. Taking command, Prince William led the finest cavalry of Prussia up the slope towards Morand's men. Infantry fire out of the squares, along with the close-range canister, emptied many saddles including Prince William's. As if by a prearranged signal, the Prussian line gave way. The cavalry went streaming back toward Auerstädt. The infantry fell back, leaving their supporting batteries to their fates; most were captured.

Prince Henry made a last counterattack with several grenadier battalions. A heroic assault took the town of Poppel, but as the attack reached the apogee of its success, the Prince was mortally wounded. Once more the commanding officer of a wing went down. Void of any instructions and facing the talented commander General Morand, the bewildered grenadiers were enfiladed and forced back after a vicious fight. The King gave the order for the Guard to cover the retreat and for the army to break off. One rearguard was placed on the high point of this section of the field, the Sonnenberg; the other was left to contest the retreat route towards Eckartsberg.

French General Debilly, leading his brigade in the assault on the Sonnenberg, overthrew the position and captured many Prussians in the process. During this attack, Debilly was killed, the only French general officer casualty. This is contrasted with the devastating officer casualties taken by the Prussians, which can again be traced back in part to the decisive French superiority in skirmishing.

To the north, Friant led his exhausted men on the assault up the Eckartsberg hill. The disciplined Prussian infantry remained willing to stand and deliver deadly volleys. The French responded by breaking their lead battalions into skirmish order and working their way up through the woods. Taking cover, they sniped at the exposed Germans and eventually wore them away to the point that they broke. Those who headed for Auerstädt fell in with the mass of panicked troops who represented what was left of Prussia's finest. Those who went to the Eckartsberg were gathered up by the French light cavalry, who had swept around the northern flank to cut them off.

Jean-Baptiste Bernadotte. Despite his disloyalty and general incompetence during the Empire, he would be chosen as Sweden's Crown Prince and succeed to that country's throne. (Ann Ronan Picture Library)

The only remaining Prussian troops in good order on the field were a handful of grenadier battalions and the Guard. These men gave ground slowly, finally falling in with the remainder of the main army. Davout's men followed till they were sure of the result, whereupon they fell down from exhaustion. Davout was to occupy the castle in Auerstädt that evening and dine at the table so recently used by the King of Prussia and his high command. He had lost a third of his men, but the devastation was complete for his opposition. The King of Prussia had lost over 100 guns and between 10,000 and 15,000 men.

Aftermath

On the night of the twin battles, Napoleon assessed the situation. Davout was victorious, but exhausted for the moment. The lead elements of his army were in Weimar. Bernadotte was in Apolda. He had sent a message that his arrival in Apolda had saved Davout – a statement that was hardly justified by the facts.

Bernadotte: what should he do about him? Orders were given to arrest him in preparation for arraigning him for a court-martial. No sooner had these been issued than Napoleon countermanded them. Bernadotte was, after all, married to his former fiancée, who was the sister of his brother's wife. This would cause no end of domestic trouble to the Emperor. Better for Napoleon to give Bernadotte one more chance for now, while leaving his options open.

After getting reports of the day's actions, Bernadotte considered the position in which his pride had placed him. He had conspired against Napoleon several times in the past, on every occasion receiving a pardon upon discovery. But there was an end to every man's patience. He felt he would have to redeem himself, and looked for an opportunity to do so.

On receiving his intelligence, Napoleon issued orders for the pursuit to commence the following morning. The process was delayed because most of his men had force-marched to the battlefields and it took time to decipher the many reports that were coming in. Even with the delay, the pursuit that followed after Jena–Auerstädt was so devastating that one would have to go back to the days of the Mongols to find its equivalent.

Leading this hunt was the vainglorious Prince-Marshal Murat. He was in his element now. His cavalry would chase down Prussian formations with an intoxicating ruthlessness. Over the next week, his command would capture as many men as the combined Prussian losses of the twin battles. While Murat was chief in this gathering up of the straggling army, the infantry corps were doing their share moving up the Saale towards Berlin. Between them and the capital was the column of the Duke of Württemberg stationed around Halle.

Napoleon, on the morrow of Jena, began to wean the Saxons away from the Prussian alliance. He sent messages of friendship to the Saxon Elector, and as a prelude to formal negotiations released his Saxon prisoners after receiving an oath of loyalty. The Saxons soon switched sides and fought with Napoleon the following year.

On the morning of 17 October, the leading elements of Bernadotte's 1st Corps attacked the dragoons attached to the Duke's forces on the outskirts of Halle. Driving the Prussians back to a series of three bridges that passed over the Saale river and then pressing

Prussian prisoners (by Myrbach). Entire Prussian armies marched into captivity, something the Prussians remembered for more than a century. (Author's collection)

on through the city, the French met supporting enemy infantry who held the three bridges. Led by the divisional general Dupont, the hero of Jungingen and Dürrenstein, the French soldiers set up a crossfire upon the enemy troops who were holding a dike, which sat above the swampy ground guarding the only approach to the outer bridge. The 32nd Line and a battalion of the famed 9th Light rolled over the bridge and quickly seized the two inner bridges under fierce fire. A panic occurred inside the city and soon all Prussian opposition had either fled or surrendered.

Dupont followed up to find that the Prussian main position was on the heights to the south of the town. Unable to press the position until reserves came up, the 9th Light sent forward a skirmish line to harass them. As more of Bernadotte's men moved into Halle, Württemberg realized that if they moved out of the city to the east, they would block his line of retreat. He therefore began to shift his troops from the heights along the front of the

Napoleon before the tomb of Frederick the Great (by Camus). Napoleon removed Frederick's sword from the mausoleum, saying, 'I prefer this to twenty millions [in plunder].' (Roger-Viollet)

city towards the north. This left them exposed to flanking fire and vulnerable to attack, which is just what Bernadotte did.

Leading his men out of the medieval gate, Bernadotte plunged into the Prussian line, committing himself to the midst of the battle. Splitting the Prussian army in two, the jubilant Frenchmen ran down whole pockets of the fleeing enemy. In an engagement lasting about two hours, half the Prussians were casualties, while they inflicted very small losses in return. Bernadotte had a victory on the scale of Saalfeld and, more importantly, Napoleon's forgiveness. This was to be his finest day fighting for the French Empire.

Between now and early November, a series of Prussian units and garrisons were caught and surrounded, and surrendered. Hohenlohe was trying to take the main army towards Stettin, where he hoped to revictual and head east to join up with the approaching Russians. On 24 October, Napoleon entered Potsdam and visited the tomb of Frederick the Great. Entering the crypt with several marshals and generals, Napoleon said, 'Hats off, gentlemen, for if he [Frederick] were here now, we wouldn't be.' On the 25th, Davout's

men had the honor of a triumphal march through Berlin, rewarding them for their performance at Auerstädt. On the 27th, the great fortress of Magdeburg surrendered after a mere ten-day siege.

Napoleon just had time to play the part of benevolent conqueror – and he knew how to play it well. Napoleon, now headquartered in Berlin, had the Governor of Berlin, Prince Hatzfeld, arrested after intercepting a letter written by him incriminating him as a spy. Facing her husband's execution, the Prince's wife went to Napoleon to plead his case. She assured the Emperor that her husband was incapable of doing the things with which he was charged. Napoleon showed her the letter and asked if that was not indeed her husband's handwriting. One look by the distraught wife made her husband's guilt clear, and she broke down weeping. Napoleon said that if she threw the incriminating evidence into the fire nearby, then there would be nothing left on which to convict her husband. This she did, and her spouse was saved.

The main Prussian army under Hohenlohe continued to retreat north, with Murat and Lannes in hot pursuit. As they chased the Prussians, both Lannes and Murat sent messages to Napoleon claiming that the other was unsupportive and slow. The old feud was pushing both marshals to have their men perform herculean feats of marching. On 27 October, General Lasalle's and General Grouchy's cavalry crushed Hohenlohe's rearguard at Zehdenick, where Queen Louisa's regimental standard was captured. On the 28th, Murat and Lasalle surrounded the town and Hohenlohe surrendered.

Lasalle went on to Stettin and tricked the garrison into surrender. Here he demonstrated around the city and claimed to have an infantry corps coming up that would show no mercy should the Prussians not surrender immediately. The ruse worked and the Prussians marched out of the city,

only to find that they had given up to fewer than 500 cavalrymen.

Marshal Murat peeled off after the surrender at Prenzlau and joined with Bernadotte's and Soult's corps in following up Blücher. They finally caught up with him at Lübeck. The previous day his Swedish ally had lost 600 men to Bernadotte. Ironically, it was Bernadotte's treatment of these prisoners that earned him a reputation for generosity that years later won him the crown of Sweden. Blücher had occupied the independent city of Lübeck in hopes of continuing the war. The French cavalry, however, stormed the two main gates of the city. While Blücher escaped with about half his men, the remainder fought a desperate street-to-street melee until they were compelled to yield. With all hope lost, Blücher

French triumphal march through Berlin. The victory parade was to set the fashion for many others over the following century. (Hulton Getty)

surrendered the remainder of the army on the following day in the village of Ratgau.

The entire Prussian army was now lost with the exception of those garrisons that had been out of the theater of war in occupied Poland and East Prussia. General Lestoq commanded the only field force in the following campaign. Additionally, the cities of Danzig, Colberg, and Stralsund would hold out for most of the next year's campaign.

On 21 November, Napoleon issued his Berlin Decrees. These closed all the occupied ports to British ships, and all British goods seized were forfeit. This was the beginning of the Continental System, an economic form of warfare that often at times seemed on the verge of success, but would ultimately undermine Napoleon's regime.

Other fronts

As the main French army operated under the Emperor, events were happening on a global scale. While Napoleon made his march against Ulm, the main Austrian army under Archduke Charles squared off against Marshal Massena. Massena's role was to entertain Charles while Napoleon destroyed

Mack and took Vienna. Throughout the month of October, the two armies maneuvered to gain advantage. Finally, they faced each other on the battlefield of Caldiero, the site of Napoleon's only defeat in his first Italian campaign. Massena knew that if he was not aggressive, Charles might give him the slip and turn the tide in southern Germany. So he attacked. The French acquitted themselves well, but Charles had almost twice the troops and was able to repulse the main attack.

The reverse at Caldiero would be salvaged by Napoleon, for word of Mack's capitulation reached Charles and ended all thought of

offensive action. Withdrawing his army in an attempt to reach Vienna to forestall Napoleon, Charles was forced to fight a series of rearguard actions and was slowed by the coming of the Alpine winter. In the end, he was miles from helping the allied armies when they were crushed on the field of Austerlitz. Massena had put Venice under siege, and when the peace with Austria came (the Treaty of Pressburg), the 'jewel of the Adriatic' was incorporated into Napoleon's Kingdom of Northern Italy.

Massena was now directed south to conquer the Bourbon Kingdom of Naples. Queen Caroline had signed a treaty of neutrality with Napoleon, but renounced it as soon as he marched north out of Vienna. A force of 13,000 Russians under General Lacy had landed along with 7,000 British troops to support a Neapolitan invasion of northern Italy. When word reached this force of the defeat at Austerlitz, the Russians and British pulled out, leaving the Queen with no option but to abandon her southern Italian holdings and retreat to Sicily under the British fleet's protection. This departure allowed Napoleon to place his brother Joseph on the Neapolitan throne. He arrived in Naples on 15 February 1806. The city of Gaëta held out and required Massena to conduct a five-month siege.

Attempting to stir up a revolt in the southernmost province of Calabria, British General Stuart landed a force of 5,000 men. Joseph dispatched General Reynier with about an equal force to attack him. The action at Maida on 4 July 1806 resulted in the French being routed by the British. Stuart failed to pursue and in fact soon retreated back to the protection of Sicily when the fall of Gaëta released Massena's troops to move against him. Calabria remained in revolt and presaged the type of savage guerrilla fighting that would be seen in Spain.

When Napoleon signed the Treaty of Tilsit with Alexander in July 1807, Britain became convinced that the Danes were about to join the French. Despite Denmark's trying to follow a strictly neutral policy, the British

Retreat of the Prussians (by Knotel). (AKG London)

attacked without provocation. Copenhagen fell, but the captured Danish fleet was found to be in poor condition. This provocation was too much for the Danes. They allied with Napoleon and would stand by him until near the end. Britain was considered a pariah for her piratical behavior. In the same year, there was another example of it. In the Argentine, a British expedition tried to seize Buenos Aires, but had to surrender in a humiliating fashion. In Egypt, another small British army landed to try to take the country. It took Alexandria, but was ambushed in Rosetta and driven from the country. At the same time a British flotilla under Admiral Duckworth was repelled from the walls of Constantinople. British military policy during this time was a series of disasters. It would take Wellington's campaigns in Spain and Portugal to reverse Britain's fortunes and reputation.

It was in 1807 that Napoleon, demanding that Portugal cut off all trade with Britain, sent an army under General Junot to occupy the country and force adherence to the Continental System. Napoleon offered to split the country with Spain and as a result the armies of the two countries occupied Portugal in the latter part of the year. Junot marched into Lisbon on 30 November 1807. The much-prized Portuguese fleet had sailed to Brazil under British escort. Disappointed, Junot was still able to set up a government and temporarily close the ports to British trade. Napoleon had taken his first steps towards the Iberian war that would sap so much of France's strength.

The Polish campaign

Following the final capitulation of Blücher and Hohenlohe, Napoleon set his sights on the Russians. He called up fresh recruits from France as well as from his allies. He had discovered that his Spanish ally had been on the point of betraying him, only waiting for any reverse against the Prussians. This had not happened, so Napoleon required that 15,000 of Spain's best troops under de la Romana be sent to support his efforts in northern Germany. They would serve the double purpose of supplying him troops and acting as *de facto* hostages.

The Emperor had sent General Sebastiani to Turkey in an effort to convince Selim III to go to war against Russia. Sebastiani had been successful and so Tsar Alexander now faced a second front. The Tsar had been slow to mobilize prior to this because he had thought that he was only acting in a supporting role to Prussia in this war. With the exception of 20,000 Prussians plus a few garrisons and the ineffectual secondary fronts of Sweden and Britain, Alexander's army was now going to have to face France alone.

Both sides now made a race for the best areas in which to winter and prepare for an anticipated spring campaign. The immediate focus was Warsaw. The Poles had risen up and celebrated the arrival of the French, seeing them as liberators. Napoleon had to play a careful balancing act, for while he was sympathetic to Poland's cause, openly embracing it could draw Austria back into the war as well as making peace with Russia impossible. His immediate answer was to strip Prussia of her Polish holdings and set up a Polish client state.

As Napoleon advanced, he had to contend with two conflicting needs. The first was to seize the left bank of the Vistula river and the second was to mop up the various garrisons left in his rear. This he did in a leapfrog fashion. Progress was slowed by the muddy roads resulting from a thaw. Murat advanced ahead of the corps of Davout, Lannes and Soult.

Bennigsen had decided that he risked being cut off from the supporting army of Buxhöwden, which was coming by way of Tilsit. He abandoned Warsaw and retreated to the right bank of the Vistula.

Murat entered Warsaw as the liberator on the evening of 28 November 1806. He held the city until Lannes and Davout arrived to support him. The town of Praga, opposite Warsaw, was taken, which gave the French a passage over the Vistula. Further downriver, Soult, Bessières, Augereau and Ney crossed with their corps.

The Russians were still holding the Bug river, which, along with the Wkra and Narew rivers, gave them a good defensive position. Napoleon was now heading to the front and ordered Murat to break the Bug line. On 10 December, Davout sent a division across and secured a bridgehead to the west of the confluence of the Wkra and Bug rivers.

The Wkra, which runs on a north–south axis, still presented a strong defensive position. On 20 December, Davout occupied the island that was formed by the junction of the Bug and Wkra. Marshal Kamenski had arrived in Pultusk on the night of 21 December to take command of the Russian army and ordered an offensive against the strung-out French army. The Russian advance was blunted at every turn and Kamenski paused to figure out his next move.

Davout was looking to force the Russian position. With Napoleon on the scene, he launched a nighttime river assault on the 24th. In an amazingly well coordinated attack, the Russians were driven back. Napoleon ordered an advance over the hastily built bridges and the Russians were driven back to the towns of Golymin and Pultusk. By this time, Augereau's and Murat's men were also over the Wkra. The muddy roads were so poor that it was virtually impossible to move artillery. The advancing French columns gathered up several Russian guns.

On Christmas night, Marshal Kamenski ordered a retreat and left the army, apparently suffering a mental breakdown. Bennigsen once more took over command and decided to stand at Pultusk. At 10 am on 26 December 1806, Lannes' corps drew up to the south of the Russian position on the high ground around Pultusk. His guns had not yet come up, but he ordered an attack anyway. The lay of the ground masked the fact that Lannes was badly outnumbered, for he was facing the main Russian army of 45,000 men. Lannes drove the outposts of

the Russians back and then brought up his main attack columns. Claparede's division hurled itself against the Russian left, pushing back the Russian first line slowly.

It was beginning to snow and vision was becoming difficult. Wedell's leading brigade, who were in the center of Lannes's line, began to wheel to their right to fall upon the troops in front of Claparede. As they did so, Russian cavalry came charging out of the snow and fell upon their flank. Hand-to-hand fighting went on, with the Russians having the better of it until Wedell's second line came up and fell on to the flank of the cavalry. Eventually falling back, they left many sabered French behind.

Lannes's cavalry were committed now, but were surprised when the Russian cavalry opposite fell away to reveal a massed battery, which unloaded a crushing canister salvo. As the French cavalry streamed back to their lines to re-form, Claparede's men succeeded in driving back the first line in front of them, capturing their guns in the process. Coming to a deep ravine running in front of the Russian reserves, they made several attempts to cross, but each time they were driven back. Bennigsen then released his reserve, and the French right flank slowly fell back under overwhelming pressure.

General Bennigsen, Russian commander at Eylau and Friedland. A master of writing communiques, Bennigsen was always able to make his defeats appear like victories. (Hulton Getty)

While this action was going on, Lannes was leading Suchet's division against General Barclay de Tolly's column. Deployed in a wood on the Russian right, Barclay's men were a formidable force outnumbering Lannes's more than two to one on this portion of the field. The French came on in skirmish order, taking advantage of the cover afforded by the trees, but Barclay's men were every bit their match. Even the inspiration of Lannes and Suchet leading their men from the front was not enough to overcome the determination of the Russian *Jäger* and line units.

As the day darkened because of the season and a relentless snowstorm, things were near breaking point. The French had all their men committed to battle and ammunition was running low after four hours of combat. Runners were sent back to replenish the ammunition, but the whole line was under pressure and the main supply wagons had not been able to get to the front because of the muddy road. The center was being held by Lannes's artillery, which after finally coming up had been engaged in a furious counter-battery fire with three times its number of Russian batteries.

At noon, several miles away General d'Aultanne, temporarily commanding Gudin's division of Davout's corps, heard the heated artillery exchange. Abandoning his plans to camp for the night, he marched to the sound of the guns. At about 2.30 pm, his men fell upon the flank of Barclay's men. Falling back on to Bennigsen's center, Barclay's men rallied and plunged back into the battle. The 34th Line was now out of ammunition and gave way. This created a gap between Lannes and d'Aultanne into which poured 20 squadrons of Russian cavalry. In the snow they were able to sweep around both divisions largely undetected. However, cries went down the French line and units formed square to repel the attack. Fortunately for the French, the snow that had aided the breakthrough also obscured the squares from a severe pounding from the Russian artillery in the center. The Tsar's cavalry, after repeated charges against the formed French, fell back through the line.

With the exception of the woods, where fighting continued in a desultory fashion for another couple of hours, the battle was over. Lannes had lost about one-third of his number while inflicting slightly fewer casualties on his opponent. The following day Bennigsen resumed his retreat and Lannes's 5th Corps was too exhausted to follow up.

While the desperate battle was going on at Pultusk, several miles away at Golymin, General Gallitzen was fighting a heroic rearguard against odds as bad as Lannes was facing. Left to cover the retreat of the Russian right, he had one small column to face three divisions with supporting cavalry. Given his instructions by his superior General Doctorov, Gallitzen deployed his men around the town. He was fortunate that the area was surrounded by heavy woods and swampy ground. The only access for cavalry or artillery was by the few roads that led into the village. In the morning, Lasalle's cavalry and the two divisions of Augereau's corps attacked Gallitzen's position. The French cavalry was thrown back by the charge of three squadrons of Russian cuirassiers. The two divisions, lacking their artillery, dissolved into skirmisher attacks about noon after their initial attacks were repulsed.

About this time, Murat and Davout arrived. Davout sent Morand's division into the attack. He drove back the Russians, but their resistance stiffened as they found the safety of the houses of the town. In an attempt to scatter the Russian cavalry who were impeding the French assault, General Rapp, an aide-de-camp of the Emperor, led a charge of dragoons down the road leading into the town. The Russian cavalry stood to meet them as the French rumbled down the road towards them. Suddenly standing up from the reeds that flanked the road were Russian infantrymen, who delivered a withering volley. Many saddles were emptied and the riderless horses fled down the road along with the remainder of the routed dragoons. As night covered the land, Gallitzen was able to break off his men and follow his withdrawing army.

When he received the report of Golymin, Napoleon was dismayed, for this ended the chance to pin the Russians against the Narew river. As it was clear that the Russians had escaped his trap, Napoleon ordered his men into their winter camps the following day.

Both sides felt pleased with their position. Bennigsen told the Tsar that he had defeated Napoleon and 60,000 men at Pultusk. He received the high command of both his and Buxhöwden's army as a result. Things would have remained at the status quo, had it not been for the aggressive actions of Marshal Ney. Hoping to increase the forage area of his corps as well as put himself in a position to be the first corps to take Königsberg, he began to extend his corps. Bennigsen caught wind of this and thought it a perfect opportunity to crush an isolated French corps. He began his winter offensive on 10 January 1807. His first contact with Ney was on the 18th. This cavalry skirmish helped to alert Napoleon to the Russian movements. Napoleon formulated a plan to move the 3rd, 4th, and 7th Corps from the south and pin the Russians against the coast and the 1st and 6th Corps.

The Battle of Eylau (by Bovinet). The church at Eylau, the highwater mark of the Russian advance, still stands there, turned into a factory building by disrespectful Russians in the 1960s. (AKG London)

The operation was well under way when Napoleon's plans were captured and Bennigsen realized his danger. Ordering a retreat, he fell back first to a position around Allenstein and finally to Eylau. There were three sharp actions at Mohrungen, Bergfried and Hof; all were indecisive, yet forced the Russians back further. All the time Napoleon was hot on their heels. On 7 February, the Russians turned and fought Soult's corps for possession of Eylau. Both sides wanted to sleep in the meager shelter that the town afforded against the bitter cold. In a tough fight, Soult's men were finally able to shelter with cover over their heads. It is most probable that the first day's actions were brought about accidentally.

Eylau

As day broke on 8 February, Napoleon had on the field 44,500 men opposite Bennigsen's 67,000. Napoleon thought that he had Ney's 10,000 men coming on fast as well as Davout's 5,500. All he wanted to do was fix the enemy in place and watch his reinforcements turn both flanks. The Russians did not intend to stand by passively and be defeated. They opened the battle with a

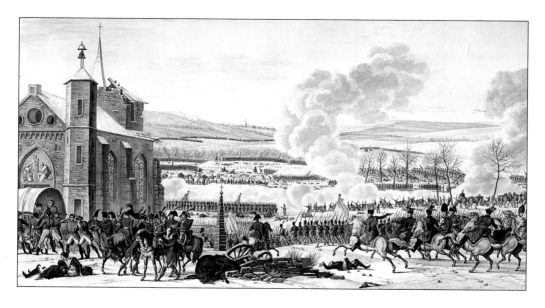

terrific barrage by a grand battery of over
100 guns. This bombardment pulverized the
French center. The French, with less then half
the guns in action, responded in kind, but
were hampered because a driving snowstorm
was blowing straight into their faces.

Napoleon had Soult attack the northern
flank in an attempt to draw away troops from
the south, where Davout was coming up.
Soult advanced and the Russians responded
effectively. Soult soon recoiled to the safety
of the main line, having unquestionably got
the worst of it. By now the first of Davout's
divisions, under Friant, was deploying.
A large Russian cavalry contingent was sent
to attack them. This forced the French to
close up to meet the onslaught and the key
assault lost its impetus.

To relieve the pressure, the Emperor
sent forward Augereau's corps in an attack
on the Russian center. The men fought
against the driving storm and waded

The cavalry charge at Eylau. By committing his superb cavalry in mass, Napoleon regained the initiative. (Roger-Viollet)

The *Grénadiers a cheval* charge at Eylau. That
Napoleon committed this regiment, the finest
regiment of his Guard, showed his determination to
reverse the tide of battle. (Roger-Viollet)

through 2 feet (0.6m) of snow. As they
moved forward they drifted off track,
exposing their flank to the line of the
Russian barrage. Equally destructive was the
fire of their own guns. The swirling snow
had so blinded the gunners that they were
firing at the last-known Russian position and
it was into this line of fire that Augereau's
men wandered. As they were hit from all
sides, confusion reigned. Bennigsen seized
the opportunity and sent a cavalry division
after the hapless Frenchmen. Coming out of
the snow, the Russian cavalry pounced upon
Augereau's men long before they could react
and form square. Behind them came two
columns of green-coated Russian infantry.

As the first fugitives came flying back to
the main line, Napoleon realized that this
was a crisis of the first magnitude. He

The Eylau campaign

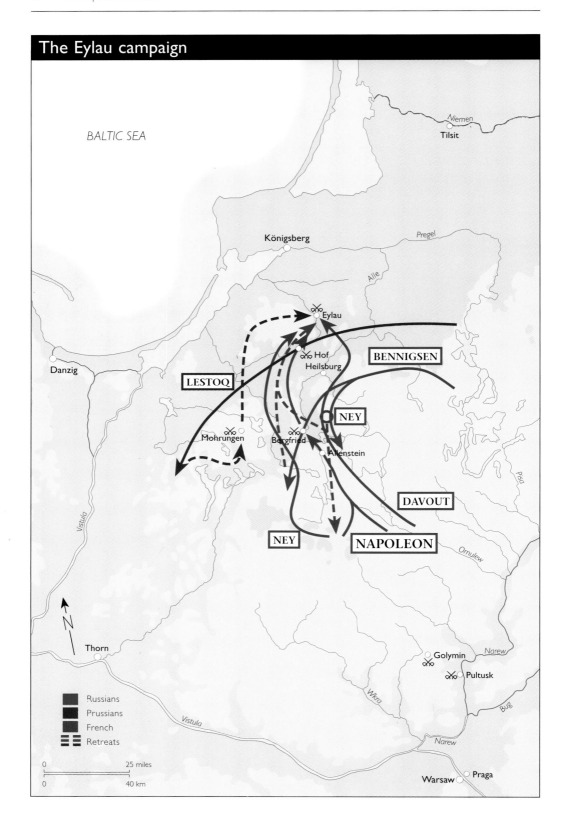

BALTIC SEA

Niemen

Tilsit

Königsberg

Pregel

Alle

Eylau

Hof
Heilsburg

BENNIGSEN

Danzig

LESTOQ

NEY

Mohrungen

Bergfried

Allenstein

DAVOUT

NEY

NAPOLEON

Omulew

Pisa

Vistula

Thorn

Golymin

Narew

Pultusk

Russians
Prussians
French
Retreats

Wkra

Bug

Vistula

Narew

0   25 miles

0   40 km

Warsaw   Praga

ordered Murat to send in his cavalry to right the situation. As the courier rode off, Russian infantry pushed into Eylau itself. The Emperor was within a moment of capture when his duty squadron charged these foes. The French were outnumbered beyond all hope, but they were able to blunt the attack until the Imperial Guard infantry arrived to hurl the Russians back.

What followed was the greatest cavalry charge in history. Murat's 10,700 men, making up 80 squadrons of line and guard cavalry, were sent forward in successive waves. The first hit the Russian infantry and cut into the army center. Here they overran several batteries before being stopped by the second line. The survivors of the first Russian line had lain down to let the French horsemen pass over them. Once clear they had stood, turned and fired into the cavalry's back. It was this type of behavior that had so often caused the French to forgo taking

prisoners. This time the French took full revenge, for no sooner had the Russians stood and begun to fire than the second wave of Murat's cavalry hit. This time it was the Guard. It struck the enemy in the rear and cut a bloody swathe through the line.

The Russians now committed a further cavalry reserve to stabilize the situation. These men got the worst of it as the final wave of the French charge hit home. But following the rout of the Russian cavalry, and finding himself increasingly surrounded by squares of enemy infantry, Murat retired; his job was done, the crisis of the battle had passed.

Murat's epic charge allowed the less impetuous Davout's attack to develop and the initiative swung over to the French. By

The Battle of Eylau (by Gros). After the battle, Napoleon surveys the field. Such cold and slaughter the French army had not experienced before. (AKG London)

1 pm, Davout had launched his attack with the support of St Hilaire's division from Soult's 4th Corps. The attack progressed as planned and the left flank of the Russian army was bending back. The heroes of Auerstädt looked like winning another improbable victory. Napoleon was following the action, but was worried that Ney had not yet made his appearance. Further, the Prussians under Lestoq, who were being pursued by Ney, were unaccounted for. As night fell, Napoleon's worst fears were realized. Lestoq arrived on the battlefield and at just the right place. Seemingly out of nowhere, his men fell upon Davout's exposed flank. The tired veterans fell back to the protection of several villages. Had the Prussian attack not come, Davout would have maintained his position astride the Russian line of retreat. The Russian army had been saved by the last remnants of the once proud Prussian army.

Ney had been trailing Lestoq for several days, but had pursued a rearguard that had been meant to draw him away from the field of Eylau. The orders sent to him by Napoleon had been lost. As he marched down the road, a corporal called to the Marshal's attention the battle going on in the far distance. Deciding to march in the direction of battle, he finally arrived at 7 pm. Ney attacked with his lead element. He took the town of Schloditten, but soon gave it up, not knowing the position of all the troops around him in the winter night.

Eylau had been a bloodbath of the highest magnitude. Napoleon suffered over 25,000 casualties, the Russians about the same. The following day, out of ammunition and supplies, Bennigsen retreated on to his supply line. Napoleon gladly let him go. The Emperor was shaken by the carnage that his army had experienced and knew that he would have to refit before once more taking on the Russians. He retired into his winter quarters and called up more reserves to the front.

Both sides tried to put a positive spin on the outcome of Eylau. Austria wavered and considered once more entering the war. Only the 'Peace Party' headed by the Archduke Charles prevented this action. Francis decided upon waiting to see the outcome of the next great battle. Napoleon offered Prussia a separate peace, which would restore all of Prussia east of the Elbe river. The King was initially disposed toward this, but his Foreign Minister, Hardenberg, opposed the offer and won over the King. War to the death seemed the only option. Europe waited anxiously for the resumption of the campaign.

Both armies spent the winter months refitting and resting. Two operations took place during the spring of 1807. Marshal Mortier had hemmed in the Swedes in Swedish Pomerania. When he marched towards Colberg with half his command, the Swedes attacked and drove back the remaining troops. Mortier rallied and in a series of running battles drove the Swedes back into Stralsund. The King of Sweden, who had lost his British support, had enough and signed an armistice on 29 April.

In March, Marshal Lefebvre invested Danzig. In perhaps the hardest-fought siege outside Spain, the city finally surrendered on 27 April. Now only Colberg held out. This could be invested much more economically than the other two cities and many of the siege troops were second rate.

The tidying up of the rear area let Napoleon plan his next offensive. Six days before he was to launch it, Sweden repudiated the armistice and renewed hostilities around Stralsund on 4 June. Next, on the 5th, Bennigsen struck, initially attacking Bernadotte and wounding him in the process, then he turned his main attention to Ney's corps. Alerted to what was coming, Ney, the master of the rearguard, drew the Russians slowly forward. While this action was happening, Napoleon issued orders to Davout to strike the Russians from the south. As the Russians took losses moving against the elusive Ney, Davout's attack got under way. Giving up, Bennigsen fell back and left Bagration as a rearguard. The wily Prince once more got the most out of his men and over a two-day retreat allowed the main army to fall back to their prepared position at Heilsberg.

Heilsberg

On 10 June, the lead elements of Napoleon's army, under Murat, arrived and attacked the outlying villages south of Heilsberg. The first village was taken, but the town of Bevernick proved more difficult. Soult's corps was committed to the fight. Forming a battery of 36 guns, they pounded the Russian avant-garde and Bagration's men were forced back. The Russians fell back contesting every foot of ground, but finally gave way and fell behind the main position. Here stood two Russian divisions in entrenchments backed by cavalry.

The French reorganized and made an assault against the Russian left. The key redoubt was taken at bayonet point. However, before more support could come up, the Russians counter-attacked with six battalions and threw out the enemy. Simultaneously, Prussian cavalry moved to the Russian infantry's right and, charging through the smoke, caught Espagne's cuirassiers at a standstill. The impetus behind them, the Prussians exacted their revenge for Jena. Many of the French were killed before they could ride off.

Another attempt was made to retake the redoubt, but once more the effort failed. All along the line, the Russian artillery blasted the French from the safety of their dug-in positions. At last the French fell back safely out of cannon shot.

At dusk, Lannes made one more effort to unhinge the Russian position. One of his divisions under General Verdier moved from

Heilsberg. The 55th Line have one of their Eagles captured by the Prussian 5th Hussars (by Knotel). (Author's collection)

the cover of the woods, came on at the double and fell upon the men defending the Russian line. Engaged in a vicious hand-to-hand fight, Verdier's men too were defeated when no support came to back up their initial success.

Heilsberg had been a needless bloodbath with the French taking over 8,000 in losses and the Russians probably something slightly less – needless because the following day the Russians were turned out of their trenches by a flanking maneuver. This battle might have had significant political effects had it not been for the events in the following few days.

At midday on 11 June, Bennigsen abandoned his position and fell away to the east. Convinced that his opponent would try to defend Königsberg, the last city of Prussia, Napoleon began to march his army in that direction. Throwing Lannes and the cavalry under Grouchy out towards Friedland, he got reports on the 13th that there was a large Russian presence in that area. Ordering the corps of Mortier, Ney, and the Guard to move to Lannes's support, he hoped that Marshal Lannes could hold on until the main army arrived.

Friedland

On 14 June, the anniversary of Napoleon's victory at Marengo, the battle started early in the morning. Bennigsen had crossed most of his army to the west of the Alle river. He thought he had caught one of Napoleon's corps isolated and viewed this as the opportunity to gain the victory that would bring Austria back into the war. At 2 am, the fighting began on both flanks. Bagration tried to push part of Oudinot's grenadiers out of the Sortlack forest. These elite troops were more than a match for Bagration's hard-fighting veterans.

On the northern flank, General Uvarov and the Russian Guard cavalry were attacking Grouchy's cuirassiers and dragoons divisions, with the support of more light cavalry. This was one of the great cavalry fights in history, with the gallant French throwing back twice their number throughout the morning. Sending forward infantry support, the Russians seized the key village of Heinrichdorf. Grouchy countered by sending Nansouty's cuirassiers forward in a perfectly timed charge that caught the Russian infantry by complete surprise. The French quickly riding among them, most were sabered where they stood. Lannes now sent his reserve brigade of grenadiers to occupy the bloody streets of Heinrichdorf.

By 7 am Mortier's men began to arrive. Sent to the hardest-pressed part of the line, they frustrated every success that the Russians gained. The forest of Sortlack would change hands at least five times, but by 11 am it was firmly in French control. Nine hours had passed and Lannes had held out against almost three times his number. Bennigsen now made one more supreme effort to break the French, only to be hurled back more viciously than before. The butcher's bill was rising for Bennigsen and he called off the attack. There are some reports that Bennigsen now experienced a gall bladder attack that incapacitated him. Report after report was sent to Russian headquarters that the French were pouring on to the battlefield, but no response came forth.

Napoleon arrived on the field at 12 noon and met with Lannes. The Marshal reported that the Russian position was divided by the swollen stream called the Mühlen Floss. Further, their only line of retreat over the Alle was by three rickety bridges. Napoleon couldn't believe his fortune. Carefully watching every movement of the enemy, he placed the troops of Ney's 6th Corps, Victor's 1st Corps, and the Guard into their positions to deliver the crushing blow. Shortly before 5 pm, Napoleon gave his signal to attack. Ney's men stormed out of the Sortlack forest and slammed into Bagration's men. The blow hit like a hammer and drove them back on to the town of Friedland. Trying to stabilize the position, Bagration threw his cavalry on to Marchand's division, but General Latour-

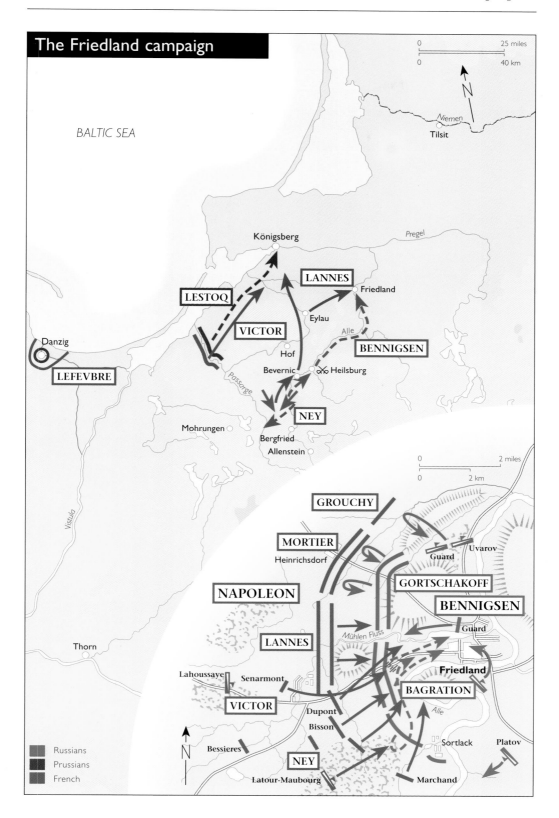

The Friedland campaign

Charge of the 4th Hussars at Friedland. The Hussars thought their swaggering panache made them the elite of the cavalry in every army. Their critics retorted that this characteristic was evident off the battlefield more often than on it. (Roger-Viollet)

Maubourg was waiting for such a move and rode down the Russians from the flank.

Ney's men pressed on, but were soon caught in a crossfire coming from the guns in front of Friedland and from across the river. Staggered by these blows, they then had to face the Russian reserve cavalry. Most regiments broke and ran. The Russian cavalry retired behind the rapidly contracting Russian center. Ney rode back and forth rallying his men and forming them back up for a final push.

As this was going on, Dupont, leading the 1st Division of Victor's corps, advanced and poured a galling fire into the massed Russians. Supporting him was Victor's chief of artillery, General Senarmont, with 30 guns. Rolling up to within close canister range of the massed Russian infantry formations, they unleashed salvo after salvo upon the hapless troops. In the smoke and confusion, the troops being so efficiently butchered could not even locate the source of their torment. Thousands died in place.

Napoleon now massed his howitzer batteries to drop shells on the town and bridges of Friedland. Soon all were on fire and in various stages of destruction. Bennigsen threw in his last reserve in the sector of this field, the Imperial Guard. Senarmont swung his guns about and swept away the cavalry in short order. The Guard infantry came on though and were met with sheets of flame as Dupont's men delivered a short-range volley. The giants of the Tsar fired back, but Dupont's men had seen much worse than this and, after wearing them down with an exchange of fire, leveled their bayonets and charged. The sight of these men coming on, having no respect or fear for their status, unnerved the Guard, who broke and fled into the overcrowded streets.

Ney's men were now pressing the advance and caught the Tsar's men against the Alle

Napoleon on the battlefield of Friedland
(by Vernet). Unlike Eylau, this was the decisive
victory Napoleon had come to expect. (AKG London)

river. Many jumped into the river trying to escape the Frenchmen's fury. Terror seized Bennigsen's men, and many who did not surrender were slaughtered or drowned.

To the north, Lannes and Mortier now advanced against the remaining Russians. With their backs to the river, the men in General Gortschakoff's column held on with a fanatical desperation. If it had not been for an opportunely discovered ford and the inactivity of Grouchy's exhausted cavalry, the result would have been the same as at Friedland. As it was, fewer then half of Gortschakoff's men could muster the following day.

Friedland had been as complete a victory as Napoleon would ever have. While taking about 10,000 in losses himself, he had inflicted nearly 40,000 on the Russians. Alexander's army under Bennigsen was in ruins. Five days later, Alexander requested an armistice in preparation for a final peace.

The Treaty of Tilsit, 1807

On 25 June at Tilsit, the Tsar met with Napoleon to make peace and divide up Europe. Prussia was left out of the initial negotiations.

The meeting was held on a raft in the middle of the Niemen river. Napoleon had a profound effect on Alexander personally. He was generous to his vanquished foe and the treaty granted Alexander much more than he could have hoped for after such a crushing defeat as Friedland. The provisions of the peace were: the recognition of all the territorial acquisitions of France and her allies; the restoration of at least a truncated Poland in the form of the Duchy of Warsaw under the protectorship of the King of Saxony; an alliance between France and Russia; and the cession of the former Prussian territory of Bialystock to Russia. Napoleon abandoned the Turks and

recognized Russia's right to take the Danubian provinces away from his former ally. The peace treaty with Russia was signed on 9 July and that with Prussia on 12 July.

Much has been written about Napoleon's callous behavior towards the Turks, but this criticism fails to take into account the fact that the Sultan Selim III had been murdered the month before by his Janissary guards, who supplanted him with a puppet ruler, Mustapha. Selim had been a friend to Napoleon, and there was no reason for Napoleon to have any faith in Mustapha, for Selim was killed in large part because of the modernizing reforms he had introduced with the urging of French advisers.

Tilsit. On a raft in the Niemen, the two Emperors, ostensibly now allied, discuss the government of the world. (Hulton Getty)

Napoleon reviews the Russian Guard at Tilsit (by Debret). The new alliance even led to giving decorations to former foes, but the new friendships were not to last. (AKG London)

Prussia was humiliated. She lost all her holdings west of the Elbe and her Polish provinces. Furthermore, Danzig was declared a free city, to be garrisoned by the French. The beautiful Queen Louisa tried to use her charms upon Napoleon in order to ameliorate the conditions, but failed.

Sweden had been promised British support. What came was much too small to face the troops freed up from the victory at Friedland. With designs elsewhere, the British pulled out leaving the hapless King to face the might of France. The Tsar abandoned Sweden and Napoleon gave him permission to take Finland from her. This offer Alexander gladly accepted.

Lannes, Marshal of France

Jean Lannes was insecure, crude, blunt and reckless, but he may have been Napoleon's greatest marshal.

Early life and career

He was born in Lectoure, France, on 10 April 1769, four months before Napoleon. His family were farmers and Lannes received his basic education from his older brother, a priest. Apprenticed as a dyer, he gladly joined the local volunteer regiment in 1792.

His early combat experience was on the Pyrenees front, fighting the Spanish. Here he rose rapidly in rank, reaching that of colonel just over a year later. This early part of his career was highlighted by continual acts of bravery. In 1795, as the war with Spain was winding down, Lannes was placed under the command of General Pierre Augereau, the future marshal. Once more his outstanding combat performance brought him to the attention of his commanding officer. This began a friendship that would last for the rest of Lannes's life.

The division was transferred to Italy, and Lannes came under the command of Bonaparte when the latter took command of the army in March 1796. Napoleon first noticed Lannes when he led the decisive bayonet charge to win the Battle of Dego. Promoted to the command of the elite grenadiers, Lannes once again carried the day with his courage at Lodi, when he led the rush over the bridge that conveyed Bonaparte one step nearer to immortality.

When he performed almost the identical act at Bassano, becoming wounded in the process, Bonaparte promoted him to general. Recuperating, Lannes hurried to the front upon hearing news of the defeat at Caldiero. Finding that Bonaparte had regrouped to

conduct a flanking battle at Arcola, Lannes resumed his command. Being wounded twice more, he rose from his ambulance bed upon hearing of the continued failures of the army. He arrived at the front just as Bonaparte had been personally thrown down a steep bank into the river, amidst the confusion caused by a failed attack over the bridge of Arcola. Rallying the men, Lannes led the charge that took the town, and saved Napoleon from capture or death. This act earned him the eternal affection of the future Emperor.

The remainder of the war in Italy saw Lannes perform diplomatic missions to the Papal States and Genoa. In both cases, Lannes shocked the opposing diplomats by his bluntness, but came away with the desired outcome.

When Bonaparte led the campaign to Egypt, Lannes followed. After the victory of Alexandria came the march to Cairo. Murat complained bitterly about the conditions and Bonaparte's mistakes. When these grumblings got back to Napoleon, Murat blamed Lannes. This started a life-long feud between the two men.

Lannes continued to cover himself with glory throughout the Egyptian campaign. His one failure was at Acre, where he led an assault on the walls. Shot through the neck, he almost perished. Fortunately, he was dragged to safety by one of his officers. He slowly recovered, and did not see action again until he captured the Turkish camp during the victory at Aboukir. It was following this triumph that he learned that his wife had given birth to an illegitimate child. This made the moody Gascon even more so.

He had become one of Napoleon's closest friends, so it was not surprising that he was one of the few chosen to accompany

Bonaparte back to France. He played a small but important role in the coup d'état of Brumaire that put Napoleon in control of the government of France. Following this event, Lannes divorced his wife and prepared to rejoin the army.

In the campaign of 1800, Napoleon turned his attention to ending the war and retaking Italy. Lannes received the key command of the avant-garde. After crossing the St Bernard Pass through the Alps, Lannes's men swept down the Aosta valley. After several successful skirmishes, Lannes daringly led his men past the impregnable Fort Bard in the middle of the night. At Chiusella, Lannes led a storming party that seized the vital stronghold. This opened the line of communications and his men were resupplied. Under his leadership, his men continued to march quickly and took the city of Pavia. Moving south, he defeated the Austrians at Stradella.

He had now marched around the Austrian army and so turned back to the west to link up once more with the main army. As he approached the town of Casteggio, he saw on the heights above twice his number of enemy. Confident of his men, Lannes launched an attack up the slopes. In a desperate struggle, the Austrians were pushed back, but had their numbers doubled by reinforcements hurrying up from the town of Montebello. The situation was critical, with Lannes riding up and down the line encouraging his men to hold on. On the verge of collapse, Lannes was relieved by the division of Victor, which was double-timing it down the road. They threw the white-uniformed Austrian infantry back to the town of Montebello.

After a lull of an hour, Lannes sent his men forward once more to double-envelop the village. Despite the commanding strength of the Montebello position, the French were irrepressible. The ground fell away sharply, and the retreating Austrians were caught with no good retreat route. Against odds of one to two, Lannes had won his signature battle. In 1808, he would be made the Duke of Montebello.

He enjoyed little respite, for five days later he and his men were fighting for their lives on the plains of Marengo. Here his troops resisted stubbornly for most of a day, but ultimately gave way. Finally, with new troops arriving on the field, Napoleon gave the orders for the counterattack that would win the day and regain Italy.

Following the Italian campaign, Napoleon rewarded Lannes with command of his Guard. He landed himself in hot water almost immediately by spending 300,000 francs out of the Guards' treasury to upgrade the men's condition. This came to the attention of General Bessières, who told his close friend Murat. The latter, itching to get back at Lannes, told First Consul Bonaparte. Infuriated, Bonaparte demanded that his friend repay the funds out of his own money or face court-martial. It was his old friend Augereau who loaned Lannes the money to get out of his fix. Lannes resigned his command of the Guard, but soon received the important diplomatic mission

Jean Lannes. Combining a shrewd tactical skill with astounding personal bravery, he was forgiven exceptional familiarities with Napoleon because of his battlefield prowess. (Ann Ronan Picture Library)

to Portugal. Remarried, Lannes headed south from Paris.

It was in Portugal that Lannes was able to win many trade concessions for France and, either from bribes or gifts, raised enough money to repay Augereau. Because of the success of his entire career, Jean Lannes was made one of the original 18 marshals in 1804. Recalled to Paris, he attended Napoleon's coronation before taking command of the newly formed 5th Corps at the camp of Boulogne.

Lannes in the Napoleonic Wars

This takes us up to the point where Lannes begins to appear in the earlier chapters on the campaigns of 1805-07. Lannes's V Corps was usually in the forefront of the *Grande Armée*.

Though Lannes was a very forthright personality, very prone to lose his temper when he felt put upon, he was capable of rising above it when necessary. Despite his animosity for Murat, Lannes gave him his best support when Murat's cavalry trapped the Austrian column at Wertingen. When Murat followed the wrong trail before Vienna and had to recuperate by stealing a bridge across the Danube, Lannes was at his side to overawe and bamboozle the Austrian bridge guards. By the time the guards realized that they had been taken, French grenadiers were within the defenses. Seldom have such high-ranking officers been ready to lead special operations from the front-line. Because Murat in turn fell for the ruse of a false armistice, Lannes was robbed of enough daylight to destroy Bagration's rearguard at Schongrabern.

Before Austerlitz Lannes fell out with Soult after the latter had put him up to challenging

Lannes at Ratisbon, 1809. When several assaults had failed to take the walls and his men would not go forward, Lannes seized a ladder himself. Shouting to his men, 'I was a grenadier before I was a marshal,' he headed towards the walls. He was overtaken by his men, who soon captured the town. (Ann Ronan Picture Library)

Napoleon's plan but then backed down when the reaction was very hostile. After a hard fight on the northern flank under the insufferable Murat, Lannes thought his achievements were underrated in the victory bulletin compared to those of the despised Soult. Lannes stormed off from the army, and no one dared tell him to return.

The "AWOL" marshal rejoined his corps on the Prussian frontier on 7 October 1806, the same day that war was declared. Three days later he crushed the corps of Prince Louis at Saalfeld, beginning the cascade of French victories. For only 172 casualties, 900 Prussians and Saxons were dead including their leader, 1800 more were captured, and 6000 scattered, even though they were good troops. Training and leadership made the difference.

Lannes was first up the escarpment at Jena, and on 13 October he was in the forefront of battle the entire day, until the French army had gained another great victory. Without sleep or rest, his corps went on to round up the scattered Prussian survivors. In fact Lannes kept pushing all the way into Poland, though as winter closed in, the mud and cold slowed V Corps. In the end it took an entire Russian army to stop him at Pultusk, though in a desperate battle he tried hard to break through that as well. Finally the pace was too much for him, and he was sent on sick leave to Warsaw for his wife to nurse him back to health. She did a good job, despite depression caused by what he saw as the intrigues of jealous rivals, for in the spring he was in his best form. He skillfully held the Russian army in play at Friedland until Napoleon could bring up enough troops to launch a decisive attack. When the moment came, Lannes led his corps from the front, and the day ended in another glorious victory.

For once Lannes was satisfied with his share of praise and rewards, and he enjoyed several months in France with his family. He was called to action once again when the best generals were needed in Spain to repair the damage caused by lesser ones. Lannes was not even given time to gather his baggage, but literally had to gallop the length of France to get to his new command. Within days he was leading it into combat at Tudela on 23 November 1808. Catching a Spanish army unready, deployed over far too great a distance, he took the opportunity to crush one half while the other looked on aghast. When Lannes's attention shifted their way they ran. Lannes moved on to Saragossa, where fanatical resistance and demoralized troops had led to a series of costly and botched attempts at siege. Despite difficult conditions, Lannes revitalized the attack in this hardest form of warfare, street fighting against a determined foe.

Victory came, but at a terrible cost for besieger and besieged. It was a hard job well done, but observers remarked that Lannes was now war weary and depressed. His spirits rose when news came of battles on the Danube front. Lannes leapt at this chance to rejoin his beloved commander, Napoleon, and once more galloped the length of Europe to get there in time. He was one of the few French commanders to leave Spain with his reputation enhanced.

In 1809 he fought the Austrians once more, crowning a legendary career with more victories and acts of heroism. Before the walls of Ratisbon (Regensburg), when the troops hung back, he grabbed a ladder and tried to scale the walls himself. Leading from the front was his one military vice. After a dogged defensive action around Essling in May, Lannes paid for this when he was mortally wounded.

Lannes had been one of the few men who could speak to Napoleon on intimate terms, and never thought his respect for Napoleon should prevent honest criticism. Napoleon could never replace him. He died with a record of no defeats on the battlefield, and more than enough victories. His battle record was enough to cover the Arc de Triomphe by itself. He had grown from being a brave uncouth grenadier to being a man highly regarded for both his personal and military virtues. So much had he grown that Napoleon said of him after that "He had found a pygmy and lost a giant."

Philippe-René Girault

Early life and career

Philippe-René Girault was a veteran by the time the *Grande Armée* marched eastwards in 1805. He joined the army in 1791 as a soldier-musician, probably aged 15. He served at Valmy and in the campaigns along the Rhine, enduring privations, enjoying adventures. By the time of Hohenlinden he was part of the band of the prestigious 5th Hussars, but soon afterward new regulations eliminated the cavalry bands. Musicians enjoyed to a limited extent the freedom of individual contractors, moving from regiment to regiment according to how much the colonel and officers wanted to subsidize the regimental music. Forced out of his billet in the Hussars, Girault drifted into a regiment that became the 93rd Line.

The 93rd was not a prestigious unit, but in its peacetime station it wanted a good band to impress the locals. Garrisoning La Rochelle and the Île de Ré in south-west France, the 93rd provided drafts for service in San Domingo, an unpopular duty where many perished from sickness. Not that the Île de Ré was much better, for it was a sickly station where many went down with fevers. Girault almost died, but he was nursed through the crisis by a girl whom he wisely married.

The Napoleonic Wars

Girault, his wife Lucile, and the 93rd Line were sent into Italy at the beginning of 1805 to provide a reserve for Massena's army. The regiment was a raw one and was not called into action, but Napoleon needed replacements to fill the gaps in his army after Austerlitz and Jena. In November 1806, the regiment was ordered to cross the Tyrolean mountains into Germany. The snow was deep, and even though Girault's wife was game, she was so short the snow came up to her thighs. She had to share a carriage with an officer's wife. The couple squeezed into an overcrowded inn in the mountains, but found they could not afford the wine or beer to go with what they had gathered for their dinner. A general of brigade chanced by, who happily invited himself to share their meal in return for providing the wine. The Giraults were happy: they calculated they had spent a mere 12 sous, whereas the General must have spent 6 francs or more.

Then it was down into Bavaria, where they settled into winter quarters in Augsburg. As Girault reported to his colonel in the city, a messenger told him that his wife, following the regiment on a *cantinière's* wagon, had fallen into the Danube when the carriage horse had panicked and gone into the river. Rushing back, he was relieved to find his wife being carried through the city gates: a *voltigeur* (the voltigeur company was the company specially designated for skirmish work) from the passing rearguard had gallantly leapt in and pulled her out of the river.

A *cantinière*, sometimes called a *vivandière*, was a soldier's wife or mistress working as a licensed sutler. Sometimes these women were very popular, especially if they extended credit, or were brave enough to bring brandy up to the regiment under fire. Under cannonfire or musketry, some *cantinières* were wounded or killed: some did not charge for brandy dispensed in action, thinking it part of their duty under fire. However, the *cantinière* riding with Lucile was obviously not one of these, because she was not popular. Perhaps because she did not extend credit or pressed her debtors too hard, or her protector might have been a bully. Whatever it was, none of the soldiers dived in to save her, and it was left to a Bavarian to fish her out.

The troops were never so happy as when they were campaigning in Bavaria or Austria. It was rich countryside in which to forage, even when the rations were regular. One officer thought that, whenever his battalion left a bivouac, it left enough food to last for 15 days. The soldiers hoped that by the time they had 'eaten' the country out, the supply services would have caught up. In billets the civilians were soon taught that if they did not serve their guests the best, the soldiers would not only help themselves, but cause waste and damage that would make it ten times worse. Of course, these habits did not make friends among the population, and the pickings were not so good in the poorer countries to the east, East Prussia and Poland.

At the end of a march, the fires were lighted, the camp kettles were put to the boil and some sort of shelter was improvised, as the army did not carry tents. Tents would slow up an army's march, and Napoleon's army marched hard. The troops had confidence in their leadership and accepted that hard marching resulted in fewer casualties. The French veteran Massena was admired for his ability to conjure shelters out of branches, straw, leaves, anything. Meanwhile, the marauders returned with food or wood for their comrades.

Recruits, however, would often arrive at a campsite so tired that they would just collapse, and unless there was someone to look after them, they would wake up to find they had to begin the next day's march after a night without warmth or food or shelter. After a few days of this, the conscripts would fall out with sickness and exhaustion, often being left to their fate and never seen again. The cold and mud of Poland, worse than they had ever seen before, soon showed the limitations of such a rough-and-ready style of warfare. The troops grew demoralized and losses from attrition soared. After Eylau, however, Napoleon pulled his troops back into warm quarters and began to rebuild his army.

To replace the losses and reinforce the *Grande Armée*, rear area troops were brought up. In their wake, even second-line formations, like the 93rd, were called forward. In the spring of 1807, the regiment marched up to Berlin, being shocked on the way at how grisly the field of Jena was even six months later. Still stationed in Berlin, the regiment had comfortable billets and the chance for some tourism: Girault visited the palace of Frederick the Great. Then they went on to winter in Stettin, again in good billets.

Usually on campaign the troops did not have such amenities, but the French soldiers were famed for their ability to make themselves comfortable if they had a little time to do so. Further to the east, the *Grande Armée* was building itself military towns of wood, straw, and canvas in the wilderness near Tilsit. More than comfortable, the streets of these towns were even elegant. One regiment, to outshine its neighbors, planted rows of fir trees along their streets, one outside every hut. Then they built a parade ground, neatly bordered with more trees. Other regiments tried to compete, but soon there were no more woods within striking range. Even the villages had been dismantled to provide wood for the huts, after their barns and flocks had disappeared to feed the troops.

For an agrarian economy, one French soldier noted, 'War, flood, hail and fire are less dangerous than the presence of an enemy army.' Later this same soldier, Captain Elzear Blaze, saw his regiment reviewed by Napoleon himself, accompanied by the Tsar and the King of Prussia. The King was very impressed by the camp. 'It would be impossible to build finer camps than yours,' he said, 'but admit that you've left some wretched villages.'

But there was work for even a despised regiment. The 93rd was called forward to join Marshal Brune in front of the fortress of Colberg, and Girault had to leave his wife behind with their newly born son. This Prussian fortress had been under siege for some time, but as it was also a port, the

French land blockade did not work. Half-hearted attacks had only served to give the garrison a sense of heroism at being one of the few Prussian forces to hold out after the debacle of 1806. Brune, however, did not intend to sit in inactivity and ordered an assault. The 93rd went forward through a wood in a vigorous attack, but stalled. It sat exposed to the fire from the Red Fort to its front and from an English frigate cruising

The Camp of Boulogne (by Bellanger). While there were many ceremonies as illustrated here, usually the camp was the scene of constant training until the troops surpassed the standards of their opponents. (Hulton Getty)

along the shoreline to its left. The musicians wisely took cover behind some sand dunes, where the surgeon was working on the wounded streaming back.

As was usual, the band was conscripted to carry back the wounded. If there were limbs to be amputated, the surgeon worked away; other cases were loaded on wagons to be evacuated. Girault had never seen an amputation before; now he saw far too many. Soon he was covered in blood from head to toe, 'like a butcher,' he said. With the standards of medical care of the time, doctors resorted to amputation as the only answer to a shattered limb: if the doctor was skillful, the wounded might survive

operation and infection. A cannonball to head or body could only be lethal, a bullet wound might be survived if not in the gut or too deep, a saber wound was almost lucky.

When the regiment finally withdrew, Girault was left to watch some conscripted peasants dig a ditch to bury the limbs left behind. Seeing an arm on a pile of straw, Girault attempted to gather it up, but found it was still attached to its live owner. After his arm had been shattered, the poor soldier had made it as far as the surgeon, but had collapsed on a pile of straw. More straw and more wounded had been piled on top of him, and unconscious he had stayed forgotten until Girault found him. The

surgeon was summoned and amputated the arm. Not a single cry escaped the soldier, who ended up staggering off on his own legs to the hospital rather than await the return of an ambulance. Girault was impressed by this display of hardness, but in the days of the survival of the fittest, these soldiers were very tough – they had to be.

The next day the 93rd was allowed to stay in cover. An Italian regiment took its place in the line. A ration of beef was issued, but it was highly unlikely that the beef was in any recognizable cut, not unless a soldier had great pull with the butcher. When the regulations specified a pound of beef, they meant it literally, even if the pound included skin, bone or offal. Usually the beef was issued in one ration for a mess of soldiers, and often there was little they could do with it other than make it into soup or stew, not only because of the quality of the meat, but also because they seldom had more than a pot to cook in over an open fire. Occasional issues of rice or vegetables would make the meal more palatable, but usually a mess would have to scrounge or buy these. Sometimes the bread ration was so poor as to be good for nothing but a stew as well.

Girault and his fellow bandsmen had the makings for soup, but lacked wood for a fire. They went searching for it in the wood where the regiment had fought the day before. The garrison was still alert, and cannonballs soon chased the band to the cover of the sand dunes. Even there ricochets from the fire hunted them down, and they had to bolt for it. One of his comrades lost a thumb and finger, but Girault lamented more the loss of wood and soup.

After a hungry night, the next day the Peace of Tilsit was announced to the troops. The good news was tainted by a rumor that Brune had known of the peace three days earlier. In his quest for glory, Brune had proceeded with the attack anyway. Within a year Brune had been dismissed by Napoleon, probably for political reasons rather than this butchery. It had cost 400 unnecessary casualties, but the 93rd was finally blooded. That was the life of a soldier.

Line Infantry: drummer of the grenadiers c.1799, print
after Maurice Orange. (Philip Haythornthwaite)

Part II
The empires fight back 1808–1812

Napoleon at the Battle of Borodino, 7 September 1812, by
Robert Alexander Hillingford. (Nassau County Museum)

Mutiny and defiance

Napoleon's popularity at home was at a low point. The treaty of Tilsit in 1807 had brought hopes of peace, but less than a year later here was France at war again, this time with Spain. A plot to overthrow Napoleon and place Murat on the throne had been hatched by Talleyrand and Fouché, Napoleon's minister of police. Napoleon had learned of this and dismissed Talleyrand. Fouché was left in place with a warning, but in later years the Emperor's leniency would come back to haunt him.

While this plot was suppressed, numerous acts of Royalist terrorism continued,

primarily in Normandy and Brittany. These staunchly Catholic provinces were fertile areas of discontent. Napoleon's relationship with the Pope, Pius VII, had seriously deteriorated since the coronation of 1804. Following his annexation of the Papal lands in 1809 Napoleon was excommunicated. He retaliated by having the Pope arrested and imprisoned for five years.

To add to Napoleon's troubles at home, a romantic nationalist revival, centered in Heidelberg, had grown strong enough to cause repeated uprisings against the French throughout the German states. In the

Europe in 1809

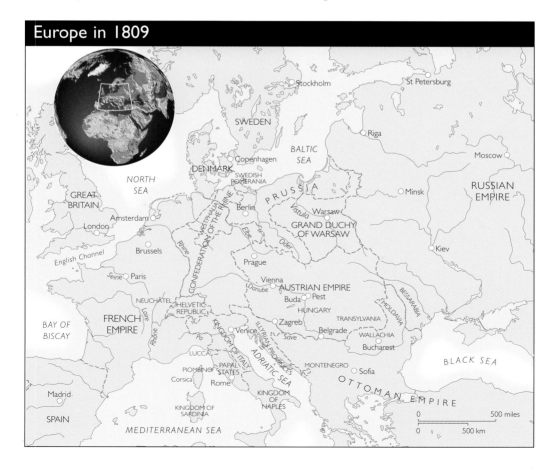

autumn of 1808 the Austrian emperor, Francis, toured his holdings accompanied by his young third wife. He received a rapturous welcome wherever he went. A war party had developed and was beating the drum to regain the Hapsburg honor by declaring war on France. So Austria put out feelers to Russia and Prussia to become allies. Russia eventually agreed to take no action against Austria, despite pretending to remain Napoleon's ally, and Prussia originally agreed to provide 80,000 men to aid in the effort.

Austria seeks reprisal

The commander of the Hapsburg forces was the Archduke Charles, Emperor Francis' brother. He had been the leader of the peace party and still had strong reservations about taking on Napoleon. Charles had been trying to reform the army ever since the defeat of Austerlitz in 1805. Much had been accomplished, but his efforts had been severely frustrated by court politics and he felt that much more was needed before they were ready to challenge the French. However, the war party was too strong, and Charles faced the choice of agreeing to the war or resigning. He chose the former.

If Austria had counted on Russian support, she was to be disappointed. Russia was successfully waging two different wars at the beginning of 1809 – with Turkey and with Sweden. Furthermore, she was ostensibly at war with Britain, though neither side was actually willing to fight. Britain had sent a large portion of its army to Gothenburg to support the Swedes, but this was not where the fighting was taking place, since all the battles were in Finland. While the Swedes fought bravely, the might of Russia brought them to the negotiating table and the Swedes were forced to trade Finland for peace.

Prussia was still led by the weak-willed King Frederick Wilhelm. Although initially he promised help to Austria, he lost his nerve and backed out before the shooting started.

Only Britain would lend support to the Hapsburg army. At first she hesitated, but once it became clear that the Austrians were in earnest, money was promised and a vague assurance given of a landing on the north coast of Europe. This was all the determined men around Francis needed to prepare for war. A report from the finance minister to Francis stated that the treasury would run out of money by mid 1809 if the army remained mobilized. It was reasoned therefore that while the army was there, it should be used. The thought that Austria should demobilize seems never to have occurred to the Austrian high command. Even Charles, while warning that the army was not yet prepared for war, did not wish to have his reformed troops demobilized.

The Austrian foreign minister to France was Prince Metternich. He made every effort to appear cordial to the French but spied and plotted with the likes of Talleyrand to undermine Napoleon. Metternich had an abiding hatred of everything for which Napoleon stood. An aristocrat of the old school, he saw Napoleon as the embodiment of the Revolution and a direct threat to his way of life. He spied successfully on the French court and gave accurate reports to Vienna of Napoleon's preparations and reactions to the Austrian mobilization. In large part, however, his warnings went unheeded.

Napoleon, meanwhile, behaved as if in a swirling mist, appearing to see clearly one moment and be completely in the dark the next. He had faith in his Russian ally, and was sure that the threat of a two-front war on Austria would deter any hostilities. However, he began to mobilize another army to meet the threat from the east. He withdrew men from Spain and called on the Confederation of the Rhine states to bring their contingents up to full war footing. He called up the recruit class of 1810 to fill his ranks. In all the theaters facing Austria he would field over 400,000 men. The Austrians had estimated his strength at only half that number.

France, Austria, and Russia

The French army

Napoleon had invaded Spain with most of his veterans from the glorious campaigns of 1805–07. When Austria threatened in 1809, he could only afford to recall his Guard and a few extra troops to meet the threat. These joined with Davout's and Marmont's veteran corps. The remainder of the army was made up of newly formed troops and various allies.

With all the demands being made upon the Empire, Napoleon had to rely increasingly upon his client states to provide manpower. Northern Italy, Bavaria, Saxony, Westphalia, Wurttemberg, Holland, and the Grand Duchy of Warsaw (Poland) each provided a corps, while other lesser states sent smaller contingents. Many of these troops saw serious fighting throughout the campaign. The remainder of the army was created by calling up the conscription classes early. On the whole the army was a grade down from previous campaigns.

The structure of the army had not fundamentally changed. The corps system was in place and all corps were led by quality fighting generals. Napoleon's infantry regiments were divided into two main classes: line (*ligne*) and light (*legère*). These were essentially identical in function, with the light perhaps getting more skirmishing duties. A regiment had two or three field battalions, with a fourth depot battalion called up to complete the new formations. Battalions were transformed from nine companies to six, leaving four center companies, one light, and one grenadier company per battalion. This demanded less training in field maneuvers.

Unlike the infantry, Napoleon's cavalry was at its height in 1809. After incorporating the superior horses captured during 1806–07, the units were expanded and improved, most notably the 30 regiments of dragoons which were transformed from mediocre to formidable. The cuirassiers had expanded too and had received additional training to make them a powerful breakthrough force. They held the advantage over their Austrian counterparts in number and in armor, having both front and back plates while the Austrians had only front.

The French light cavalry, hussars and chasseurs, gained a reputation for battlefield prowess, but their scouting skills were poor and Napoleon was often left blind as to the whereabouts of the enemy.

The artillery had been reformed since 1804. The Gribeauval system was replaced by the *An XI* (Year 11) models. These put 12lb and 6lb guns in place of the 12lb, 8lb, and 4lb guns of the former system (the weight referring to the cannonball used). The new carriages were lighter and more mobile, standardized to include the field guns and howitzers. This made for more efficient artillery parks. Although not all of the older guns had been replaced, the process was well under way. As the campaign progressed, a number of captured Austrian guns were added to the reserves. The artillery had been Napoleon's arm as a young lieutenant, and as a result many talented men sought out this branch of service. This resulted in the French artillery being unquestionably the best in Europe.

The Guard Corps was made up of all three arms. The infantry had the new regiments of the Young and Middle Guard added to their number. These new formations, while not having the prestige of the Old Guard, served very well during the campaign.

The Guard Cavalry gained the Polish Light Horse. These Poles had added a lance to their equipment following Wagram, where they had fought a regiment of Austrian lancers (*Uhlans*) and taken several lances as trophies. The other regiments of the Chasseurs and Grenadiers à Cheval and Empress Dragoons, and the sub-units of Mameluks and Gendarmes, made up the most feared cavalry in the world. Although rarely used, their effect was devastating.

There were two types of artillery of the Guard: horse artillery (*Volante*) and heavy foot, nicknamed Napoleon's 'beautiful daughters'. The horse could fly into position and produce an incredible amount of firepower at a critical point; the heavy guns could outshoot any enemy artillery and pulverize opposing formations.

The Confederation of the Rhine troops were organized upon either the French or German model but gradually all adopted the French six-company formations. The troops were of variable quality but usually adequate. The cavalry was usually mediocre, with the exception of the Saxons, who were very good. The artillery was never up to French standards but usually well matched to the enemy.

Napoleon's army in 1809 was good, but nowhere near the quality of the French army at Austerlitz in 1805. As Napoleon prepared for the invasion of Russia he pulled troops from every available source. In addition to the Confederation, Italians, and Polish troops used in 1809, he incorporated the Kingdom of Naples and Spanish troops. Furthermore, his reluctant allies, Prussia and Austria, sent a corps each to the front.

There is little to distinguish Napoleon's armies of 1809 and 1812 other than increased size of the latter. Regiments acquired a 4th, 5th, or even 6th field battalion, cavalry regiments were brought up to an average of six squadrons, and a new class of light cavalry was introduced – lancers. These were converted dragoon regiments. There was no change in the artillery batteries except that they were given their full complement of men. In all, the army that started out in 1812 was the largest Napoleon had ever assembled and showed the variations in quality expected in such an all-out muster of force.

The Austrian army

Austerlitz and the subsequent Treaty of Pressburg were further confirmation that the Austrian army needed an overhaul. The obvious choice for the job was Emperor Francis' brother, Archduke Charles, who was acknowledged to be the finest general in the realm. However, Francis mistrusted his brother because Napoleon had offered Charles the Austrian throne following Austerlitz. While Charles had loyally refused, the seeds of fear had been planted and Francis kept the Military Advisory Board (*Hofkriegsrat*) in place to oversee his brother's activities as supreme commander. This led to an atmosphere of mistrust and a situation in which the two camps spied on each other, initiating a series of court intrigues. This further slowed a reform process which was already hampered by a natural Habsburg conservatism.

Between 1806 and 1808 the Habsburg empire swung back and forth between calls to join a war effort against France and the peace party, led by Charles, who said more time was needed to complete the army reforms. By the end of 1808 the war party gained the upper hand when the Habsburgs interpreted Napoleon's Spanish woes as a chance for revenge. Thus the country began preparations for war.

In 1806 Charles had issued a new guide to army and unit tactics. Changes were small and incremental, yet in the context of the entrenched attitudes in Austria they were seen as very advanced. The primary tactical reform was the 'mass'. This was an anti-cavalry infantry formation created by closing up the spacing between ranks. This modest tactical device was rarely used outside of the immediate sight of Archduke Charles, reflecting the reluctance of the generals to try anything new.

Following the defeats of Ulm and Austerlitz, Mack's earlier 'reforms' were considered to have been a failure in action and Charles abandoned the four-company battalion and returned to the six-company formation used prior to the 1805 campaign.

The army was divided into five categories of infantry: Line, Grenzer, Grenadier, Jaeger, and Landwehr.

The Line had 61 regiments (46 German and 15 Hungarian). Each was made up of three battalions.

The Grenzers from Croatia had 17 regiments with two field battalions and one reserve battalion. The skirmish skills of the mountain troops had slowly eroded and by 1809 there was little difference between mountain troops and Line regiments.

Hungarian and Austrian infantry. (Ottenfeld)

The Grenadier battalions were officially composed of companies taken from the Line regiments, but by 1809 they had in effect become separate formations. These were the elite of the army and were brigaded into their own shock formations.

The Jaegers – elite rifle-armed troops – had taken on the army's skirmishing duties and performed very well throughout the campaign. With only nine battalions, they left the Austrians woefully short of skirmishers to match their French opponents.

The Landwehr was sub-divided into volunteer and militia units. This measure had been considered for many years, but had always been shelved for fear of arming the general populace. By 1809, however, it was clear that new sources of manpower would have to be found to fight the war and even this new plan would only provide a portion of what was needed; only the volunteer units showed much value in combat.

Charles' cavalry remained largely unchanged. Efforts to expand the number or capacity of the mounted arm were curtailed for economic reasons. In general, this left the Austrians' *arme blanche* outnumbered and outclassed. The cavalry's efforts were further undermined by the practice of distributing it in small units throughout the army. This left only the Cuirassiers as a massed force for shock purposes. These eight regiments of breast-plated cavalry would prove too little to make a decisive impact in battle.

The Austrian artillery, once the finest in the world, had fallen behind the times. Charles sought to reform this arm and re-organized the cannon into more effective batteries. He militarized the transport service – a marked improvement – but still the doctrine of massing guns at the point of decision was one which was followed more in theory than practice; although Aspern-Essling would be the best day for the Austrian artillery in the entire war, such massed artillery tactics were not institutionalized. The weight of the Austrian shot was less than that of their French counterparts and

Hungarian Grenadiers. (Ottenfeld)

therefore lacked hitting power. Finally, there was no prestige to the artillery so the best officers gravitated to other arms.

Charles imitated the superior French model of the corps structure, but not in time to familiarize the commanders with its workings and possibilities. Used to a rigid structure, often based on elaborate planning and long-winded written orders, the Austrian corps commanders remained fixed in place, waiting for orders rather than taking advantage of the resources at their disposal.

The General Staff was in a constant state of reform, yet change came at a snail's pace. The average field general was in his sixties – a marked contrast to the youthful French. The older the general, the less likely they were to lead from the front. This gave them a greater chance of survival, but lessened their ability to react. An additional problem was the small number of staff at army and corps level, which meant that changes to orders were not always possible in the time available.

The Russian army

The Russians had been fierce but lumbering opponents of Napoleon in 1805–07. They had defended well, but had been unable to match the French in a battle of maneuver. Following the Peace of Tilsit it was clear that the organization inherited from the Seven Years' War needed to be overhauled.

This task was originally given to Alexei Arakcheev, a sadistic martinet who showed little interest in reform except in his artillery. He replaced the old, slow-moving artillery with lighter, better, 12- and 6-pounders and improved the Licorne, the Russian answer to the howitzer. These new models still lacked the mobility and hitting power of the French, but they were a marked improvement.

Arakcheev did little else to change the army other then terrorize his contemporaries and give his favorites positions of power. In almost all matters he was a reactionary and a xenophobe, so he did the Tsar a great service when he resigned in 1810 over a power

struggle. His replacement was Barclay de Tolly, who reorganized the army and introduced a corps structure similar to that of the French. He also tried to install a staff system like Napoleon's but with less success.

The army of near a million men was scattered over the vast Russian empire. Many were in depots and many more were levies waiting to be called up. In the field at the start of 1812, there were over 600,000 men, equal to Napoleon's entire force, with another 500,000 men waiting to be called up. However, mobilizing this army would prove to be a lengthy process, so initially Russia faced Napoleon with only a third of his force.

The Russian infantry was obedient and stalwart. The officers lacked imagination and initiative, but the peasant infantrymen, used to hardship, had few complaints about a military lifestyle that was often draconian and they fought hard when put into battle. The infantry was particularly adept at digging in when in defense, offering tenacious resistance, and enduring a heavy pounding from the superior French artillery.

The infantry was divided into three types: line, jaegers, and grenadiers. The line and jaegers were essentially the same, designated for light infantry duties but ill-trained for the job (although at Borodino almost all the Jaeger regiments broke down into skirmish formation). The grenadiers were sub-divided into two types: grenadier regiments and converged grenadier battalions. The regiments were true elite formations that had earned their title on the battlefield and continued to justify this honor. The converged battalions were a merger of companies taken from the line regiments and elevated to elite status. These men were good, reliable troops, but not markedly better than their brethren in the line.

The cavalry, the most aristocratic of the Russian arms, had needed least by way of reform. It was organized into permanent divisions and had begun to practice large formation maneuvers when the war broke out. The cavalry was steady if unremarkable. It performed well against many of the allied

Charge! Hurrah! Hurrah! by V. Vereshchagin. An idealized picture of Russian Grenadiers going into the attack.

the battlefield and amassed as much as possible for the battle of Eylau in 1807, providing a frightful example of the carnage Russian cannon could inflict. While Russian officers had not developed Napoleon's skill in deploying huge batteries on the move, they firmly believed in pounding an opponent into submission.

Finally there was the Russian Guard. This combined arms formation, modeled upon Napoleon's Guard, was made up of elite formations. They received the best of everything Russia could provide and were the Tsar's shock troops. None in the world could match them, save the French. They were used more liberally than Napoleon's Guard, because to do so never risked the entire regime.

It was in command that the Russians failed most. Rivalry and bickering led to a series of near-disastrous appointments. Often generals were put in place more for their political acumen than their military skills and were replaced because of a loss of political influence rather than for any failure. The responsibility for this lay with the Tsar, but even he was often looking over his shoulder, fearful of a coup!

troops, but usually gave way when matched against an equal number of French. In these encounters, their lack of training above the squadron level proved costly.

The one cavalry force that made a real difference on campaign was the Cossacks. These steppe horsemen could outmarch any of their rivals and they were mounted on sturdy ponies which could withstand the hardships of the Russian weather and terrain. While rarely useful against anything approaching an equal number of cavalry, they were a nightmare to stragglers and scouts, and could occasionally destroy smaller isolated enemy units. The lure of booty made them lose discipline, but they were ready to attack to find their loot if the odds were good. In 1812 Cossacks appeared in great numbers.

The artillery was the backbone of the army. The Russians were the first to recognize the changing role of artillery on

The Austrian campaign to the march on Moscow

The Austrians invade Bavaria

With the decision to go to war made, Archduke Charles planned the main Austrian advance along the upper Danube River. The 1st through 5th Corps, along with the 1st Reserve Corps, would advance north of the river out of Bohemia. The 6th Corps and the 2nd Reserve Corps would advance south of the river from a starting position on the Bavarian border. When reports arrived that the French were beginning to concentrate in the Augsburg area, the specter of an unprotected Vienna being taken by a rapid advance along the south bank of the Danube caused Charles to rethink his plans. Accordingly, he shifted the main body of his troops south of the Danube to the Inn River line on the border with Bavaria. While this countered the perceived threat, the decision cost the Austrians one month of critical time. Even so, by 10 April 1809, the army was in position.

On other fronts, Archduke Ferdinand was to lead the 8th Corps and additional troops against Napoleon's Polish allies in the Galicia region, while Archduke John with the 8th and 9th Corps would attack the French and Northern Italian army commanded by Napoleon's stepson, Prince Eugene de Beauharnais. The Austrians believed that by applying broad and constant pressure, French resources would be stretched to breaking point.

Napoleon believed that he had until mid-April to concentrate his forces, but left Marshal Berthier instructions to fall back on the lines of communications should an attack come earlier. Berthier, a superlative chief of staff, struggled when commanding an army. When crucial orders from Napoleon were delayed, Berthier's confusion only worsened.

Archduke Charles was considered the only general who could match Napoleon, but he was prone to inaction at the most inappropriate times. (Roger-Viollet)

In the early morning of 10 April, the leading elements of the Austrian army crossed the Inn River. The opposing cordon of Bavarians fell back, but bad roads and freezing rain delayed the Austrian offensive during the first week. The Bavarians made a brief stand on the Isar River at Landshut on 16 April, before once more retreating and yielding the passage of the critical river line. Beyond the Bavarians, only Marshal Davout's 3rd Corps, deployed around Regensburg, remained guarding the key bridge over the Danube that linked the north and south banks.

Charles stopped to analyze the intelligence he had received on the evening of 17 April. By concentrating his forces north of the Danube and delivering a thrust from the south, Charles could drive Davout's forces back and the whole of the French defensive position would come unhinged. The archduke ordered the two wings of the Wurttemberg army to converge on Regensburg, but his plans had to be altered the following day when he learned that Davout was heading south along the Danube and attempting to link up with supporting French corps further to the south and west. Davout had been placed in this precarious position through a combination of bad luck and poor timing, and Charles had a golden opportunity to crush the 'Iron Marshal' by pinning his 3rd Corps against the river.

The arrival of Napoleon

Napoleon arrived at Donauworth, the French headquarters, on 17 April 1809. He immediately began to assess the disastrous situation facing his army. Until now the French army had been badly out-scouted by the numerically superior Austrian cavalry. The most reliable reports were coming from spies and civilians reporting to Davout's men. The 3rd Corps was clearly in extreme danger, and aid could not arrive for a couple of days. The best solution seemed to be for Davout to abandon his position around Regensburg and link up with the Bavarians further to the east. Unfortunately, when these orders from Napoleon arrived, Davout required an additional day to gather up his corps as they were scattered and fatigued from marching and counter-marching as a result of Berthier's confused orders. Davout set off early on the morning of 19 April to link up with his allies.

Davout's 3rd Corps moved south out of Regensburg on the direct road that ran along the Danube and toward Ingolstadt. In the initial stages of this maneuver his corps, formed in two parallel columns of march, were strung out with no line of retreat if the Austrians attacked from the east. Davout had left a regiment behind the walls of

Regensburg to prevent any passage of the Danube by the Austrians and to protect his rear. Charles' plan of attack was to wheel with his 3rd Corps attacking along the Danube while the 4th and 1st Reserve Corps swung on the pivot.

Teugen-Hausen

On the morning of 19 April, both armies got under way, the French with a two-hour head start. By 8.30 am, Davout had nearly escaped the trap. Two of his four divisions had moved past the choke point, but the marshal received word of strong enemy activity moving up from the south and his supply train was not yet through the key village of Teugen. The Austrian 3rd Corps, under Field-Marshal the Prince of Hohenzollern, was rapidly arriving upon the battlefield and trying to cut them off. This force had been partially weakened out of fear that the Bavarians might fall upon their flank so more than one division had been detached to act as a flank guard. These men would be sorely missed in the day's contest.

The action opened with the French skirmishers being thrown back toward Teugen as the advance guard of the Austrian 3rd Corps crashed forward. Davout, realizing that his flanks were in peril, sent the 103rd Line forward to buy time and give the remainder of St Hilaire's division a chance to deploy. He sent them in skirmish order toward the town of Hausen and the 6,000 Austrians waiting for them. At the same time, Davout ordered Friant's division to advance to St Hilaire's left and support the effort. Friant had his own problems: elements of the Austrian 4th Corps were going in to the attack as well. However, fortunately for the French, at the rear of the column, General Montbrun's cavalry would mesmerize Field-Marshal Rosenberg's 4th Corps for most of the day.

The men of the 103rd were doing well considering they were outnumbered three to one and all the artillery on the field was Habsburg. As they finally gave way, the

'Terrible 57th', arguably the finest regiment of line infantry in the French army, swung into action. They took a position upon the ridge overlooking the town and the Austrian assault ground to a halt.

Now checked, the Austrians failed to see the 10th Light Regiment creep up through the woods. This elite force fell upon the Austrian artillery and drove it from the field. Hohenzollern committed some of his reserves in response to this reverse, and as the white-coated Austrians came forward, they tipped the balance back to their side in this running fight. Davout had to commit all available troops on the field to stem the tide.

Sensing victory, more Austrians were released and this time cavalry charged the beleaguered 57th, which lay down a withering fire and formed square with its flank battalion. The battered cavalry withdrew and played no further part in the day's actions. Under the cover of this cavalry assault, a fresh regiment came up to attack the French line. The Manfredini regiment advanced in column through a swale in the ground and turned on the flank of the

One of Napoleon's aides, Mouton, stormed the bridge at Landshut despite the defended barricade and buildings. Napoleon was so impressed he punned, 'My Mouton (sheep in French) is a lion.' (Roger-Viollet)

57th. Fortunately for Davout, General Compans saw what was about to happen and led newly arriving troops forward. The two columns collided and the French came off better. The Austrians fell back, rallied, and came on again, led by the dashing General Alois Liechtenstein. The 57th, out of ammunition, finally gave way. The French fell off the ridge and down to the town of Teugen. There Davout rallied the men and, sending in his last reserve, retook the ridgeline. The Austrians were almost completely played out on the ridge, when Friant's men appeared upon their right flank. This was too much, and the Habsburg line gave way. Streaming down the ridgeline toward the town of Hausen, they rallied behind the last reserves that Hohenzollern had to commit on the field.

Once more General Liechtenstein led the attack, carrying the Wurzburg regiment's

1809 Austrian campaign, Regensburg: Part 1

1. Davout withdraws from Regensberg, leaving garrison behind (2).
3. Archduke Charles advances against Davout, engages at Teugen and Hausen on 19 April (4).
5. Hiller advances with Austrian left wing.
6. Napoleon's counterattack towards Abensberg, 19–20 April.
7. Massena and Oudinot advance, Massena towards Landshut upon which Napoleon hoped to drive the Austrian left wing.

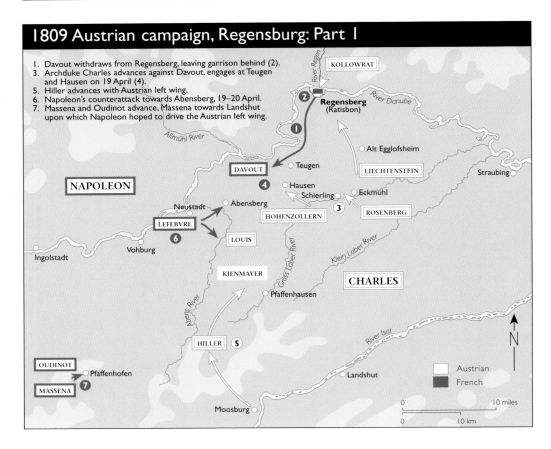

(IR 3) flag to inspire the men, and stormed the woods. While his attack drove back the French line, more of Friant's men and the arrival of the long-awaited French artillery restored the situation. For his efforts, General Liechtenstein lay severely wounded. The Austrians had retreated behind the protection of their guns deployed in front of Hausen when a violent thunderstorm started and the battle ended.

Davout had defeated a force twice his size and had been able to re-open communications with the rest of Napoleon's army. Charles had spent the battle only a couple of miles away with a reserve of 12 elite grenadier battalions. It is difficult to determine who was at fault for the failure to commit these troops. Clearly, communication was poor, but the blame must be shared between Hohenzollern for not begging for the men and Charles for not finding out what was happening to his front. As it was, the Austrians knew they had fought well but had

still lost: demoralization began to set in.

As the battle of Teugen-Hausen was drawing to a close, Napoleon switched to the attack. He ordered Marshal Masséna's 4th Corps to advance on Landshut. Masséna advanced from Ingolstadt with the heavy cavalry, linked up with the Bavarians and Wurttembergers, and ordered the 2nd Corps to hurry to the front. By 9.00 am the following day he was in place. To give him even more flexibility Napoleon made an ad hoc corps from two of Davout's divisions and placed it under Marshal Jean Lannes, who had just arrived from Spain. Davout and his two remaining divisions would press the forces in front of him.

Napoleon's plan was to drive the Austrians back to Landshut, which he assumed was their line of communication. There they would be pinned by Masséna's Corps coming up from the south.

The battle of Abensberg, 20 April 1809, was a running battle, with the Austrians

1809 Austrian campaign, Regensburg: Part 2

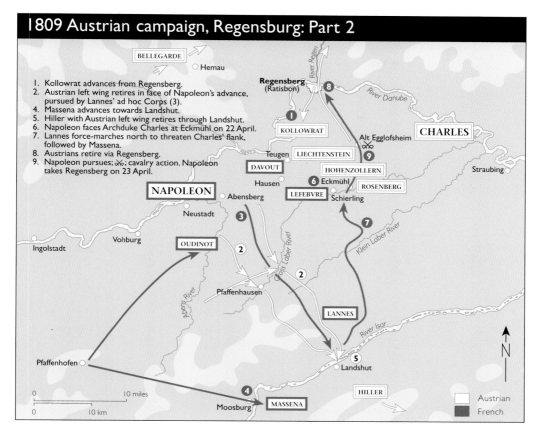

1. Kollowrat advances from Regensberg.
2. Austrian left wing retires in face of Napoleon's advance, pursued by Lannes' ad hoc Corps (3).
3. Massena advances towards Landshut.
4. Hiller with Austrian left wing retires through Landshut.
5. Napoleon faces Archduke Charles at Eckmühl on 22 April.
6. Lannes force-marches north to threaten Charles' flank, followed by Massena.
7. Austrians retire via Regensberg.
8. Napoleon pursues; ⚔: cavalry action. Napoleon takes Regensberg on 23 April.

being driven back throughout the day. By nightfall the Austrian 5th, 6th, and 2nd Reserve Corps were well on their way to Landshut. They arrived the following morning, having marched through most of the night. General Hiller, commander of the Austrians in this sector, did his best to put them in good defensive positions.

Napoleon was close on their heels. At Landshut, on 21 April, Napoleon assembled his forces and attacked through the town and over the two bridges that spanned the Isar River. This daring assault saw more than 8,000 Austrians surrounded and forced to surrender in the town. Strategically the attack may have been irrelevant, because the Austrian position had already been flanked by the French 4th Corps. Masséna's men crossed over the river quickly, closing on the position from the south. They narrowly missed cutting off the retreating Austrians who had been foiled by bad roads, a lack of initiative in the

Davout (Job). At Auerstadt in 1806 and at Eckmühl in 1809 Davout proved to be tough enough to score victories over superior numbers of enemies. (Edimedia)

aging marshal, and pockets of determined enemy resistance. Compromised by the hard-driving French offensive, this Austrian wing fell back to the east and to the next defensive line.

Early next morning, Napoleon received the last of several desperate messages from Davout. This time the news was delivered by the trusted General Piré, who finally managed to persuade the Emperor that he did not face the main Habsburg army. Napoleon now grasped that his left flank stood in the greatest peril.

Throughout 21 April, Davout attacked the retreating Austrians with the help of a Bavarian division under Marshal Lefebvre. The further back the Austrians fell, the stronger their line became, for in fact they were falling back on their main force. General Montbrun's cavalry, off to the north, was reporting massive formations heading Davout's way. The combat on the first day of the Battle of Eckmühl, as this fight was to become known, was sharp, with each side giving as much as they took. However, that night Davout faced a terrible predicament. While a fresh division had come up to his support and the artillery train would be present for any fighting in the morning, his infantry was low on ammunition. Davout

knew that at least three Austrian corps remained in front of him. In fact the situation was even more desperate than he realized, for Regensburg had fallen and two more Austrian corps would be able to cross the Danube and enter the fight.

Charles saw this great opportunity, but his spread-out army would take half a day to get into position. He, like his opponent, was reading the situation wrongly. He assumed that Davout was the leading element of the main French army. Charles' forces were aligned on a north-south axis, and his reinforcements were coming from the north, through Regensburg. If the plan worked, his new arrivals would fall upon the French far left flank. The archduke wanted the two wings of his army to coordinate with each other, so he would allow the French to expend themselves upon his defensive position around Eckmühl and take no offensive action himself until his reinforcements were in position.

Eckmühl

As dawn broke on 22 April, the two sides faced each other and except for some skirmishing, neither side made an attack. Morning turned to midday and still an uneasy calm hung over the battlefield.

While Charles looked for signs of his 2nd Corps, Davout had a better grasp of the developing situation. Napoleon had sent General Piré back with the message that the Emperor was coming with his army. Davout was to maintain contact and expect Napoleon to launch his attack at 3.00 pm. Every minute that Charles delayed increased the marshal's chances of survival and victory.

At about 1.00 pm the leading elements of the Austrian attack collided with Montbrun's cavalry. The hilly and wooded terrain great aided the French in slowing down the impetus of the attack. As the French horsemen retreated, the Austrian commander of the left flank, General Rosenberg, felt concern as he observed Davout's main force opposite him. Instead of quickly shifting to meet the threat caused by Charles' attack, they remained in place and were watching him! Rosenberg knew this could mean only one thing. He began to shift troops to meet a threat from the south. It was not long before his suspicions were confirmed. His small flank guard had caved in under a massive French force that was heading his way.

Napoleon had achieved a most remarkable march, one of the finest examples of turning on an army's axis in all of history. After receiving the intelligence at

The outnumbered Austrian cavalry attempted to delay the pursuing French.

around 2.00 am he had set into motion the orders to turn his army to the north and to march the 18 miles to the help of his beleaguered marshal. In short order, the plans were set in motion. Remarkably, Napoleon would arrive even earlier than promised.

The tip of his hammer blow was General Vandamme and his Wurttemberg troops. These Germans came on with the greatest élan. Led by their crack light battalion, they stormed across the bridge at Eckmühl and into the town. There they seized the chateau despite dogged Austrian resistance.

As the first of Napoleon's attacks got under way, Davout launched his own attack against the center of Rosenberg's position, the village of Unterlaiching and the woods above. Davout had sent in the 10th Legere to carry out the task. This elite unit paused only momentarily in the village before continuing on against the woods. There they faced several times their own number, and a vicious fight ensued tree to tree. Eventually, Davout reinforced the efforts of the light infantry regiment with the Bavarians under General Deroy and the position was taken.

To the north of Unterlaiching, Davout's men under Friant and the remaining troops of St Hilaire slowly pushed back the defenders around Oberlaiching and the woods to its north. A redoubt held by Hungarian grenadiers was overrun, the whole line began to give way, and Charles ordered a retreat.

Between the town of Eckmühl and the woods above Unterlaiching was a ridgeline called the Bettelberg. Astride the ridge was some of the best cavalry in the Austrian Empire, including the Vincent Chevaulegers and the Stipsic Hussars, and several batteries of guns. After deploying on the marshy plain below, the Bavarian and Wurttemberg light cavalry launched a charge uphill against the position. Briefly overrunning one of the batteries, they were thrown back by the two crack cavalry regiments of Hussars and Chevaulegers. The countercharging Austrians were in turn stopped by the Bavarian infantry.

A stand-off developed. The Austrians were determined to hold this position until the rest of the army got away, and Napoleon was equally determined to break the position and destroy the retreating adversary. To accomplish this goal, Napoleon now committed his heavy cavalry. The divisions of St Sulpice and Nansouty deployed in the soft ground. Their ranks were pummeled as they maneuvered under the continuously firing heavy guns on the Bettelberg. Slowly the magnificent cavalry moved forward, picking up speed. As they hit the ridge and began to ascend the heights, they were in a full canter. Finally, in the last hundred paces they broke into a gallop. The tired, outnumbered Austrian cavalry was overthrown and the heavy guns were taken. The lighter guns limbered and broke away, and many of their gunners were sabered. Now established on the ridge, the cuirassiers stopped to catch their breath. Others would have to do the immediate follow-up.

The French victory had been won by late afternoon, but Charles was able to pull off his infantry with few captured. While the French organized their pursuit, the Austrians found a choke point in the road to buy time. Napoleon urged on his troops and sent his heavy cavalry into the van to run down the enemy. They caught up with Charles' final rearguard a couple of miles from Regensburg at Alt Egglofsheim.

What followed was an enormous cavalry clash. Charles had left cuirassiers and his now exhausted light cavalry to delay the French. Napoleon committed his three divisions of cuirassiers with the support of Bavarian and Wurttemberg light cavalry. The French swept down, but the Austrian heavies were fresh and plowed into the French with great effect. The entire fight turned into a swirling melee, with each side feeding in more and more troopers. The Austrians fought magnificently and for a while more than held their own with the exhausted French, but in the end the French superiority in numbers was too much. Seeing more French appear and realizing that it was quickly becoming dark, the Austrians tried to break off. It was at this moment that the next wave of oncoming French shattered the tired Austrians. Panic resulted and the frantic horsemen streamed back toward Regensburg and the safety of her walls. The French too became confused in the gloom and the pursuit was ineffectual. This was lucky for the Archduke Charles, since he had been swept up in the rout.

Napoleon is wounded

The following day, 23 April, found the Austrians retreating as fast as possible over the Danube and the protection of her left bank. A sizable rearguard was left to defend the walls of Regensburg. Napoleon was disappointed when he learned that the French garrison had fallen. He had hoped to trap the Austrians against the river. Instead he launched a massive assault in an attempt to catch as much of the retreating army as possible. The medieval walls would easily fall

to a prolonged bombardment, but time was short. Napoleon's infantry rushed forward with ladders to scale the walls. Each time the firepower of the Austrians drove them back. At the height of the battle, a bullet struck Napoleon in the heel. Rumors spread quickly amongst the French that he had been seriously hurt. Wishing to stop the panic, he had his wound quickly bandaged and rode along the lines to show himself. A crisis was averted.

Even with the panic quelled, every renewed assault was driven back. Finally, the fiery Marshal Lannes grabbed a ladder and exclaimed: 'I was a grenadier before I was a marshal, and still am!' His men, shamed into another attempt, grabbed ladders and made one final attempt. This time it succeeded and the French were in. The Austrians fought

Napoleon rode amongst his troops before Regensburg to show he was not wounded. In the background, the French are preparing to assault the city walls. (Myrbach, Roger-Viollet)

desperately in an attempt to prevent the French from working their way through the city and reaching the critical stone bridge over the Danube before Charles' engineers could destroy it. House-to-house, hand-to hand fighting followed. Five Austrian battalions were to perish or surrender, but their sacrifice was not in vain. The French broke through to the river just in time to see the charges explode. Charles and his main army had escaped, and Napoleon had lost his opportunity for a quick knock-out blow. The following day the Emperor turned his attention to trapping and destroying the enemy forces still south of the Danube.

While developments in Bavaria saw the repulse of the main Austrian offensive, things had gone better for the House of Habsburg on other fronts. In the Tyrol region, which had been ceded to Bavaria following the disastrous Austerlitz-Ulm campaign, General Chasteler had invaded with 10,000 men and the region had risen in revolt to support his efforts. His movement was coordinated with Archduke John's invasion of Italy and Dalmatia. Chasteler had advanced on Innsbruck and captured virtually all opposing forces with the help of bands of patriotic Tyrolian rebels, whose most notable leader was Andreas Hofer. Within three days almost all of the Tyrol was retaken by the Austrians. It would be May before any response could be organized.

Actions in Italy

Archduke John's army advanced against Napoleon's stepson, the viceroy of Italy, Prince Eugene de Beauharnais. Although the Franco-Italian army outnumbered John's, it was scattered throughout northern Italy. This was Napoleon's fault, for he had believed that the Austrians would not attack until later, if at all, and that to assemble the army ahead of time would in itself have been a provocation which might have ignited a war. This meant that as John advanced, only about half of Eugene's troops were available at the battlefield of Sacile on 15/16 April

1809. Eugene was aching for a fight, in order to 'win his spurs.' Furthermore, Chasteler's success was threatening his northern flank, and he felt that if he could defeat John, he could deal with the threat in the Tyrol at his leisure.

The first day of the battle saw John maul Eugene's advance guard at Pordenone. The following day, Eugene tried an outflanking attack that became bogged down in the soggy, broken terrain. John calmly watched as the French spent themselves trying to seize the village of Porcia. Once it had finally been taken, after several attempts, the Austrians launched an attack against the French left and drove it back against the Livenza River. Staring at the threat to his line of retreat, Eugene broke off the battle. Marching through the rain-soaked night, Eugene's army outpaced the lackluster Austrians in pursuit.

After several stands to make a rearguard, Eugene fell back to Verona and the line of the Adige River. On this familiar ground, held by the French in 1796 under Napoleon and 1805 under Masséna, Eugene gathered his army together and prepared to go over to the offensive.

Other fronts

In Dalmatia, Marmont, under the nominal command of Eugene, was told to attack the enemy in front of him. His mountain offensive on 30 April was repulsed by General Stoichewich's force, with most of the serious damage being caused by the skilled mountain troops, the Grenzer. The French retreat that followed was harassed by locals who sprang several ambushes.

To the north, things were going equally badly for Napoleon's allies. Prince Poniatowski had tried to stop Archduke Ferdinand's army as it headed for Warsaw. Deciding to make a stand just south of the city, the Poles were defeated by the Austrians at the battle of Raszyn on 19 April. Despite a heroic effort, Poniatowski's army had to abandon Warsaw and retreat beyond Ferdinand's reach.

Perhaps as ominous as any of the other developments, Major Schill, a firebrand Prussian Hussar leader, gathered his men around him and begin a ride across northern Germany trying to raise a revolt against the French. Fortunately for Napoleon, Schill was largely ignored and his actions disavowed by the Prussian king. Still he had Jérome Bonaparte's kingdom of Westphalia in a state of confusion and near revolt. All these setbacks made Napoleon's victories all the more crucial, for if they had taken place without the Eckmühl campaign, they may have been the spark to bring Prussia into the war.

The pursuit of the Austrians

The initial pursuit of the Austrians south of the Danube was the responsibility of Marshal Bessieres. He commanded a combined force of cavalry and Bavarian infantry. Pursuing too rashly, part of his command was attacked and mauled at Neumarkt on 24 April. Bessieres halted and it was only the arrival of Marshal Lannes that the advance could resume. Another command, Marshal Masséna's, caught up with Hiller's men and,

Engraving of Archduke Charles de Habsbourg at the battle of Aspern. (Roger-Viollet)

Napoleon's camp before the battle of Ebelsberg. Many doubted that this costly little battle was necessary. (Painting by Antoine Pierre Mongin, Edimedia)

on 3 May, faced them across the Traun River at Ebelsberg.

Masséna wanted to gain laurels by running down the retreating Austrians, so he quickly ordered an assault across the long bridge over the river. The French were pounded by batteries that had been positioned to maximize damage to anyone daring to cross. These were some of the best troops in Napoleon's army though, and they kept on coming. They broke into the town where they soon learned that most of Hiller's force had been hidden from view. Pinned by the withering fire, Masséna's men held on desperately to their foot-hold. More French crossed as their artillery swung into action to counter the Austrian batteries. The tremendous fire served to ignite the town, adding further horror to the ghastly carnage that sickened even the most hardened veterans. Pressing on through the smoke and flames, the French soldiers finally arrived at the castle on the hill above the town. There a vicious and heroic fight finally left the French in control of the castle and the town. Hiller broke off and retreated. While

ultimately victorious, Masséna's costly win was largely superfluous since Lannes had already outflanked Hiller's river line and would have dislodged them in a couple of hours without a fight. Masséna's men were too spent to launch an adequate pursuit and Hiller was able to retreat and cross the Danube largely unmolested.

Charles' army had escaped, but now Vienna was left exposed. Napoleon and his army had occupied the Habsburg capital on 12 May after only the smallest show of resistance by the home guard. The greatest triumph of the Viennese had been the destruction of the bridges over the Danube. At least they could comfort themselves that they had not been captured intact, as had happened in 1805.

As Napoleon's army advanced up the Danube toward Vienna, to the south events had also turned in the French favor. Eugene had sparred with John at Caldiero on

30 April, and the now outnumbered archduke had been forced into a retreat by a combination of pressure to his front and the collapsing situation on his northern flank.

The Austrian army of this era still depended on a large supply train, which slowed its advances and retreats. Many times Austrian commanders had to offer battle to protect the train, even when defeat seemed the most probable outcome. This was the situation John found himself in a little over a week later. At the Piave River John held his ground while Eugene assembled his army on the opposite bank. On the morning of 8 May, Eugene launched an assault across two fords. The leading forces established themselves and waited for more support. John had little in the way of options and sent his men forward to destroy the French on the northern bank. Eugene was ready for them and after repulsing the Austrian assaults, counterattacked and broke John's line in several places. By evening the victory was complete and Eugene had avenged his defeat at Sacile. Exploiting his advantage, Eugene advanced rapidly and pushed John's army out of Italy and towards Hungary. In a series of small actions, one after another of John's rearguards were overwhelmed, so that by 20 May, Eugene had reached Klagenfurt and was in a position to either join Napoleon or continue the pursuit of John.

While Eugene was following up the remnants of John's army, Marshal Lefebvre had reassembled his Bavarian Corps and set out to retake the Tyrol. With fire and sword the road to Innsbruck was cleared in a number of small actions. With the situation collapsing all around him, Chasteler began to retreat, leaving the Tyrolians to their fate. The Bavarians were too much to overcome and Innsbruck fell on 19 May. The Tyrol seemed pacified.

The Battle of Linz

As Napoleon advanced up the Danube, he left key crossing points guarded by corps-strength commands. At Linz the Wurttemberg Corps, under General Vandamme, was given just such a task. Vandamme was able to cross the Danube and create a *tête du pont* (a fortified bridgehead). This was a dagger pointed directly at the heart of Charles' army in Bohemia. In response, Charles sent General Kolowrat with the 3rd Corps to drive this incursion back over the river. The Austrian commander planned a three-pronged converging attack.

The Battle of Linz was a disjointed affair because the three Habsburg columns arrived and were repulsed one at a time. Furthermore, to disrupt Kolowrat's plan, Marshal Bernadotte, with elements of his Saxon Corps, arrived throughout the day. The result was complete failure on Kolowrat's part and his men retreated to lick their wounds. Napoleon's German allies had once more proved of great service, and for the time being Napoleon's supply line was secure.

From the Palace of Schönbrunn, Napoleon made plans for his next move. His line of supply was overextended, and while the line of the Danube was protected by the corps of Bernadotte, Vandamme, and Davout, his adversary was making no overtures toward peace. There were rumors of a British invasion, Archduke John's army could appear at almost any moment, and the Russians (French allies by treaty) appeared more menacing than reassuring. Since there was no word of any large formations near the river, Napoleon assumed that Charles and his army were somewhere near Brunn. French intelligence had completely broken down, for Charles was a few short miles away near Wagram.

Aspern-Essling

Napoleon planned and started the crossing of the Danube, first to Lobau Island, three-quarters of the way across, from where he could easily bridge the narrow channel to the northern (left) bank. He arranged several diversions, but Charles recognized them for what they were. From late on 18 May to

French infantry desperately trying to hold Essling from sustained Austrian attacks. (Myrbach, Roger-Viollet)

noon on 20 May, the French engineers worked to finish the pontoon bridges. Their work was badly hampered by the rising waters of the Danube, swollen by the melting snows of the Alps. Even so, the work was completed and two divisions of Masséna's Corps were hurried over to Lobau island. Molitor's division crossed over the further stream and occupied the towns of Aspern and Essling. Lasalle's light cavalry joined Molitor and took up a position between the two towns.

Masséna climbed to the top of the steeple of Aspern's church to view the surrounding countryside and look for signs of the Austrians. He spotted the campfires of the small reserve corps, but no others. Things seemed acceptably in order, so early on the morning of 21 May, he ordered the men of Boudet's and Legrand's divisions to the north bank in support of Molitor. Marshal Bessieres' cavalry crossed too and waited for the rest of the 4th Corps to arrive before expanding their perimeter. Carra St Cyr's division and Lannes' Corps were scheduled to cross next, but a large barge crashed into and ruptured the bridge, preventing the crossing.

From a hill overlooking the river the Habsburgs were able to watch every development. Charles saw a golden opportunity: if he could interrupt the flow of men to the north bank of the river his massive army should be able to crush the force in front of him. To accomplish this goal, barges, logs, and toppled windmills were set alight and floated down the Danube. With the help of the high rushing waters, these makeshift rams smashed the bridge several times over the next two days. Each time the French sappers repaired it, the Austrians would send down another flaming ram.

With the flow of Napoleon's soldiers now interrupted, Charles closed in on Aspern and Essling with 100,000 men. At about 1.00 pm an alarmed messenger reported to Napoleon that a massive force of white-coated men was closing in on the French position. Napoleon sent an aide for confirmation, and learned that the number of the enemy was at least 80,000. He considered a withdrawal. Events were moving too fast for the French, for Charles had caught them ahead of plan.

The first to receive the brunt of Charles' attacks was Molitor's division, deployed in Aspern. The focal point of the Austrian attack was the church and cemetery on the west edge of town. Hiller's men came in before the two supporting corps could react, but advancing to the walls of the church they were hurled back by a tremendous fire. A second attempt, just before 3.00 pm, swept past the church into the town, but again was sent back as Molitor committed the last of his reserves. Hiller re-formed his men. By now the 1st and 2nd Corps were in position throughout the town. As their guns unlimbered and began to pound the French positions, Bessieres sent part of his cavalry to disrupt the fire and Charles countered with his own cavalry. In the swirling melee which followed, Charles fed in more regiments until the French cavalry withdrew.

By 4.30 pm a new assault has been launched from the three Habsburg columns aimed at Aspern. The church was once more the focal point and this time the bloodied French *fantassins* were expelled after a vicious hand-to-hand struggle. Much of the town was occupied and Napoleon's left flank was in danger of collapse. The Emperor sent Masséna forward with Legrand's division, to support Molitor's weary men. At bayonet point the Austrians were again thrown back.

The few guns the Emperor had were holding a critical portion of the line near Essling and providing covering fire to support the center between the two towns, so the Austrian cavalry had to be sent in once more on the left. This time they overran many of the French guns, but were halted by support infantry drawn up in massed formation behind the guns. Unable to break this formation, the Austrians flowed impotently around the infantry until driven back by the musketry. Their sacrifice had bought critical time but little else.

At 6.00 pm another attack was launched towards the town and was repelled. Charles himself rallied the repulsed troops and sent them in once more. This time they took the blazing town. The loss of this position spelled doom for Napoleon's army, so the Emperor sent in St Cyr's recently arrived division with the remnants of the two other previously decimated divisions to re-take Aspern. The spent Austrians were hurled back, rallied, and returned, but their impetus ran out half-way through the town and a French counter-attack had them slowly retreating. With stubborn defense they kept the strong-point of the church.

While the attacks were continuing around Aspern, Rosenberg's 4th Corps, divided into two columns, was moving into position. Without waiting for the supporting column, half of Rosenberg's men attacked. Waiting for them was Boudet's division under the direct command of Marshal Lannes. Boudet had arranged his men in the gardens and buildings that made up the village of Essling. The best fortification there was the granary, a massive structure with walls over three feet thick. Built at the end of the last century following riots caused by famine, it had been created with defense in mind. Boudet and a couple hundred of his best troops used it as a breakwater against the Austrian's assaults.

This strategy worked perfectly against the Habsburg first wave. It was easily repulsed and Lannes sent d'Espagne's heavy cavalry to run the fleeing enemy down. Many were caught from behind, but the pursuit was called off so that the metal-plated cavalrymen could respond to General Liechtenstein's counter-attacking cavalry. As the two forces closed on each other, General d'Espagne was killed by a round of canister. Deprived of their leader, the cuirassiers fought on, but, as would happen throughout the battle, the Austrian numbers proved decisive. However, the pursuing cavaliers were pulverized by the massed French artillery that Napoleon had placed in anticipation of such a reverse.

As night closed in on the village, the second half of Rosenberg's men were finally in position and came on. They took several of the outlying houses along with Essling's 'long garden'. Lannes was able to organize a force to storm these positions and soon all of

Often the infantry had little choice but to stand under artillery bombardment. (Sergent)

Essling was in French hands again. Marshal Lannes then held a meeting with Marshal Bessieres. The two men had detested each other since the Egyptian campaign of 1798, and Bessieres had been angered by Lannes' throughout the day, ordering Bessieres' cavalry to 'charge home.' The suggestion that he and his men had been hanging back was sufficient grounds for Bessieres to challenge his antagonist to a duel. The hot-headed Gascon was happy to accept, but Marshal Masséna came along and demanded both men put away their swords.

By nightfall, sporadic firing was all that remained of the day's combat. Essling was still in French hands, as was most of Aspern. Napoleon crossed the 2nd Corps and his Guard during the night and ordered Marshal Davout to prepare his men to cross too. Napoleon planned to take the initiative and break the Austrian center, using Lannes to attack with the newly arrived corps and the support of Bessieres' cavalry. Davout's men would exploit the success

and the Guard would be thrown in for the *coup de grâce*.

First Aspern would have to be re-taken again. Masséna, at the head of St Cyr's men, went over to the attack at 4.00 am. Driving the surprised Austrian occupants before them, they were halted by Austrian reserves coming up and were in turn driven back. The struggle continued, but by 7.00 am the town was in French hands once more.

While the fight had been going on around Aspern, Napoleon had sent Lasalle's light cavalry to attack south of Essling, so as to expand the deployment area and relieve any pressure coming from that direction. At first the fearsome cavalry had succeeded in driving back the opposing cavalry, but then they were stopped by the Austrian massed infantry. Not wishing to become the target of Rosenberg's many guns, Lasalle retired behind Essling toward the bridges, leaving Essling exposed. Rosenberg saw this as an invitation to seize the vital town once more. His men swept forward, but once again the two columns were not coordinated and met defeat.

Napoleon now sent Lannes forward, supported by the heavy cavalry. He was trying to repeat his victory of Austerlitz four years earlier by breaking the center and rolling up the two flanks. However, this time he was not using the crack troops of the camp of Boulogne but, with the exception of St Hilaire's men, new recruits. Even so, the attack went off well at first. Spearheaded once again by the ubiquitous 'Terrible 57th', the French smashed into the Froon Regiment (IR 54), captured one battalion, and sent the other two fleeing to the rear.

As the French came on, the Austrian artillery plowed great swaths through their ranks. This had to be stopped, so the French cavalry was committed against the Austrian guns. The cavalry came on brilliantly and quickly silenced the offending batteries. Breaking through, they encountered the infantry and cavalry of the center. The Austrian cavalry gave way, but the infantry stood firm and the French cavalry was forced to fall back. As it did so, on came Lannes' infantry.

Charles had watched developments and now committed his last available reserve in the area, the elite Grenadier Corps. They marched to fill the gap created by the wavering center, but they would still take critical minutes to arrive. Charles rode over

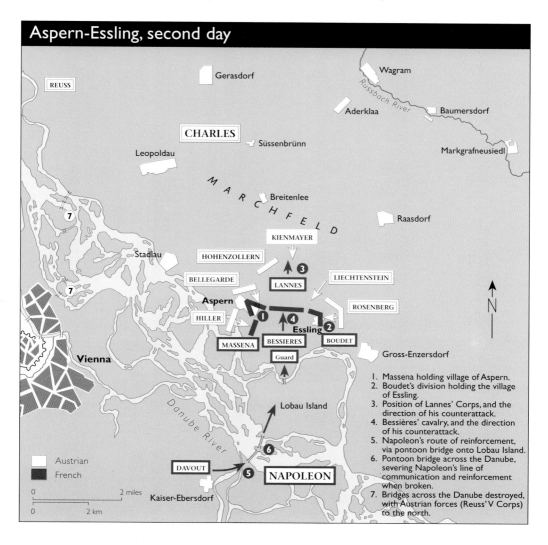

Aspern-Essling, second day

1. Massena holding village of Aspern.
2. Boudet's division holding the village of Essling.
3. Position of Lannes' Corps, and the direction of his counterattack.
4. Bessières' cavalry, and the direction of his counterattack.
5. Napoleon's route of reinforcement, via pontoon bridge onto Lobau Island.
6. Pontoon bridge across the Danube, severing Napoleon's line of communication and reinforcement when broken.
7. Bridges across the Danube destroyed, with Austrian forces (Reuss' V Corps) to the north.

to where his men were falling back and, grabbing the flag of the Zach Regiment (IR 15), rallied the men and led them back against the French. Lannes had now advanced almost a mile, but he received orders to call off the attack.

Austrian attempts to break the pontoon bridge had once again succeeded, this time using a floating mill set alight, and it might be a day before it could be restored. Worse, Davout's men had not managed to cross before the rupture, so Lannes' men represented the freshest fighting troops between Napoleon and annihilation. They had to be preserved.

Lannes' men held their position hoping for a quick repair of the lifeline. After confirming the disaster, Napoleon ordered the slow retreat of 2nd Corps. As the men fell they came under a devastating artillery barrage. General St Hilaire, perhaps the finest divisional general of France, had his left foot taken away by one of the rounds. The troops of the two conscript divisions began to leave the ranks in clumps and head to the rear, but Lannes remained calm and the line held. Finally they were back to their starting positions.

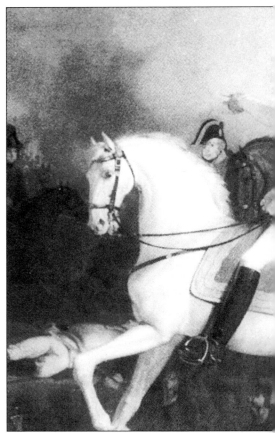

General Espagne was killed while leading one of the sacrificial charges of his cuirassiers.

With the crisis in the center averted, Charles once more sent forward attacks on the two towns. Aspern had changed hands twice already during Lannes' attack, and now the Habsburg's troops' effort was renewed. Charles had his howitzers converged into a single battery and set about pulverizing Aspern. The town once more ablaze, an assault took it but was again thrown back. Once more they came on, and by 1.00 pm Aspern was in Austrian hands for good. The defeated French set up a ring of fire to prevent any sallies from the town, but if Essling now fell, the artillery could be brought up to pound Napoleon into submission. Charles set about trying to make that happen.

Renewed attacks threw Boudet's men from all of Essling except the granary. There

Boudet remained with several elite companies, repelling all attempts to evict him. If the granary fell, all French hope would be lost. Charles sent in his elite grenadiers, but Boudet held on. Napoleon now sent in two battalions of Young Guard and one of the Middle Guard, under Mouton, to re-take Essling. The Guard came on and drove out the Austrians. Rosenberg committed more troops to surround the town and compel surrender. Napoleon responded by sending in General Rapp with two more battalions of Middle Guard to break out the beleaguered Guardsmen. Rapp, sizing up the situation, disobeyed the Emperor's orders

Archduke Charles with his staff in 1809. Years after rallying the Zach Infantry Regt he talked down the incident, saying 'You don't think a little fellow like me could carry one of those heavy flags, do you?' (Ian Castle)

and, rather than breaking off, defeated all comers. Charles had seen enough and ordered the attack on Essling discontinued.

With Napoleon pinned in Essling, the Austrians decided to decimate the French army using their superior number of guns. Almost 150 cannon began to pound the French center. Taking the brunt of the fire was 2nd Corps. Further behind them the battalions of the Old Guard had whole rows removed from their ranks under the incredible barrage. There was nowhere to go and the army was spent. Finally, Marshal Bessieres rallied some of the retreating men of the 2nd Corps and led them forward on foot as skirmishers to open fire upon the Austrian artillerists. The marshal's calm demeanor steadied the men and their fire took its toll upon their adversaries. However, by 4.00 pm Napoleon had returned to Lobau and accepted the inevitable. He would have to call off the battle and accept defeat. He left Marshal Lannes in command and began to organize the retreat, but soon after that Marshal Lannes was struck by a cannonball in the right kneecap, shattering his leg. He was carried to the rear past the Emperor, and as he was one of the small handful of Napoleon's personal friends, the Emperor wept openly upon seeing the wounded hero.

Charles was satisfied to let Napoleon retreat. His ammunition was low and his men were spent. During the night, the French evacuated to Lobau, where they spent a miserable night.

Napoleon licks his wounds

From a tactical point of view Aspern-Essling had been a draw, with both sides taking about the same casualties (22,000) but there was no mistaking the French strategic defeat. Napoleon did his best to disguise it, but the news spread throughout Europe, and the Allies hoped that perhaps now the 'ogre' could be brought down.

Following the battle, Napoleon made Lobau Island a massive fortified camp. He built sturdy bridges to bring over supplies

and reinforcements, and he called up the reserves to strengthen the army. Bernadotte's Saxons arrived, and the forces from the Italian front – including Marmont's Dalmatian Corps – began their march to join him.

Napoleon had wanted Eugene to protect his southern (right) flank and had ordered him to move into position to accomplish this goal prior to the battle of Aspern-Essling. The importance of this move was doubled as a result of the defeat. As Eugene moved north with his troops, he caught General Jellacic retreating from the Tyrol to link up with Archduke John in Hungary. At the battle of St Michael on 25 May, the badly outnumbered Austrians were mauled and very few of Jellacic's men made it to Hungary. Soon these regulars would be sorely missed.

The victory removed any immediate threat to Napoleon's strategic right flank, and Eugene was now free to pursue Archduke John and attempt to annihilate him before he could join Charles north of the Danube. John had divided his army after his defeat at the Piave River. One force remained under his command, while the other, under Gyulai, was to defend the Habsburg province of Carinthia against Macdonald's wing of Eugene's army, which now operated independently. Supporting Macdonald's efforts was the force of Marmont.

Marmont had fallen back to Zara on the Adriatic coast following his defeat on 15 April and had gathered his troops together for a counterattack. He struck on 13 May at Mt Kitta, initiating a series of actions that destroyed Stoichewich's division. He was aided in no small part by the huge number of guns he had assembled – 78 in all. Marmont had come up through the artillery, as had Napoleon, and he was regarded as the premier artillery specialist under the French emperor.

Following the defeat of Stoichewich, Marmont set off in the direction of Vienna. His first goal was to link up with Macdonald, one of whose divisions was besieging the citadel at Graz. Unknown to Marmont, Gyulai had made a relief effort and the

French had retreated rather than face a two-front battle. As a result Marmont's leading element marched on Graz unaware that the town was no longer in French hands. The 84th Line, two battalions strong, advanced against Graz and, after recovering from the shock of being fired upon, threw out the advance guard of Gyulai. Taking up a position in a church and its cemetery, they repelled attacks by an entire division before finally cutting their way out of their encircled position when their ammunition gave out.

Marmont's main force soon came up and Graz was retaken from the weary defenders. The 84th Line's legendary defense earned them the motto *'Un contre dix,'* (One against ten), which was later inscribed upon their eagle. Following Graz, Marmont and Macdonald marched to join Napoleon's army on Lobau.

While Marmont was heading north, Eugene had caught John near Raab. John had been reinforced by the Insurrection, the Hungarian militia, but was still outnumbered and outclassed. He had chosen a strong position, however and felt confident of his line of retreat. The Battle of Raab, fought on 14 June, was a vicious little battle in which the Habsburgs initially made good use of the terrain and inflicted losses upon Eugene's men. Then the tables turned and the Austrians got the worst of it. Once the stronghold of the Kis-Meyer farm had fallen for good, all hope of victory was lost to John

Tyrolian insurgents revolt against Napoleon. Despite many victories over Bavarian and French troops, eventually Napoleon's victories on the Danube left them exposed and alone (Painting by Franz von Defregger, Roger-Viollet)

and he called a retreat. John's army had suffered twice the losses of Eugene's but had fought well enough for no effective pursuit to take place. His army retreated to the north bank of the Danube and established contact with Charles' army. Eugene and his men joined Napoleon.

To the north, Prince Poniatowski was leading the Polish forces to victory. After losing Warsaw, he had appeared to melt into the countryside but had reassembled behind Ferdinand's line of communication and incited the Austrian (formerly Polish) province of Galicia to rise in revolt. The Austrian situation grew steadily worse but they were given a reprieve by the Poles' Russian 'allies,' who so devastated the areas they operated in that Poniatowski had to dispatch large parts of his army to protect his own people from their 'friends.' There was no question though, that given time, Charles would have to watch his northern flank as well as his southern.

The stage was now almost set for Napoleon to attempt another attack on Charles. He called up Wrede's Bavarian division, but could not bring up any more Bavarian troops, because the Tyrol had once more exploded in revolt. Innsbruck had again fallen to the Tyrolian insurgents and raids were being made into the Danube valley in an attempt to break the French line of communication. This problem would not be solved until the Austrians were knocked out of the war.

As Charles waited for the hammer blow he was sure would come, he looked to the west for help. Britain had promised the Habsburgs a raid in force on Germany. This plan had evolved into an attack on Antwerp, now the major French naval arsenal, which was much more to London's liking. To accomplish this goal, a huge armada had been assembled and supplies gathered – a force that Wellington would have envied. However, May became June and June became July with no sign of the British. Intelligence was such that there was no doubt of the invasion coming, but when it would happen was unknown even to Parliament. Napoleon made what provision he could to repel an attack, and then carried on with his plans for Charles.

Wagram

Lobau had become a huge warehouse. By the day of the battle the army had grown to 190,000 men. Charles had only 140,000 to oppose them. Napoleon had retaken his former *tête de pont* on the north bank and it was from there that Charles expected the attack to come. However, Napoleon was planning to drop bridges from the east edge of the island and swing around the Austrian positions from the south and east. Then in a huge wheeling motion, he would drive the Austrians away from the Danube and bring over the remainder of his army from the now undefended *tête du pont*. He put this plan into effect on the morning of 5 July 1809.

Under cover of a violent thunderstorm, the French constructed the bridges needed to transport the corps of Davout, Masséna, and Oudinot. The Austrian skirmish line was driven off or captured and the crossing took place with only light opposition. Marshal Berthier, when issuing the orders to the corps, had accidentally given the same crossing to two corps. This caused a several hour delay to sort out the traffic jam, but finally all three corps were across. Deploying on an east-west axis the French drove all enemies before them. Supporting these efforts, Napoleon opened up a terrific bombardment from his prepared positions on Lobau.

All was going well for Napoleon. Instead of finding the main Austrian army in positions around Aspern-Essling, all he faced was the outpost divisions of Nordmann and Klenau. The main Habsburg army was positioned five miles away, centered on the village of Wagram. The few battered troops to deal with the French onslaught were driven back and by noon all enemies opposite Lobau were gone. By this time, Bernadotte's Saxon Corps had joined the other three and they began an advance over the *Marchfeld* towards the main Austrian

position, with more French and Allied troops entering the plain from the Lobau bridges.

Charles had sent a message to his brother John to move from his positions near Pressburg and hurry to the battlefield, but John's men were scattered along the Danube and he failed to appreciate the urgency of Charles' request. It would be early the next morning before he would get his force on the road. While John dawdled, Charles and Emperor Francis watched the French advance with increasing trepidation.

As the four leading corps fanned out over the *Marchfeld*, the heavy cavalry positioned on the Austrian right tried to disrupt the advance by charging the Saxon cavalry opposite them. Although initially successful, they were soon driven back by the lighter Saxon horse. It had been a brave attempt by the Austrians, but they had had the misfortune to face the finest line cavalry in the world. There would be no further

After the failure of the bridges over the Danube during the battle of Aspern-Essling, Napoleon did not intend to be dangerously exposed again. He supervised the bridge building himself before the battle of Wagram. (Myrbach, Musee de l'armee)

attempts to stop Napoleon's deployment.

It was now approaching evening and Napoleon decided to try to exploit the gains made during the day. Ever fearful that his adversary would slip away during the night, he ordered an assault along the line. His mistake would be a lack of effective effort to coordinate the several corps.

At about 7.00 pm Oudinot's Corps, with the support of Dupas' small division from Bernadotte's Corps, attacked the center of the enemy line. The defense was centered around Baumersdorf. Spearheading the assault was Grandjean's division, the best in the army apart from the Guard. The 'Terrible 57th' Line attacked the southern end of the village and drove out two regiments facing it, capturing many Austrians. They continued over the little Russbach stream and into the northern half of the town. Here their furious attack ran out of steam, for Hardegg's men dug in and would not budge. The Austrians knew that if the town was taken, their position would be hopelessly compromised. Both sides laid down a withering fire and casualties mounted.

While this action was taking place, the 10th Legere had crossed the marshy stream and had begun to climb the slopes beyond. Charles was there and knew that if the heights were taken, Baumersdorf would be quickly surrounded and would certainly fall. He ordered one of his cavalry regiments, the Vincent Chevaulegers, to charge. Here was a fight between one of the best cavalry regiments in the Habsburg army and one of the best French infantry regiments. The first round went to the French and the cavalry recoiled. Charles regrouped them and they came on again, only to suffer the same result. While the 10th Legere repulsed the charges, their progress was temporarily halted. They waited for two more divisions of Oudinot's Corps to come up on their flank. These two divisions were made up of the conscripts of the 4th battalions. They had little stomach for the murderous artillery barrage that was pouring down on them. After a brief attempt to advance they halted, then fell back.

The retreat of Oudinot's two divisions left Grandjean's men isolated. It was at this moment that Charles turned to the twice-repulsed Vincent Chevaulegers and said: 'It is clear that you are no longer Latour's dragoons.' This was a reference to their heroic past. Stung by the reproach, the regiment charged once more, with the corps commander, Hohenzollern, leading. The 10th could no longer hold on. They fell back, firing as they went, and were driven across the stream. The repulse of the 10th Legere left the flanks of the 57th Line open to attack, so they too had to retire. The French assault in the center was over, with nothing to show for it.

To the left of this action the elements of the army of Italy now attempted to assault the Russbach heights. Led by General Macdonald, three divisions crossed the stream and attacked. Pressing uphill against the Austrian gun line, they were on the verge of breaking through when fresh Habsburg reserves counterattacked. Macdonald's men recoiled down the slope but regrouped and were beginning a fresh advance when the Vincent Chevaulegers attacked from the right flank. The heroic cavalry unit had rallied from their assault on the 10th Legere and, seeing the opportunity, charged. Seras' division gave way and routed to the rear. While Macdonald's right flank was collapsing, his left was doing no better. General Dupas' division had crossed the Russbach and had become mired in the swampy ground. Finally extricating themselves, they made a first assault up the slopes. The Austrian fire drove them back, and as they retreated, Macdonald's reserves mistook the white-coated Saxons attached to Dupas as Austrians and opened fire. Since it was Italian troops initiating the fire, they too were clad in white and the Saxons returned fire. Before the generals could restore the situation, the Italians had been badly shaken and the hapless Saxons had completely dispersed. When the panic caused by the situation on its right flank rippled down the line, the entire army of Italy dissolved into a rout. A disconsolate Eugene was comforted by Macdonald with the words that the attack had been ill-considered and that Napoleon would soon realize it. He did.

With half of his small division destroyed, Dupas could not hold on for long. Soon his men began to flee to the rear. As they headed back, they were passed by a brigade of Saxons aiming to take Wagram. It was now nearly 8.00 pm and Bernadotte had sent forward his three remaining infantry brigades one at a time. Napoleon had realized that if the Saxon attack was to have any hope of success, it had to have artillery support, so he deployed the horse artillery of the Guard and the Saxon and Bavarian batteries to pulverize Wagram. The effect was

Wagram, second day

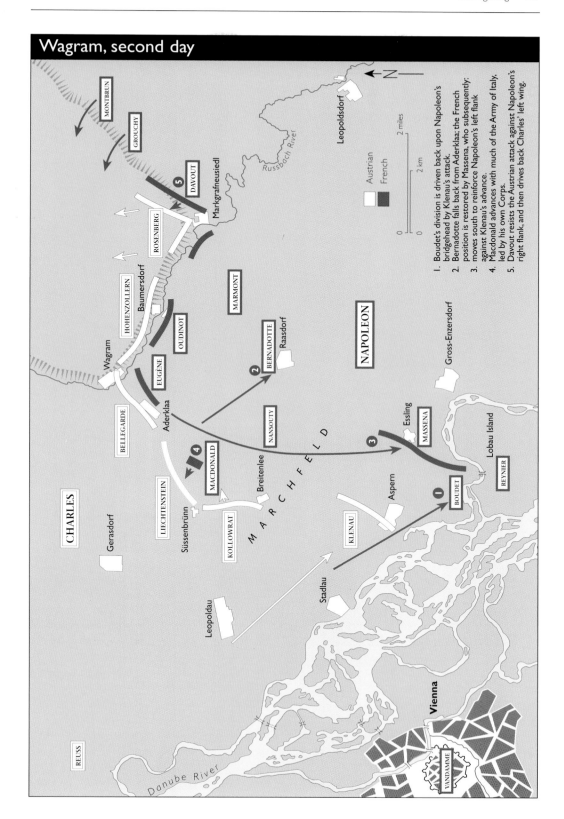

Austrian

French

0 ___ 2 km
0 ___ 2 miles

1. Boudet's division is driven back upon Napoleon's bridgehead by Klenau's attack.
2. Bernadotte falls back from Aderklaa; the French position is restored by Massena, who subsequently moves south to reinforce Napoleon's left flank against Klenau's advance.
3. moves south to reinforce Napoleon's left flank against Klenau's advance.
4. Macdonald advances with much of the Army of Italy, led by his own Corps.
5. Davout resists the Austrian attack against Napoleon's right flank, and then drives back Charles' left wing.

MONTBRUN

GROUCHY

DAVOUT

ROSENBERG

Markgrafneusiedl

Russbach River

Leopoldsdorf

HOHENZOLLERN

Baumersdorf

OUDINOT

MARMONT

EUGÈNE

BERNADOTTE

Raasdorf

Wagram

NAPOLEON

BELLEGARDE

Aderklaa

NANSOUTY

Gross-Enzersdorf

MACDONALD

Breitenlee

Essling

MASSENA

LIECHTENSTEIN

Lobau Island

Süssenbrünn

KOLLOWRAT

M A R C H F E L D

Aspern

BOUDET

REYNIER

CHARLES

Gerasdorf

KLENAU

Stadlau

Leopoldau

REUSS

Danube River

Vienna

VANDAMME

devastating and allowed the single Saxon brigade to gain a foothold in the town. Caught in a fierce firefight, the outnumbered Saxons held on until the next brigade came up. These men penetrated to the other side of Wagram but a counterattack threw them back. Retreating through the gloom and smoke, they fell back to the third and final brigade of Bernadotte's troops which had finally entered the battle. Once more, the Saxons were mistaken for Austrians and were fired upon by their own side. With fire from friend and foe alike, their morale collapsed and they fled. This rout started a general panic and soon all hard-won gains were gone. The panicking infantry fell back toward Aderklaa under the protection of their cavalry and guns. This attack had been as dismal a failure as the others.

As Bernadotte's men had stepped off on their attack, Davout on the far French right had crossed the Russbach and had met stiff resistance. Aware that darkness would make coordination of any attack impossible, Davout wisely called it off and retreated to his starting position.

The first day ended with the French army unnerved by the mauling they had received. They were, though, firmly on the *Marchfeld* and still under their Emperor. During the night, Charles surveyed the situation. Things had gone well, but it was too late to change the orders for the next day. These called for a double envelopment attack on the French. He had a sizable force that could attack on his right, but unless Archduke John arrived soon, his left attack stood no chance. Napoleon planned for Davout on his right to be the main attack, and for his other corps to be committed as Davout's attack developed.

Napoleon felt confident that with Aderklaa held and several corps in reserve, ready to fill any gaps that might develop, his plan could succeed. What he did not know was that Bernadotte had pulled out of Aderklaa at 3.00 am and fallen back a thousand yards. While it was true that the Saxon Corps had been roughly treated, to pull out of such a key position was to invite disaster. Bernadotte felt his men had been

One of the finest French generals, André Masséna. Wagram was his last victory, and owed much to his performance, though he was confined to his carriage by a previous wound. (Ann Ronan Picture Library)

mistreated and deserved reinforcements which had not come. Telling anyone who would listen that he could have turned the Austrians out of their position by a 'telling maneuver,' he would earn Napoleon's wrath the following day when these words reached the Emperor's ears.

The morning of 6 July 1809 broke hot and sweltering. Several of Charles' corps had been on the march since the early hours. The key to Charles' attack was to turn both of the French flanks and drive to the bridgehead at Lobau. There he could cut off the French retreat and hopefully induce panic in the enemy. The main attack on the French left would be spearheaded by Klenau's 6th Corps, with the support of Kolowrat's 3rd Corps. Charles further hoped that John would appear on the French right

Portrait of General Macdonald. He wore his old Revolutionary War uniform for Wagram, emphasizing that he had only just been rehabilitated after a long period of disgrace. After the battle he was compensated with the award of a marshal's baton.

and close the trap from that direction. To support this he ordered Rosenberg's 4th Corps to attack Davout's 3rd Corps. John's arrival would fall on Davout's flank and seal the victory.

Klenau's initial cannonade broke the morning stillness at about 4.00 am. Facing them initially was Boudet's single division of Masséna's 4th Corps. Seeing the attack begin, Masséna sent Legrand's division to aid Boudet. They would face the full wrath of Kolowrat's men. Badly outnumbered Legrand's division stood for a brief time before being overwhelmed, and a hole several miles wide was opened in the French line.

While this was taking place, Boudet's men were grimly holding on to the charred ruins of Aspern. Supporting their defense were two batteries of guns, which poured fire into the powerful tide of white-coated Austrians. When Legrand's division gave way and the French line was breached, Austrian cavalry flooded into the gap, circled around the northern flank of Boudet, and came charging down his flank and rear. The exposed

gunners were sabered and when an infantry regiment went into the plain to rescue the artillery, it too was cut up. At the same time the left flank of Boudet was turned and soon almost all of his division panicked and broke for the rear. A brief stand was made at Essling, but there was to be no repetition of the hotly contested fighting of two months earlier. Essling was soon clear of the French. It was only as Klenau's men approached the *tête de pont* that the vast number of guns left on the island stopped the pursuit. The first half of Charles' plan had been achieved, but Klenau had no support, for Kolowrat had stopped his advance and was lending lukewarm support to the action developing around Aderklaa. Further there was no sign of a closing pincer coming from the other flank.

Rosenberg had made a good start. His attack has surprised Davout's men and sent the outposts streaming to the rear in panic. However, once stability had returned to the French ranks, the attack petered out and quiet fell in that part of the field.

Napoleon had intended the attack by Davout to be a decisive blow. While the Austrian attack had failed to drive Davout from his position, it had cost the French in the area much of their ammunition. It would now take several hours of re-supply and prepare for the planned attack. Perhaps more important was that news of Rosenberg's attack caused Napoleon to shift his reserves to the French right, away from the area where later it would be needed most.

The village of Aderklaa was a key position on the battlefield and both commanders recognized this. Charles had ordered his I Corps under Bellegarde to attack and take the village. Napoleon believed that the Saxon Corps under Bernadotte was still in possession of Aderklaa and he sent most of Masséna's Corps to support them, but Bernadotte had pulled his battered men from the position as he felt that it was too exposed to the tremendous artillery concentration in the area. That danger was real enough, but the loss of this key position posed an even greater threat.

Bellegarde's troops were able to take the village with few losses and began to dig in. When Napoleon returned from his ride to Davout's position, he ordered Bernadotte's men to retake Aderklaa. The Saxons came on but were devastated by the Habsburg guns that the marshal had so feared the night before. Soon the shaken men gave way and fled to the rear. Bernadotte was carried along with them, frantically trying to rally his men, with little effect, when he came into the Emperor's presence. Napoleon shook his head and asked if this was the 'telling maneuver' of which Bernadotte had spoken. The marshal had little

time to wallow in this humiliation, however, as the Saxon infantry retreat continued for some time.

In truth much of the French left had effectively ceased to exist. The only organized force was some cavalry and the remaining two divisions of Masséna's 4th Corps. These were now sent to attack Aderklaa. Carra St Cyr's division went into the attack to Masséna's call to 'throw out that *merde.*' The men came on through a hail of cannon shot and at the points of their bayonets ejected the Austrians from the houses. Following up their victory, St Cyr's

Napoleon snatching a moment's rest on the battlefield of Wagram, his staff and household at work around him. (Edimedia)

burning village. Yard by yard, Aderklaa fell into Molitor's hands, despite several attempts to reclaim it for the Habsburgs. It was just past 9.00 am and the battle hung in the balance.

As Napoleon's reserves made their way back from their march to the right flank, Charles organized a massive assault against Aderklaa. He committed his 1st Reserve Corps of elite grenadiers to support the efforts of Bellegarde's attack from the north and Kolowrat's from the south. This attack came after a two-hour pounding from over 100 Austrian guns. Seeing that their retreat would soon be cut off and down to almost half their number, Molitor's troops evacuated the village, firing as they went. Unlike the Saxons, however, they remained a cohesive force.

Napoleon now needed to buy some time. With Davout's attack at last underway, Napoleon needed to hold his front long enough to allow Davout to win the battle. His first concern was to deal with the threat to his rear from Klenau, so he sent the remains of Masséna's Corps south. He then ordered much of his center to swing to the west and align themselves to face the advancing troops under Kolowrat and Liechtenstein's reserve grenadiers. This maneuver would take over an hour. To buy this time, Napoleon sent in his heavy cavalry under Nansouty. The 4,000 cuirassiers and carabineers swept across the open plain. The Austrian cannon rounds plowed the earth around them and tore holes through their ranks, but the cavalry came on, and after crushing one battalion, dashed themselves upon the grenadier squares. Here they had no effect. They swung around the squares and charged the Austrian gun line from the flank. Before they could do much good, however, they were themselves charged in the flank by Austrian cavalry which had hurried up. The melee was brief, and soon the remaining French horse were flying back

men carried on past the village. They had gone beyond their effective support and were counterattacked so successfully that two of their 'sacred' eagles were lost. Charles had been on the spot to rally his retreating men and led them forward to retake Aderklaa. Charles was wounded in the conflict, taking a bullet in the shoulder.

As St Cyr's men reeled back from the fighting, Masséna sent in his last reserve, Molitor's division. These were the men who had held on to Aspern against all odds in May. They first repelled a vicious cavalry attack, then fell upon the defenders of the to the safety of their lines. The charge had done little more than stall the Austrians.

While the cavalry was creating this costly diversion, Napoleon ordered a massive battery to be formed opposite Rosenberg's men. Made up mostly of Imperial Guard artillery, it had 112 guns and was commanded by General Lauriston. Galloping into position under a hail of fire from the Austrian guns, the grand battery set up and began to bombard the luckless 3rd Corps. This was the largest concentration of artillery ever assembled during a field battle and its effect was devastating. First Kolowrat's guns were silenced, then the massed Austrian infantry was targeted. The solid rounds tore through the Austrian formations, taking out entire files with a single shot. To add to these horrors, the dry grass ignited and many of the wounded on both sides were burned alive. Several times the Austrians tried to dislodge the guns, but they were pulverized before they could have any real effect. The tide was finally turning in Napoleon's favor.

Davout had prepared his attack against Markgrafneusiedl, the linchpin of the Austrian left, with a heavy artillery bombardment. After pounding much of the village into rubble and setting many of the buildings alight, Davout sent forward his four divisions. Those under Morand and Friant swung to the right of the village, while the other two, under Puthod and Gudin, went straight in. Morand and Friant advanced in echelon to the right and hit the back of the village. The leading troops were stopped and the Austrian general Nordmann saw an opportunity to turn Morand's flank. Driving off one regiment with his attack, Nordmann was in turn hit in the flank by Friant's men. In the fighting Nordmann was killed, and soon his men were running to the rear.

Markgrafneusiedl was still in Austrian hands though, and the divisions of Puthod and Gudin were making slow progress. In desperate house-to-house fighting Davout's men eventually evicted Rosenberg's men. The fighting continued past the village to the medieval tower above. This was taken

and retaken several times until it was finally in French hands.

It was now around noon and the wounded Charles arrived with fresh troops to stem the French tide. His cavalry was able to repel the first assault, but was finally overwhelmed by superior numbers. The whole of the Austrian line on the Russbach heights began to give way and retreat to the west.

When Napoleon received the news of the capture of Markgrafneusiedl, he assumed, correctly, that any enemy reserves were being sent in that direction to try to stop Davout. Knowing that the Habsburg line was stretched to breaking point, he launched General Macdonald's three small divisions at the Austrian center. Macdonald formed his men into a huge square and began the advance. Supported by Wrede's Bavarian division on his right, the huge phalanx lumbered forward. The remaining Austrian guns turned all available fire upon them. It was impossible to miss a target of this size, and Macdonald's men paid a fearful price. On they came, nevertheless, and soon the devastated Austrian line began to yield. A hole was created, but soon closed because there were no cavalry to exploit the victory. With the Guard cavalry commander, Marshal Bessieres, badly wounded in Nansouty's earlier attack, the orders to bring on the Guard cavalry were never executed. Isolated, Macdonald's men had to finally give way and fall back the way they had come. The moment passed and the complete victory slipped away.

In the south, Masséna had evicted Klenau's men from Essling and Aspern and Klenau was now in full retreat, having come within a hair of winning the day, but having received no support.

Victory was in the capable hands of Davout and he was making the most of it. Austrians in one position after another on the Russbach heights had to turn and face his flanking attack, while the French opposite these positions added their weight to the onslaught. These were Oudinot's 2nd Corps and Marmont's Corps. The pressure from two sides was too much and Charles ordered a retreat toward Bohemia. By 2.00 pm the field was in French hands, but the decimated French-Allied army had no appetite for pursuit. Once the victory was assured, many men collapsed in place and rested.

It was about 4.00 pm when Archduke John's first troops arrived on the field. Besides scaring some understandably skittish Saxons, he could do no good. After sizing up the situation, he too ordered a retreat to Bohemia.

The cost of the fighting

Losses on both sides were staggering, approximately 40,000 killed, wounded and missing from each army. Among the upper ranks losses had been equally devastating. The French lost five generals killed and 38 wounded. The Austrians, less apt to lead from the front, still had four generals killed and 13 wounded. As a result of the battle, Napoleon honored three generals on the battlefield. He made Oudinot, Marmont, and Macdonald into marshals. Bernadotte was dismissed from command after he issued a letter of congratulation to the Saxons, giving them great credit in the preceding day's battle. This was the Emperor's purview and Bernadotte had once more overstepped his authority. The act was particularly galling given that his withdrawal from Aderklaa had cost the French so dearly, but his earlier comments had not been forgotten either.

The following day the French reorganized their army while Charles retreated toward Znaim. Marmont's Corps caught up with the Austrians on the evening of 10 July and tried to pin the Habsburgs before they could retreat across the Thaya River. Though he took heavy losses, Marmont succeeded in pinning much of the army until Napoleon showed with reinforcements. The battle was in full progress the following day when an Austrian rode out between the lines with an armistice request. Many French veterans wept at the thought of their old enemy

escaping once more with a punitive peace treaty.

Napoleon met with Liechtenstein and a one-month truce was signed. Napoleon needed the rest to recoup from this bloody campaign, as did the Austrians. The latter hoped though that they could gain some leverage from the now imminently expected British invasion of the Dutch coast.

After months of dithering, the British force finally set sail in the last week of July 1809. Their object was the port of Antwerp and its naval base, but first the British had to take the island of Walcheren. Located at the mouth of the Scheldt River, they needed the island as a base of operations from which to launch the attack on Antwerp. The army, under the Earl of Chatham, was the strongest Britain could muster and the naval support enormous.

A 20,000-strong force landed on the island and advanced on Flushing. Defending this fortified town was a rag-tag force under General Monnet. While delays allowed the French to send over more troops, the final outcome seemed predetermined. Monnet flooded the island, which is mostly below sea level, delaying the British advance, but when the massive fleet ran the French fort at the mouth of the Scheldt, the British bombardment secured the outcome. On 15 August, the French asked for surrender terms.

Chatham's victory was in vain, for he took far too long organizing his force to push up the Scheldt for Antwerp. Probes were made in several directions, but no firm decision was taken about which path to take. Meanwhile Bernadotte had been appointed to take over command of the district defenses. Sensing that this was perhaps his last chance to recover his reputation, Bernadotte pitched in and organized his forces so that every British attempt was frustrated.

As continued attempts were made to seek a weak spot in the French defenses, a virulent fever broke out in the British army. The marshy ground of Walcheren was a perfect breeding ground for mosquitoes and soon 100 men were dying each day. After more than a month of terrible losses the British gave up and set sail for home. There recriminations waited for all the leaders involved.

In the Tyrol, Napoleon sent in troops in such numbers that the outcome was no longer in doubt The rebels were suppressed one band at a time. Finally, Andreas Hofer was captured and sent to his trial and martyrdom. After that, all rebellion was quelled.

As the months dragged on, Napoleon waited for the negotiations in the Viennese Palace of Schönbrunn to reach a conclusion. There he put on parades and entertained his Austrian counterparts. He even had time to re-visit the battlefield of Austerlitz, scene of his greatest triumph. Once the Walcheren expedition had failed, it was merely a matter of working out the details of the penalty to be suffered by the Habsburgs for their violation of peace and their alliance with the hated British.

It was during one of many reviews at this time that General Rapp noticed a young man acting suspiciously. Searching him he found a large knife. The young Saxon, Friedrich Stapps, soon confessed to planning to assassinate Napoleon. Brought before the Emperor, he explained that the reason for his plan was to liberate his subject country. Napoleon offered clemency for an apology, but Stapps refused. His plot and subsequent execution deeply troubled Napoleon. This was the tip of the iceberg, a symptom of growing German nationalism. The French Revolution had spread the modern ideas of liberty, but the young men of Europe did not necessarily believe that it should happen under French rule. However, these were specters of the future: for the time being, there was peace to be settled.

Heading up the negotiations for Francis was Prince Metternich. He had the same goal as Charles, the preservation of the Habsburg Empire. Promising peace and friendship, he succeeded in fooling Napoleon into making more modest demands for peace than he could have exacted. Napoleon received

Carinthia, Carniola, and the Adriatic ports; part of Galicia was regained by the Poles; the Salzburg area of the Tyrol was given to the Bavarians; and the small Tarnopol area was given to the treacherous Russians. However, most of the hereditary lands remained with Francis' crown.

Napoleon made the critical error of believing that a permanent peace with the great monarchies of Europe was possible. Austria, Russia, and Prussia believed that peace should only be made in order to regain lost strength, but that ultimately the 'Corsican usurper' had to be removed. It would have been better for Napoleon had he dismantled the Habsburg holdings, perhaps giving Bohemia to Bavaria or Saxony, making Hungary independent, and leaving the Habsburgs with Austria alone. This arrangement would have left Austria in no position to turn against him, as they would do four years later. Metternich understood all this, and directed negotiations towards a more moderate conclusion.

A false peace

The year 1809 had been difficult for Emperor Napoleon. He had withstood threats on every front. When peace was finally signed, on 14 October 1809 at the Schönbrunn palace, Napoleon was already planning to take the Austrian princess Marie-Louise as his new wife. Josephine could no longer bear children, and Napoleon believed that a son and heir was needed to continue the regime. Originally, Napoleon had approached Tsar Alexander with the idea of marrying his sister Catherine, but because the dowager empress rejected the idea of a family alliance with heretic France, or because of a possible incestuous relationship with her, Alexander had spurned the offer. He quickly married off Catherine to the Prince of Oldenburg and kept her at close quarters. The offer to marry the younger sister Anne was put off until she was older.

Napoleon was no fool and knew he had been rejected a second time. So when peace

One of the greatest armadas Britain had ever seen bombarding the fortress of Flushing on the Dutch coast. (National Maritime Museum)

came with Austria, he turned his attention to creating an alliance with them instead. Metternich could not have been happier, as this sacrifice assured that Napoleon turned his eyes away from the Habsburgs. Married by proxy, the princess was brought to France where Napoleon met her near Compiegne and hosted the bridal party prior to the formal church wedding held in the Louvre. While the marriage was hailed as a harbinger of peace for Europe, many of Napoleon's men felt that the ideals of the Revolution were being lost and that their good luck charm, Josephine, had been discarded.

Josephine went to Malmaison where she lived out most of her remaining life. Napoleon saw her little, for Marie-Louise resented the continuing friendship. Napoleon clearly loved his new bride and she him. He became much more domestic and housebound, and the pace of his previous frenetic activity slackened. The war in Spain was not going as well as it should, but he never managed to pull himself away from his bride long enough to take the field in Spain again.

The new empress fulfilled her part in the bargain as she was soon pregnant. It was on 19 March 1811 that the King of Rome, Napoleon II, was born.

The war with Russia, 1812

Causes
While Napoleon and his new bride visited sights around his empire in 1810 and 1811, the relationship with Russia was deteriorating. Tsar Alexander had been under pressure ever since Tilsit in 1807 to break the restrictions on trade that the treaty had imposed. His first response was to permit open smuggling, but this was soon decried by the French and he looked for another answer.

Napoleon was well aware of Alexander's duplicity. The rejection of Napoleon's marriage proposal and the lackluster performance of the Russians in 1809 had irritated Napoleon so much that he struck back by incorporating large parts of Germany and the Balkans into the French empire. Included in this was the Duchy of Oldenburg, whose ruler had just married into the Tsar's family.

Alexander resented these actions intensely. He was even affronted by Napoleon's marriage to an Austrian princess. He declared in December of 1810 that he would no longer refuse to trade with neutrals

Napoleon had difficulty in believing that Alexander wanted war, but he prepared to assemble his army in Poland to deal with the errant ally. Napoleon approached the Swedes with the prospect of regaining Finland should they join the war effort. Bernadotte had become the Swedish crown prince and *de facto* ruler, and he was more than willing to listen to these proposals, but the French ambassador in Stockholm became incensed that Sweden continued to trade with neutrals and broke off relations. Bernadotte went to Tsar Alexander looking for a better deal. He was offered Norway, a Danish possession, for his cooperation. Bernadotte accepted and turned his back on his homeland. Alexander would find that Bernadotte was as unreliable an ally in 1812 as he had been a marshal for Napoleon.

Russia wanted war by the beginning of 1811 and was making plans to invade Poland. Only poor finances made this impossible. A signal success in Turkey led to a peace that released Russian troops in the south for use against Napoleon. Alexander had a million men under arms by 1812, but they were scattered throughout the vast Russian territories. It took enormous time to mobilize them, but this had some advantages for the Tsar.

In Paris a spy ring had been discovered, which particularly embarrassed Napoleon. One of the key players was Alexander Tchernishev, a Russian colonel who had made friends with Napoleon. The Emperor was particularly chagrined to discover, after the Russian's return to Moscow, that a worker in the French Ministry of War had been handing over to the spy every return of the troops in the field. When this was announced, it was treated as proof of Russia's bad faith.

Napoleon had his own successes. The French Foreign Minister Champigny showed a forged document to the King of Prussia indicating that the Tsar proposed the elimination of Prussia in the near future. This threw the King into France's arms and he provided a corps for the war effort against Russia. Austria was equally compliant. When promised that they would be able to keep their existing territories if they contributed 30,000 men, they quickly agreed.

Napoleon had received repeated warnings that to invade Russia could be disastrous, particularly from Caulaincourt, his recent ambassador to St Petersburg. But Caulaincourt had been fooled before by Alexander's protestations. Napoleon assumed that threats of war to the death should the Russian borders be violated were nothing more than bluster. What Napoleon did not know was that the vacillating Tsar had experienced a mystical vision in which he saw himself as God's shield against the Antichrist Napoleon. This gave the barely-sane Tsar a new resolve.

By August 1811 Napoleon had accepted that war was inevitable. He began to plan for the campaign the following year, with 600,000 men beginning their march to the borders of Russia, with few knowing their final destination.

Napoleon enters Russia

The French-Allied invasion force designated for the campaign was divided into five commands. The three central armies were commanded by Napoleon, his brother Jérôme, who was King of Westphalia, and his stepson Eugene Beauharnais, Viceroy of Italy. One of the two flanking armies, the southern, was commanded by the Austrian Prince Schwarzenberg, while Marshal Macdonald led a combined French and Prussian corps. Napoleon's main force was made up of the Guard, Davout's 1st Corps, Ney's 3rd Corps, and two reserve cavalry corps under Montbrun, and Nansouty. On his right Jérôme had Poniatowski's (Polish) 5th Corps, Vandamme's (Westphalian)

Marie-Louise, Napoleon's Austrian princess bride. (Ann Ronan Picture Library)

8th Corps, and Reynier's (Saxon) 7th Corps, plus a cavalry corps under Latour-Maubourg. Eugene commanded his own 4th Corps, the 6th Corps under St Cyr, and a cavalry corps under Grouchy. In all, the central forces totaled some 320,000 men. The central army began to cross the River Niemen early in the morning of 24 June 1812. The flanking armies, with another 115,000 men, also began their advance. Less than half Napoleon's men were French.

The Russians were divided into three armies: the 1st, 2nd, and 3rd Armies of the West, deployed over a wide front. The largest

of these armies was the 1st, commanded by
Barclay de Tolly. His 126,000 men were
further subdivided, for the 1st Corps under
Wittgenstein was separated by 100 miles
from the main army, and Platov's Cossacks
were even further away forming a link with
Bagration's 2nd Army. Bagration had about
47,000 under his command, divided into
two corps. The 3rd Army, under Tormasov,
some 45,000 men, was so dispersed that it
would take several weeks to bring it together.
A further 30,000 reserves under Admiral
Chichagov would be called up from the
Crimea during the campaign. All told the
Russian field armies were outnumbered
almost two to one.

Napoleon's strategy was to advance upon
Barclay and then turn and crush Bagration
when his anticipated advance into Poland
brought him into range. Ironically, this fitted
well with General Phull's plan for the Tsar.
Phull, a Prussian in exile, had convinced the
Tsar that a fortified camp at Drissa would act
as the anvil to Bagration's hammer. Just prior
to Napoleon's invasion, however, others in
the Russian high command convinced the
Tsar that an initial defensive strategy was
required when new intelligence revealed that
Napoleon's army was much larger than
previously believed. So Bagration's offensive
was cancelled. When Barclay fell back toward
his camp at Drissa, Bagration began to fall
back as well.

The French failure in the 1812 campaign
can be attributed to a number of factors.
Much of the Franco-Allied army was made
up of recent conscripts. These soldiers were
not yet accustomed to the rigors of the
extended marches that Napoleon required of
his troops. Secondly, the supply system broke
down. While Napoleon had assembled the
greatest logistical train in history, the poor
roads and lack of forage prevented the
supply wagons from keeping up with the
main army. As the supply train failed,
discipline went too. Men left the ranks to
find food and shelter, and many never
returned. The long marches caused the men's
health to break down and they died
ingloriously from various maladies.

While the terrible hardship of the winter
retreat is legendary, the stifling heat
alternating with chilling thunderstorms
caused more deaths on the march into the
interior of Russia than on the exit. Finally,
the French were out-scouted throughout the
entire campaign. The Russians knew the
terrain and the French had few reliable
sources of information. Murat, the King of
Naples, while dashing and the envy of every
allied cavalier as well as the Cossacks, ran his
cavalry into the ground. French cavalrymen
complained that they seldom had a chance
to unsaddle their horses, and the loss of most
of the good mounts would undermine many
of the later efforts of Napoleon's army and
haunt it for the rest of the Napoleonic era.

All these factors combined to doom
Napoleon's enterprise. Many losses might
have been avoided by a slower advance with
frequent stops to rest and allow the supply
to catch up. However, that would have
eliminated any chance of catching the

Russian army and bringing them to the decisive battle that Napoleon sought. While we are ahead of our story, these causes of the destruction of the Grande Armée were pervasive and had begun to tell from the first day of the invasion. Indeed, the army's exhaustion was already appreciable on the advance to the frontier through Poland.

While his intelligence reports were slow and not very reliable, Napoleon soon came to recognize that his best opportunity for a quick victory was to pin Bagration's army against the Pripet marshes. He devised a pincer movement, hoping to catch the Russians between Davout's 1st Corps, on the left, and Jérôme's army, on the right. Once he arrived in Vilna, recently vacated by the Tsar and the main Russian army command, Napoleon sent Davout and two divisions with cavalry support to move toward Minsk. At the same time, Jérôme was to keep in contact with Bagration's force and trap and destroy Bagration between the two French commands. However, Jérôme had made little progress, and by the time he got his men moving, a violent thunderstorm made the roads virtually impassable. He fell further behind schedule, and compounded his failings by not keeping Napoleon informed of his progress. Jérôme quarreled with his corps commander General Vandamme and then relieved him. This was the only information forwarded to the French emperor. Napoleon's response was to send a blistering letter back, berating Jérôme for letting a wonderful opportunity slip away. He also sent a secret message to Davout, putting him in command should a battle with Bagration appear to be imminent. Jérôme did little to communicate with headquarters and sat in Grodno for a week awaiting orders, despite instructions to press Bagration.

Napoleon commencing the campaign, crossing the River Niemen which was then the Russian frontier. (Musée de l'armee)

Jérôme Napoleon, posing here before one of his palaces, enjoyed a
reputation as a playboy prince. But not content as the King of
Westphalia, he wanted to rival his brother Napoleon as a general.
His failure to perform his role was an important factor in
Napoleon's defeat in Russia. (Roger-Viollet)

For over two weeks Napoleon stayed in Vilna trying to gather the information required to formulate a new plan of attack. He called upon Schwarzenberg to move his army to support Jérôme, leaving only a small corps under Reynier to watch Tormasov's 3rd Army. The latter had been badly underestimated because of poor intelligence. As these orders went out, there was little Napoleon could do but wait. The rain continued and supply suffered.

To the north, Macdonald was slowly advancing on Riga. There was little to oppose him besides the Cossacks, but again the French and Prussian troops proved ineffective in scouting. South of Macdonald, Oudinot was advancing upon the Drina River. Ney was ordered to support him, but in the wooded countryside was unable to keep contact with his fellow marshal.

On 4 July, Napoleon was still in Vilna and Barclay was approaching the fortified camp of Drissa, along with Phull's adjutant, von Clausewitz. He was horrified when they at last arrived upon the scene. The camp was completely inadequate for their purposes and to try to defend it would surely result in a Russian disaster. Barclay's army was being drained of men, like the French, and he needed to rest for several days in order to stop the hemorrhaging.

Alexander was in a nervous state and torn by conflicting advice he was receiving from all sides. Barclay advised retreat upon the line of supply, while Bagration and others would not consider giving up one more foot of Russian soil. Two political camps had developed. One centered on Barclay and various 'foreign' advisors around the Tsar; the other centered on ultra-nationalists who followed Arakcheev and Bagration. These two factions sent advice and poison-pen letters to the Tsar, who vacillated in order to try to keep the peace.

One aspect where the inconclusiveness of Alexander's policies was shown most tellingly was in unity of command. The two main armies under Barclay and Bagration

The *Grande Armée* crossing a river during the advance into Russia. Many of the losses to horses and men occurred during this exhausting march.

1812 Russian campaign to the French invasion of Moscow

1. Napoleon advances across the Niemen.
2. Barclay withdraws to Drissa, declines to defend it, detaches Wittgenstein and continues to withdraw to Smolensk.
3. Davout and (4) Jérôme try to intercept Bagration.
5. Bagration retires on Smolensk.
6. Reynier and (7) Schwarzenberg contain Tormasov, who retires.
8. Macdonald advances on Napoleon's left flank towards the Russian garrison of Riga.
9. Barclay and Bagration unite at Smolensk; French attack on 17 August.
10. Wittgenstein engages Oudinot at Polotsk, 19 August.
11. Russian army, now under Kutusov, retires to Borodino and gives battle there, 7 September.
12. Kutusov permits Napoleon to occupy Moscow, 14 September, and takes up a position to the south.

needed to act in concert to have any hope of stopping the invader, but no general-in-chief was appointed. Barclay theoretically commanded Bagration by virtue of being minister of war, but Bagration outranked Barclay by seniority and had been Barclay's commander in a previous campaign. It seems that Alexander wanted the coordination to be handled by Barclay, but to avoid the wrath of the ultra-nationalists, he never made this formal. To further complicate the situation, Bagration believed that Barclay was behind a campaign to discredit him and allow the 2nd Army to be crushed. There is no evidence of this, but Bagration was obsessed by the thought.

One thing was certain: as long as Alexander failed to lead, yet remained in the field, Russia's prospects were bleak. A party of generals, led by Arakcheev, and

statesmen, notably the secretary of state Shishkov, convinced the Tsar to leave the front and rally the country to the cause. He left on 19 July and hurried to Moscow, where he called for a raising of more militia.

By 9 July, Napoleon had issued new orders, beginning a concentration between Bagration and Barclay. By now Davout had taken Minsk and was preparing to advance on Borisov. On 12 July Jérôme finally re-established communications with Davout and the two forces were in a good position to attack Bagration. Seeing the opportunity, Davout apprised Jérôme of Napoleon's secret order giving the marshal overall command on this front. Most likely transmitted in Davout's usual blunt manner, the insulted Jérôme quit the army and left the command to Marchand. The latter had no instructions and understandably took several days to sort out the mess. In that time, the opportunity slipped away.

Bagration fought a small battle against Davout's lead column at Saltanovka on 23 July but did not manage to break the French. He retreated and tried to slip around Davout's southern flank.

Barclay's first goal, after Alexander's departure, was to link up with Bagration and interpose himself between Napoleon and Moscow. He headed south-east toward Vitebsk, where he hoped the junction would occur. To protect the route to St Petersburg, he left General Wittgenstein to support General's Essen's men in Riga.

Napoleon had been maneuvering his army to make a strike at Drissa. It took some time before his reconnaissance discovered that the blow would strike air. Finally divining that it was Vitebsk that Barclay was heading for, he turned his army and made for the city. He recalled Oudinot to protect his line of communications. As Oudinot withdrew, Wittgenstein actively harassed him and fought a series of inconclusive actions. This had the effect of pinning Oudinot's men and preventing them from close coordination with the main army. After the first battle of Polotsk, on 18 August, where the outnumbered Russians attacked Oudinot and fought him to a standstill, the front settled down, with both sides digging in.

Barclay barely beat the French to Vitebsk. Marshal Murat had defeated a cavalry rearguard at Ostrovno on 25 July and learned from prisoners that Barclay was ultimately headed for Smolensk. Napoleon's army was in bad shape and exhausted, so Napoleon halted the advance on 29 July and waited for his army to close up and for the lagging supply to arrive. This pause of a week allowed Bagration to swing around Davout's men and head for Smolensk to join Barclay.

Word now reached Napoleon that Tormasov had defeated a portion of Reynier's Corps, a small Saxon force at Kobrin. Napoleon ordered Schwarzenberg back to support Reynier against this unexpected threat. The initiative temporarily passed to the Russians.

Once united with Bagration, Barclay's mind turned to the offensive. He was well aware that the poison tongues of St Petersburg society were railing against the 'foreigner' who had abandoned so much of Mother Russia. If he could now strike successfully, his critics would be silenced, but the continued lack of cooperation from Bagration and then a failure of resolve on Barclay's own part brought the plans to nothing. In the meantime, Napoleon was closing in on the Holy City of Smolensk. Only a heroic stand by General Neverovsky's division at Krasnoi on 14 August prevented the Russian army from being split in two and destroyed.

Smolensk

Neverovsky fell back into Smolensk, a city defended by massive ancient walls, and sent desperate appeals for help. Barclay rushed General Docturov's Corps to the rescue and the French halted to plan for an assault.

The attack began just after noon on 17 August. Leading his men, Marshal Ney drove the Russians out of the surrounding suburbs and several times nearly cut the bridges over the Dnieper River. Napoleon called off the attack at 4.30 pm and brought up more men to continue the next day.

That night, the Russian council of war saw a heated debate between Barclay, Grand Duke Constantine, and Bagration. It was clear that they were getting the worst of the fight, but the Tsar's thick-headed brother and the hot-headed Bagration could think of nothing besides the loss of another provincial capital. Despite the opposition, Barclay ordered the retreat. Smolensk was abandoned. Bagration started his 2nd Army of the West on the road, but in doing so, left a key ford uncovered. After Bagration's withdrawal, Barclay was horrified to find that Ney had crossed many of his men over the river. The Russian counterattack failed to dislodge Ney's men, and much of the 1st Army's supplies had to be abandoned. Barclay started his hurried retreat on the night of 18 August, and his men immediately got lost.

As morning broke on 19 August, Ney's men suddenly came upon Barclay's rearguard about three miles from Smolensk. Probing through the broken terrain, Ney had no idea that he had caught Barclay's main column and was driving in its rear. Barclay turned his men to face the growing threat. The Battle of Valutino swung back and forth for much of the day, as more French troops arrived. At about 4.00 pm Napoleon arrived and ordered Gudin's division of Davout's Corps into the attack. This broke the Russian line. They fell back further to the east and established a new position, and Ney began a bombardment to prepare for yet another assault.

Junot's 8th Corps had arrived on the field to the flank and rear of Barclay's men. Junot had been ordered to cross the Dnieper further downstream and move to support the crossing of the remainder of the army. The moment Napoleon sought had arrived. The fate of the entire campaign might hang in the balance. If Junot sent his men forward, a victory was assured, the only question would have been its magnitude. Murat had moved with Junot and urged him to attack, but Junot said he had no orders. Murat, who himself did not fully appreciate the opportunity, rode off to find better terrain in which to operate his cavalry. Several local attacks were made by Junot's cavalry, on their own initiative, and all were successful. Yet Junot would not budge.

A mile away Ney made his attack as dusk was descending and once more dislodged the Russians. Darkness ended the battle, with the French never knowing how close they had come to winning the war. One more tragic note for the French was that in the final assault, General Gudin was fatally wounded. Gudin was one of the very best French divisional generals, a hero of 1806 and 1809, and from the beginning a stalwart support to Davout.

As the two Russian armies streamed eastwards, their retreat was aided by a five-day rainstorm which allowed them to break contact. Napoleon rested his men prior to resuming the advance on Moscow on 24 August. He had received word that Schwarzenberg had defeated Tormasov at Gorodeczna on 12 August. This had relieved the pressure on the southern flank and left Napoleon in an aggressive mood. His last chance to avoid disaster may have been to halt and spend the winter in Smolensk, but it always appeared that his foe was just within reach. A great victory like Austerlitz or Friedland and the campaign would be his. Three times he had the Russians within reach, only to watch them slip away. While his army was dwindling, were not the Russians also watching their army drain away?

These same questions were haunting the Tsar. With the failure to hold Smolensk, the drum-beat for a 'proper Russian' to lead the army became too much. St Petersburg was militant, demanding a change, and Alexander remembered all too well that his father had been murdered after losing the support of the nobles. He cast about for a general-in-chief and finally, but reluctantly, chose General Mikhail Kutusov. While Kutusov was a hero of the Turkish War and a refined aristocrat, Alexander saw him as an intriguer and moral degenerate, all probably true. Still, the newly created prince had the devout loyalty both of his men and of the xenophobic nobility. Barclay and Bagration kept their positions as commanders of the 1st and 2nd Armies respectively.

Kutusov arrived with the Russian army on 29 August 1812. He held several counsels in which he explained his determination to fight before Moscow while wanting to retreat until he found a proper site to offer battle. It was at Bagration's suggestion that the fields around Borodino were chosen. Kutusov began to deploy his army on the sloping terrain and had redoubts dug on several rises.

Borodino

The leading elements of the French began to arrive on 5 September. They discovered a redoubt near the village of Shevardino,

The battle of Vyazma on the way to Smolensk.
(Roger-Viollet)

which was occupied by Russian artillery and protected by a division of infantry with strong light infantry and cavalry supports. Afternoon was passing, and Napoleon needed to take the position so that he could deploy his men to face the rest of the Russian army waiting for him a mile-and-a-half beyond the redoubt. He ordered in Compans' 5th division of Davout's 1st Corps, supported by two cavalry corps. At the same time the Emperor ordered Poniatowski's Polish Corps to circle to the south and take the position from the flank.

The French came on in skirmish formation and poured a terrific fire into the Russians. The latter responded as best they could, with most damage coming from their cannon. The time had come to take the redoubt, and Compans sent in his best troops. At the point of the bayonet, the Terrible 57th line swept the flanking defenders away and entered the redoubt.

They found not a single man standing left to oppose them. The sun was setting and Prince Bagration mounted an attempt to retake the bloody position. His cavalry had a terrific clash with the French and got the best of it, but could not follow up in the darkness. Bagration claimed to have taken the redoubt and then withdrawn, but their relatively small losses suggest they did little more than skirmishing. What is clear is that the Russians had a stiff fight over a relatively useless position.

Night fell cold and damp, and the French could only look on the Russian campfires with envy as there was little firewood for them to light their own. Napoleon worked through much of the night, making sure that the corps coming up moved to their proper battle positions.

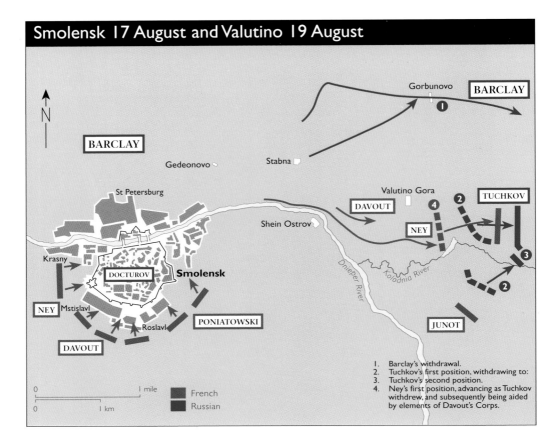

Smolensk 17 August and Valutino 19 August

1. Barclay's withdrawal.
2. Tuchkov's first position, withdrawing to:
3. Tuchkov's second position.
4. Ney's first position, advancing as Tuchkov withdrew, and subsequently being aided by elements of Davout's Corps.

The following day both armies reconnoitered their opponent's positions and made plans for the battle. Kutusov had deployed his men on a north-south axis with Barclay's 1st Army in the north, behind the Kolocha River, and Bagration's 2nd Army in the south, anchored in a series of well built redoubts. The lynchpin to Bagration's line, indeed the whole of the Russian position, was the Great Redoubt. This overlooked the crossing point of the river above the village of Borodino. It would have to be taken before Kutusov could be made to yield. Its southern flank was protected by three smaller redoubts called the Fleches, positioned several hundred yards to the left.

Napoleon rode along the front examining the green-clad enemy and watching for any sign that they might once more slip away. He saw none and returned to his tent to rest, for he was feeling ill. There he presented a painting of his son to the Guard. After a while he had the portrait put away, saying that his son was 'too young to see the carnage of the battlefield.' These words were prophetic. An unwelcome omen arrived at about this time. Napoleon received word from Spain of Wellington's defeat of Marshal Marmont at Salamanca.

In his headquarters, Kutusov was spending his time drinking and trading stories with his staff. Most of the final details were left to his chief of staff, Bennigsen. This was not altogether ideal since Bennigsen had no firm idea of what Kutusov had in mind. In several instances he realigned troops to fit his own concepts, not knowing that they disrupted his commander's plans. The most critical among these changes was Bennigsen's moving Tuchkov's Corps out of a hidden reserve position and into an exposed position near the town of Utitsa. This would mean that when Poniatowski's Poles attacked the next day, they fell upon the exposed troops.

During the night, Napoleon had his reserve artillery arrive on the field, adding to the already sizable number of guns. He positioned most of it to begin the battle with a bombardment. At about 6.00 am on 7 September the earth shook as the French line of guns opened fire. The Russians answered with their own cannon and soon the field was covered with a thick blanket of blue-gray smoke. Thousands of solid shot plowed the earth and made bloody messes of those that blocked their path.

Napoleon opened with Eugene's 4th Corps attacking Borodino itself. The French came through the smoke and fell upon the Russian Guard Jaegers. These troops had been battered by the artillery and quickly gave way. The French rashly pursued too far, however, and were themselves defeated. Eugene still held the town and used this position to deploy his guns so as to bring flanking fire upon the Great Redoubt.

Napoleon now ordered his main effort to begin. He wanted to attack the whole of the Russian left flank. To accomplish the assault he sent in three divisions of Davout's

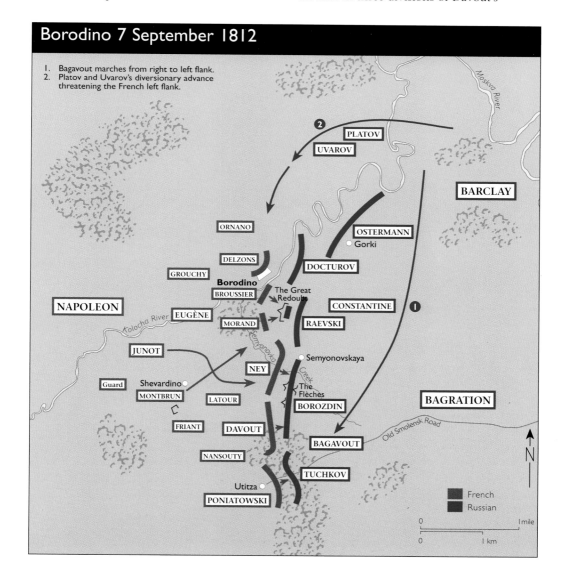

Borodino 7 September 1812

1. Bagavout marches from right to left flank.
2. Platov and Uvarov's diversionary advance threatening the French left flank.

PLATOV
UVAROV
BARCLAY
ORNANO
OSTERMANN
Gorki
DELZONS
DOCTUROV
GROUCHY
Borodino
BROUSSIER
The Great Redoubt
NAPOLEON
CONSTANTINE
EUGÈNE
Kolocha River
MORAND
RAEVSKI
JUNOT
Semyonovskaya
NEY
Guard
Shevardino
The Flèches
MONTBRUN
LATOUR
BOROZDIN
BAGRATION
FRIANT
DAVOUT
Old Smolensk Road
BAGAVOUT
NANSOUTY
TUCHKOV
Utitza
PONIATOWSKI
Moskva River

French
Russian

0   1 mile
0   1 km

1st Corps against the three Fleches, and he ordered Prince Poniatowski's 5th Corps to attack the position around Utitsa further to the south. In support of both, he had Junot's 8th Westphalian Corps.

Poniatowski had done little fighting in the campaign so far, and was anxious to come to grips with the hated Russians. In his impatience, he drove his men into constricted terrain and had to retrace his steps to meet the enemy. This caused approximately a two-hour delay. Napoleon was unaware of this delay because of the smoke and terrain. The lack of an immediate threat to his front allowed Tuchkov to shift one of his divisions north to aid Borozdin's VIII Corps defending the Fleches. Bagration, whose army was taking these assaults, was riding along his front and feeding in reserves as fast as he could.

Davout's leading division, Compans', drove forward against a terrific pounding delivered by massed Russian guns. Yet his elite 57th was able to seize the first of the redoubts, consolidate, and await the support coming up from Dessaix's division. This support was not forthcoming since Dessaix was intercepted by troops sent by Tuchkov. In a vicious fight along the Utitsa wood-line, Dessaix went down with a critical wound and his men first faltered, then fell back, leaving Compans' men unsupported. Compans went down wounded and Davout took personal command. He too was slightly wounded and his French were ejected by Bagration's grenadier reserves. Seeing the French fall back before him, Bagration sent his supporting cavalry forward in pursuit.

The splendid cavalry dashed down the slope and sabered the running infantry. Their charge carried into the squares formed by Friant's division, held in support by Davout. A swirling melee developed, but was cut short by Murat's French cavalry riding to the rescue. The French cavaliers plowed into the disordered ranks of the Russians and sent them streaming back toward their own lines.

Napoleon now sent forward Ney's 3rd Corps to renew the attack. Moving around Davout's northern flank, he advanced

through the same barrage that had taken such a toll on Davout's first wave. This attack would match the two greatest firebrands in Europe; Ney and Bagration. The red-headed Ney, sword in hand and leading from the front, charged with his men and swept all before them. This time all three Fleches were taken and the supporting guns overrun. Bagration countered by sending in his massed cuirassiers. The pride of the Russian cavalry swept forward and ejected Ney's men from the hard-won positions. Marshal Murat had come forward with his cavalry and was cut off by the unexpected fury of the Russian heavy cavalry charge. Jumping into the middle of a friendly Wurttemberg infantry battalion, he rallied the shaken Germans so that they fended off every attack and were able to withdraw safely.

Kutusov conferring with his generals. Patriotic myth so soon obscured the truth of the 1812 campaign it is hard to tell what Kutusov actually did during the Borodino battle. (Painting by A.V. Kivchenko, Roger-Viollet)

Poniatowski and his Poles were now drawing near to Utitsa. The prospect of coming to grips with the 'defilers' of their homeland gave them all the *élan* needed. Tuchkov had an elite grenadier division waiting for them. The Poles closed to point-blank range and started a firefight. The Russians held on grimly, but when Poniatowski used his superior numbers to overlap the flanks of the grenadiers, Tuchkov ordered his men to set fire to Utitsa and fall back to the woods to their rear. It had been a vicious fight and the Poles now paused to reorganize.

Barclay had been up early and riding the field. He worried about French strength on the left. When the bombardment started, Bagration immediately called for help. Wishing to respond, Barclay ordered Bagavout's II Corps to move to support Bagration. He also shifted more of his army to a central position. The animosity between Bagration and Barclay did not deter the latter from his duty.

It took two hours before Bagavout could get underway and a further hour for him to get into a useful position. This made the delays in Poniatowski's morning attack all the more regrettable: when he was once more able to renew the attack, Bagavout was already arriving on the scene.

The Polish prince had massed his corps' guns and began to pound the hill position behind Utitsa. Tuchkov's artillery was on the point of annihilation when a fresh battery heralded Bagavout's arrival. These guns took up the duel and momentarily stalled the assault. Soon, though, the Poles came on with their infantry and the Russian guns had to retreat. Onward came the two divisions. As they reached the wood-line, they were met by a crushing volley, for not only were the elite grenadiers waiting for them, but many of Bagavout's men had taken up positions. The determined fighting again proved expensive for all involved. Tuchkov took a position at the head of the Pavlov Grenadiers and charged. These troops, perhaps the finest in Russia, swept forward into the Poles. As brave as Poniatowski's men were, the Pavlovs were not to be denied. Soon the entire Polish corps was being pressed back to beyond Utitsa. It was at this point that Tuchkov was struck in the head by a bullet and fell mortally wounded; the Russian counterattack subsequently waned.

Russian officers. (Engraving after Finart, Roger-Viollet)

Napoleon now sent Junot's Westphalians to Poniatowski's support. The North Germans advanced and entered the woods. There they encountered the Jaegers responsible for putting flanking fire into both Poniatowski's and Davout's corps. Pushing them steadily back, Junot's men relieved some of the pressure on the Poles and allowed them to re-form for another effort.

While the combat in the woods was progressing, Ney and Davout had come on again and taken the Fleches once more. Bagration counterattacked and took the positions one last time. As this last attack was sweeping over the redoubts, Bagration was hit in the leg by a shell fragment. He remained on the field to see this last Russian success in his sector and then retired. He died of the wound seven days later.

Ney was in a frenzy and led his men forward once more. Davout did the same and this time the blood-soaked Fleches were taken for good. It was about 11.30 am.

To the north, Prince Eugene had organized his forces to prepare an assault across the river on the Great Redoubt. He first launched a probing attack at mid-morning with Brossier's division. While this made little impact on the Russians, it did provide the intelligence needed to make a more determined assault. This was delivered by Morand's division, who swept up the rise and caught the gunners working the 18 guns by surprise. A fierce hand-to-hand left most of the gunners dead and the French in control of this key position.

General Yermolov, Barclay's chief-of-staff, was leading troops toward the crisis to the south when Morand's attack occurred. Rallying the fleeing troops and calling for all local support, he charged the redoubt. Sensing the crisis, the Russians attacked with a fanatic zeal and overwhelmed the French before further supports could arrive to secure their gain. During this attack General Kutaisov, who commanded Barclay's artillery reserve, heroically led forward an infantry regiment whose flag he grabbed. Killed a moment later, his death meant that the substantial 1st Army artillery was paralyzed for the remainder of the battle.

Eugene now prepared to make an assault three times stronger than before, but a cry went up that a large Russian force was descending on him from the north. This was Platov's Cossacks and Uvarov's line cavalry. Platov, the Ataman of the Don Cossacks, had gone to Kutusov early in the battle and pointed out that nothing opposed him. 'Would it not be a good idea to try and turn the French flank?' Kutusov had approved the plan and Platov had started back to his position to prepare the advance. This decision is the only one that can be definitively attributed to Kutusov during the battle.

The two Russian cavalry formations crossed the Kolocha River and slowly made their way toward Eugene's troops in Borodino. Their attack caused few French losses but cost them a great deal in panic and lost time. It also caused Napoleon to send over some of his reserves to meet the threat. Further, Eugene put off all plans for another attack on the Great Redoubt until he was satisfied that the

The Battle of Borodino, 7 September 1812. Napoleon's illness after the battle meant that there was no pursuit of Kutusov, who withdrew to Moscow. (Engraving by Le Beau, after Naudet, Roger-Viollet)

The appearance of unexpectedly large numbers of Cossacks like these upset the French plan of campaign. Uvarov's use of them in his flanking maneuver at Borodino cost the French valuable time they needed to achieve a decisive result. (Roger-Viollet)

The last Russian stronghold, besides the Great Redoubt itself, was the small village of Semyonovskaya. Ney had earlier made an attempt to take it, following the final seizure of the Fleches, but had been repulsed. Next came Murat's cavalry. The troopers of Nansouty and Latour-Maubourg were now committed against the position. Nansouty attacked south of the town and found the ground less than ideal for cavalry. His men ran into firm infantry, and despite their best efforts could not make them give way. To the

threat had disappeared. 'Uvarov's diversion' had delayed the French by nearly two hours.

This gave the Russians time to restore their line and pound the French opposite them with a merciless bombardment. The brunt of this fire fell upon the cavalry assembled for the anticipated attack on the Great Redoubt. During this barrage General Montbrun, commander of the 2nd Reserve Cavalry Corps, was directing his men when a cannonball tore across his stomach. He looked down at the gore, said: 'Good shot,' and fell dead from the saddle. A similarly terrible fate faced Latour-Maubourg's 4th Reserve Cavalry Corps, who stood impotently by and watched their numbers dwindle.

Kutusov's army held the key position of the Great Redoubt but was being threatened by developments occurring to the south. The final taking of the Fleches threatened Bagavout as his flanks could now be turned, but he also faced a new attack by Poniatowski and Junot. While the tired Russians made the French pay for the ground dearly, the French pressure was now irresistible. Finally driven through the protective woods, Bagavout's men quickened their retreat and fell a mile to the rear astride the Old Smolensk Road.

north of Semyonovskaya, Latour-Maubourg's men had fared better. Catching several grenadier regiments out of square, they rode them down and were only stopped when Russian cavalry hit their disordered formations. However, coming fast on their heels was Friant's division from Davout's Corps. Despite a fearful pounding from the Russian guns, Murat urged them on. Friant hurried to the aid of the hard-pressed cavalry and the position was theirs.

Barclay now sent his IV Corps to try to re-take Semyonovskaya. Napoleon had himself come up and he ordered the Guard Horse Artillery to open up on the dense formation of IV Corps. The initial rounds stopped their advance, and the continued fire by the finest artillery in the world had the expected terrible results. In fact, Napoleon now had almost 500 guns pouring fire into the area between Semyonovskaya and the Great Redoubt. Virtually all the remaining troops in good order of Kutusov's army were in this area. Any round fired into this spot could hardly fail to find its mark.

It was now almost 2.00 pm and the French made a massive push to take the Great Redoubt. The three infantry divisions of Broussier, Morand, and Gerard attacked from the front while the cavalry of Montbrun, now under General Caulaincourt, and of Latour-Maubourg hit the flanks. The honor of being the first unit to enter the fort

French and allied cavalry finally storm the Great Redoubt to finish the battle. (Charpentier, Roger-Viollet)

seems to have belonged to the Saxon Zastrow cuirassiers from Latour-Maubourg's Corps. This superb unit slaughtered the gunners as the supporting French quickly joined in the fight. The resisting Russian units were destroyed. Caulaincourt chased off the Russian supporting cavalry opposite him before swinging in from the rear of the redoubt to close the trap. Unfortunately, he would pay for this success with his life.

Grouchy's cavalry, following up the French attack, now charged into the remaining Russians. Barclay committed the Russian Guard cavalry in order to stop them.

The entire Russian line was now shattered. Barclay re-formed the remaining units on a ridgeline a mile to the rear. There he waited for Napoleon's next move. Several marshals urged their Emperor to send in the Guard and complete the victory. Napoleon hesitated, then declined. He reasoned that he was a long way from home and that his Guard ensured his survival. It was also not clear to him that the Russians were entirely beaten. Napoleon,

tired and ill, was satisfied that a victory had been won. For that day, it was enough.

That night Kutusov sent a message to the Tsar announcing a great victory. When his generals asked to retreat he was at first angered by the suggestion, but as the evening wore on, it was clear the Kutusov's army had taken a fearful beating. He had lost 45,000 men out of 120,000. While he did not know Napoleon's losses (about 30,000), it became clear that the French were prepared to fight the next day. The Russians were low on artillery ammunition as well. Reluctantly, Kutusov ordered the retreat.

Napoleon had trouble even rising the next day, 8 September. His illness and the terrible carnage of the battle had caused a lethargic depression to set in. It was some time before he ordered the army to prepare to resume the advance to Moscow.

When the final reckoning was done it was clear the Kutusov could not face Napoleon

The fire in Moscow forced even Napoleon to flee.

1812 Russian campaign: The retreat from Moscow

1. Kutusov attacks Napoleon's outposts at Vinkovo, 18 October.
2. Napoleon leaves Moscow, marches south and is blocked at Maloyaroslavets, 24 October.
3. Napoleon retreats; pursued by Kutusov (4), with action at Krasnoe (5), 15 November.
6. Chichagov advances north to intercept Napoleon at the Beresina; Schwarzenberg and Reynier (7) are unable to stop him, and retire subsequently.
8. Napoleon reaches the Beresina on 25 November; Chichagov and Wittgenstein are held off by Victor and Oudinot while Napoleon crosses the river just north of Borisov.
9. Napoleon's retreat continues, reaching Königsberg mid-December; Napoleon himself leaves the army at Smorgonie, 5 December.
10. Macdonald withdraws, and
11. Macdonald's Prussian contingent under Yorck defects at Tauroggen, 30 December.

again until fresh reinforcements had swelled his ranks. So the decision was taken not to defend Moscow. On 14 September the Russian army passed through the city, taking what they could, and marched to the east. The French army entered the capital that same evening. The object of so much hardship was now Napoleon's, but where were the messengers from the Tsar asking for terms?

The French enter Moscow

That same evening Napoleon received an answer of sorts. Fire had broken out in several places in the city. The governor-general of the city, Rostopchin, had ordered that Moscow should burn to the ground rather than be possessed by the French. Ironically, this act of a man driven insane by his responsibility almost saved Napoleon's army. For had much more of the city been incinerated, the Emperor would surely have

started his withdrawal west earlier.

After the first day, the fire seemed to be contained, so Napoleon rode into the city and entered the Kremlin. From here he saw the fire leap up in several new spots and reports came back to him that it was the Russians deliberately setting the fires. Incredulous that men would do that to their own cherished city, he ordered all men caught setting fires shot. He surveyed the situation until it was almost too late. It was only with repeated urgings of his staff that he consented to leave the inferno, barely escaping as the flames closed in around him.

The fire burned for four days and destroyed three-quarters of the city. The French were able to preserve some of the most historic buildings, but the ancient city of the Tsars of Russia was no more. Re-occupying the burnt-out shell, the French sat down and waited for the Russian surrender that they were sure would come.

Napoleon deployed his army in a ring around the city and guarded the approaches from which any attacks might come. The problem was that while the troops immediately around Moscow were still getting regular food, the outlying units were not. This left these men vulnerable to attack as they spread out desperately foraging for something to eat.

Following his retreat from Moscow, Kutusov had taken his army in a wide circle to the south. This left him in a position to receive reinforcements coming up from the Orel region. He also had the option of moving against Napoleon's supply line.

Napoleon sent out several feelers for peace but received no response. Finally he sent General Lauriston on a mission to Kutusov. After meeting with the aged general, Lauriston delighted Napoleon with the news that an emissary had been dispatched to the Tsar. This surely would bring about the desired end to war, so Napoleon decided to put off any thoughts of withdrawal until an answer arrived. This delay proved fatal.

As Napoleon sat in the Kremlin, sending letters to govern his vast holdings, his men had begun to fraternize with the Russians in an informal truce. This laxness led to a surprise attack on Sebastiani's cavalry at Vinkovo. Here were some of the men left to fend for themselves, and they had become scattered when the attack came. It was only the quick thinking of Murat that prevented a major defeat. The dashing King of Naples put himself at the head of the Carabiniers and charged the enemy. The attack sent the Russians reeling back and by the time that they had recovered, the French had restored their order. Seeing this, the Russian attack was abandoned.

The defeat at Vinkovo convinced Napoleon that no peace was in the offing, and he made plans to leave Moscow. Examining the possibilities, the best direction seemed to be a march to the south-west, where he could either take the unravaged route to the west or possibly bring Kutusov to a decisive battle while the French army could still fight. Planning his departure

for several days he slipped out of Moscow on 19 October. This proved to be far too late.

The retreat begins

As Napoleon was pulling out of Moscow, the Russians were going over to the offensive. While Kutusov watched Napoleon's main army, the other armies were to strike the strategic flanks north and south. Admiral Chichagov had joined Tormasov and took command of the combined force. He swung west around the Pripet Marches and moved against Schwarzenberg's rear. When the Austrian gave way and positioned himself to protect Warsaw, Chichagov sent Sacken with 25,000 men to pursue and took his remaining army of 38,000 around to the north of the marshes and headed toward Napoleon's rear. Schwarzenberg reacted by defeating Sacken and heading off in pursuit of Chichagov, but it was clear the Austrian's heart was no longer in the campaign.

To the north, the Russian commander Wittgenstein, who had received large reinforcements, advanced on St Cyr, but divided his command into two parts. Wittgenstein himself was defeated at Polotsk, while his other wing, under Steingell, lost a battle to the Bavarian General Wrede. However, Wittgenstein did succeed in temporarily diverting Marshal Victor's Corps from moving to support Napoleon.

Napoleon planned to make his way back to Smolensk via a southern route. Marching out of Moscow, he headed south for the key town of Maloyaroslavets, which guarded the crossing of the Lutza River. Prince Eugene led with his French troops and upon arrival at the town, on the evening of 23 October, found it free of any enemy. He placed two battalions in Maloyaroslavets, south of the river, and kept the remainder on the better camp site north of the river. What Eugene and Napoleon did not yet know was that their maneuver had been detected by General Docturov and that he had been shadowing the French on a parallel road. Furthermore, he had alerted Kutusov, and

The army of France on its return from Moscow.
(Engraving, Roger-Viollet)

the remainder of the Russian army was in hot pursuit.

Docturov launched an attack on the two isolated battalions before dawn the following day. His men threw back the surprised French and headed for the bridgeheads over the Lutza. Eugene reacted by counterattacking with Delzon's division. They pushed their way into the town but were repelled when they tried to exit on the other side. The Russians were coming onto the field quickly and deployed in a strong position on a ridge above the town. The battle continued throughout the day, with the final outcome much in doubt. Finally, Napoleon, who arrived at the scene, committed sufficient troops to widen the bridgehead so as to allow his army to cross. The battle sputtered to a close with nightfall. The following day, Napoleon rode out to survey the field and consider his prospects. A body of Cossacks swept down and took his small escort by surprise. The outnumbered Guard cavalry was able to repulse the attack, but not before several of the enemy had come very close to the Emperor. Napoleon was visibly shaken by this incident. The prospect of being captured so unnerved him that he ordered his doctor to prepare a pouch of poison that he could take should this ever happen again.

That night Napoleon ordered a council of war to discuss the options with his commanders. This extremely unusual occurrence shows how unsettled he was: he had lost his confidence. Only Murat suggested a renewed attack. The others proposed various courses of retreat. Napoleon ordered the retreat. Ironically, Kutusov had ordered a disengagement as well, for he was sure that his raw army could not withstand another full battle.

The two armies broke away from each other, with Kutusov heading west and Napoleon heading north-west toward Mozhaisk. This line of retreat would take him over the same devastated route that he had taken on the way to Moscow.

Kutusov divided his army, with one wing moving parallel with the French, ready to strike at any opportunity, and the main force

Ney's heroic command of the rearguard made him a legend. (Edimedia)

following a similar course outside of striking distance. He also pushed his cavalry ahead to raid the French outposts and depots.

The French army was strung along 40 miles of road. The troops with intermixed, at least in the beginning, with caravans of carriages bearing loot, camp followers, and French actresses rescued from Moscow. Davout was bringing up the rear, trying to gather all the stragglers and wounded. Kutusov in a earlier correspondence with Napoleon had made it clear that prisoners could expect no mercy from the Russians because of the impassioned feeling against the invaders of Mother Russia. This meant that any French soldier who fell out of line would probably die.

When Napoleon learned that Kutusov was trying to make an end run around his army and destroy the essential depots, he increased the pace and drove his Guard on to Vyazma. This preserved the key depot, but strung out his army even more. The Russians attacked the rear on 31 October and 3 November, but with little effect.

On 4 November, it began to snow. The weather worsened over the next few days and the last semblance of order within the French supply system disintegrated. Every night hundreds of men froze to death. There was little, if any, shelter and men huddled together for warmth. Setting villages on fire became common practice in order to provide some respite from the cold.

As supply broke down, the men began to wander off in search of food. Most would never return, falling victim to the cold or to Cossacks. The French had little left by way of organized cavalry, so any small contingent of men were susceptible to the great bands of Cossack raiders that swooped down on the shivering enemy, slaughtered them, and looted the bodies. In one incident a brigade under General Baraguay d'Hilliers was surrounded and annihilated. Images of Cossack depredations terrorized Napoleon's men.

On the retreat, illness was an almost certain death sentence, and disease became rampant as the men were increasingly malnourished. A healthy well-fed man could have dealt with the cold, but the soldiers of the Grande Armée were starving, sick, and forced marching. A fatalism set in among the ranks and the French high command, as each day they stumbled upon a dead man in the snow who only the day before had been among the 'healthy' ones.

Napoleon halted in Smolensk to try to reorder the army. Discipline had become so bad that the stores of food and clothing were broken into and looted by his men. Vast amounts of supplies were thus wasted. With the army losing cohesion, the Emperor resumed the retreat in an effort to save what he could. His army was now only half the strength it had been in Moscow and dwindling fast. The various corps left Smolensk over the

next four days on the road to Krasnoi.

There Kutusov prepared a trap for the French. As Napoleon and his Guard caught up his army's leading troops on 15 November, the Russians attacked to the French front, flank, and rear, in an effort to split the army in two. The first two attacks failed but the third cut the road.

In the army's vanguard, Napoleon went over to the attack. He sent in his Guard artillery and it more than held its own against the Russians, who were driven from Krasnoi and the battle subsided. That night Napoleon sent his Guard Infantry in a risky night attack against several Russia encampments, reflecting his increased desperation. The bitter cold prevented the enemy from properly deploying pickets, and the Guard exacted a terrible revenge upon the dazed Russians. This French success made Kutusov cautious and he went back to

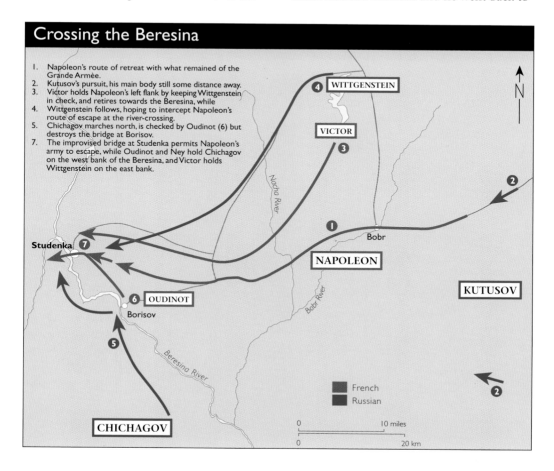

Crossing the Beresina

1. Napoleon's route of retreat with what remained of the Grande Armée.
2. Kutusov's pursuit, his main body still some distance away.
3. Victor holds Napoleon's left flank by keeping Wittgenstein in check, and retires towards the Beresina, while
4. Wittgenstein follows, hoping to intercept Napoleon's route of escape at the river-crossing.
5. Chichagov marches north, is checked by Oudinot (6) but destroys the bridge at Borisov.
7. The improvised bridge at Studenka permits Napoleon's army to escape, while Oudinot and Ney hold Chichagov on the west bank of the Beresina, and Victor holds Wittgenstein on the east bank.

striking only when Napoleon was in the process of retreating. The road was open again, at least for a time.

The victory at Krasnoi allowed Napoleon once more to gather his army, with the exception of Ney's Corps. Ney had lingered too long in Smolensk to gather up stragglers and had been cut off. Called on to surrender, he refused and tried to fight his way out. Failing in this, he lit fires to fool the Russians and slipped around the Russian northern flank in the darkness.

The Beresina

When Ney's tiny command rejoined the main army there was rejoicing. The marshal was now lauded by Napoleon as 'the bravest of the brave.' By now Victor had joined Napoleon, swelling the ranks, but Admiral Chichagov had cut off the army at the Beresina River. He had surprised the garrison at Borisov and stood between Napoleon and safety. A thaw had not proved kind, leaving an impassable river. Oudinot, who had taken over St Cyr's command when the latter was wounded, surprised Chichagov's garrison at Borisov and took the depot. The Russians burned the bridge and still had their main force on the western bank of the Beresina. As Napoleon

approached, he was being encircled by three Russian armies: Wittgenstein's, Chichagov's, and Kutusov's. Time was of the essence and it was clear that Schwarzenberg was not going to arrive to attack Chichagov from the rear. A ford had to be found and quickly. By 24 November Napoleon arrived ahead of the main army. Victor was deployed to slow Wittgenstein, Oudinot was demonstrating in front of Chichagov, and the remainder of the army struggled onward towards Borisov.

On the night of 25 November, engineers began building three bridges over the Beresina at Studenka, about 10 miles north of Borisov. Standing in chest-deep freezing water, many of the men sacrificed their lives for these constructions. By late afternoon of the 26 November they were complete and the troops began to cross. Both Oudinot's and Ney's men crossed and took up positions to oppose Chichagov's expected attack. What little remained of the army fought well.

The crossing points were a confused mass of the wounded and stragglers crowding to get over the bridges. Victor's Corps were deployed as a rearguard and for over a day

Many failed to cross the Beresina bridges when they had a chance because they were exhausted mentally and physically. When they realized time had run out, the chaos at the bridges was brutal. (Lithography by V. Adam, Edimedia)

withstood the weight of Wittgenstein's men. By the night of 27 November it was clear that Victor could not hold out much longer. Ammunition was running low and more Russians were arriving by the minute. Just after midnight Victor evacuated the east bank of the river and passed to the other side. There he stood guard over the bridge in order to allow as many stragglers as possible to reach safety. Many were too exhausted and apathetic. Victor preserved the bridge as long as possible, but finally set it on fire, abandoning many to their fate.

The remnant of the French and allied army headed toward Vilna. It was then that the temperature plummeted, and many who had survived that far now died. The Cossacks were about the only troops that could operate off the roads, and daily they added to the French casualties.

Napoleon had received word of an attempted *coup d'etat* in Paris orchestrated by a madman, General Malet. For a day he had taken the reins of power before being arrested, claiming Napoleon had died in Russia. This plot, along with the knowledge that new troops would be needed to continue the campaign, prompted Napoleon to leave the army and return to Paris. On 5 December, he left the army at Smorgonie. While his generals had agreed with the decision, many in the ranks felt abandoned. Murat was given overall command.

When the army arrived at Vilna, it was a repeat of Smolensk. Stores were sacked and food and supplies wasted. With disorder rampant, Murat ordered the retreat to continue. Ney fought several rearguard actions and kept the Russians at bay. When the army reached the Niemen, it was Ney who on 9 December stayed behind to destroy the last baggage. He then crossed the river and in so doing was the last Frenchman to leave Russian soil, making himself a legend.

One final piece of bad news for the French was that Count von Yorck had defected to the Russians with his men. Yorck, who had led the Prussian half of Macdonald's command, even failed to alert Macdonald of his actions. Macdonald met most of the remaining army in Konigsberg where the retreat finally ended on 13 December. The news of Yorck's defection panicked Murat and he left the army, turning over command to Eugene. It was a typical act for the mercurial marshal.

The Grande Armée was dead. Prussia was clearly beginning to rebel and Europe saw Napoleon as vulnerable. The campaign of 1812 was over and the campaign of 1813 was beginning.

Barclay de Tolly and Jacob Walter

Barclay de Tolly: Portrait of a commander

The popular history of the Russian campaign of 1812 comes from Tolstoy's novel *War and Peace*. It is Marshal Kutusov who is portrayed as the great Russian hero of the campaign. This is a great disservice to the real hero, Michael Andreas Barclay de Tolly.

Barclay de Tolly was born on 24 December 1761 in Polish Lithuania. He was descended from a minor Scottish nobleman who had gone to the Baltic to seek his fortune. The Barclays had prospered in the Germanic Lutheran provinces and Michael's father had served in the Russian army prior to receiving his patent of nobility from the Tsar.

Michael grew up in St Petersburg where he was raised by his aunt. This was a common occurrence among the German Protestants and gave the young man the exposure to upper society unavailable in the Baltic provinces. His foster-father was also in the military and enrolled the young Barclay in a cavalry regiment at the age of six. He would spend the rest of his life within the military.

Barclay's schooling was basic, but he was a voracious reader and pursued studies beyond the normal requirements. Among his acquired talents was a fluency in Russian and French, to accompany his native German. He also devoured anything that would expand his military knowledge.

During his youth he developed a quiet, taciturn personality quite in keeping with his German upbringing. His contemporaries described him as meticulous, brave, honest, modest, bright, and somewhat humorless.

Barclay joined the Jaegers in 1787 and his unit joined the army of Prince Potemkin (of Potemkin Village fame). Here the captain caught the attention of his superiors and became an aide to one of the wing commanders, Prince Anhalt-Bernburg. During the victorious siege of Ochakov against the Turks, Barclay participated in the desperate sortie in which most of his fellow officers were casualties, including the severely wounded Mikhail Kutusov.

Barclay continued to serve with distinction until 1789, when he was transferred to the Finnish front. The ongoing hostility between Russia and Sweden turned to war when King Gustavus decided to take advantage of Tsarina Catherine's Turkish war to move troops into his Finland province with an eye toward taking St Petersburg. The addled king lacked good organization, however, and when Russia's ally, Denmark, invaded Sweden in support of Russia, Gustavus' attention was diverted, giving Catherine time to move enough troops into place to counter the Swedish threat. The war was bloody and inconclusive on both sides and came to a halt when Sweden's internal problems caused the king to end the war with things back to pre-war status.

For Barclay, marriage to his cousin followed the next year before a posting as major and battalion commander of the St Petersburg Grenadier Regiment sent him to Poland to participate in its partition. The war lasted till 1793 and flared up again the following year when the Poles under Kosciuszko revolted. Distinguishing himself at the battles of Vilna and Grodno, he continued the campaign under General Suvorov when the Warsaw suburb of Praga was stormed. This brutal event ended the rebellion and led to the final destruction of what remained of Poland. Barclay was promoted to lieutenant-colonel for his conduct and to full Colonel in 1796. He remained in Russia commanding the 3rd Jaegers, missing Suvorov's campaign in

Barclay de Tolly, to whom the lion's share of the credit should go for a reformed and reinforced Russian army for the 1812 campaign. (Roger-Viollet)

Italy and Switzerland but performing with such efficiency that he was promoted to major-general in March 1799.

When war against Napoleon came in 1805, Barclay was posted under Bennigsen. Fortunately Bennigsen's army avoided the debacle of Austerlitz, though its arrival there may have swung the balance. There was to be no promotion for battlefield heroics, but neither was there any blame.

The war came to life again for the Russians in 1806 as they moved to support their Prussian allies. Unfortunately, they were unable to arrive before Napoleon crushed the Prussians at Jena-Auerstadt and

the pursuit that followed. The leading Russians took up their positions around Warsaw and awaited the French and their supporting armies. Napoleon moved upon them quickly and after forcing a river crossing fought the twin battles of Pultusk and Golymin. It was at the battle of Pultusk that Barclay, by now a lieutenant-general, received his baptism of fire as a commanding general. Leading one of the advance guards, his men faced the brunt of the redoubtable

Barclay's great rival, Prince Bagration. Despite his great suspicions of his fellow general, Bagration did finally join Barclay at Smolensk. He became a Russian martyr for his mortal wound at Borodino. (Roger-Viollet)

Marshal Lannes' attack. A desperate fight in the woods swung back and forth. Lannes, realizing the French were facing the main Russian army and not a rearguard, broke off the attack. Barclay won praise for his calm, skillful performance

The three advance guards were consolidated under the command of Prince Bagration. Barclay led the most active troops of this command. He continued the campaign and covered himself with glory for several rearguard actions. At Eylau on 7 February 1807, his men defended the village against determined assaults by the

French. It was only an attack of the Old Guard that finally expelled Barclay's men. Once more he mounted a counterattack. Barclay, leading cavalry, was hit by canister in the arm and narrowly avoided being crushed by the stampede of horses before one of his men scooped him up.

After being rushed to a hospital in Konigsberg, Barclay's arm was saved. However, this wound would never fully heal, nor would Barclay ever again have the full use of the arm. It was serious enough that he would not be fit for action again until after Friedland and the Russian surrender at Tilsit. During his convalescence Barclay became friends with the Tsar. Visiting his wounded general in the hospital, Alexander was struck by Barclay's modest and honest character – a welcome contrast to the vain, preening degenerates who so often surrounded the young Tsar.

Following the Peace of Tilsit, Napoleon suggested to his new Russian allies an attack on Sweden. This served the French needs in two ways: first it would close one of Britain's most lucrative ports left in Europe; and secondly it would draw Russia away from central European affairs. Still, an attack on this traditional enemy was very appealing to Tsar Alexander. The campaign got underway, with Barclay commanding a column in the main army. After initial successes the tide turned against the Russians as all of Finland rose up in a guerrilla war. Barclay showed initiative to the point where he disobeyed a direct command in order to save a contingent which was about to be crushed. Demands were made in the army hierarchy to have him court martialed, but defenders arose to support Barclay. In the end the Tsar sided with Barclay and he was promoted to Governor of Finland.

The second phase of the war called for a crossing of the frozen Gulf of Bothnia. This scheme seemed insane since it called for crossing the frozen waters– a march of 24 miles, a brief rest on a snowy islet, then another 36 miles over the ice. Throughout they would be subjected to the near-arctic winter with no possible protection. Despite these tremendous obstacles, Barclay led his men safely to the Swedish side of the gulf and captured the fortified city of Umea. This legendary effort was temporarily lost in the news that a coup d'etat had overthrown the King of Sweden and peace had been declared.

Barclay remained as Governor of Finland until the end of 1809. His careful and efficient performance earned him Alexander's praise and promotion to Minister of War on 20 January 1810. He immediately set about reforming the field regulations. This massive effort was compiled and distributed in what became known as the 'Yellow Book' because of the color of its cover. This was the first change to be made to the regulations since the days of Peter the Great in the early 1700s.

He next lobbied to establish a series of defensive fortifications along the frontier. While he started the program, little was completed prior to the 1812 campaign. It was his belief that the Russians should be passive in the campaign and grudgingly fall back upon their lines of communication until they could effectively counterattack. This is not to say that he advocated a total Fabian strategy, rather that he believed that trading space for advantage was a sound option. This policy set him at odds with Bagration, who felt that any abandonment of Russian soil was a sin.

When the war began, he was directly under the command of the capricious Tsar and dutifully fell back on the camp of Drissa. It was only after the Tsar's departure that he was able to formulate his own plan. He fell back toward Smolensk and prepared to take the initiative. Bagration joined him with his army and graciously placed himself under Barclay's command.

It was only now that Barclay seemed to lose his nerve. He vacillated between attack and a further retreat. He sent confusing orders and had his troops marching in circles. When Napoleon made a move on Smolensk he regained focus and orders became firm and clear. Following the battle, Barclay decided on a further retreat, and the generals around him became enraged.

He had been under suspicion for being a 'foreigner' and his behavior brought this criticism to a new height. Tsar Alexander felt a change was required and placed Mikhail Kutusov in overall command. Barclay took this demotion with equanimity and performed heroically at the following battle of Borodino. At that battle, Bagration was mortally wounded. With his great rival gone, Barclay continued to act as the 1st Army commander. A fortnight after the fall of Moscow the two armies were consolidated. Soon thereafter Barclay left the army and Kutusov for reasons of health, but in reality, with the joining of the two armies, his role was at an end.

He took no further part in the 1812 campaign, but was placed in charge of the Russian 3rd Army in February 1813. He maneuvered skillfully and once more earned the confidence of the Tsar. Following the twin defeats of Lutzen and Bautzen, Barclay was made commander-in-chief of all Russian armies. He remained in the field at the Tsar's side throughout 1813 and entered France for the campaign of 1814. He was promoted to field marshal for his service.

In 1815, Barclay organized the army for a second invasion of France following Napoleon's return. Though he saw no fighting, he was made a prince of Russia. He continued his role as commander-in-chief for the next three years, when ill health caused him to ask for a leave of absence. The Tsar, wishing to reward this most loyal servant, granted him a two-year leave and 100,000 rubles for expenses.

Barclay was not to enjoy this rest, for on his way to a spa in Bohemia he stopped at one of his homes near Riga for a rest. He died that night, 25 May 1818, apparently of a heart attack.

In the end it was his organizational skills, more than his bravery, that had proved the more valuable to Russia. By preserving the Russian army, he set the stage for Napoleon to make the fatal error of advancing too far and remaining too long in Russia. His steadying influence may have made the crucial difference in Russia's struggle.

Jacob Walter:
Portrait of a common soldier

Jacob Walter, from Wurttemberg (now in south-west Germany) was drafted into the army in the autumn of 1806. He was inducted into the 4th (or Franquemont) Infantry Regiment and sent to guard Napoleon's line of supply as the campaign moved into old Poland. During 1809 he fought the rebels in the Vorarlberg who were attacking Napoleon's rear. During the campaign of 1812 his regiment was part of Ney's Corps. Apart from fighting at the battle of Smolensk, he participated in no major action. He followed the army during the retreat and was mustered out of the regiment for reasons of poor health upon returning home in 1813.

There was nothing remarkable about him and he contributed little to the war effort, but he was an honest chronicler of his experiences and he recorded the attitudes common among the German soldiers of his day.

Walter had been brought up a Catholic, the brother of a priest. This had allowed him the opportunity to learn to read and write. While he considered himself devout, he exhibited relative or situational morals. Stealing was wrong, unless you needed something. Kindness to your fellow men was to be shown at all times, unless they were peasants in an enemy land. It is interesting that Walter sowed his wild oats in 1806, 'an element of my youth', but became religious during the retreat from Moscow.

In 1807, Walter was guarding a rear area when a spy was brought in. The evidence seemed clear enough, so the man was whipped 150 times prior to being shot. There seemed to be no purpose for the flogging other than the amusement of the soldiers and officers, but Walter found nothing odd in this. Following this incident, he was sent out to requisition food from the local villages. Not having a map, he sought a local guide. Naturally, he picked on the most down-trodden section of society to find his man, the Jews. The man tried to hide but was found and dragged down two flights of stairs. His misery was of great amusement. Walter's attitude was typical of the time, and he never noted any disapproval among his comrades.

The process of finding food often differed little from outright theft. The peasants in their huts made of straw could not defend themselves against pillaging troops. On one occasion, Walter shot a pet dog for his own amusement and then was surprised that the locals were uncooperative.

Walter had contempt for other beliefs, including the Prussian Lutheranism. He observed that these people were superstitious, while exhibiting his own superstitions on repeated occasions. The ideas of the Enlightenment had not penetrated far beyond the upper and educated classes.

Walter's fondest recollections were of his family. The highlight of a campaign was when his regiment was stationed in the same place as his brother's.

In 1809 Walter's battalion was sent to put down the rebellion in the Vorarlberg, which had risen in sympathy with the Tyrol. He saw action in the fighting around Bregenz on 29 May, where he gained experience as a skirmisher. Taking a position on the staircase of a building, he shot off most of his ammunition before making a mad dash to the rear. In the subsequent fighting in the town, he shot a man at point blank range. At no other time does he mention that he actually hit an opponent. At Bregenz, where his men made a hurried withdrawal, Walter makes it quite clear that he considered his running ability his key asset.

Complaints about the local breads and grain, which differed from those at home, were typical among soldiers at the time and Walter makes repeated comments throughout his memoirs.

In 1812 his regiment marched to the Russian border. Throughout the march, he was unaware of the ultimate destination. This was the only time he remembered seeing the high command. The Crown Prince ordered his Wurttembergers to go through maneuvers when it was a holiday.

This was pointed out by one of the lesser ranking Wurttemberg generals and the prince threatened to arrest him. It seems that the prince was annoyed that he had had his command placed under Ney, and was taking out his displeasure on his men.

Walter remembered the march into Russia for its heat, choking dust, and long downpours. He soon began a campaign-long effort to find food. Often the only food available had to be purchased from the despised Jews. The irony that his salvation lay in their willingness to sell to him was lost on him.

At Smolensk, Jacob Walter fought in the only major battle of his military career. His blue-coated comrades and he assaulted the bridgeheads in an effort to cut off the city's defenders. Breaking into the city, he saw the devastation of the fires caused by the battle. His impression was one of total chaos. Finally he rested near a hospital station, to be treated to the sight of piles of amputated limbs.

Walter did march past the carnage of the battle of Borodino, but made little comment about it. By the time he reached Moscow, his company was down to 25 men, from a starting strength of about 175.

During the retreat, Walter became the servant or batman of a major. This he hoped would provide him with a better chance of survival, but it soon was clear that the major depended more on Walter than vice-versa. Hunger was a daily concern and the resulting weakness led to disease and death all along the march. Lice covered every part of his body and the cold wore him down. If he had not stolen a horse, he thought he would have perished; instead someone else did. Indeed, Walter claimed that no-one survived without a horse. This was an exaggeration,

but clearly it was important, since the soldiers kept stealing each others' horses.

Near Borisov he was reunited with a fellow Wurttemberger, cold and wet from fording a river, who shared his loaf of bread with Walter. For this Walter pledged a lifetime's devotion. They finished their meal and mounted their horses to continue the journey, but the generous friend was dead by morning.

The horror of the Beresina crossing is told, with dazed men sitting down in the snow, never to rise. It was here that Walter saw Napoleon. He comments on the unmoved expression on the Emperor's face, though it is hard to believe that he got close enough to get a good look. It is more likely that he projected his own disillusionment.

Near Vilna, he was with a small group of men when the Cossacks came upon them. At first he tried to flee, but he was stabbed at and knocked off his horse. He lay in the snow and did not move while his compatriots were massacred. Finally the Cossacks rode off and Walter stole away to rejoin the army.

At the Niemen he met up with some Westphalian soldiers. Offered hospitality by some local peasants, the men were plied with alcohol and soon set upon and murdered. Walter escaped only by sensing a trap at the last moment.

On Christmas eve, he finally reach a place where he could bath and get a change of clothes. The filth and lice were caked on like 'fir-bark.' Soon he had his first square meal in months and headed back home with a supply and hospital train. On reaching Wurttemberg his was mustered out of the army for reasons of ill health. He returned home and made a full recovery within a couple weeks.

Louise Fusil

Napoleon's army had found a flourishing French colony in Moscow. Some of these émigrés had fled the political persecutions of the French Revolution, but many others were artists and tradespeople seeking to tap the Moscow market. Among the Russian aristocracy, fashion and the arts still imitated French styles, so there had been plenty of opportunities for ambitious French people. While Fedor Rostopchin, the governor of Moscow, had taken the director of the French theater company as a hostage, the rest of the troupe had been left behind. The French decided to celebrate their victory by enjoying some good plays.

The performers had suffered growing hostility from the suspicious Moscow populace. Now they had the honor of performing for Napoleon himself and his glittering entourage. Some officers sniffed that the performance was not up to Paris standards, but the actors must have thought their luck had changed. The 38-year-old actress Louise Fusil enjoyed not only a new protector, an urbane soldier-diplomat, General Armand de Caulaincourt, but also the distinction of being asked by Napoleon himself for an encore of a song.

Distracted by the company of the most powerful men in the world, it came as a complete surprise to Louise when a French officer told her the army had to leave Moscow. Fearing what the Russian soldiers would do when they saw the wreckage of Moscow, Louise decided it would be wise for her to leave. She hoped she could find sanctuary in Minsk or Vilna until calm was restored and she could safely return to Moscow. Many other actresses and French and allied civilians also decided that safety lay in following the French army. She thought herself fortunate to be offered a ride in the splendid carriage of Caulaincourt's

nephew, also on Napoleon's staff. Though the weather struck her as beautiful, fortunately she remembered to bring her furs.

The carriage was designed to allow its occupant to sleep in comfort, so Louise was comfortable during the first stage of the retreat. The pace was punishing, and outside the wounded were being abandoned, food distribution had ceased, and the nights were getting very cold. The horses began failing, and some were not even dead before the starving troops clamored to cut them up before the flesh froze. At this stage women and children were still getting help, but the bonds of comradeship were fraying fast.

Louise, close to headquarters, was spared much of this. Nothing would have been funnier at other times, she thought, than the sight of an old grenadier, with his mustache and bearskin, covered in pink satin fur. But the poor fellow was perishing from cold. She narrowly evaded disaster when the coachman carelessly let two of the horses freeze to death one night. The two remaining could not pull the carriage and she desperately considered ways to continue, but the driver managed to turn up with two replacements, obviously stolen.

Another general took pity on her and detached a gendarme to see her through the chaos that surrounded the column. Outside Smolensk, a Guard colonel held up her carriage, accusing it of blocking his regiment, threatening to have it cast aside despite the servant's insistence of the august rank of its owner. The sight of Louise softened his heart: 'Oh, I'm sorry, I didn't realize there was a lady inside,' he said.

Louise had to smile at him, for the grenadier colonel was covered in blue satin fur. He had not lost his sense of humor yet, and soon turned into another protector. He shared his dinner with her in his quarters,

The sight of Napoleon, like this, without his famous hat and showing the strains of campaigning demoralized one of Louise's fellow actresses. (V. Vereschagin, Roger-Viollet)

but in the cold there was nothing romantic about it. In the end she had to abandon her carriage to get through the crush at the gates of Smolensk. Yet to her surprise, the carriage turned up again though it had been looted, by Cossacks it is said, though probably by the servants. What food was available in Smolensk was selling at famine prices and even the servants of prominent courtiers were in danger of starving.

In Smolensk, Louise regained the company of her fellow actresses. One of them was rattled. Napoleon himself had come over to give her some words of comfort, but his headgear, a green velvet bonnet trimmed with fur, instead of his trademark hat, struck her as incongruous and sinister.

Still, the actresses were able to get out of Smolensk as far as Krasnoi. There the Russians had cut the road: Louise saw cannonballs bouncing across it. The carriage was abandoned again, and the horses were used to carry the actresses cross-country. However, the horses were exhausted and the snow very deep, and soon they were able to go no further. Louise struggled into town on foot. Remarkably the Polish coachman, who Louise regarded as a careless brute, was resourceful enough to go back later and recover the carriage.

Krasnoi was a nightmare. Alone amongst the mob, Louise found no-one who could direct her to Imperial Headquarters. An officer told her it had already gone. Knowing she was not able to catch up with it, her strength failing, Louise resigned herself to die. She found herself falling asleep. Death by cold seemed very gentle, and the shaking given to her by a savior seemed very annoying. She passed out, and woke to find herself in a room surrounded by officers. One of the Emperor's surgeons had saved her life by wrapping her in furs and placing her in a quiet corner. Placing a frozen person next to a big fire, as some officers had tried to do with her, could have been fatal.

Marshal Lefebvre, the grizzled war-horse, regarded her with interest. He was one of those who had picked her up out of the snow in the street. As she thawed out, he brought her some coffee. Louise had found a new protector. Soon she was in the marshal's carriage, following behind a Guard detachment. Behind, the road was littered with abandoned wagons and artillery and many corpses. Ney and his corps were far behind, presumed lost. One of her actress friends made it out of the debacle perched atop one of the few remaining cannons.

On to Liady, where the dignitaries of the Imperial Headquarters packed into some of the squalid houses of the poor Jewish inhabitants. A few miserable potatoes were extorted from the Jews with threats or gold. Louise was more considerate than most: 'They were Jews, but at least living beings. I'd gladly have embraced them.' Outside the crowded shelter, the unlucky ones were dying by the battalion.

On to the Beresina. The old warrior Marshal Lefebvre had grown a white beard, and leant on a knobby stick. At the bridges, Napoleon himself stood, seeming to Louise to be as calm as he would be at a Paris review. 'Don't be frightened, go on, go on,' Napoleon said, presumably to her as she was the only woman present.

Characteristically, Murat did not miss a chance to flirt with a pretty woman. He stood at her carriage door, chatting, dressed like a hero in a melodrama she thought, even to the undone collar in the biting cold. The favored Louise experienced a different Beresina than most, but even she thought she heard from a mile or so away the scream of the many stragglers lost on the far bank when the bridges were broken and the Russian artillery opened on them. Marshal Lefebvre was as tough as a soldier could be, but she saw even he turned pale at the ghastly sound.

Some of her fellow actresses did not make it across the Beresina. Some were rounded up by the Cossacks and spared perhaps, as were many of the officers. The rank and file were given no quarter. At Vilna was another bottleneck where more of the French civilians from Moscow died, unable to get through the crowded gate to the shelter within. Louise did get through thanks to Lefebvre and Murat, and there she repaid one of her benefactors, volunteering to stay behind to nurse and protect Lefebvre's sick son. Besides, she was sick, exhausted too, and the French army, abandoned by Napoleon, had still a long way to go to safety, beset by Cossacks all the way.

Twenty thousand French were left behind in Vilna to fall into Russian hands, three to four thousand of them officers, some of them the poor civilians who mistakenly left Moscow in the army's protection. Even after the Russians arrived, many were to die of privations and an epidemic of typhus. Louise survived to write her memoirs. If it was like that for a pampered actress, what must have it been like for the less fortunate?

Napoleon under pressure

The destruction of the *Grande Armée* in Russia was the greatest disaster, both militarily and politically, to have befallen Napoleon since he came to power. With his enemies determined to continue the fight, Napoleon had to find a way of opposing them. That he did so is testimony both to his own determination and to the resources of his empire.

Although the retreat from Moscow had ended at Konigsberg, this was not a position that could be held. Before leaving the army, and before turning over commmand to Eugene, Murat had placed most of his serviceable troops into Danzig, where a considerable force was to remain besieged until they were compelled to surrender on 29 November 1813. These troops were thus denied to Napoleon for operations in the field; but having called off the pursuit of the remnant of the *Grande Armée*, the Russians waited until the spring of 1813 before recommencing major offensive movements. This gave Napoleon a respite of a few months in which to assemble a new army to support the troops already in Germany, a force insufficient on its own to resist a determined Russian advance.

Napoleon's problems were not even concentrated in this one area of operations. Since 1807 increasing numbers of French troops had been engaged in the Pensinsular War, which had arisen from Napoleon's attempt to occupy the Iberian peninsula by deposing the Spanish monarch and replacing it with his brother Joseph, who had been proclaimed as king of Spain in June 1808. This was so unpopular that most of Spain rose in revolt which, aided by the presence of the energetic and successful British army commanded by Arthur Wellesley (later Duke of Wellington), had turned the French occupation into a running sore, a 'Spanish ulcer' as Napoleon described it, which constituted a severe and continual drain upon his resources. By the end of 1812, the war in Spain had turned decisively against the French; by the end of the following year they would be expelled from the Peninsula, and southern France would be threatened with invasion (see Osprey Essential Histories, *The Napoleonic Wars: The Peninsular War 1807-1814*, by Gregory Fremont-Barnes). Napoleon's decision to withdraw numbers of experienced troops from Spain, to assist him in continuing the fight in Germany, served only to make the French position in Spain even worse, and confirmed the fatal difficulty of attempting to maintain campaigns upon two widely separated fronts.

For the remainder of his new army, Napoleon drew some troops from internal security units and recalled retired veterans, but assembled most from newly or recently conscripted men. In the following months, such was the demand for troops that conscripts were called up years before they were due officially, resulting in regiments filled with increasing numbers of ever-younger recruits; experienced officers and NCOs trained them, but they did not possess either the experience or the physical abilities of the battle hardened men lost in Russia. Nevertheless, in numerical terms Napoleon was able to field an impressive army for a campaign which was to begin in spring 1813, even if it was deficient in cavalry, the most difficult troops to replace.

Napoleon's defeat in Russia also had the most profound political consequences, beginning with the Convention of Tauroggen (30 December 1812) by which General Hans David von Yorck's Prussian contingent of the *Grande Armée* signed a pact of neutrality with the Russians. This was done without reference to King Frederick William III of Prussia, nominally Napoleon's ally, and together with elements within the Prussian military and civil establishments which were strongly anti-French, it placed great pressure upon the king to take a stronger stance against Napoleon. The situation was compounded when Austria also adopted a position of neutrality, and Schwarzenberg's troops, which had formed the right flank of the advance of the *Grande Armée* against Russia, retired to Austrian territory, compelling the remaining French and allied forces in Poland to retire further west. These measures caused great concern among Napoleon's German allies of the Confederation of the Rhine, many of whose troops had been lost in Russia, but despite their misgivings, these states remained loyal to Napoleon at least for the earlier stages of the 1813 campaign. This was not the case with Prussia: emboldened by the catastrophe that had overtaken Napoleon in 1812, on 28 February 1813 that state secretly joined Russian by the Treaty of Kalisch, and as French forces withdrew westwards to regroup, Prussia declared war on Napoleon (16 March 1813).

Napoleon still enjoyed some advantages as the campaign of 1813 opened, notably 'unity of command' in that all his resources were under his control, whereas his enemies were to some degree mutually distrustful and lacked co-ordination. Thus upon the renewal of hostilities, Napoleon was to enjoy some successes, but the entry of Austria into the war against him (12 August 1813) was to cause a fatal shift in the balance of power. Supported by a tide of public enthusiasm, the 'War of Liberation' in Germany was to cause the collapse of the Confederation of the Rhine as Napoleon's allies changed sides, and France itself was to be laid open to invasion; all consequences of Napoleon's catastrophic decision to invade Russia in 1812.

Part III
The Peninsular War 1807–1814

Perennial foes: Britain, France and Spain

The centuries that preceded the Peninsular War were marked by regular periods of confrontation between Britain, France, and Spain in a series of constantly shifting alliances and loyalties. Anglo-French hostility, however, was consistent. These powers were known as 'hereditary' enemies by contemporaries with good reason. The table below summarizes the conflicts waged in the century before the Peninsular War between Europe's three oldest unified nations.

Up to 1792, these conflicts were, of course, those of kings, and followed the pattern of eighteenth-century warfare: sovereigns sought limited objectives and entertained no desire to overthrow their adversaries' ruling (and indeed usually ancient) dynasty. The outbreak of the French Revolution in 1789 altered this pattern forever and international relations underwent some radical changes as a result.

In the realm of power politics the eighteenth century was a period of nearly continuous rivalry between France and Britain, fueled by colonial and commercial rivalry, and

heightened by the basic tenet of British foreign policy that the Continent remain free from a single hegemonic power. In short, Britain would not tolerate an imbalance of power that furnished an overwhelming advantage to any of the other Great Powers – France, Austria, Russia, and Prussia. As France had consistently sought to upset this balance, most particularly since the accession of Louis XIV, Anglo-French hostility was a natural and frequent product of Bourbon French ambitions.

Many British contemporaries held that the changing nature of international relations brought about by the French Revolution would eliminate the grounds of suspicion between these traditional rivals. Yet on the contrary, they became fiercer opponents than ever, more strongly opposed by the introduction of radically different political ideologies, now fused with the same old colonial and commercial disputes and, above all, with the French revolutionaries' desire for territorial expansion. All this was a much more potent mix than had been the traditional ingredients of Anglo-French enmity. The occupation of the Low Countries

Conflicts between Britain, Spain, and France 1702–1808

1702–1714	Britain vs. France and Spain	War of the Spanish Succession
1718–20	Britain and France vs. Spain	War of the Quadruple Alliance
1739–48	Britain vs. Spain	War of Jenkins's Ear
1740–48	Britain vs. France	War of the Austrian Succession
1756–63	Britain vs. France	Seven Years' War
1778–83	Britain vs. France	War of American Independence
1779–93	Britain vs. Spain	War of American Independence
1793–1802	Britain vs. France	French Revolutionary Wars
1793–95	Spain vs. France	French Revolutionary Wars
1796–1802	Britain vs. Spain	French Revolutionary Wars
1803–14/15	Britain vs. France	Napoleonic Wars
1804–1808	Britain vs. Spain	Napoleonic Wars

Death of General Wolfe at Quebec, 13 September 1759. Anglo-French rivalry in the eighteenth century involved hostilities throughout the world, particularly in North America, where French Canada and Britain's 13 colonies provided a fertile killing ground. When the Seven Years' War ended in 1763, having been waged in Europe, North America, India, and across the oceans of the world, Britain emerged supreme, annexing Canada and parts of India from France. (Ann Ronan Picture Library)

1790 Britain and Spain nearly went to war over the Nootka Sound crisis, a territorial dispute concerning the coast of present-day British Columbia. France and Spain had an alliance, but the National Assembly refused to honor a treaty signed prior to the Revolution. The feeble position of Louis XVI, still king but with restricted powers, attracted the sympathy of the Spanish ruling house which was Bourbon, like that of Louis. Yet the Revolution meant that the French and Spanish sovereigns could no longer rely on the 'Family Compact' established between them. Increasing humiliations perpetrated against Louis, and the steady stream of French emigrés crossing the Pyrenees, inevitably turned Spain against the revolutionaries. Spain offered sanctuary to the French royal family but the revolutionaries twice refused to allow this before finally declaring war on Spain on 7 March 1793.

Spain enjoyed initial success in the campaign that followed. One army defended the western Pyrenees against all French incursions, while another invaded Roussillon and western Provence. However, Spanish conduct at the siege of Toulon at the close of the year was disgraceful, and in 1794 Spain's two best commanders died. Later that year the French counterattacked with superior strength, taking the border fortresses and penetrating nearly to the line of the River Ebro. Military reverses and economic dislocation led Spain formally to withdraw from the war by concluding the Treaty of Basle on 22 July 1795. She ceded Santo Domingo (the present-day Dominican Republic) to France in exchange for French withdrawal from Spanish territory.

In the following year, 1796, the Treaty of San Ildefonso allied Spain to France, against Britain. As this required Spain to furnish

during the French Revolutionary Wars posed, for instance, an insuperable barrier to good relations between the two countries. In short, Britain considered any power with a strong navy which controlled the Low Countries to be a threat to her very existence.

After nearly a decade of conflict between 1793 and 1802, Britain and France concluded a very tenuous peace at Amiens, but Napoleon's continued incursions into Switzerland, Holland, Germany, and Italy, and Britain's refusal to evacuate Malta as protection against French expansion in the Mediterranean meant that the renewal of hostilities in May 1803 was inevitable. This opening phase of the Napoleonic Wars, confined until the summer of 1805 to Britain and France, was by the nature of their respective armed forces largely restricted to naval activity. The Peninsular War changed this dramatically by offering Britain the opportunity to confront France on the soil of a friendly power, easily accessible by sea.

Yet relations between Spain and Britain had, historically, been far from amicable. In

British surrender at Yorktown, 1781. The War of American Independence (1775–1783) offered France the opportunity to avenge her losses in the Seven Years' and the French and Indian War (1756–1763) by assisting the rebellious American colonists. Indeed, French military, naval, and financial aid proved decisive, particularly at Yorktown, where General Cornwallis surrendered 7,000 troops not merely to American, but to thousands of French troops, who had isolated the British army on the Virginia coast with the vital support of a French fleet under de Grasse. (Ann Ronan Picture Library)

25 ships to the war effort, the stage was set for a period of worldwide naval confrontation between Spain and Britain which lasted from 1796 until the Peace of Amiens in 1802.

Spanish ties with France were strengthened when on 7 October 1800 the two countries signed the Convention of San Ildefonso, which was later confirmed by the Treaty of Aranjuez on 21 March 1801. British interests were further damaged when, by the Treaty of Badajoz with France, Spain agreed to wage war against Britain's long-standing ally, Portugal. The so-called 'War of the Oranges' was short (May and June 1801) but by the peace signed on 6 June Spain annexed the small frontier district of Olivenza and

Portugal was forced to close its ports to British ships and to pay France a reparation of 20 million francs.

During the period of Anglo-Spanish hostilities from 1796 to 1802, operations were almost exclusively naval. On paper, at least, Spain appeared a formidable opponent. In 1793 the Spanish Empire stretched over vast reaches of the Americas, including a million square miles (2.6 million square kilometers) west of the Mississippi, and extended to possessions in the Caribbean (chiefly Cuba) and in the Pacific (chiefly the Philippines). She was the third ranked naval power in the world, with 76 ships-of-the-line (of which 56 were actually in commission) and 105 smaller vessels.

Nevertheless, the Spanish navy proved no match for the Royal Navy. In practically every encounter, from cutting-out operations to ship-to-ship actions to fleet engagements, the Spanish were defeated, both in home and in colonial waters. Notable exceptions included an unsuccessful British attack against San Juan, Puerto Rico in 1797 and Nelson's foray against Santa Cruz de Tenerife in the Canary Islands in the same year. Nevertheless, the

Battle of Cape St Vincent, fought in February 1797, was a notable British triumph. Indeed, the defeat suffered at St Vincent was enough to force the Spanish fleet back to Cadiz for the remainder of the war, and notwithstanding Nelson's bloody repulse at Tenerife, the Spanish fleet had been effectively neutralized. This situation not only adversely affected Spain's trade with, and administration of, her overseas colonies, it halted ship building altogether: Spain launched its last ship-of-the-line in 1798 and the last frigate two years later. To crown the country's misfortunes, British troops easily captured Minorca in 1798.

Although the Treaty of Amiens brought peace, albeit short-lived, between Britain and Spain in March 1802, the Anglo-French contest resumed only 14 months later, and it was not long before Spain was once again drawn into the conflict. On 9 October 1803 France effectively coerced Spain into an alliance which required her to supply a monthly payment of 6 million francs, to enforce Portuguese neutrality and to provide France with between 25 and 29 ships-of-the-line. Napoleon intended to use these to protect his cross-Channel invasion force.

Nevertheless, this agreement did not oblige Spain to enter hostilities against Britain and therefore its existence was as yet unknown by the Admiralty in London. Yet as the months passed Spain's repeated claims of neutrality in the Anglo-French conflict rang increasingly hollow and it became impossible for Britain to tolerate what amounted to Spain's funding of Napoleon's war against her: confrontation with Spain was only a matter of time. The approach off Cadiz of a fleet carrying treasure from Peru precipitated it, and, without a previous declaration of war a Royal Navy squadron attacked on 5 October 1804. Outraged, Spain formally declared war on 12 December, thus providing Napoleon with the opportunity he had long hoped for to make use of the sizable, though decrepit, Spanish fleet. By combining it with his own he hoped to draw the Channel fleet out to sea and thus provide the short interval needed to thrust his army of invasion, which was camped at Boulogne on the north coast of France, across that narrow stretch of water which for centuries had protected his rivals. As is well known, Vice-Admiral Horatio Nelson (1758--1805) shattered Napoleon's plans at Trafalgar on 21 October 1805, when the Franco-Spanish fleet was virtually annihilated in one of the greatest contests in the history of naval warfare.

This did not, however, spell the end of Anglo-Spanish hostility, and in the following year a British expedition to Spanish America captured Buenos Aires and Montevideo (in present-day Argentina and Uruguay, respectively). Both cities fell to British troops, but the garrisons quickly found themselves confronted by overwhelming numbers of colonial militia and Spanish regulars and were forced to surrender. A relieving force arrived in January 1807 and retook Montevideo, but it was defeated at Buenos Aires and all British troops were withdrawn the following month. Thus, in 1807, on the eve of the Peninsular War, Britain and Spain remained at war. Quite how the relationship between Britain and Spain could have undergone such a radical shift in the course of a single year will be covered later.

Opposing forces

The British Army

Throughout the eighteenth century and into the Napoleonic Wars Britain remained a largely self-reliant nation whose strength derived mainly from the Royal Navy, unquestionably the greatest maritime force of its day. Geography and superior naval power had meant that only a small standing army was necessary for the country's defense. In any event the size of the army was limited by financial and above all political considerations. A mistrust of the military amongst Parliament and nation was a legacy dating back to the Commonwealth, under

Lieutenant-General Sir John Moore (1761–1809). Adored by his men, Moore was instrumental in improving light infantry training before becoming C-in-C of the British Army in the Peninsula in 1808. While advancing into Spain to confront overwhelming French forces he found himself badly unsupported by the Spanish and forced to make a disastrous retreat to Corunna, where he was killed. His victory there, however, ensured the army's safe evacuation. (Ann Ronan Picture Library)

Cromwell, who had used the army as an instrument of despotism. Suspicion continued under the Restoration, making the army feared and in some cases even despised as the enemy of liberty. The regular army lived on the margins of society, supplying garrisons for the colonies and Ireland. New units were raised on the outbreak of war and disbanded at the peace. Home defense was the responsibility of the Navy as the first line of defense and the Militia as the second.

Recruiting methods and the social make-up of the British Army remained effectively unchanged from its eighteenth-century forebears, such that the professional and mercantile classes scarcely appeared in the officer corps, making the army highly divided on class lines. The officer corps was the preserve of the aristocracy (mostly confined to the Guards and cavalry) and, above all, the gentry. This situation was perpetuated by the purchase system: gentlemen aspiring to an officer's rank had to possess sufficient funds to buy their regimental commissions. The monopoly of wealth and social connection all but guaranteed that the upper ranks remained in the hands of the ruling classes. In this respect it bore no relation to its French counterpart. The reforms of the Revolution had swept away such forms of privilege and it was said that every soldier carried a marshal's baton in his knapsack – an allusion to meritocratic promotion.

British officers were generally brave and possessed a social status that commanded respect and obedience from the men under their leadership. Officers were expected to lead from the front, with predictably high rates of casualties. The ordinary ranks were, unlike the French, volunteers, drawn to the colors by bounty and, being the poorest elements of society, shared nothing in

Sir Arthur Wellesley, 1st Duke of Wellington (1769–1852). Born into an aristocratic Anglo-Irish family, Wellington remains the greatest of many exceptionally skilled commanders produced by the British Army, including the accomplished Marlborough. Highly intelligent and hard-working, Wellington first distinguished himself in India before leading Anglo-Portuguese and, later, Spanish forces in the Peninsula. He conceived the brilliant defenses of Torres Vedras and though he was not adept at siege warfare he won every battle in which he was present. (Oil by Sir T. Lawrence, Edimedia)

wished to escape from poverty or to seek adventure. Whatever their background, over time Wellington molded them into a first-rate fighting force and he was impressed by the change wrought in his men by army life: 'It is really wonderful,' he wrote during the war, 'that we should have made them the fine fellows they are.'

The British Army had its reformers in men such as Sir Ralph Abercromby (1734–1801) and Sir John Moore (1761–1809), but no personality put a greater stamp on this period than Wellington. Wellington embodied eighteenth-century stability, and

common with their officers. Indeed, the only link between them were the sergeants and other non-commissioned officers.

Although officially a volunteer force, the British Army certainly contained an element of unwilling recruits: criminals and vagabonds, thugs and ruffians who were only serving to avoid a prison sentence. It is however important to rectify a common misconception on this subject: when Wellington wrote of 'the scum of the earth,' he was referring not to the army in general, but to that element which plundered in the wake of the Battle of Vitoria. It is probably fair to say that most ordinary soldiers simply

Wellington and his generals, 1813. Remarkably little in the Duke's performance in the Peninsula can be criticized, apart from his failure to provide his subordinates with opportunities for independent command. As C-in-C he refused to appoint a second-in-command and until the very end of the war he rarely delegated authority over the troops except at divisional level – possibly the consequence of Beresford's near disaster at Albuera. (After Heaphy, National Army Museum)

Major-General Sir Edward Pakenham (1778–1815). Wellington's brother-in-law, Pakenham took a prominent part in the victory at Salamanca, where he assaulted the head of the French column of march. The C-in-C said of him afterwards: 'Pakenham may not be the brightest genius, but my partiality for him does not lead me astray, when I tell you he is one of the best we have.' He was killed at New Orleans in 1815 during the war against the United States. (National Army Museum)

did not undertake any fundamental change to a system which appeared to function well.

However it is easy in hindsight to assume that when the British Army landed in Portugal in 1808 victory was only a matter of time. This was by no means the case, and the record of the army since 1793 was not a wholly unblemished one. Apart from the campaigns in Egypt in 1801, and Copenhagen in 1807, many of the expeditions had achieved only limited success, or, such as at Buenos Aires and Rosetta as recently as 1807, were outright failures. The reputation so tarnished in the War of American Independence had yet to be fully restored, despite the reforms and inspiration of such men as Abercromby and Moore.

Nevertheless, Wellington maximized the effectiveness of the system he inherited. As Commander-in-Chief in the Peninsula, Wellington chose to have a tiny staff headquarters and no second-in-command, keeping matters in his own hands and those of a few key officers, particularly the

Quartermaster-General, the Adjutant-General, the head of the Commissariat, the Chief of Artillery, and the Chief Engineer. He relied heavily on his intelligence network, acquiring useful information on French strength, plans and dispositions from his own superb intelligence officers, 'correspondents', and observers throughout the Peninsula, and from civilians and guerrillas, who provided much useful information through simple observation or by interdicting French dispatches.

Wellington took great pains to see that the Commissariat kept his army well supplied with the necessities of war: food, clothing, and ammunition. In this he held a significant advantage over the French army, which suffered a chronic shortage of all matériel and could not feed itself without recourse to plunder. The Peninsula lacked the fertile plains of Germany and Italy, but Wellington could compensate by using unrestricted access to the sea to obtain supplies and, however poor the inhabitants of Iberia, at least they were friendly. He developed an effective system of depots which provided for the needs of tens of thousands of men and animals, both horses and the livestock which supplied meat for the army.

The result of Wellington's personal attention to the administration, supply and training of the army was the creation of one of the greatest fighting forces of modern times. As he himself claimed in 1813: 'It is probably the most complete machine for its number now existing in Europe.' Their record on the battlefield is a worthy testament to Wellington's achievement, for they never lost a battle. Their commander proudly acknowledged: 'I have the satisfaction of reflecting that, having tried them frequently, they have never failed me.'

The French Army

The French armies in the Peninsula in the early years of the war were large, but most of the men were raw recruits, about one third drawn early from the levies of 1808 and 1809. They also contained soldiers of many

Joseph Bonaparte (1768–1844), King of Spain. In 1808 Napoleon's eldest brother reluctantly left the throne of Naples in exchange for that of the Empire's most recent conquest. He lacked popular support in a country he could never wholly subdue, received constant criticism and interference from Napoleon, and held no authority over French generals in the field. As a result, Joseph repeatedly sought to abdicate – a wish the Emperor did not grant until after the disaster at Vitoria in 1813. (Ann Ronan Picture Library)

needs, with many people already living at subsistence levels, the French found their freedom of movement severely impaired and relied ever more strongly on plunder and requisitions of the civilian population. As there was no overall commander in the Peninsula there was often no coordination between the various armies, which were scattered across Spain and struggled to maintain communications along its primitive and often nonexistent roads.

French generals were shameless in stripping the assets of the towns they occupied, stealing art and raiding treasuries as they went. It is not surprising that French soldiers in their disillusionment would decry their leaders' avarice while they themselves struggled just to keep themselves fed. 'This war in Spain,' ran the popular sentiment of the ordinary ranks, 'means death for the men, ruin for the officers, a fortune for the generals.'

nationalities, many of whose countries had been absorbed into the Empire. Poles, Swiss, Germans from the states of the Confederation of the Rhine, volunteer Irish, Italians, and Neapolitans, all served in the Peninsula, with different degrees of willingness and skill. Over 50,000 Italians alone fought as French allies. Many of the Germans deserted when opportunity presented itself, joining the King's German Legion, a fine corps of Hanoverians formed in 1803 during the French occupation of this north German patrimony of George III.

The French employed those tactics that they had used with such consistent success in the past on the battlefields of western and central Europe: concentration of artillery and massed attack in column. Their armies were accustomed to 'living off the land,' and as such did not establish the network of supply depots which Wellington wisely did. As the land was found woefully deficient for their

Marshal André Masséna (1758–1817). Though distinguished in numerous campaigns since the 1790s, he was far less successful in the Peninsula. Defeated at Busaco in 1810, Masséna failed to penetrate the Lines of Torres Vedras and was beaten again at Fuentes de Oñoro in 1811, before being recalled. Wellington nevertheless considered him a worthy opponent: 'When Masséna was opposed to me I could not eat, drink or sleep. I never knew what repose or respite from anxiety was. I was kept perpetually on the alert.' (Ann Ronan Picture Library)

Marshal Nicolas Soult (1769–1851). Commander during the later stages of the pursuit of Moore to Corunna, Soult was later defeated at Oporto in 1809 and ejected from Portugal. Although he subsequently enjoyed great success against the Spanish at Ocaña and elsewhere, he performed badly at Albuera in 1811. Recalled for service in Germany in 1813, he returned to Spain after the Battle of Vitoria and was appointed C-in-C, in which capacity he demonstrated considerable skill in opposing Wellington's advance. (Ann Ronan Picture Library)

The Spanish Army

In 1808 the army stood at slightly over 100,000 men and about 30,000 troops mobilized from the militia. Spain's regular forces were amongst the worst in Europe at the start of the Peninsular War, but by the end of the conflict had improved on their appalling record. Administered by corrupt and incompetent officials, the infantry was severely lacking in officers, who themselves received virtually no training. Surtees, a soldier in the 95th Rifles, called them 'the most contemptible creatures that I ever beheld … utterly unfit and unable to command their men.' Leith Hay, another British soldier, described the army as '… ill-commanded, ill-appointed, moderately disciplined and in most respects inefficient …' Units were composed of volunteers and of conscripts, who came from the lowest classes. Promotion was all but impossible in a system

where rising through the ranks effectively ceased at the rank of captain. Higher ranks were held by aristocrats and landowners who had neither knowledge of nor interest in soldiering. Not only were the officers deficient in training or motivation, the army authorized no official drill, leaving every unit commander to devise his own field instructions as he saw fit. Unit effectiveness was further undermined by insufficient numbers, equipment and food, and the cavalry suffered from an acute shortage of mounts, with fewer than one third of its troopers supplied with a horse.

The most respectable units of the Spanish army were those of the Marquis de la Romana, whose division had been sent to north Germany to serve with Napoleon's troops. On hearing of the uprising in Madrid, Romana's men revolted, were evacuated by the Royal Navy, and returned for service in Spain. Even these relatively well-led and well-equipped troops were described by one British soldier as having '… more the appearance of a large body of peasants … in want of everything, than a regular army.' During the retreat to Corunna Surtees found them '… [even] in their best days, more like an armed mob than regularly organized soldiers.'

If the soldiers were bad, the commanders were beyond contempt. With few exceptions they were a liability in the field, not merely to their own troops but to the British as well. They provided erroneous information to Moore, which led to the disastrous retreat to Corunna, they failed either to support or to supply Wellington after Talavera, and they were widely known for their corrupt practices. Eventually Wellington took personal command of the Spanish armies, and only then was he able to rely upon them.

The cavalry consistently performed so badly that any success was seen with astonishment. The infantry was prone to panic and flee, casting away their weapons in the stampede for the rear. Contempt for such men in the British ranks was not surprising, though it must be remembered that low morale was the natural result of poor leadership, irregular pay and food, and a chronic lack of equipment and clothing.

When properly led and supplied the Spanish could perform well, as at Vitoria and in the Pyrenees and toward the close of the war standards had improved sufficiently to allow a small number of Spaniards to join the ranks of British regiments.

If the regular forces were abysmal, the civilian defenders of cities like Saragossa and Gerona were an entirely different breed, demonstrating immense courage in the face of French troops and heroic feats of resistance and hardship under siege. The Church and landowners supported all such forms of resistance as well as the guerrillas,

Spanish guerrillas. As shown, guerrillas were variously armed and clothed, depending on the availability of Spanish, British or captured French weapons and uniforms and the particular tastes of the partisans themselves. The figure on the left is dressed entirely in civilian clothes and carries an antiquated blunderbuss, while the other two men wear vestiges of military dress, particularly the cavalryman on the right. (Roger-Viollet)

who were infamous for their cruelty. The French retaliated in kind with revenge on a grand scale. These will be described elsewhere.

The Portuguese Army

General Andoche Junot (1771–1813) disbanded the Portuguese army during his occupation of the country and it was not resurrected until Wellington assigned General William Beresford (1764–1854) the task of raising and organizing new units which were then incorporated into British brigades. Like the Spanish, the Portuguese officers were badly paid and had no opportunity for advancement. A man could remain a captain for literally decades. William Warre, a Portuguese-born British officer, noted in 1808 that the Portuguese were '... cowards who won't fight a

one-sixteenth of a Frenchman with arms, but plunder and murder the wounded ...' The following year he found the men '... well enough, very obedient, willing, and patient, but also naturally dirty and careless of their persons ... The Officers ... are detestable, mean, ignorant ...'

Beresford found the army numbering half its establishment, with only 30,000 instead of nearly 60,000. This was changed through conscription, while Beresford instituted wide-ranging and effective reforms, including the retirement of inefficient and indolent officers, and the addition of British officers to the regiments and higher command structure. These men were so positioned as to have Portuguese officers above and below them; likewise, all Portuguese officers had British superiors and subordinates. A Portuguese regiment might therefore have a British colonel, but below him Portuguese majors. Non-commissioned officers and men received better pay, training, food, and equipment, which in turn raised morale and produced improved results on the battlefield. Warre remarked in the spring of 1809 that, 'The Portuguese immediately under the instruction of British officers are coming on very well ... The men may be made anything we please of, with proper management ...' Others noted over time that the Portuguese bore the fatigues and privations of campaigning without complaint and showed considerable bravery in action.

By 1812 a number of British observers commented that the Portuguese were fine soldiers and in some cases fought on a par with their British counterparts, and Wellington would call them 'the fighting cocks of the army.' As early as at Busaco in 1810 Schaumann remarked how 'The Portuguese fought with conspicuous courage ... They behaved just like English troops.' Apart from the regular soldiers there were the mule-drivers and camp-followers, who gained a dreadful reputation for pillaging and the murder of French wounded after battle. Unlike the infantry, the Portuguese cavalry and siege train never improved. A shortage of horses plagued the former and obsolete equipment the latter.

The Portuguese contribution to the war was important, and while it is natural to think of Wellington's army as 'British', it is only right to observe that by 1810 it was nearly half Portuguese. Beresford performed his task well, and his soldiers made a solid contribution to the Allied victory.

Origins of the conflict

June 1807 marked the high water mark of Napoleonic fortunes. On the 14th Napoleon routed the Russian army at Friedland and on the 25th he and Tsar Alexander met on a raft in the Niemen River at Tilsit to make peace. Not only did Russia conclude peace (together with Prussia), she went so far as to form an alliance with France against Britain, thus leaving Napoleon supreme in Europe. He had cowed the three great continental powers, Austria, Prussia and Russia, in three successive and brilliant campaigns, and only Britain, Sweden, and Portugal remained to oppose him. Trafalgar, fought two years before, had not only saved Britain from imminent invasion, it had established her as mistress of the seas, leaving France no means of striking at her most implacable foe except by severing her trade links with the Continent. This Napoleon duly attempted when, immediately after subduing Prussia in 1806, he issued the Berlin Decrees, which banned British and British colonial goods from all territory under French control. This was the beginning of his 'Continental System', a novel attempt first to isolate and then to starve Britain into submission. Britain instituted a novel reply: rather than eliminate French trade through blockade, she sought to regulate it. Vessels flying the tricolor or those of the French satellites were fair game for British warships; those of neutral countries wishing to trade with France could only do so under heavy restrictions.

British maritime policy was to have serious implications for Anglo-American relations and ultimately led to war between the countries in 1812. As British and British colonial goods were in great demand on the Continent, Napoleon's system became increasingly unpopular throughout the Empire – and even in France herself – making smuggling rampant along practically

every coast. This, in turn, drove Napoleon to tighten and, above all, expand his control over the few remaining territories not yet subject to his rule. He had little trouble conquering southern Italy in 1806, but this left neutral Portugal as the last country still defying his plan. Control of Portugal meant control of her colonial trade, above all with Brazil. Access to Spain's colonies was even more coveted, encompassing as they did most of South and Central America.

The opportunity to plug this gap in the Continental System came after Tilsit, when Napoleon and Alexander agreed to cooperate in the closure of continental ports to British trade. This agreement extended as far west as Portugal, and here may be found the origins of the Peninsular War. With the sole exception of Portugal, France already controlled the European coastline from the Niemen to the Adriatic, and thus Napoleon relied on his Spanish ally to allow the passage of French troops across the Pyrenees. Only in this way could he compel Portugal to adopt the Continental System.

Long at odds with her more powerful neighbor, Spain, Portugal, with her extensive Atlantic coastline, had since the Middle Ages depended on maritime trade with Britain, which by 1807 accounted for almost half that trade. Over the centuries Portugal had remained steadfastly linked to Britain, and had defied French attempts to coerce her cooperation. Portugal had remained neutral since the start of the conflict in 1803, but she had irritated the French emperor by permitting ships of the Royal Navy to use the Tagus estuary as a base for shelter and provisioning. This, in combination with her total defiance of the Continental System, rendered Portugal a natural target for French occupation, not least because Tilsit had put an end to fighting elsewhere, releasing

Principal battles and sieges

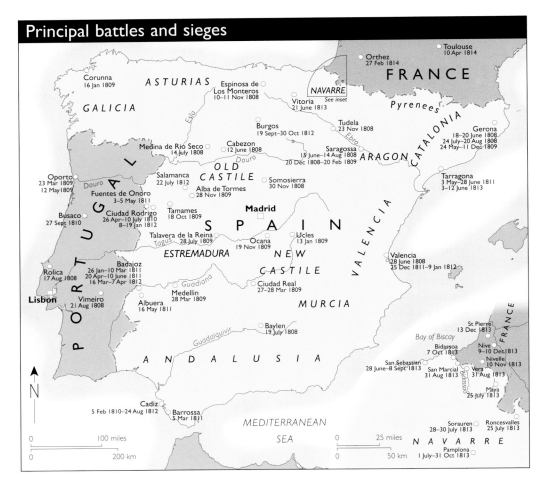

Every province in Spain and Portugal experienced fighting in one form or another, ranging from minor skirmishes between companies or battalions to major battles and sieges, involving tens of thousands of combatants on both sides. Most of the principal actions fought in the Peninsular War are shown here. In contrast to many other Napoleonic theaters of war, the Peninsula witnessed numerous major – and often extremely bitter – sieges, some conducted between Anglo-Portuguese and French forces, others solely between the French and Spanish. Some of the main sieges included: Cadiz, Valencia, Gerona, San Sebastian, Saragossa, Tarragona, Burgos, Badajoz, and Ciudad Rodrigo. The last two were of particular strategic importance, being the key points of passage between Portugal and Spain.

French forces for operations against a weak country which also shared a long frontier with an ally of France.

Portugal was ruled by the Prince Regent, John (1767–1826), of the House of Braganza.

His parents, King Peter III and Queen Maria I, had succeeded to the Portuguese throne as joint rulers in February 1777, but the King died in 1786. From 1792 onward their son acted as regent for the Queen, who had gone insane and remained so at the time of the French invasion. Tilsit had no sooner been signed than John received a series of threats and ultimata demanding adherence to French demands for the closure of Portuguese ports to British ships, commercial as well as naval. John had no wish to comply and made several futile attempts to placate the French with a series of concessions. Napoleon remained firm and orders were issued to Junot to cross the Pyrenees and invade Portugal. Needless to say, this required the cooperation of Spain, which had been obtained in the Treaty of

Fontainebleau, concluded on 27 October, and authorizing the passage of French troops across Spanish territory.

The subjugation of Portugal quickly followed. Spain duly granted permission for French troops to pass through the country, and on 17 October, 10 days before the agreement at Fontainebleau, Junot advanced with 24,000 men across the Pyrenees. On 19 November they passed through Alcantara into Portuguese territory. The Portuguese could offer only feeble resistance, but the march over appalling roads and horrendous terrain took a heavy toll on the invaders. When, at last, Junot entered Lisbon unopposed on 30 November, he did so with little more than 2,000 bedraggled men, the remainder strung out along the primitive roads. It was a hollow victory. The previous day the Regent, the royal family and its vast suite had abandoned the capital and taken refuge aboard a Royal Navy squadron in the harbor. They then departed for the Portuguese colony of Brazil, taking with them the Portuguese fleet and most of the state treasure.

If Napoleon did not, therefore, achieve all his objectives, he could be satisfied by the swift and practically bloodless conquest of Portugal, whose army Junot disbanded and whose territory Napoleon divided with Spain in accordance with Fontainebleau. He had achieved the closure of the Tagus to the Royal Navy and the termination of all trade between British and Portuguese home ports (although, of course, not those of the Portuguese empire).

The invasion of Portugal, as we have seen, had depended on Spanish cooperation, the inducement being the partition of the country. Yet the Treaty of Fontainebleau hid Napoleon's real intentions regarding Spain, with whom he was becoming increasingly frustrated. As noted earlier, Spain had fought revolutionary France from 1793 to 1795 when, after a poor performance on the Pyrenean front, she had withdrawn from the First Coalition and, in the following year, joined France against Britain until the conclusion of peace in 1802. In 1801 Spain had invaded Portugal and annexed territory.

Charles IV, King of Spain (1748–1819), and his family. His reign, which began in 1788, marked an end to the period of enlightenment under his father. Charles was a political nonentity who spent much of his time hunting and ignoring political matters large and small, thus allowing Prince Godoy and his half-mad queen, Maria Louisa, to bungle state affairs. After the conference at Bayonne Charles lived in exile in France and died in obscurity. (Goya, Prado Museum/Edimedia)

Yet apart from that gain her alliance with France had cost her the loss of Trinidad to Britain and the virtual destruction of her fleet. She was badly beaten at St Vincent in 1797 and then again at Trafalgar in 1805. Spanish policy thereafter was inconsistent: in February 1806 the First Minister, Godoy, made a proposal to Napoleon for the dismemberment of Portugal which came to nothing. After that Franco-Spanish relations began to sour, and when in the autumn Napoleon became embroiled in conflict with Prussia, which Godoy erroneously believed would win, Spain secretly planned to leave the unpopular French alliance.

Partly to ensure Spain's loyalty, Napoleon required the country to supply its best division, under the Marquis de la Romana, for service in Bernadotte's corps, which was then watching the Baltic coast. Spain was then rendered weaker, for the march to Portugal had provided Napoleon with an excuse to garrison key Spanish towns between Bayonne and the Portuguese border, in theory to secure the line of communications but in reality a cover for a full-scale occupation of Spain.

King Charles IV had assumed the Spanish throne on the death of his father in December 1788. Charles III, although a despot, had presided over a period of *Ilustracion* (enlightenment) during which the arts and sciences were encouraged and the economy thrived. In the two decades which followed until the Peninsular War Charles showed himself to be kind, though stupid and completely unfit to rule a major nation. His chief interest was hunting and he ruled Spain in nothing more than a nominal role, for he was strongly influenced by his wife, Maria Louisa of Parma. It was the Queen's favorite minister (and lover), Manuel de Godoy, who became chief minister in 1792 and held the reins of power. Godoy, dishonest and ineffective, had led the country into financial ruin, military incompetence and bureaucratic corruption. Over time he built up support within the court by carefully appointing his supporters and arresting or exiling those who opposed him. He grew rich through corruption and misappropriation of public funds. As chief minister it was Godoy who had persuaded Charles to sign the Treaty of Basle in 1795 which took Spain out of the war against France (hence his title 'Prince of Peace') and made the nations allies. The three leading political figures, the King and Godoy on the one hand, and the heir-apparent Crown Prince Ferdinand (1784–1833) on the other, hated one another. Each had the support of their own factions, creating a political vacuum which not only prevented any unified front against Napoleon, but gave the Emperor the opportunity to meddle in Spanish internal affairs.

Throughout the winter of 1807 French agents in Spain became increasingly involved in Spanish internal affairs, encouraging friction between the King and Godoy, and Ferdinand, all as a means of creating an atmosphere of chaos that the French could manipulate into requiring formal intervention on the pretext of mediating. Spain, under French control, would become a reliable partner within the empire, her long Atlantic and Mediterranean coastlines could be sealed against British trade, and the remainder of her fleet would be at French disposal. The Spanish political crisis

Manuel Godoy, Prince of Peace (1767–1851). Corrupt, immoral and an arch-schemer, Godoy became the lover of Queen Maria Louisa of Spain, and a close confidant of her idiot husband, King Charles IV. As First Minister Godoy concluded the Treaty of Basle, which ended the conflict with France in 1795. During the royal intrigues of 1807–1808 he backed the king against his son Ferdinand, thus encouraging French intervention in Spanish internal affairs. Here he is flushed out of hiding after the riots at Aranjuez in March 1808. (Ann Ronan Picture Library)

Ferdinand VII, King of Spain (1784–1833). Constantly at odds with his father, Charles IV, Ferdinand particularly opposed the influence of the First Minister, Godoy, whom he unsuccessfully sought to depose in 1807. Further conspiracy, mutual recrimination and suspicion between father and son led to requests for Napoleon's mediation. Ferdinand briefly became king in March 1808, but on being himself forced to abdicate by Napoleon, the foundations of French intervention in Spain were finally established. (Goya, Roger-Viollet)

deepened when, on 29 October, Godoy persuaded the king to arrest Ferdinand, claiming that he was behind a plot to dethrone his father and murder his mother. Later, on 17 December, Napoleon issued the Milan Decree, reaffirming his other policies on the continental blockade and banning all British trade with the European mainland. Spain, as France's ally, officially supported the blockade, but in practice smuggling through her ports and extensive coastline was widespread and often ignored or even condoned by local or provincial officials. This did not go unnoticed in Paris.

Napoleon's plan was formally instituted on 16 February 1808 when he announced that, as Spain's ally, France was obliged to intervene to restore order in Spain's domestic affairs and would mediate between the rival political factions within the royal family. First, French troops were dispatched to occupy key points and fortresses in the northern provinces, including Pamplona, San Sebastian, Barcelona, and Figueras, to secure the passes through the Pyrenees; next Marshal Joachim Murat (1767–1815) proceeded into Spain with 118,000 troops, ostensibly to reinforce Junot in Portugal. They received a warm welcome as

they passed through the towns. Meanwhile, on 17 March, Charles, at Aranjuez, was confronted by a popular uprising against him and Godoy (the *Motin de Aranjuez*) led by the Royal Guards. This marked the first *pronunciamento*, or coup, carried out by soldiers in the country's history. With the encouragement of Ferdinand, a large mob sacked and burned Godoy's palace. Godoy, who barely escaped alive, was arrested, deposed, and forced into exile. The King's connection with Godoy made his position untenable and he abdicated on 20 March in favor of his son, who became Ferdinand VII.

A few days later, on 24 March, Murat entered Madrid. Charles had attempted to flee to Cadiz some days before but had been prevented from doing so by an angry mob. Continuing his ruse, Napoleon called the rival members of the royal family to Bayonne, just across the Franco-Spanish border, ostensibly for a conference of arbitration. Notwithstanding anti-French riots in Madrid on 1 April, Ferdinand left the capital on 10 April to meet Napoleon. The conference was convened on 5 May. In a matter of days Napoleon had forced both Charles and Ferdinand to abdicate their claims to the Spanish throne in favor of his own brother, Joseph (1768–1844), who, with the backing of pro-French elements in Spain, was created king on 6 June. Crowned on 7 July at Bayonne, he entered Madrid on the 20th. Charles meanwhile retired to Rome and Ferdinand was placed under house arrest in Valençay, where he would remain until 1814. Thus, as the Spanish Bourbons were interned, Joseph duly proceeded to Madrid to take up a throne whose illegitimacy was plain for all of Spain to see.

A war of contrasts

Operations in 1808

Napoleon's decision to overthrow Bourbon rule in Spain proved a great miscalculation. Open defiance against the treacherous occupation of the country, exacerbated by the attempts of French troops to escort the King's youngest son, Don Francisco, to France, led to an uprising in Madrid on 2 May 1808. Infuriated mobs of *Madrileños*, armed with knives, clubs, and makeshift weapons, slaughtered 130 French soldiers before Murat's cavalry ruthlessly cut them down in their hundreds in order to restore order. Reprisals followed the next day: those believed complicit in the revolt were shot outside the city. Meanwhile, Francophile

Popular uprising in Madrid, 2 May 1808. When rumors reached the capital of Ferdinand's deposition and a plan to remove the remainder of the Royal Family to captivity in France, the crowd gathered in the Puerta del Sol grew hostile and began to attack the French garrison. Violence rapidly spread throughout the city, to be finally quelled by Murat's cavalry. Here, the inhabitants, armed with muskets, blunderbusses and knives, confront a body of dragoons. (Lithograph by Raffet, Roger-Viollet)

elements were said to have called on Napoleon's brother Joseph to be 'elected' king. Infuriated by the imposition of a foreign monarch, Spaniards across the provinces raised the standard of revolt. Starting on 9 May at Oviedo, capital of the Asturias, they held Ferdinand up as a martyr to French political machinations and established *ad hoc* military forces through regional 'juntas', or legislative assemblies. These sprang up across the country at Oviedo (24 May), Saragossa (25 May), Galicia (30 May), Catalonia (7 June) and elsewhere. They appeared rapidly, but the juntas failed to coordinate their efforts or agree on a common objective except for the extirpation of the French from Spanish soil. The strength of feeling was great and the conflict would soon come to acquire a highly emotive charge distinctly its own, carrying the evocative name of *La Guerra de la Independencia* (the War of Independence). Within a few weeks entire armies sprang up. In Andalusia alone General Francisco Xavier Castaños (1756–1852) raised 30,000 men.

That the French should employ a heavy-handed policy in sacking several major towns only increased the numbers of volunteers flocking to join the new armies. The war took on an altogether wider scope when the insurgent juntas appealed to Britain for help through a delegation led by the Count de Toreño, who arrived in London on 8 June and was enthusiastically received. George Canning (1770–1827), the Foreign Secretary, promised weapons, ammunition and funds. Other regional emissaries followed and the time had now come to intervene. On 14 June Sir Arthur Wellesley was appointed to command an expeditionary force of 9,500 men. Ironically, these were originally intended for operations against Spain's colonies in South America, to reverse General Whitelocke's complete failure at Buenos Aires of the previous year.

As discussed earlier, since 1793 Britain had had mixed success in her amphibious operations on the Continent, with little impact on the overall course of the campaigns fought by her allies. The French invasion of Portugal and Spain at last provided an opening on the European mainland into which British military resources could be channeled, and in many ways this opening was ideal. First, Britain could exploit to the full her complete mastery of the seas by safely transporting troops and all the requisites of war; second, the Peninsula was accessible from three directions by sea, whereas practically everything the French army required – men and matériel – had by necessity to cross the Pyrenees. Finally, a British expeditionary force could operate in friendly country, a particularly important factor in a land inhospitable to large-scale military operations. Campaigning on friendly soil would also facilitate supply, communication and intelligence gathering.

Notwithstanding these considerable advantages for Britain, in military terms Spain herself was in a wretched state. Her best troops – 15,000 men under La Romana – remained in Denmark, while, as noted earlier, the remainder of the army consisted of underfed, ill-clothed and poorly paid men led by idle and incompetent officers and corrupt generals. Moreover, many of those who might have provided some element of cohesion and leadership backed Joseph's liberal policies and wished to discourage popular resistance, whatever its cause.

But if the French had little to fear from the regular Spanish forces, there were still considerable natural obstacles to overcome. Indeed, geography and climate could hardly have been more forbidding to an invader than in the Peninsula. High mountains with narrow defiles served as ideal places of ambush; primitive unpaved roads produced clouds of dust in the summer and became churned into mud in the winter; bitterly cold nights and blisteringly hot days tormented troops exposed both on the march and in camp; and passes choked with snow seriously impeded the progress of both man and horse. In vast stretches of the country the soil was so deficient in moisture and nutrient that it barely kept the inhabitants alive much less provided forage for hundreds of thousands of foreign troops. The French had no choice but to detach thousands of troops to protect their vital lines of communications back over the Pyrenees. These, in turn, were vulnerable, in Portugal and, especially, in Spain, to irregulars of various descriptions. Some were patriot guerrillas and others just plain bandits, who began to operate first as individuals, rising to small groups and finally to larger *partidas*, or bands, murdering stragglers, hounding foraging parties, and intercepting couriers.

Meanwhile, as the revolt spread and Spanish armies rose seemingly from nowhere, Napoleon took swift action against this wholly unexpected tide of resistance. From Bayonne he issued orders to destroy the juntas and their military forces. General Merle routed the Army of Estremadura under General Don Gregorio de la Cuesta (1740–1812) at Cabezon, but Marshal Bon Adrien de Moncey's (1754–1842) 9,000 men were ejected from Valencia, and when General Charles Lefebvre-Desnouëttes

(1773–1822) attempted to seize the key Aragonese city of Saragossa he encountered extraordinarily bitter resistance on the part of its brave inhabitants, led by the 28-year-old General José Palafox (1780–1847) and backed by a small contingent of regulars. When the French summoned him to surrender, Palafox, with great bravado, returned a curt 'War to the death!', and the bitter struggle went on with quarter neither asked nor given. Twice the garrison forced their assailants to abandon the siege, leaving 3,500 French dead. Also under siege was Gerona, in eastern Catalonia, where in July the inhabitants courageously held off 6,000 French troops, rising to 13,000 the following month.

Further reverses lay in store for the French. In July Cuesta assumed command of the Army of Galicia and, though the Spanish were utterly routed at Medina del Rio Seco

French capitulation at Bailen, 21 July 1808. While attempting to pacify Andalusia General Dupont, with 17,000 men, unexpectedly encountered overwhelming regular and irregular forces, which obliged him to surrender his entire force. Bailen held enormous political significance extending well beyond the Pyrenees, for in addition to lending heart to resistance in the Peninsula itself, it completely dispelled the myth prevalent throughout Europe that the French could not be beaten. (Roger-Viollet)

on the 14th, only nine days later General Pierre Dupont (1765–1840), finding his army of 17,500 men isolated at Bailen, deep in Andalusia, capitulated his entire force to Castaños on condition that they would be repatriated to France. The victors, however, treacherously murdered many of the prisoners and confined the remainder to almost inevitable death aboard the prison-hulks at Cadiz. Dupont's surrender had a dreadful effect on French morale and a correspondingly positive effect on that of his adversaries, for not since General Menou's surrender in Egypt in 1801 had a French army laid down its arms. French prestige, and above all the myth that the army was invincible, suffered a shattering blow. That these were, in the main, not the same men who had triumphed at Austerlitz, Jena, and Friedland mattered little. That they were Napoleonic soldiers was sufficient for contemporary observers to appreciate the significance of the French debacle.

Quite apart from attracting British attention, Bailen and the rapid creation of new Spanish armies seriously upset French plans, and without reinforcements readily available to protect Madrid, King Joseph withdrew northwards to the protection of the strategic line behind the River Ebro.

With remarkable rapidity, by the end of the summer of 1808, the Spanish had inflicted 40,000 casualties on the invaders and had driven them from most of the country. Joseph soon recognized that his task of ruling would be near impossible. Writing to the Emperor he declared despondently:

It would take 200,000 Frenchmen to conquer Spain and 10,000 scaffolds to maintain the prince who should be condemned to reign over them. No, sire, you do not know this people; each house will be a fortress, and every man of the same mind as the majority ... Not a Spaniard will be on my side if we are conquerors.

With cruel irony, Joseph evidently failed to realize that French troops in Spain already numbered 200,000, an impressive figure which, by October, would rise still further to 286,000 with the arrival of the reinforcements brought by Napoleon himself.

Arrival of the British

With the withdrawal of French troops behind the Ebro, Junot now lay isolated in distant Portugal where, though he faced insurrection rather than organized opposition as in Spain, his task was nonetheless an unenviable one. There were no Portuguese armies in the field, but holding down a seething population was not a task for which Napoleonic armies were trained. The situation worsened dramatically in August. Wellesley's expedition had left Cork on 13 July. His instructions from the Secretary of State for War told him to support the Portuguese and Spanish in 'throwing off the yoke of France, and [securing] the final and absolute evacuation of the Peninsula by the troops of France.'

Wellesley landed at Mondego Bay, 80 miles north of Lisbon, on 1 August and was joined four days later by 5,000 men conveyed from Cadiz by General Sir Brent Spencer (1760–1828). Wellesley began his march on the capital on the 10th, learning on the way that, though he was to be reinforced by another 15,000 men, he was to

be superceded in command by Lieutenant-General Sir Hew Dalrymple (1750–1830) and Lieutenant-General Sir Harry Burrard (1755–1813). Before this took effect, however, Wellesley achieved his first, though minor, victory at Roliça on 17 August, suffering 479 casualties to General Henri Delaborde's (1764–1833) 600 men and three guns. The army continued its march on Lisbon. Three days later Burrard arrived and, much to Wellesley's displeasure, ordered a halt. As Burrard was still aboard ship and therefore had not yet assumed command in the field, Wellesley was pleased to discover that Junot was in fact advancing against him from the south. He therefore took up defensive positions along a ridge and a hill at the village of Vimiero, near the mouth of the Maceira River.

At 9.00 am on the 21st Junot appeared and launched four attacks against Vimiero Hill, all of which Wellesley's infantry, deployed in line, repulsed with heavy loss. Two other attacks against the eastern ridge also failed, and when the battle ceased at midday the French had lost 1,000 men and 14 guns to Wellesley's 720. British morale soared and the route to Torres Vedras and the capital now lay unopposed. Nevertheless, Burrard, who now arrived on the scene, refused to permit Wellesley to follow up his victory, and the army halted to await the arrival of Lieutenant-General Sir John Moore. Junot therefore withdrew without interference, leaving Wellesley bitter at his superior's ineptitude. Still, the victory proved significant: Wellington had made excellent use of natural cover, temporarily deploying his infantry behind the crest of a hill to conceal its position and to protect it from artillery fire, before unleashing disciplined firepower at the head of advancing French columns. Properly handled, a two-rank British line could defeat the headlong French assaults which had hitherto proved so successful on battlefields across Europe. The superiority of French tactics had now been called into question.

Two days later Dalrymple and Junot opened negotiations for surrender. Failing to appreciate the full extent of Junot's predicament, Dalrymple concluded the

Battle of Vimiero, 21 August 1808: The first major action between British and French troops in the Peninsula, Vimiero demonstrated the superiority of the two-deep British line over the hitherto virtually invincible French column. By successfully opposing French skirmishers with his own screen of light infantry, which could protect his more vulnerable formed units, Wellington stripped the column of its main advantage: shock power against an enemy already demoralized by preparatory skirmish fire. Moreover, by deploying his men on the reverse side of the slope, Wellington effectively shielded his troops from artillery, while simultaneously concealing his dispositions and strength. (Madeley, Philip Haythornthwaite)

disgraceful Convention of Cintra on 31 August. This not only permitted Junot to evacuate his troops back to France, rather than confine them as prisoners of war, but also provided for their conveyance, together with all their weapons and booty, in British ships. Portugal would thus be freed of French troops, but such favorable terms granted to an army manifestly incapable of further resistance provoked a storm of public outcry in Britain which led the War Office to recall the three generals involved to face a court of inquiry. Only Wellesley survived the experience with his reputation intact, since he had shared no direct part in this lamentable arrangement. Nevertheless, on receiving no new command he returned, intensely disappointed, to his political duties in Dublin as Chief Secretary of Ireland.

In the meantime command of the 30,000 British troops in Portugal passed to Lieutenant-General Sir John Moore, an experienced commander who had established a solid reputation for efficiency, professionalism, and innovative reforms of infantry tactics, above all, light infantry training, much of it carried out at Shorncliffe in the years immediately preceding the war. Moore was ordered to march into Spain to operate in conjunction with Spanish forces in driving the French out of the country. Accordingly, he began his advance in September, supported by another 15,000 under Major-General Sir David Baird (1757–1829), but his government's expectations were grossly unrealistic. The Spanish juntas had approximately 80,000 men in the field, but these were broken down into separate armies (of Galicia, Castile, Léon, Andalusia, Aragon, and Estremedura), each of which consisted of the poorly led, badly disciplined, ill-armed and ill-supplied rabble described earlier. To make matters worse, no coordinated plan existed between these armies, nor had the Spanish appointed a commander-in-chief with whom Moore could consult and cooperate. It soon became apparent that none of the various independent Spanish commanders was inclined to cooperate with, or properly supply, Moore.

Notwithstanding these serious disadvantages, on 18 October Moore began an advance on Burgos, where, in addition to joining Spanish forces watching the French across the Ebro, he planned to combine with the 10,000 men under Baird who had been transported to Corunna, on the northwest coast of Spain. Moore's army pushed on toward Salamanca over appalling roads, minus its complement of cavalry and artillery. Advised by the Spanish that the direct, northern route through Ciudad Rodrigo was impassable to artillery, Moore had sent them, under Sir John Hope (1765–1823), by an extremely circuitous southerly route via Badajoz and Madrid, to meet up with him in Salamanca. Worse still, Moore was as yet unaware that on 4 November Napoleon had arrived in Spain at the head of 125,000 men under his personal command, intent on expelling the British from the Peninsula and crushing the Spanish once and for all.

Incensed by Spanish resistance and the bunglings of his subordinates, the Emperor had shouted to Dumas: 'I can see very well that I must return and set the machine in motion again.' And from Erfurt on 13 October he wrote: 'The war must be terminated by a single *coup par manoeuvre* … My presence will be necessary.' Superior numbers led by the Emperor himself ought, Napoleon believed, to be more than sufficient to crush Spanish resistance decisively.

Accompanied by some of his greatest commanders, including Marshals Ney, Lannes, Jourdan, and Soult, and a host of other well-known generals, Napoleon and his *Grand Armée* opened an offensive on 6 November, sweeping aside all contenders, smashing the defenses at Burgos and arriving at Valladolid, midway to Madrid, on the 13th. At the same time Moore was reaching Salamanca, there to await Baird and Hope. From Valladolid Napoleon pushed on virtually unopposed toward the capital until, on the 30th he found the narrow defile at Somosierra blocked by 9,000 Spanish and a few pieces of artillery. Outflanking them was impossible without considerable delay. 'My Guard will not be stopped by peasants,' the Emperor declared, and, with scant regard for the lives of his men, ordered forward the 87 troopers of his Polish light cavalry escort in an attack that can only be described as suicidal. The horsemen, confined to a space only permitting four men to ride abreast, charged headlong into the guns, cut down the crews and galloped on to the crest, obliging the infantry to flee. The charge, followed up by further attacks by other units, succeeded, and passed into legend, but it cost the intrepid Poles half their number. The *Grande Armée* continued its inexorable advance, and entered Madrid on 4 December.

On 26 November, meanwhile, Moore learned that the bulk of Spanish forces had melted before the Emperor's advance. Thus abandoned by his inept allies to face the Napoleonic onslaught alone, Moore concluded that he must abandon attempts to advance on Burgos and order a withdrawal, a decision that met immediate and vociferous opposition not merely from the Spanish, but from his own subordinates and troops, who were itching to get to grips with the French.

Napoleon entering Spain, November 1808. Frustrated by the failure of his marshals to destroy the British Army, the Emperor determined to settle matters himself once and for all. 'The hideous leopard,' he announced to his soldiers in the flamboyant vocabulary reminiscent of his early campaigns in Italy and Egypt, 'contaminates by its presence the peninsula of Spain and Portugal. Let us carry our victorious Eagles to the Pillars of Hercules [Gibraltar].' (Roger-Viollet)

Moore found himself in a dreadful predicament: Hope arrived with the cavalry and artillery on 4 December, but Baird had reached no further than Astorga. Two days later, with enormous pressure building for him to continue the advance on Burgos and confront the French, Moore countermanded his orders for a withdrawal and again set the troops in motion. 'I was aware that I was risking infinitely too much,' he wrote, 'but something must be risked for the honour of the Service, and to make it apparent that we stuck to the Spaniards long after they had given up their cause for lost.'

A serious lack of intelligence left Moore unaware that Napoleon had entered Madrid on 4 December with an army of 80,000 men intent on destroying him. On the 11th Sir John therefore moved north with his meager 20,000 troops and finally linked up with Baird at Mayorga on the 20th, bringing his force up to 30,000. Two days later Napoleon, with the pick of his best troops, reached the snow-covered Guadarrama mountain range, whose high passes, though swept by a blizzard, he crossed with his army in pursuit of his still unsuspecting prey. All seemed well to Moore when, on Christmas Eve, with all his forces finally united, his army was *en route* for Carrion, where Marshal Nicolas Soult (1769–1851) lay temptingly vulnerable with a mere 16,000 men. Late that evening, however, Moore learned of Napoleon's advance from a captured dispatch. Now aware of the vastly superior forces threatening him, the British commander had no option but to order a general retreat.

The retreat to Corunna

Moore hoped to confront Soult's army before it combined forces with that under Junot, but when on 4 December he learned that Madrid had fallen, he concluded that the Spanish would never materialize to support him. With Napoleon in pursuit, Moore began a desperate winter retreat to Corunna on Christmas Day. Conducted over icy and snow-bound roads and abysmal mountain tracks, the march became a nightmare as discipline broke down and men collapsed from hunger, cold and exhaustion. The sick and wounded had to be left behind in the villages through which the army passed or sometimes literally abandoned on the roadside to face inevitable death from hunger or exposure, all for the lack of transport or strength to carry them. The rearguard, the elite Light Brigade, initially under Brigadier-General Robert 'Black Bob' Craufurd (1764–1812) and later Major-General Edward Paget (1775–1849), nonetheless offered a magnificent defense against the French van whenever it made contact, always managing to keep it at bay and allowing the main body to escape. The cavalry, under Lord Henry Paget (1768–1854) (Edward's brother), also played a vital role in holding back the pursuers. As the retreat progressed, much of Moore's formations disintegrated into a mere rabble which took to pillage and drink; in one instance, the column was obliged to abandon 1,000 drunken soldiers in the village of Bembibre, where most were massacred where they lay by French cavalry. One senior commissary officer observed that:

All orderly distribution was at an end. No officer or non-commissioned officer was respected … every soldier took what he liked, everything was plundered, carried away and trampled under foot … Although Villafranca is not small, every corner of it was soon full of men …Fresh troops were always streaming in, the stores of depots were also violently raided … In the end Villafranca was literally plundered, and the drunkenness that prevailed … led to the most shameful incidents.

Later during the retreat he added:

The road was strewn with dead horses, bloodstained snow, broken carts, scrapped ammunition boxes, cases, spiked guns, dead mules, donkeys and dogs, starved and frozen soldiers, women [soldiers' wives] and children … Discipline became ever more and more relaxed … Every hour the misery of the troops increased.

All along the route to Corunna the army trudged through knee-deep snow and mud with a line of frozen bodies marking the passage of the retreat.

On the 30th the army reached Astorga, 200 miles (322 km) from Corunna, where it was possible to stand and fight. Moore concluded, nevertheless, that a victory would achieve nothing, while a defeat would certainly destroy his demoralized army. Against bitter opposition from his generals, who advocated a stand, he therefore decided to press on, first dividing his force and sending south to Vigo the 3,500 men of the Light Brigade and the King's German Legion. Napoleon had meanwhile passed command of the army on to Soult, while he himself returned to quash political intrigue brewing in Paris. Though the Emperor promised to return to Spain he never did, and the conquest of the country was left in the hands of men who would never, for reasons which will become clear later, complete this formidable task.

At last, on 11 January 1809, Moore's ragged but unbroken army – they had not lost a single gun or color – reached Corunna, where Shaumann saw the shattered remnant

of men '... all in tatters, hollow eyed, and covered with blood and filth. They looked so terrible that the people made the sign of the cross as they passed ...' The promised transports were not yet in the harbor, but, fortunately for Moore, by the time Soult's main body of 20,000 (with the same number *en route*) appeared, the ships had arrived and an orderly disembarkation was already under way, covered by a force of 15,000 men and 12 guns. Soult attacked on 16 January in a pitched battle outside the town, in the course of which Moore, at the cost of his own life, first repulsed and then drove back his assailants several miles. By dusk the fighting was over, with 800 British casualties, including the much-loved Sir John, whom his men interred in the ramparts of the city. The embarkation duly continued and was completed on the 19th, when the remnants of the army sailed for England.

On its surface the campaign appeared to have ended in unmitigated disaster for the British, having cost them 6,000 men and a large quantity of weapons and equipment. The French remained in possession of most of Spain and Portugal and the British government, under the Duke of Portland, was justifiably reluctant to undertake any future offensive operations. On the other hand, notwithstanding their relentless

Battle of Corunna, 16 January 1809. Following its horrific retreat from Sahagun, Sir John Moore's army reached the northwest coast of Spain with the French close in pursuit. Soult nevertheless unwisely chose to concentrate his forces before launching an attack, thus providing Moore with a two-day respite in which to rest, re-supply and evacuate much of his army by sea. Sir John's superb defense, which cost him his own life, obliged the French to retire and enabled the remaining British troops to embark without further harassment. (Ann Ronan Picture Library)

pursuit, the French had failed to destroy Moore's army, and though it had endured a terrible campaign, its march and subsequent retreat was to shape the future course of the war decisively. In short, by continuing his advance on Burgos, Moore had obliged Napoleon to focus his attention on the British rather than the Spanish forces. This provided the British vital time with which to consolidate their defenses in Portugal and their Spanish allies with an opportunity to recuperate and prepare for the next campaign season. The vital British base at Lisbon was therefore preserved and the French had yet to conquer southern Spain. Moore's actions, therefore, may well have prevented a complete French victory by the end of 1808.

But if the French had found themselves unable to destroy Moore's army, they were nevertheless successful elsewhere, utterly

Retreat to Corunna

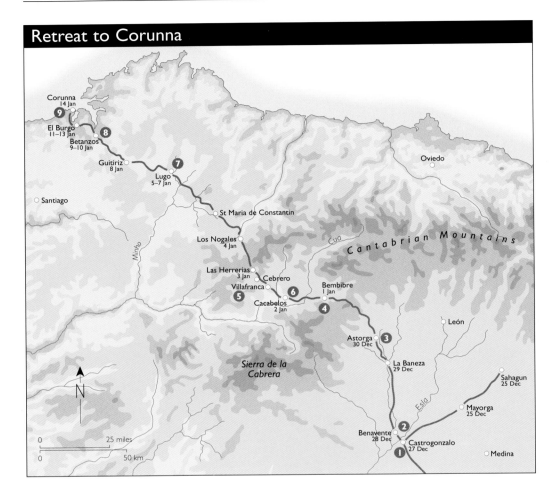

1. Castrogonzalo. Moore crosses River Esla, blowing the bridge behind him. Enters Galician mountains.

2. Benavente. Demoralized by retreating rather than facing the French in battle, troops loot and pillage the town. On 29 December 600 Imperial Guard cavalry are defeated by British cavalry, losing almost 200.

3. Astorga. Moore chooses not to stand; detaches two brigades by different routes to Vigo.

4. Bembibre. Troops raid wine cellars and get exceedingly drunk. 1,000 left behind are mostly massacred by French cavalry.

5. Villafranca. Starving vanguard raids depot containing fortnight's supply of food.

6. Cacebelos. Moore's rearguard puts up stiff resistance against Soult's pursuing vanguard.

7. Lugo. Moore halts and prepares to fight, but Soult refuses to oblige him.

8. Betanzos. Troops emerge from the mountains.

9. Corunna. Survivors reach their destination after a 312 mile (499km) march. Royal Navy transports arrive 14 January. Embarkation begins immediately. Soult defeated outside town on 16th, but Moore killed.

crushing the Spanish at Ucles in January and at Medellin in March. Defeating in open battle the sometimes sizable though nevertheless feeble regular armies of the juntas was no great challenge for veteran French forces, but siege operations proved altogether more vicious and bloody undertakings. Nowhere was this more true than in the capital city of Aragon, Saragossa, whose people, supported by a contingent of regular troops and large numbers of the local peasantry, grimly resisted the siege laid against them in December. As Marbot recalled:

The town was surrounded by immense and solidly built convents; these were fortified and guns placed in them. All the houses were loopholed [the walls being perforated to facilitate small arms fire] and the streets barricaded;

powder, cannon-balls, and bullets were manufactured, and great stores of food collected. All the inhabitants enrolled themselves ... The besieged only agreed on one point: to defend themselves to the death ... Religious fanaticism and the sacred love of country exalted their courage, and they blindly resigned themselves to the will of God.

Manuela Sanchez, the 'Maid of Saragossa'. After the crew of a cannon, including her fiancé, was wiped out by French fire, she boldly lit the fuse with a party of advancing infantry only yards away. Thousands of Spanish women took an active part in civilian resistance, particularly in the defense of cities like Saragossa and Gerona. Most tended the wounded, cooked, and brought forward ammunition and water, but others took up arms beside the men. (Ann Ronan Picture Library)

In the course of two months the city was reduced by sappers employing a systematic combination of mining and desperate assaults. 'Never have I seen such keen determination,' Marshal Lannes informed the Emperor by dispatch. 'I have seen women come to be killed in the breach. Every house has to be taken by storm ...' At last, on 20 February, after a horrendous trial in which the citizens, even in the midst of starvation and disease, had engaged in savage house-to-house fighting at a total cost exceeding 50,000 lives, fewer than half of whom were soldiers, the city capitulated. Such instances of unmatched civilian resistance highlighted the incompetence of the regular Spanish armies and marked a new and dreadful chapter in

warfare. If any single episode in the Peninsular War symbolized Spanish defiance, it was the siege of Saragossa.

Operations in 1809

Despite the evacuation of Moore's army the British government decided to continue the war in support of Portugal, where 16,000 British troops still remained defending Lisbon. Renewed effort came in the form of a second expeditionary force, dispatched in April under Wellesley, who, delighted by his return, had prepared an 'Appreciation of the Situation' for his superiors in which he had laid out the clear strategy that was to guide him for the remainder of the war. Since the government was only prepared to commit a small force, Wellesley had to assure ministers that he could defend Portugal with 20,000 British troops in conjunction with a reorganized Portuguese army. Protecting Portugal, he argued, could be achieved provided that Spain continued to resist occupation and supported Britain's efforts. He further maintained that Spain's sheer size and the ferocity of her population to foreign occupation would make it impossible for the French to subdue the country entirely.

Wellesley's strategy also depended on continued British control of the sea and, critically – and this could not be guaranteed – he had at all costs to preserve his small force from defeat or severe loss, whether in action or from disease. This highly uncertain condition, Sir Arthur argued, partly depended on his being able to prevent the French from concentrating overwhelming strength against him. Finally, he concluded, severe supply difficulties, exacerbated by overextended lines of communication, and coupled with continuous attacks by partisans, would all hamper the French and favor his own prospects for defending Portugal and eventually carrying the campaign into the heart of Spain.

Wellesley landed at Lisbon on 22 April, a mere three months after Moore's army had embarked at Corunna. The British controlled southern Portugal, but to the north Marshal Soult, with 20,000 men, controlled the area from Coimbra stretching north, including the important coastal town of Oporto. With exceptional speed Wellesley reorganized his army in an effort to improve its mobility and fighting capability. Chief amongst the changes he introduced was the amalgamation of his various brigades into divisions which, with their own commanders and staff, could operate with considerably more independence than hitherto. He also began to rebuild the Portuguese army, placing British officers at all levels of command and assigning a Portuguese battalion to each of his exclusively British brigades. Thus began a

process which, over the course of the next several years, would witness the rapid growth of competently trained and led Portuguese forces as an integral part of the allied effort.

Within a fortnight of his arrival Wellesley's preparations were complete. He was ready to march against one of the three armies opposing him: Marshal Soult in the north, General Pierre Lapisse (1762–1809) near Ciudad Rodrigo, and Marshal Claude Victor (1764–1841) to the south at Talavera. Both Lapisse and Victor could cross into Portugal, and were the three forces to combine, Wellesley would face double his own numbers. On the other hand, the French armies were separated by considerable distances and rough terrain, and Wellesley confidently believed he could defeat each in turn before they could oppose him as a combined force. He intended to confront Soult first, ejecting him from Portugal before confronting Victor in the south. Thus, leaving 12,000 troops under General Mackenzie to defend Lisbon, and sending 6,000 men under General William Beresford (1764–1854) to march east to block Soult's line of retreat, he set out on 8 May with 16,000 British, 2,400 Portuguese and 24 guns. His object was to cross the River Douro at Oporto, which Soult had occupied on 29 March.

Reaching the Douro early on 12 May, Wellesley discovered Soult ensconced on the opposite side, having destroyed the only bridge across the river and moved every boat to the north bank. Confident that he was protected from an attack across the river, the French commander was therefore caught completely unprepared when Wellesley boldly ferried several hundred men across in barges – wine-barges, appropriately enough in this city – provided by the populace. By the time the French discovered the presence of the British, their chance of driving them into the water was lost, and every counterattack was repulsed. Further upstream meanwhile, at Avintas, more British troops effected a crossing, preventing Soult and his 11,000 men from withdrawing in that direction. The best route of escape lay to the east, blocked by Beresford; Soult therefore had no option but to leave behind most of his transport and retreat into the mountains to the north.

The crossing of the Douro and the victory at Oporto demonstrated Wellesley's ability to act boldly and decisively, and to conceive and execute plans with little preparation time. As a result, the French were forced to abandon Portugal for a second time, having sustained heavy losses in men and equipment. The resulting blow to French morale gave a boost to the Allies, and with Soult out of the way Wellesley was free to proceed south against Victor. Elsewhere, the French, finding themselves constantly under guerrilla attack, as well as by La Romana's regulars, withdrew from Galicia.

Wellesley's operations in Spain were now to involve him in collaboration with the military forces of that country. This posed a number of problems, for without any unified command the Spanish armies had no coherent strategy, leaving Wellesley unable to coordinate his efforts with the various Spanish generals in the field, each of whom jealously operated on his own terms with little inclination to support his own colleagues, much less Wellesley. Yet operating on Spanish soil obliged the British commander-in-chief to cooperate with the Spanish generals, insofar as they permitted it, in particular with Cuesta. Thirty years Wellesley's senior, ill-tempered, stubborn, and utterly unfit to command, Cuesta neither trusted Wellesley nor wished to accept his advice, and only communicated through his own chief of staff. Rifleman Harris described him as 'that deformed-looking lump of pride, ignorance and treachery … He was the most murderous-looking old man I ever saw.' If Cuesta were not bad enough, the junta was worse, having promised Wellesley food and transport which in the end never materialized.

On 10 July, with his army of 20,000 at Plasencia, Wellesley met with Cuesta, who was in command of 35,000 men, to negotiate a joint strategy. Relations between the two were prickly, but they nonetheless agreed to join forces at Oropesa and to move their combined 55,000 troops against Victor's much smaller force of 22,000 at Talavera. The French had other forces, in Madrid and just south of the

capital, but measures were taken to try to prevent them from uniting with Victor. Thus, on 21 July, British and Spanish forces united as agreed and Cuesta, as planned, proceeded towards Victor's position at the River Alberche, while Wellesley stood in reserve. The two allied generals agreed to attack together on the 23rd, but when at sunrise Wellesley's forces were ready to open the engagement, the Spanish were nowhere to be seen. Wellesley found their commander three hours later, sleeping soundly. When awakened Cuesta announced that his troops were too tired to attack, and by this off-hand and unaccountable manner a splendid opportunity was thus lost to the allied cause. Wellesley, livid, not least because lack of the promised Spanish supplies had left his troops without adequate food for two days, was powerless to stop Victor from withdrawing, which that marshal did that evening entirely unopposed.

In a bizarre move Cuesta then decided to follow the French on his own, and on the 24th he proceeded towards the capital, only to be confronted and routed on the following day at Alcabon by 46,000 French, who then pursued him to the Alberche. Local circumstances had suddenly shifted in favor of the French, who now possessed a united force comprising both King Joseph's forces and those of Marshal Victor, which had been brought together in order to defeat Cuesta. Together these well outnumbered Wellesley, who was obliged quickly to take up a defensive position. At this Wellesley was clearly adept, and he accordingly chose a strong post north of the town of Talavera. Firmly fixed, he awaited the inevitable attack.

Wellesley had a theoretical strength of 55,000, but only 20,000 of these, plus 36 guns, were his own troops, the remaining being Cuesta's unreliable Spanish. The army under King Joseph was composed of 46,000 troops and 86 guns – twice the size of the British and King's German Legion (KGL) force. The French attacked the allied left on the night of the 27th, but were repulsed. They resumed the offensive on the following day, when several thousand Spanish ran off at the outset of the fighting. The French

Charge of the 48th Foot at Talavera. The collapse of Sherbrooke's division in the course of the fighting left an enormous gap in the British line that threatened the whole army with imminent defeat. Unable to spare an entire brigade from the Cerro de Medellin, Wellesley deployed only the 800-strong 48th Foot and two regiments of Light Dragoons as a temporary plug. The 48th lost nearly a quarter of its strength in killed and wounded – not untypical of Napoleonic battles. (Ann Ronan Picture Library)

assaulted several points along Wellesley's line, but successive attacking columns were driven off by British volleys, and at last the French withdrew.

Lieutenant Simmons recorded the appalling sight of the field of Talavera in the aftermath of the carnage:

Thousands dead and dying in every direction, horses, men, French and English, in whole lines who had cut each other down and I am sorry to say the Spaniards butchering the wounded French-men at every opportunity and stripping them naked.

The following day his brigade was assigned the unenviable job of 'collecting the dead bodies and putting them into large heaps mixed with faggots and burning them. The stench from so many dead bodies was volatile and offensive beyond conception as the heat of the weather was very great.' The sound of the wounded was dreadful, as well. August Schaumann, a British commissary officer, encountered a convent in the town requisitioned as a hospital:

Never shall I forget the heart-rending cries which could be heard coming from the windows … [from one of which] … the amputated arms and legs were being flung out upon a small square below. In front of the door lay the wounded, who had been deposited there as fast as they arrived, awaiting their turn. Many of them were already dead.

The defensive tactics employed by Wellesley at Talavera proved, like those used at Roliça and Vimiero, to be highly effective against massed French columns of attack. British skirmishers had shown themselves to be the match of their French counterparts: Wellesley had once again positioned his men behind the crest of a hill to shield them from the more numerous French artillery, and, most significantly, once again a pitched battle revealed the superiority of the British line against the French column. Infantry firepower, when withheld until the attacker was

Battle of Talavera, 27–28 July 1809

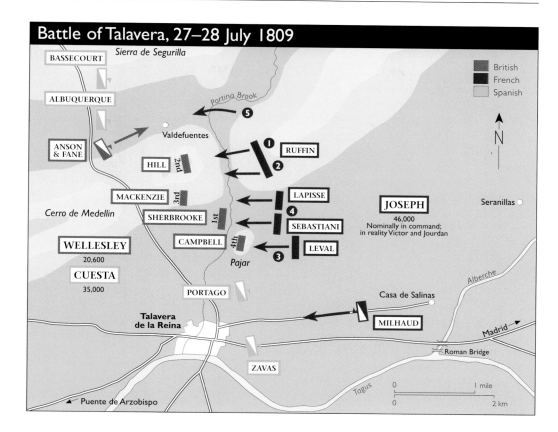

1. 27 July 9.00 pm. As a prelude to the main action to open on the 28th, Ruffin launches a surprise night attack against a ridge called the Cerro de Medellin and narrowly fails to take it.

2. 5.00 am 28 July. After an intense bombardment by 53 guns, Ruffin's division of 4,300 again attacks Hill's position on the Medellin; repulsed with heavy losses from musketry by infantry deployed in line. Informal truce of several hours follows.

3. 1.15 pm. As a diversion for the main attack to be made against the Medellin, Leval assaults Campbell's 4th Division on the Pajar, but is repulsed.

4. 1.30 pm. After a bombardment by 80 guns, Sebastiani and Lapisse launch main thrust, but are repulsed.

5. 2.40 pm. Ruffin attacks again. British cavalry charge.

close at hand and immediately followed by a spirited bayonet charge, had proved devastatingly effective. Lastly, Wellesley had made himself conspicuous to his troops under fire, constantly moving from one section to another, encouraging the men, issuing orders directly and observing the progress of the fighting.

Having said this, Wellesley's achievement, though a victory, was dearly bought,

costing a quarter of his effective strength (5,300 casualties) compared to the French, who lost less than a fifth of theirs, or 7,200. Though French losses were higher in absolute terms, they could afford these much more than could Wellesley, who also suffered a particular shortage of cavalry at this time. Indeed, numerical inferiority, especially in terms of cavalry and artillery, would constantly plague the Allied war effort in the Peninsula, and it would become a testament to Wellesley's eventual greatness that he consistently devised successful methods and strategies to compensate for these deficiencies. News of the victory created a sensation back in Britain, whose hero was raised to the peerage as Viscount Wellington.

Despite his victory at Talavera, Wellington could not afford to be complacent. He withdrew across the Tagus when, on 3 August, he was informed that an army of 50,000 under Soult was marching south from Salamanca in a bid to block his communications with

Portugal. On the 20th he retreated still further, to Badajoz, on the Spanish-Portuguese border, from which he could defend the southern route to Lisbon. The retreat was a dreadful affair; not, perhaps, comparable to Corunna, but Wellington's troops suffered badly from shortages of food. Refuge just over the border in Portugal would have suited Wellington better, but, recognizing the importance of preserving the delicate Anglo-Spanish relationship, he remained on Spanish territory.

Wellington well appreciated that the war would not be won overnight and that he must take a long-term view of the situation. The French might yet invade Portugal a third time, and if they did so with sufficient strength the Allied armies could not, unaided, hold back the tide. Therefore, in October, to compensate for his numerical inferiority he devised what in time would prove a brilliant plan of defense. In that month he left the army cantonment in Spain and, in the company of his engineers, surveyed the area around Lisbon. After extensive planning they devised a scheme for a series of fortifications which, in three lines, were to run north and west of Lisbon and to be manned by a small contingent of British troops and tens of thousands of Portuguese militia, known as the *Ordenenza*. These defensive works were to become the famous Lines of Torres Vedras. Work began immediately, and tens of thousands of Portuguese laborers toiled to construct the Lines, a task which occupied them for the next 12 months. So effective was the veil of secrecy surrounding the project that the French would have no inkling of its existence until they actually arrived before the Lines towards the end of the following year.

Having safely ensconced himself in and around Badajoz, Wellington did not undertake any major operations for the remainder of the year, and so incensed was he with the antics of his Spanish allies that he adamantly declined to operate jointly with them. They had failed to seize the opportunity to defeat the French in July and when, a few days later, Wellington was confronted alone at Talavera, he had been lucky to withstand the assault. Worse still, even while the British were in the midst of the

battle, fleeing Spanish soldiers had looted British baggage wagons in the rear. Nor had Wellington received the promised supplies and food. In short, he was unwilling to jeopardize his army when the Spanish had repeatedly proven themselves both incompetent and unreliable. 'Till the evils of which I think I have reason to complain are remedied …,' he wrote in agitation, 'I cannot enter into any system of co-operation with the Spanish Army.'

Still, to their considerable credit, the Spanish continued to fight on, albeit independently, and defeated the French at Alcaniz on 23 May and again on 18 October at Tamames. But these successes, like those few before them, were short-lived. They were defeated at Almonacid on 10 August and, on 19 November, 52,000 Spanish commanded by General Areizago were routed at Ocaña, losing 18,000 men, 50 guns and 30 colors. Only 10 days later, at Alba de Tormes, they were trounced again, with 3,000 casualties to the tiny loss to the French of just 300. Moreover, on 11 December Gerona finally surrendered after an eight-month siege – another epic defense, albeit on a somewhat smaller scale than Saragossa. Such consistent Spanish reverses put the French in a better position to threaten Portugal, leaving Wellington little option but to re-cross the border on 9 December and await the new season for campaigning in the spring.

If Spain's fortunes appeared to be on the wane, for Wellington the campaign of 1809 ended on a fairly satisfactory note. With a small army he had, in consequence of Oporto, evicted the French from Portugal for the second time, and though his campaign in Spain had miscarried, he had managed to defeat his opponent's counteroffensive at Talavera. His army remained intact, its morale, training, and efficiency were constantly rising, and Beresford's reforms were gradually taking effect in the Portuguese ranks, though they had not yet been tested in action. As for the Spanish, though their armies continued to suffer successive defeats, they always returned to the contest, diverting sizable French forces from operating against Wellington or subduing the guerrillas, and inflicting casualties in battle.

Operations in 1810

With the end of Napoleon's campaign against Austria, culminating in the Battle of Wagram on 5–6 July 1809, substantial numbers of French troops could be shifted for service in the Peninsula. By early 1810 there were 325,000 men in Spain – far more than the Allies. With peace reigning throughout the Napoleonic Empire except in Spain, Joseph ought to have had greater success; but holding down an entire hostile population was proving impossible. 'My power does not extend beyond Madrid,' he complained to the Emperor, 'and at Madrid itself I am daily thwarted … I am only King of Spain by the force of your arms.' To Napoleon winning the hearts and minds of the Spanish by the introduction of liberal political and social reforms was not the answer. Only a military solution would suffice: 'You will not succeed in Spain except by vigour and energy. This parade of goodness and clemency ends in nothing.'

Wellington, of course, faced his own problems. French forces outnumbered him by many times and against such odds he had to remain on the defensive. His policy was severely criticized by both the British and Spanish governments for his apparent inactivity, yet he wisely spent the first nine months of the year preparing his army and the country for an anticipated third invasion of Portugal. A French advance could come from three possible directions: from the center down the River Tagus, where Wellington placed Beresford's Portuguese troops; from the south via Badajoz, where he put Sir Rowland Hill with 7,000 British and 13,000 Portuguese; or from the north, through Ciudad Rodrigo and Almeida, which Wellington thought was the most likely direction of attack. Therefore, he marched his remaining troops to protect this route. In front of this position the Light Division provided both a screen for the army and intelligence on French movements. These tasks they performed extremely well, and the French were unable to probe Wellington's position to assess his strength or dispositions.

Wellington spent much of his time improving his defense, his intelligence network and in reorganization and training. At the same time Beresford continued to improve and expand the Portuguese forces under his command, and in the course of the year he integrated whole Portuguese brigades into most of the all-British/KGL divisions. He also improved and expanded the Portuguese militia, thus freeing up regular troops for service in the line. In addition to relying on Portuguese and Spanish guerrillas and other civilians for intelligence, Wellington also acquired information from his own intelligence officers, sent deep behind hostile lines to gather information on French strength and dispositions. And, as part of his general defensive measures in Portugal, he received permission from Portuguese officials to implement a policy of what would now be known as 'scorched earth'; in short, should the French actually invade as expected, they would find themselves deprived of crops, equipment and transport. Throughout this period the construction of the Lines of Torres Vedras continued steadily, supervised by the Chief Engineer, Lieutenant Colonel Sir Richard Fletcher (1768–1813), all unbeknown to the French.

It was now only a matter of time before he would confront the French in battle, and as he was to do many years later at Waterloo, Wellington set out to select a particularly strong defensive position for just such a purpose. The direction of his adversary's approach was, of course, unknown, but it became immediately obvious to the British C-in-C that if the French obliged him, the 11 mile (18 km) long, 1,000 ft (315 m) ridge at Busaco would be an ideal position to defend, rising as it did extremely sharply from its base. On the reverse side of the summit he therefore constructed a road running the length of the ridge, thus facilitating the movement of troops from one sector of the battlefield to another – completely out of sight of the attacker.

The French were not idle during this period. In April 1810 Napoleon sent Marshal

Masséna to the Peninsula with orders to reconquer Portugal. This clear objective notwithstanding, the French system of command would nevertheless continue to be hampered by the absence of an overall commander in Spain and the consequent necessity of communicating with Paris. This was a time-consuming and expensive practice which often meant that changing circumstances rendered reports and orders completely obsolete by the time they were issued or received.

The campaign opened in May when Masséna proceeded to besiege the vital border fortress of Ciudad Rodrigo, which controlled the northern corridor between Spain and Portugal. The fortress, held by 5,500 Spanish troops under Herrasti, surrendered on 10 July. Against the wishes of the Spanish government as well as his own troops, Wellington had refused to come to the city's relief, as the risks seemed clearly to outweigh the benefits. But British forces were not wholly inactive, for a fortnight later Marshal Michel Ney (1769–1815), with 24,000 troops, advanced and fought the Light Division, which narrowly escaped disaster along the rocky banks of the River Coa. The Portuguese counterpart to Ciudad Rodrigo was Almeida, another strong fortress, but it fell prematurely when on 26 August French artillery fire ignited loose powder, causing a catastrophic explosion in the magazine that left 500 dead and obliged the garrison commander to capitulate on the 28th. With the fall of Ciudad Rodrigo and Almeida the French had succeeded in opening the northern invasion route between the two countries. Nonetheless, Wellington had reason for some hope, for when Masséna finally continued his march west on 15 September, he chose precisely the route that Wellington had hoped and marched straight toward the ridge at Busaco.

Wellington duly positioned his troops according to the plans he had devised months before and summoned the 20,000 men under Hill to reinforce him. That completed, Wellington had a formidable 52,000 men, half of whom were

RIGHT Busaco demonstrated not only the superiority of the British line versus the French column but the benefits of a strong defensive position, even without earthworks.
1. 5.45 am Merle's division (11 btns) attacks in column; repulsed.
2. 6. 00 am Heudelet attacks with four battalions; also repulsed, in part by spirited charge of the 88th Foot (Connaught Rangers).
3. 6.00 am Foy attacks Picton's 3rd Division with seven battalions north of San Antonio; repulsed.
4. 8.15 am Loison attacks with 12 battalions (6,000), unaware that the Lt Div. (1,800) lay behind the crest; also repulsed with a loss of 1,200.
5. 9.00 am Marchand attacks with 11 battalions versus Packs' Portuguese Brigade; repulsed.

now Portuguese, as against 65,000 French. Though outnumbered, Wellington had had more than a year to train his troops, and though the Portuguese were as yet untried, they too had undergone extensive training. On 27 September Masséna flung his columns against the ridge in wave after wave, all to no avail. Every assault was repulsed and the Portuguese, for their part, fought creditably. Rather than pursue his beaten foe, Wellington implemented the strategy he had planned for just such a situation: withdrawal to the protection of the Lines of Torres Vedras, destroying everything in his path that could be of use to the French. The army suffered less during this withdrawal than during the retreats of 1809, but the civilians who accompanied it underwent terrible hardships: Schaumann noted in his diary that

The retreat … from Coimbra to the fortified lines presented a sad spectacle. The roads were littered with smashed cases and boxes, broken wagons and carts, dead horses and exhausted men. Every division was accompanied by a body of refugees as great as itself and rich and poor alike, either walking, or mounted on horses or donkeys, were to be seen all higgledy-piggledy – men and women, young and old, mothers leading children, or carrying them on their backs, nuns who had left their convents, and, quite strange to the world, either wandered about helplessly, beside themselves with fear, looking timidly for their relations, or else, grown bold, linked arms with the soldiers and carried the

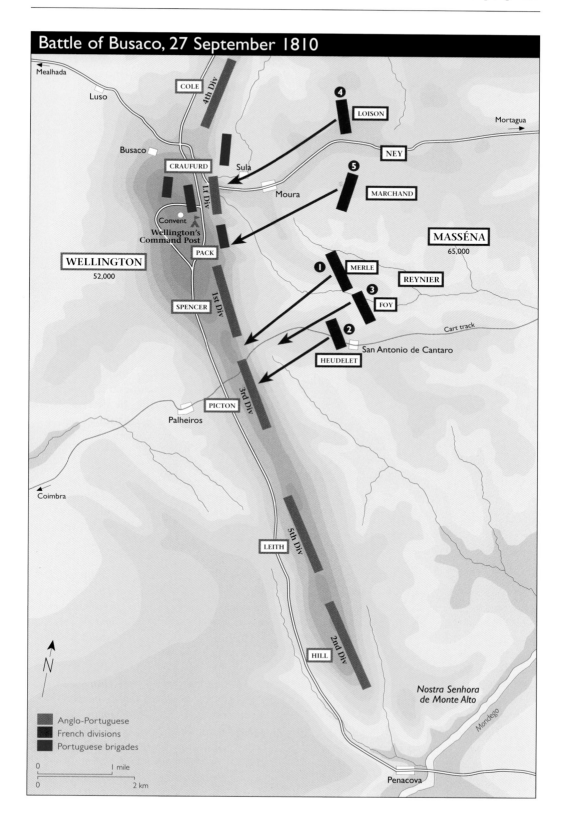

Battle of Busaco, 27 September 1810

Mealhada
Luso
COLE
4th Div
Busaco
CRAUFURD
Sula
Moura
LOISON
Mortagua
NEY
MARCHAND
Lt Div
Convent
Wellington's
Command Post
PACK
MERLE
REYNIER
MASSÉNA
65,000
WELLINGTON
52,000
1st Div
SPENCER
FOY
Cart track
HEUDELET
San Antonio de Cantaro
PICTON
3rd Div
Palheiros
Coimbra
LEITH
5th Div
HILL
2nd Div
Nostra Senhora
de Monte Alto
Mondego
Penacova

Anglo-Portuguese
French divisions
Portuguese brigades

0   1 mile
0   2 km

Battle of Busaco, 27 September 1810. French infantry struggling uphill against severe artillery and small arms fire. At one point they could see nothing but the lone figure of Major-General Robert 'Black Bob' Craufurd, commander of the Light Division, unaware that concealed in a sunken road behind him lay the 43rd and 52nd Foot. As the attackers approached the summit Craufurd turned round and cried, 'Now Fifty Second! Avenge Moore!' With a mighty 'Huzza!' the 52nd bounded forward with the bayonet, forcing the French to flee in disorder. (Roger-Viollet)

latter's knapsacks. Monks, priests and invalids – everybody was taking flight. The nearer the procession came to Lisbon, the greater the number of animals belonging to the refugees that fell dead either from fatigue or hunger; and very soon the ladies were to be seen wading in torn silk shoes, or barefoot through the mud. Despair was written on all faces.

Masséna accepted the bait and followed closely on Allied heels, still unaware of the existence of the Lines until they hove into view on 10 October. These fortifications had been constructed with such skill that they required only 2,500 British troops, 25,000 Portuguese militia and 8,000 Spanish regulars to defend them. The French marshal recognized their strength immediately, but sought confirmation by probing them on the 14th. This proved a costly failure, and with no prospect of penetrating the defenses Masséna declined to try again. Instead he established his camp to their front, hoping to coax Wellington out. But he prudently remained in place, well fed and supplied by the Royal Navy. Masséna, by contrast, with his supplies exhausted and facing the devastation deliberately wrought on the countryside by Wellington's retreating troops, was forced to withdraw to Santarem on 15 November. Wellington emerged from the Lines and advanced by degrees, but chose not to attack, for he dared not risk his army until the opportunity was right. His strategy proved successful, for starvation and disease that winter cost the French 25,000 men – all without a fight. Thus, the Lines of Torres Vedras had served their purpose brilliantly, completely frustrating French hopes of taking Lisbon, and rendering northern Portugal effectively untenable.

Operations in 1811

While Masséna's men languished on meager rations at Santarem, Wellington's army remained in complete safety and well supplied in its camps behind the Lines of Torres Vedras. Soult continued his siege of Badajoz, while other forces captured Olivenza on 22 January and defeated the Spanish at the Gebora River on 19 February. As for the Anglo-Portuguese, the year 1811 was to be a more active one for these forces than the previous year, with three pitched battles: Barrosa (5 March), Fuentes de Oñoro (3–5 May), and Albuera (16 May), two of which would be fought by Wellington's subordinates.

Since January 1810 an Anglo-Spanish force of 26,000 had been besieged in Cadiz, in the extreme south of the country and the seat of the Supreme Junta. In February 1811 the commander decided to use 13,000 of these in an attack by land and sea against the investing army. But General La Peña, leading the Spanish contingent, bungled the operation, leaving Sir Thomas Graham's 5,000 British troops unsupported at Barrosa, where on 5 March Marshal Victor struck

with 9,000 troops. Despite numerical inferiority Graham risked everything in a daring counterattack and succeeded.

That same day Masséna, unable to confront Wellington while he remained behind the Lines, incapable of feeding his starving and disease-ridden army around Santarem in a region devastated by the Allied policy of 'scorched earth', and continually dogged by guerrilla activity, began withdrawing his dejected men into Spain, reaching Salamanca on 11 April. In the process he had had to leave behind most of his transport and had lost 25,000 out of the 65,000 men with which he had started the campaign, fewer than half of whose losses were accounted for by battle losses and prisoners. Thus the Lines of Torres Vedras

Torres Vedras, the main area around which Wellington ordered construction of what proved to be impregnable 'Lines' extending across Portugal from the River Tagus to the Atlantic. The Lines served two purposes: to prevent the French from taking the vital supply base at Lisbon, and to enable Wellington time in which to evacuate the country in the event of unforeseen disaster. They proved brilliantly successful in 1810–1811. Here French troops are shown engaged in an unsuccessful probe near Agraco on 14 October 1810. (Ann Ronan Picture Library)

proved exceptionally cost effective to the Allies. As soon as Masséna had begun his retreat from Santarem the Allies followed, amused by the straw dummy sentries which the French had left behind to try to trick them. Except for the garrison at Almeida, the French had now been forced out of Portugal for the third time.

Nonetheless, Soult had managed to effect the surrender of the key frontier city of Badajoz on 10 March, and with its possession and that of Ciudad Rodrigo, the French held both routes connecting Spain and Portugal. In order to defend the latter, Wellington had therefore to observe both cities, thus dividing his small army of 58,000 by 120 miles (193 km). Masséna and Soult, were they able to join their respective forces, could mass a minimum of 70,000 men. With his forces divided and his lines of communications dangerously long, Wellington established 38,000 men under himself at Frenada in the north, while General Beresford, with 20,000, marched south. On 25 March Beresford defeated the French in a minor action at Campo Mayor and the following month he besieged Badajoz, though without a siege train the prospects of success were very slim indeed. Wellington advised Beresford, should Soult attack him, to consider establishing his defense at Albuera, a village 14 miles southeast of Badajoz.

At the beginning of May Masséna led his 48,000 troops west, with the intention of relieving the garrison at Almeida, the only French troops left in Portugal. Wellington had, as noted, only 38,000 with which to oppose him, but he employed his time as before, seeking an advantageous position of defense where he could meet the French on his own terms. He chose the area around the village of Fuentes de Oñoro, just over the border in Spain. It was nothing like as strong a position as he had enjoyed at Busaco, but he hoped Masséna would employ the same unimaginative tactics as before: a simple frontal attack.

On 3 May the marshal did precisely that, and Wellington's infantry drove back the attackers with the same methods employed elsewhere in the Peninsula. A lull followed on the 4th, but on the next day Masséna tried again, now from the south, where he nearly turned the allied flank. Anglo-Portuguese troops fought stubbornly and though pushed back, the Light Division performed well, and the cavalry, brilliantly. Once again Wellington's unique defensive tactics, his close supervision of the action and the dogged resistance of his infantry yielded another victory, and in the end the French withdrew. The narrow streets and alleys were clogged with heaps of dead, fallen in bitter hand-to-hand fighting. It was not long before Napoleon sent the more competent Marshal Auguste Marmont (1774–1852) to succeed Masséna.

Wellington's victory was significant, but it was tempered by two less fortunate events later that week. Major-General Sir William Erskine (1769–1813), commanding the force investing Almeida, bungled the operation so badly that on the night of 10/11 May, General Antoine-Francois Brennier (1767–1832) blew up the fortifications and managed to force his way through the blockade with 900 of his 1,300 French troops. Wellington was livid, declaring: 'I have never been so much distressed by any military event as by the escape of even a man of them.'

The Battle of Fuentes de Oñoro, 3–5 May 1811. Hoping to relieve the besieged Portuguese border fortress of Almeida, Masséna ordered a colossal frontal assault on this village, which failed. A day's pause followed, and a second attack on the third day nearly succeeded. Wellington described his narrow victory as 'the most difficult one I was ever concerned in and against the greatest odds.' (Roger-Viollet)

Battle of Albuera, 16 May 1811. An extremely bloody engagement fought between an Anglo-Portuguese force under Beresford, reinforced by Spanish troops under Cuesta and Blake, and a French army under Soult that had marched north from Cadiz in order to break the Allied investment of the key fortress city of Badajoz. Beresford's mismanagement of the action cost him enormous casualties and led to his return to administrative matters. Here, Beresford grapples with and unsaddles a Polish lancer. (Engraving by Sutherland after William Heath, Philip Haythornthwaite)

For Wellington Fuentes de Oñoro put paid to a worthy adversary, but further south Marshal Soult had undertaken the conquest of Estremadura and Andalusia, in the course of which he had captured both Olivenza and Badajoz. These were solid achievements, bolstered by victory at the Gebora.

The following day, further south, Beresford had to lift his siege of Badajoz in order to prepare his defense against Soult, who with 25,000 men and 50 guns was moving up from the south to relieve the beleaguered French garrison. Beresford adopted Wellington's plan and established his 35,000 men and 38 guns around Albuera. Yet this time the French were more imaginative, and rather than a simple frontal assault, moved instead against Beresford's right, where Spanish troops, known for their unsteadiness, were positioned. The battle soon developed into a series of extremely destructive firefights fought at close range. The French might have won the day had not Sir Galbraith Lowry Cole (1772–1842), commander of the 4th Division, launched a counterattack at a critical time, obliging the French to withdraw.

The near disaster at Albuera left half of Beresford's men killed or wounded. Wellington could not contemplate a repeat of this bloodbath. Still, the battle confirmed the deserved reputation of the British soldier for receiving excessive punishment yet standing his ground: the 2nd Brigade lost 1,054 men out of 1,651, with a captain the senior surviving officer. As for Beresford, he was soon replaced by Sir Rowland Hill (1772–1842) and transferred to command the growing Portuguese army. This organizational responsibility suited Beresford far better than a field command, and he was to prove himself a great success in this role.

Albuera enabled the Allies to resume the siege of Badajoz, but when Wellington learned on 19 June that Soult and Marmont had united their armies and were marching towards the city with 58,000 men, he quickly abandoned the operation and crossed the River Guadiana. The French did not pursue – perhaps the consequence of bitter experience. By the end of the month, with Badajoz still firmly in French hands, Wellington switched his attention to Ciudad Rodrigo. Without a siege train this operation was very unlikely to succeed, and on 20 September he was obliged to withdraw when, once again, the combined forces of Soult and Marmont advanced to counter his operations. Bowing to superior numbers, Wellington raised the siege and crossed the frontier into Portugal, bringing the year's operations to a close.

Two sides to war: 'Gentlemen' and the guerrillas

The Peninsular War was a conflict of striking contradictions, for two radically different attitudes between adversaries existed side by side. Off the field of battle, and even sometimes on it, British and French troops often fraternized with one another, even to the point of dining inside each other's lines and especially to barter food, alcohol, tobacco, and clothing. Both sides occasionally arranged unofficial truces, sometimes at an individual level between rival sentries or between field commanders who wished to remove casualties from the field for medical treatment and to bury the dead. Colonel Vivian noted how 'we now ride along side by side, within five yards of each other, without any more danger of being shot than you are when hunting on the town burrows. This is doing as gentlemen should. They really are devilish civil, honourable fellows, and know how to make war …' Colonel Napier, for his part, appeared to have little reason even to dislike the French: 'I should hate to fight out of personal malice or revenge, but [have] no objection to fight for Fun and Glory.' The paradox reached truly ludicrous proportions when

one French general received through opposing lines copies of London newspapers so that he could check the fluctuating value of his investments in British government stock.

Nothing could be more further removed from this 'gentleman's war' than the nebulous but nevertheless very important 'second front' posed by the bands of guerrillas who operated against the French wherever and whenever opportunity offered itself. Although guerrilla warfare has its origins in ancient times, it was in fact the Peninsular War which made it the phenomenon familiar to us today. The Spanish word *guerrilla* means 'little war', the individual participant a *guerrillero*, which has since been revised to *guerrilla*. These were often tough, hardy men, one of whom a British soldier described as 'a swarthy, savage-looking Spaniard … armed to the teeth with pistols, daggers … a long gun, … crimson sash and free bearing, [which] at once proclaimed him as a guerrilla.'

By the very nature of their activities and loose-knit (or indeed often nonexistent) structure, guerrilla numerical strength cannot be estimated with any accuracy, as their bands could range from a handful to several thousand. What is known is that there were many separate *partidas* under numerous leaders sometimes sporting colorful nicknames such as 'El Empecinado' and 'El Medico'. While guerrilla leadership varied in character, from simple patriots to bandit leaders and even priests, their purpose, targets, and methods remained generally constant: to sever communications, cut up small detachments, ambush convoys, pick off sentries, and intercept couriers and messengers. Guerrilla numbers multiplied as the war progressed and rendered effective French rule in the provinces difficult at best and impossible at worst. In short, French authority remained in a constant state of flux, with every region unsafe to the occupier. It is no exaggeration to say that the countryside was infested. Every rock and tree became a potential place of concealment or site of ambush; every seemingly innocent peasant a possible look-out or cut-throat.

One British soldier accurately and colorfully described the guerrilla war thus:

Night and day, the French troops were not only open to attacks from the British, but in constant alarm from the natives, whose animosity made them alive to the slightest opportunity of doing them mischief. No Frenchman, however fatigued, dared to straggle or fall back because it was instant death to him. At this time the Spanish guerrillas wore their own peasant dress, not uniform, so the French could not recognise friend from foe. The guerrillas and the peasantry watched with the thirst of wolves, and slaughtered all who fell into their hands.

The countermeasures employed by the French give some idea of how effective the guerrillas were: eventually 200 cavalry would accompany a messenger to ensure safe passage, and as many as 1,000 men would escort a French general wishing to travel independently of his army. By the summer of 1813 dispatches sent by King Joseph to Paris had to be escorted by 1,500 men to guarantee safe passage to the French border.

Much of the guerrillas' ferocity was the natural consequence of French depredations,

for occupying armies frequently devastated towns and villages through pillage and wanton destruction. In 1809 a British officer encountered such a place in Portugal, but the scene he describes echoes that of countless other instances occurring the length and breadth of the Peninsula:

I passed a field where the French had bivouacked. All the furniture and even the crockery had been taken from the houses of a neighbouring village and had been brought into the field. The beds and mattresses lay in rows in the mud. The drawers from the various articles of furniture had been used as mangers. Wardrobes had been transformed into bedsteads and roofs for the huts; all the crockery and glass lay in fragments on the ground. The chairs, staircases and window frames had been used partly as fuel for the kitchen fires and partly to feed huge bonfires which had been lighted when the French had withdrawn ... In the churches

Executing a monk. A not uncommon practice which did much to incense the deeply religious Spanish and increase the cycle of atrocity and counter-atrocity. Many clergy were at the forefront of encouraging resistance to the 'heretic' French, and often joined the guerrillas or fought side by side with the citizens of such cities as Saragossa and Gerona. (Goya, Roger-Viollet)

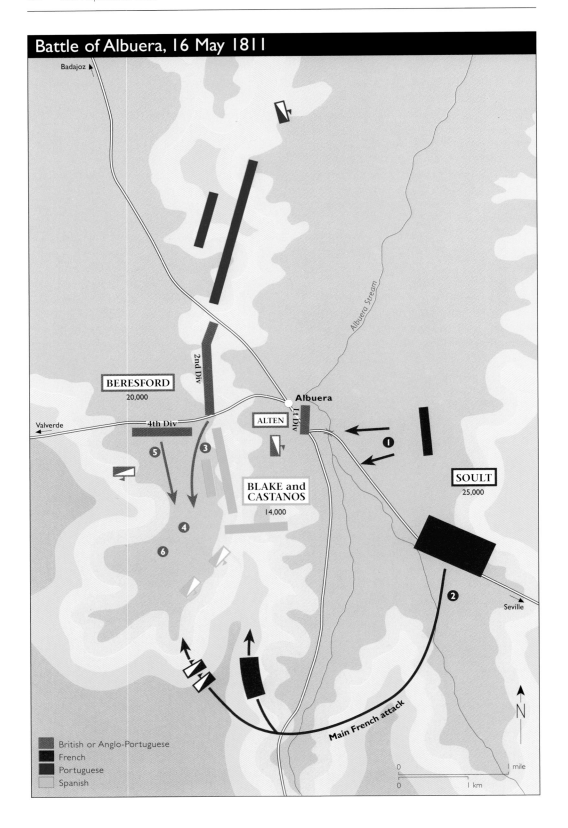

Battle of Albuera, 16 May 1811

Badajoz

BERESFORD
20,000

2nd Div

Valverde

4th Div

ALTEN

Albuera

Lt Div

BLAKE and
CASTANOS
14,000

Albuera Stream

SOULT
25,000

Seville

Main French attack

N

British or Anglo-Portuguese
French
Portuguese
Spanish

0   1 mile
0   1 km

LEFT

1. 8.00 am. French launch two feint attacks; Beresford reinforces his center.

2. 9.00 am. Main French attack with 12,000 of all arms crosses stream to threaten Spanish right flank. Spanish redeploy to face this threat and stand firm despite heavy losses.

3. 9.00 am. Part of 2nd Division moves to support Spanish.

4. 10.30 am Successful defense until sudden rainstorm prevents musket fire, leaving British infantry helpless against 3,500 cavalry. One brigade, with no time to form square, loses 1,300 out of 1,600 in a matter of minutes. Two more brigades from 2nd Division arrive to bolster defense. Storm settles; intense firefight at close range; terrible losses on both sides.

5. 4th Division (4,000 men) advances to join action.

6. 12.15 pm. French cavalry charges defeated; attacking infantry also driven off. 12.20 pm Soult commits reserve of 6,000. British attack its flanks and drive off. French retreat across river; exhaustion prevents Allied pursuit.

BELOW A French blockhouse. Built along important roads in northern Spain, these massive wooden structures housed infantry used in escorting couriers and guarding convoys. Adequate against musket fire, by 1812 they were rendered obsolete when the British supplied the guerrillas with light cannon. Ironically, at the end of the century the British themselves would be obliged to build blockhouses in order to combat their own guerrilla problem during the Boer War. (Bacler d'Albe, Roger-Viollet)

even the graves had not been spared ... Altar candlesticks ... torn vestments, chalices, prayer books and the like mixed up with straw and filth lay all about them.

Forcible requisitioning and looting by the French encouraged the peasantry to flock to the partisan bands, but it was the ill-treatment of the inhabitants themselves – documented instances of which were legion – which contributed most to fuel guerrilla activity. On entering Santarem in 1811, for instance, Rifleman Costello discovered a fountain contaminated by the mangled remains of dead Portuguese. In the town plaza he found '... murdered and violated women, shrieking and dying children. All in the village that had possessed life, lay quivering in the last agony of slaughter and awful vengeance.'

On another occasion Schaumann noted in his diary:

Never during the whole of the war did I again see such a horrible sight ... Death and destruction, murder and fire, robbery and rape

lay everywhere in the tracks of the enemy ... the burning villages, hamlets and woods ... told of the progress of the French. Murdered peasants lay in all directions.

One must not, however, discount the influence of money on those committing atrocities, for there was plunder to be acquired not merely from individual soldiers, but from their baggage wagons and convoys. One British soldier, encountering a guerrilla fresh from the kill, noted that from a silk purse he produced several human ears and fingers bearing gold rings which he claimed to have cut off from his victims in battle. 'Napoleon,' the guerrilla is reputed to have said, smiling grimly. 'Napoleon loves his soldiers, and so do the ravens. We find them plenty of food. They shall never want, so long as a Frenchman remains in Spain.'

The French for the most part found themselves unable to come to grips with such small and fluid bodies of men who fought out of uniform. The occupiers were driven to employ increasingly brutal methods in order to suppress the guerrillas, and a ferocious cycle of atrocity and counter-atrocity was begun. Outrage followed outrage as French civilian camp-followers were massacred, with villagers shot and their homes burnt in retaliation – a sharp contrast with the conduct of war in the eighteenth century, but an unmistakable foretaste of that of the twentieth. Both sides committed abominable acts of torture and murder, the French excusing their conduct on the grounds that

Fighting guerrillas. A good impression of the type of landscape that provided ideal conditions for partisan warfare. Primitive mountain tracks, dense forests, narrow gorges, steep passes, and high cliffs left French columns, especially convoys, extremely vulnerable to ambush, sometimes by guerrilla forces large enough to annihilate forces numbering in the hundreds or even, on a few notable occasions, exceeding a thousand. (Roger-Viollet)

Guerrillas surprise and massacre a convoy of French wounded. Combatants and noncombatants alike were treated mercilessly in this ugly side of the war in the Peninsula, and even Wellington, whose operations greatly benefited from ubiquitous partisan activity, remarked that once roused a Spaniard became an 'undisciplined savage.' While guerrillas were frequently responsible for such acts of butchery as shown here, the French committed their own fair share of atrocities. (Philppoteaux; Roget-Viollet)

guerrilla violations of the normal rules of war justified all counter-measures against 'brigandage', while the partisans could hide their own repulsive measures under the guise of national liberation. In many cases, however, the guerrillas were nothing more than cut-throats intent on pillage and receiving the financial rewards offered by Wellington for intercepted French dispatches. But whatever the motives of either side, the guerrilla war rapidly became a bloodthirsty cycle of violence, costing the French an estimated 100 men a day during the course of the war and causing unquantifiable damage to the troops' morale.

French soldiers unfortunate enough to be captured by the guerrillas rarely survived the experience for long. Schaumann noted that vengeance was severe: 'The cruelties perpetrated by the Portuguese hill folk against the French soldiers who fell into their hands

are indescribable,' he observed on discovering men nailed alive to barn doors. One leader is said to have hanged every male, and disemboweled every female, prisoner. Captain François encountered 'French officers and soldiers, even women disemboweled ... Some men were put between two boards and sawed asunder ... others were buried alive up to their shoulders, or hung up by their feet over fireplaces, so that their heads burned.' There was also the grisly sight of the bodies of 400 French hospital patients, massacred after the place fell into guerrilla hands. Later he met a soldier driven insane by his experiences as the only survivor of 1,200 murdered invalids.

Some victims were stoned, others blinded with pikes, disabled and left to die in the scorching heat of the sun, or tied to trees and castrated, there left to perish from blood loss. Captain Schumacher, a cavalry trooper in the Imperial Guard, discovered the burnt remains of a military hospital set on fire with nearly 200 mutilated patients still inside. In another instance General René met an agonizing fate when his captors suspended him, feet first, over a cauldron of boiling water and lowered him by increments over the course of several hours. In short, a horrible and painful death awaited stragglers,

Surprise attack by guerrillas on a French convoy in the Salinas Pass, Navarre, 9 April 1812. One of the greatest triumphs of the celebrated leader Francisco Espoz y Mina, this exploit was nothing short of spectacular: 500 infantry of the Polish 7th Regiment, bound for Russia, were killed, 150 men were captured, 450 Spanish prisoners were released and a huge store of plunder was seized. (Philippoteaux, Roger-Viollet)

couriers, small parties of soldiers, sentries – almost anyone who fell into guerrilla hands. French retaliation, in turn, was harsh. François observed that when a party of stragglers were found tortured and murdered, the perpetrators' village was burnt while the inhabitants were lined up and shot until the guilty were identified by the next man waiting to be killed.

Operations in 1812

This year was to mark a critical point in the war, for preparations were being made by Napoleon for the invasion of Russia, a colossal undertaking which had important implications for operations in Spain, where King Joseph assumed overall command of the five French armies, totaling about 230,000 men. Napoleon's projected campaign in Russia, for which 27,000 of his

troops in the Peninsula were withdrawn, was to be waged on an unprecedented scale. Moreover, Marmont was obliged to detach 10,000 of his men to bolster the operations of Marshal Louis Suchet (1770–1826) in Valencia. Wellington now saw the opportunity he had long awaited: a general offensive into Spain. As before, this required gaining access to the northern and southern corridors, the fortresses of Ciudad Rodrigo and Badajoz, respectively. Having received intelligence of the French troop withdrawals and transfers, Wellington promptly prepared to seize Ciudad Rodrigo before the two marshals could march to its aid.

The siege began on 8 January in the depths of winter. Lieutenant Simmons recorded the hazards he encountered on the night of the 14th:

I had charge of a party to carry earth in gabions [wicker baskets] and plant them upon the advanced saps [trenches] in places where the ground was an entire rock and could not be penetrated. The enemy fired grape and consequently numbers [of men] fell to rise no more from the effects of it. I ran the gauntlet here several times and brought gabions of earth, always leaving some of my poor fellows behind when I returned for more and glad enough I was when the Engineer said 'We have now sufficient.'

Two practicable breaches were made and on the night of the 19th British troops stormed and captured the fortress at relatively low cost (500 men), but General Craufurd, the charismatic and skillful commander of the Light Division, was mortally wounded on the glacis encouraging his men in the attack. Many others died when the French exploded a mine beneath them. The troops behaved disgracefully in the aftermath, sacking the city. Simmons described a shocking practice which more than once sullied the reputation of the British Army in the wake of this and other of its bloody sieges:

… men who have stormed a town are seldom fit for anything but vice and irregularity for some time afterwards if left within its walls. The soldiers were laden with all sorts of things and looked like a moving rag-fair. Some liking their bellies better, had their swords fixed and stuck upon them large chunks of corned beef, ham, pork, etc.

Less than a week later, amid torrential rain, Wellington prepared to take Badajoz as well. He invested the place on 16 March and captured part of the outlying defenses by storm on the 24th. Without an adequate siege train Wellington's operations slowly ground on, but a sense of urgency overcame him when he learned that Soult was advancing from the south and that Marmont was moving against Ciudad Rodrigo.

Therefore, on the fateful night of 6 April, after having blasted two breaches in the bastions of Santa Maria and La Trinidad, and a third in the connecting curtain wall, a storming party was organized with the forlorn hope – a small party of men sent ahead to spearhead the main assault – led by Major O'Hare. Officers who volunteered for such perilous tasks were promised a rise in rank if they survived, and thus O'Hare's statement to a friend before setting off: 'A Lieutenant-Colonel or cold meat in a few hours.' On the signal, waves of infantry assaulted the improvised barricades placed in the breaches, put scaling ladders against the high walls of the fortress and clambered up to take the place by escalade. At least 40 attempts were made. Losses were horrendous, thousands of the besiegers falling in the storm of musketry, grapeshot, and even masonry and brick hurled down by the stalwart defenders. In the end the city was taken after a secondary attack succeeded in penetrating the rear of the town, but by the time the French surrendered allied losses had reached 5,000 men – 30 percent of the total force.

On the following morning even Wellington, known for his severe countenance, wept at the sight of so many fallen infantry. Their shock heightened by the horrendous 'butcher's bill', British troops then feasted themselves on drink and ran amok through the streets of the fallen city, defying all attempts by their officers to bring the mob under control. The French governor, Armand Philippon, and his two daughters only survived under the escort of sword-wielding British officers, while the hapless Spanish inhabitants bore the brunt of the sacking, which included numerous

British troops storm a breach at Ciudad Rodrigo, 19 January 1812. A key objective for Wellington, this fortress commanded the northern invasion route between Portugal and Spain. Major George Napier, who led one of the storming parties, recalled: 'We all mounted the breach together, the enemy pouring a heavy fire on us.' Badly wounded by grape shot, he urged his men to 'Push on with the bayonet!' – which they did, driving off the defenders. (Ian Fletcher)

British troops storming Badajoz, 6 April 1812. Costello numbered amongst those in the main assault and barely survived the experience. 'Three of the men carrying the ladder with me were shot dead in a breath … and fell upon me, so that I was drenched in blood.' This particular attack failed, but two others elsewhere eventually succeeded. Nonetheless, the combined cost of the assaults was horrific: 3,350 men, bringing the total for the siege to nearly 5,000. (Caton Woodville, National Army Museum)

dreadful instances of looting, rape and murder. The city's ordeal continued for three days before fresh troops were brought in to subdue the frenzied soldiers, and gallows were erected as a grim warning against future acts of indiscipline.

With the capture of both routes into Spain, Wellington could advance via either one, and by an offensive into central Spain he could sever communications between Marmont and Soult, endanger the French presence in Madrid and possibly take Burgos, a key point in the lines of communication back to France. Thus, detaching Hill with 18,000 to watch Soult in the south, Wellington advanced north with 48,000 men

to confront Marmont, with 40,000. Wellington himself reached Salamanca on 17 June, and as neither side had a clear numerical advantage, they each sought to achieve a superior position. Several weeks of maneuvering between the rival armies followed. Many marches and countermarches were conducted in close proximity to one another, with neither side able to secure a superior position or to find a favorable opportunity to strike. At last, by late July, Wellington was ready to strike, for intelligence told him that Marmont was shortly to receive 13,000 men, sent from Madrid by King Joseph. Battle had therefore to be joined before the reinforcements arrived if Wellington was to succeed.

He chose to fight around the small village of Los Arapiles, five miles south of Salamanca, on 22 July. Both armies were marching on a parallel course about a mile apart. In the afternoon Wellington observed Marmont dangerously extending his troops over four miles and thus exposing them to defeat in detail. Wellington immediately launched an attack against the French flank, in the course of which the French were decisively defeated, losing 14,000 casualties to Wellington's 5,000. Marmont, himself wounded, retreated ignominiously and might have lost his whole force had not the Spanish, without orders, abandoned their watch over the only bridge spanning the River Tormes, thus leaving open the only possible escape route for the fugitives. Nevertheless, Salamanca was a tremendous blow to the French, and forever discredited the sobriquet 'defensive general' unfairly applied to Wellington. The battle had been won by maneuver, not merely by holding ground and repulsing the attacker. On 12 August the Allied command-in-chief entered a jubilant Madrid, where the army rested for several weeks and looked forward to regular supplies.

The next strongpoint to be attempted was the castle of Burgos, to the north of the capital. Wellington invested the place on 19 September but in the course of the following five weeks his operations suffered from woefully inadequate numbers of heavy guns and other siege equipment. Every assault launched against the defenses failed dismally and on 21 October he abandoned

the siege as French armies totaling 60,000 men converged to relieve the city. Burgos was a severe disappointment and Wellington's only major defeat of the war. The subsequent retreat, all the way back to the Spanish–Portuguese border, was a dreadful affair, like several others before it, and was conducted in appalling weather and aggravated by the loss of supplies. The march, which deprived him of nearly 10 percent of his force of 35,000 men, Wellington described as 'the worst scrape I ever was in.' At almost the same time Napoleon had left Moscow on a far more catastrophic retreat of his own. Hill was ordered to move north and Madrid was left to the French. Nevertheless, the main body eventually reached Ciudad Rodrigo on 20 November and the French pursuit had halted well before then.

Battle of Salamanca, 22 July 1812. After Vitoria, the most decisive battle of the Peninsular War, fought between Wellington and Marshal Marmont. Wellington, shown here, sought to defeat his opponent before the arrival of French reinforcements, while Marmont hoped to confront the Anglo-Portuguese army in the process of forcing it back to Portugal. Wellington caught the French in a highly vulnerable line of march, routed their forces and occupied Madrid. (AKG Berlin/British Library)

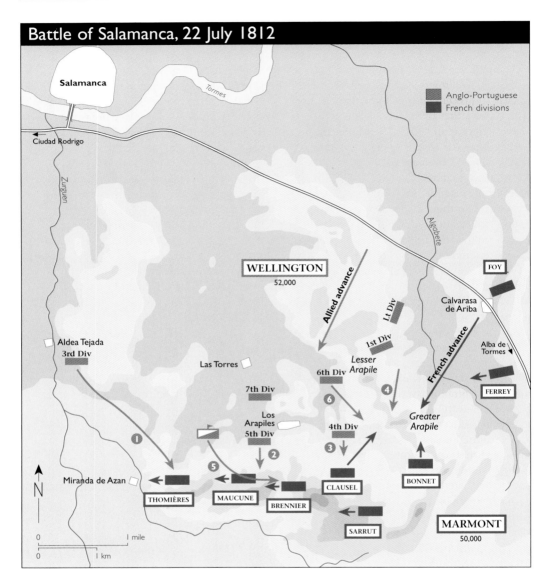

Battle of Salamanca, 22 July 1812

Salamanca

Tormes

Anglo-Portuguese
French divisions

Ciudad Rodrigo

Zurguen

Algabete

WELLINGTON
52,000

Allied advance

Lt Div

FOY

Calvarasa
de Ariba

Aldea Tejada
3rd Div

Las Torres

1st Div

French advance

Alba de
Tormes

Lesser
6th Div Arapile

FERREY

7th Div

❻

❹

Los
Arapiles
5th Div

4th Div

Greater
Arapile

❶

❺

❷

❸

Miranda de Azan

N

CLAUSEL

BONNET

THOMIÈRES

MAUCUNE

BRENNIER

MARMONT
50,000

SARRUT

0   1 mile
0   1 km

If Oporto had not convinced his detractors, Salamanca plainly demonstrated that Wellington was not merely a defensive tactician. He seized a superb opportunity for attack when a gap of about a mile opened between the two leading French divisions marching parallel to the Allied position. This weakness, and the fact that Marmont's remaining divisions were strung out for several more miles, enabled Wellington to achieve local superiority by launching a series of successful assaults throughout the day: 1) 3.30 pm. 3rd Division (7,000 men) attacks. 2) 4.15 pm. 5th Division (8,300) attacks. 3). 4.30 pm. Two brigades of 4th Division (3,900) attack. 4) 4.30 pm. Pack's Brigade (2,500) attacks. 5) 4.45 pm. 2,000 British/KGL cavalry attack. 6) 5.30 pm. 6th Division (5,500) attacks, with additional brigades in support.

Notwithstanding the failure at Burgos and the subsequent retreat, Wellington's campaign closed with some solid achievements: all French forces had been driven north of the Tagus, he had taken both vital border fortresses of Cuidad Rodrigo and Badajoz albeit at great cost in the latter case, he had severely defeated the French at Salamanca, had briefly retaken Madrid, and had captured 20,000 French prisoners and 300 guns. His army was now battle-hardened and more than confident in taking on the French, whereas French morale was low and future prospects for success had all but disappeared. Greater still for the Allies, the catastrophe which Napoleon's army had suffered in Russia not only turned the tide of the war firmly against France; for Wellington it ended all prospect of French reinforcements arriving in Spain. On the contrary, the coming campaign would actually siphon off badly needed veterans for service in central Europe. Wellington was also finally created Commander-in-Chief of the Spanish armies, totaling 160,000 men. In reality, this was more of a burden than an advantage, for they were situated across the length and breadth of the country and continued to suffer from an antiquated form of organization.

Operations in 1813

After five years on the strategic defensive, largely necessitated by the numerical superiority of the French, by 1813 Wellington was finally able to move to the offensive. Combined French forces still outnumbered those of the Allies, but the initiative had clearly passed to Wellington, and with the Russians and Prussians preparing their campaign in Germany, France would soon face a two-front war from adversaries determined to carry the conflict through to the bitter end.

In the course of the winter of 1812–13 Wellington drew up plans for the spring campaign, which were to incorporate another 5,000 men sent from home. In all, the Allied army numbered 81,000, plus 25,000 Spanish troops under Wellington's immediate control. The French, finally under King Joseph as overall commander, had 200,000 at their disposal, mostly concentrated in northern Spain and thus largely available for operations against Wellington. Wellington planned to advance north in a wide arc that would proceed around the flank of the French, who stood on the River Douro between Zamorra and Valladolid. To support this strategy Wellington planned to shift his base of supply from Lisbon to Santander, on the coast of northern Spain. In so doing he would not only

shorten his lines of communication, but place himself in a position to outflank the French well north of their present positions. To assist his operations, he organized a number of diversionary operations intended to keep French forces separated and occupied. Guerrilla operations were to be stepped up, while 18,000 men under Sir John Murray (1768–1827) would conduct an amphibious landing against Tarragona.

The new campaign season began with a rapid Allied advance in three columns which outflanked the French main defensive line and enabled Hill to take Salamanca on 26 May. The following day King Joseph fled the capital for the third time, and on 2 June Graham captured Zamorra. Caught entirely by surprise, and with their right flank continually vulnerable, the French retreated to Burgos. Wellington was not to be drawn into another costly assault, and this time he bypassed the city, obliging Joseph to retreat once again, this time to the line of the Ebro. When Graham threatened this line of defense, Joseph withdrew even further, to Vitoria, where he took up positions on 19 June. Wellington pursued closely and, in expectation that Joseph was shortly to receive reinforcements, decided to attack on the 21st.

Joseph and Jourdan, anticipating an attack, took up defensive positions with their 66,000 men near Vitoria. Expecting a straightforward assault to their front, French resistance crumbled when Wellington, with 79,000 men, assailed both flanks and pierced their center. Although some French units stubbornly held on, by 5.00 pm a rout ensued, the fugitives moving eastwards. French losses were comparatively light at 8,000, with the Allies losing 5,100, but King Joseph escaped capture by the narrowest of margins when he jumped out of one side of his coach just as a British hussar reached the other side. His army abandoned all but a handful of the 153 guns with which it had begun the battle, as well as the King's entire baggage train, including his treasury. This accounts for the failure of a vigorous pursuit, for thousands of Allied soldiers wasted several hours plundering the abandoned baggage,

Battle of Vitoria, 21 June 1813. The decisive battle of the war, it was the highlight of Wellington's bold offensive that had begun in May and culminated with Allied forces across the Pyrenees and into France herself by year's end. Anecdotes connected with the battle abound: while leading the 3rd Division in an attack on the bridge at Mendoza the fiery Sir Thomas Picton shouted to his men, 'Come on, ye rascals! Come on you fighting villains!' (German engraving, Edimedia)

making off with money and all manner of other items valued in excess of £1 million. All discipline broke down as soldiers roamed the field in search of spoil. 'In some cases,' Schaumann recalled, 'particularly over the plundering of the wagons carrying the war treasure, our men fought to the death. No officer dared to interfere. In short, more thorough and more scandalous plundering has never been known … Our men were loaded with spoil.' At the jumble sale that followed the battle Schaumann paid bargain prices for candlesticks, teapots, silver ingots, plates and cutlery.

Although the Allied pursuit completely foundered, Vitoria proved the decisive action

of the war and the liberation of Spain now remained only a matter of time. Southern and central Spain were free of French troops, and the only garrisons remaining held the northern cities of San Sebastian and Pamplona. The wider political implications of Vitoria were great. In Germany the Russians and Prussians had arranged an armistice with Napoleon; this was broken when news of Wellington's victory reached Vienna and Austria decided to enter the struggle on the Allied side, going so far as to offer Wellington a military command in central Europe. Vitoria was, therefore, not merely decisive for the Peninsular War, but for the wider Napoleonic conflict as well.

Advancing toward the Pyrenees, Wellington appreciated that he could not undertake an invasion of southern France without first securing the border-fortresses of San Sebastian and Pamplona. He also had to consider the possible liabilities of his 25,000 Spanish troops, who were likely to pillage or worse in retribution for French atrocities committed in the Peninsula over the years. Wellington had seen the effects of guerrilla operations and did not wish to stir up a similar movement against him amongst the French populace. He therefore decided to leave behind all but a small portion of his Spanish contingent and issued stern warnings that anyone caught looting on French soil, irrespective of nationality, would meet with summary justice. Shaumann noted how, in at least one instance, General Pakenham, 'supported by a powerful guard and the provost marshal ... began to ride up and down our columns like a raving lion ... His command, "Let that scoundrel be hanged instantly!" was executed in a twinkling. Over 200 men, chiefly Spaniards and Portuguese, were put to death in this way.'

Meanwhile, Soult, re-appointed to supreme command of the remaining French forces in Spain which still numbered over 100,000 men, could still lead an offensive across the Pyrenees or maintain the advantage of defending home ground with this mountain range as a formidable – though not impenetrable – barrier. Although there were dozens of minor passes through the Pyrenees, only three routes would permit the passage of large bodies of men: the coast road at Irun, the Pass at Maya, and the Pass at Roncesvalles, all of which stood on the Spanish side of the frontier. With only 60,000 men against Soult's immediately available force of 80,000, this left Wellington to defend a front 50 miles (80 km) in length. Rather than divide his troops between the passes, he maintained a nominal force along the front and held the balance in reserve, where it could react to any French incursion. He deployed the bulk of his forces to the northeast near San Sebastian, where he believed Soult would strike first. This plan was ambitious: with limited forces he proposed to capture two fortresses while simultaneously securing the border from attack.

While Wellington busied himself deploying his troops Soult assumed command over a single army of 80,000 men which he fashioned out of the four armies (those of the North, South, Center and Portugal) which had either been withdrawn or expelled from Spain. Aware that the Allied

army was overstretched and that it was expecting a French attack to relieve San Sebastian, Soult planned a counteroffensive intended to seize the passes at Maya and Roncesvalles as a prelude to the relief of Pamplona, now blockaded. Should he succeed in this, he planned to move north, defeat the Allied force besieging San Sebastian and in so doing place himself between Wellington's main force and the smaller formations elsewhere in northern Spain. Accordingly, on 25 July the French opened a surprise offensive in which General le comte d'Erlon (1774–1847), with 21,000 men, assaulted the Allied force at the pass at Maya. Despite the attackers' determined effort they faced a stout defense and the French only managed to hold the pass but not break through. On the same day, 20 miles to the south, 40,000 troops under Soult struck at Roncesvalles, seizing that strategic pass.

On hearing of the actions at Maya and Roncesvalles, Wellington made for Sorauren, 5 miles north of Pamplona, where on 27 July he took command from Cole, who had been closely pursued by the French. On the following day Soult attacked in force but was defeated, putting an end to his plans of relieving Pamplona and re-supplying his army there. Now determined on one last attempt to maintain a presence in Spain, Soult ordered three of his divisions to move west against Hill, and on 30 July d'Erlon pushed that general as far as Lizaso. On the same day, however, Wellington forced the French in the same sector to flee back to the safety of the Pyrenees. Soult had no choice but to withdraw. However, as the Allies now barred the routes through Maya and Roncesvalles, the French had to struggle north to Vera in order to make their escape. By the end of July, having suffered losses of 13,500 men from a total force of 61,000, the French stood on native soil, weakened and demoralized.

About this time, on 25 July, the Allies attempted an assault against San Sebastian. This failed, but when Graham tried again on 31 August he took the town, but not without first losing 2,300 men, followed by the castle

Battle of Vitoria, 21 June 1813

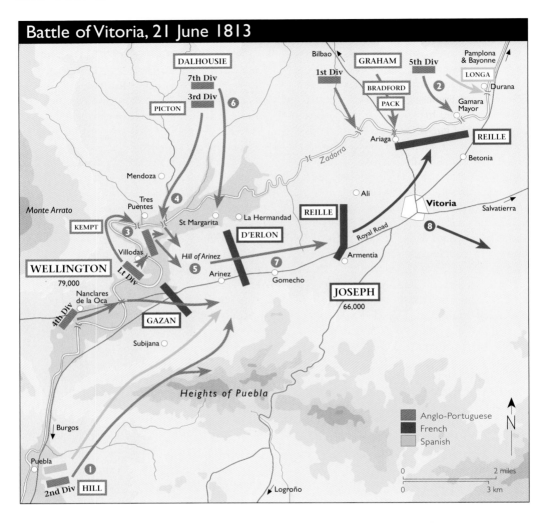

1. 8.00 am. Hill's corps, containing British, Portuguese, and Spanish divisions, attacks Heights of Puebla.

2. 10.00 am. Graham advances from hills and within two hours cuts French escape route along Vitoria–Bayonne road.

3. 12.00 pm. Kempt's brigade of the Light Division seizes virtually unguarded bridge at Tres Puentes.

4. 2.00 pm. Without orders, Picton's 3rd Division launches attack and seizes bridge near Mendoza.

5. 3.00 pm. Attacking from three sides, Allies capture hill and village of Arinez.

6. 3.00 pm. Dalhousie's 7th Division moves against St Margarita, but the Light Division takes it first.

7. 4.00 pm. Pressing the French on three sides, Allies advance east, breaking through.

8. 5.00 pm. French begin eastward retreat, which then dissolves into a rout.

on 7 September. As at Badajoz, the town was sacked and, perhaps unintentionally,

destroyed by fire. Also on 31 August Soult launched an attack across the Bidassoa, the river constituting the Franco–Spanish frontier to the west. His final effort to prevent an invasion of France failed when his attacks at Irun, near the coast, and at Vera, slightly inland, came to nothing. By September Austria had joined the Allied cause and French fortunes in Germany were rapidly declining.

On 7 October Wellington made his historic passage of the Bidassoa, soon crossed the mountains and entered France. The Austrians, Prussians, and Russians, meanwhile, decisively defeated Napoleon in the three-day epic Battle of Leipzig on 16–19 October, which cost the French 100,000 casualties and 100 guns and obliged the survivors to make rapidly for the Rhine.

Pamplona finally capitulated on 31 October, enabling Wellington to expand his campaign into France, all the while taking pains to treat French civilians with courtesy in order to avoid his own army being plagued by the kind of guerrilla war that had dogged the French in Spain. In fact, so scrupulous was the conduct of Allied troops that they received a better reception than did Soult's. Anyone caught looting was hanged or shot; anything acquired from the French population was paid for on the spot. Thus, with no campaign of civilian resistance to impede his progress, Wellington had little need to detach troops for static duties and could concentrate on opposing Soult.

On 10 November he overcame the marshal's strong position along the River Nivelle, forcing him to withdraw to a new defensive line along the Nive which extended from Cambo-les Bains to Bayonne and then to the Biscay coast. Wellington resumed his relentless advance on 9 December, moving on Bayonne, which he intended to invest. Yet Soult refused to abandon the initiative, and on the 10th he launched an unexpected attack near the sea against Hope, forcing him back several miles. Three days later Soult, with a 2-to-1 numerical superiority, attacked again, this time against Hill's force at St. Pierre, east of the Nive. Hill narrowly escaped a serious defeat when reinforcements appeared at a critical time, obliging Soult to withdraw. Suchet, for his part, was obliged to abandon control of Catalonia and cross the Pyrenees with his remaining force of only 15,000 men. French fortunes were now on the wane and Napoleon himself effectively admitted that the war in the Peninsula was all but lost when, in December, seeing France invaded for the first time in nearly 20 years, he wrote with disgust: 'I do not want Spain either to keep or to give away. I will have nothing more to do with that country …' He had even greater worries to attend to personally: far to the northeast, elements of the combined armies of Russia, Prussia, Austria, and Sweden, together with numerous German allies who had finally defected from the French cause after Leipzig, had begun crossing the Rhine and were poised for a full scale invasion.

For Wellington the year had ended extremely successfully. From Portugal he had marched his army back into Spain and decisively defeated the French at Vitoria before resuming his advance northward. He had taken the last remaining fortresses, had defeated Soult in a series of actions along the Pyrenees, and had pursued his forces into France herself as far as Bayonne.

Private Edward Costello, 95th Rifles

Edward 'Ned' Costello, was born in Ireland in 1788 and joined the 95th Rifles in 1808, while a shoemaker. His battalion embarked in May 1809 for the Peninsula, where his experiences over the next five years were a series of hardships, adventures, narrow escapes, wounds, and desperate combats. Throughout his many years' of unbroken campaigning he remained a private, and his experiences, recorded for publication in 1841, provide a valuable insight into the lives of ordinary British soldiers in Wellington's army.

The 95th was a recently raised regiment, armed with the Baker rifle rather than the Brown Bess musket, and sporting distinctive dark green uniforms trimmed with black leather. 'I was highly delighted with the smart appearance of the men, and with their green uniform,' Costello wrote. The 95th (nicknamed the 'Sweeps' because of their dark appearance) not only wore different uniforms from the line regiments, their weapons provided unrivalled accuracy and their loose open-order tactics, known as skirmishing, quickly brought the 95th into prominence as an elite unit within that already distinguished element of the army, the Light Brigade, later renamed the Light Division. One of its more flamboyant riflemen was Private Tom Plunkett, who, near Astorga, had responded to General Paget's financial incentive to shoot General Colbert, who, though conspicuous on horseback, had eluded death at the hands of soldiers armed with hopelessly inaccurate smooth-bore muskets. Lying on his back in the snow and placing his foot in the sling of his weapon, Plunkett unseated the French general before running back to friendly lines, pursued by a dozen troopers.

Hardly had Costello arrived than the Light Brigade began one of history's greatest forced marches when it left to join Wellington's main body at Talavera, where a battle was shortly expected. 'Our men suffered dreadfully on the route, chiefly from excessive fatigue and the heat of the weather. The brain fever soon commenced, making fearful ravages in our ranks, and many dropped by the roadside and died.' Despite being light troops, the 95th still carried 70–80 lbs of equipment, provisions, ammunition, and a rifle, and the blistering July heat took a terrible toll. In 26 hours the Light Brigade had marched 62 miles (100 km), only to arrive at Talavera after the battle was over. But it had been an epic achievement.

As we advanced … the heights of Talavera burst upon our sight. With three loud huzzas, we hailed the news … The scene, however, was appalling … The field of action … was strewn with the wreck of recent battle. The dead and dying, thousands of them, conquerors and conquered, lay in little heaps, interspersed with dismounted guns, and shattered ammunition waggons. Broken horse trappings, blood-stained shakos [infantry helmets], and other torn paraphernalia of military pomp and distinction, completed the battle scene.

After suffering a severe fever for six weeks Costello rejoined his regiment at Barba del Puerco in March 1810. There, on the windy night of the 19th, while defending the bridge over the River Agueda over a deep chasm studded with jagged rocks, the French attacked, taking the sentries prisoner and surprising Costello and 43 other riflemen, who were on picket duty. The men sought cover in the rocky and broken ground and kept up a regular fire at those attempting to take the heights from below. Costello's company kept 600 French infantry at bay for half an hour until the colonel of the regiment brought three more companies to assist.

In July 1810, following the French capture of Ciudad Rodrigo, the French attacked the

Light Division with overwhelming numbers, in the course of which Costello and a small group of riflemen became surrounded by cavalry. 'While hotly engaged with the French infantry in our front, one or two troops of their hussars ... whipped on our left flank ... A cry of "The French cavalry are upon us" came too late, and they charged in amongst us. Taken unprepared, we could offer little or no resistance, and our men were trampled down and sabered on every side.' A French dragoon grabbed hold of Costello's collar and aimed his saber at his chest, only to be killed by a volley fired by soldiers of the 52nd Foot.

This tumbled the horse of my captor and he fell heavily, dragging me down with him. The animal was on the dragoon's leg. Determined to have one brief struggle for liberty, I freed myself from his grasp, dealt him a severe blow on the head with the butt of my rifle, and rushed up to our 52nd.

Costello, however, was shot in the right knee and while being evacuated on the back of a comrade, that man was shot, whereupon Costello dragged himself over the bridge spanning the Coa. He was lucky to have escaped with his life and this was only one of a number of similar occasions.

The retreat was typically awful, and Costello eventually reached the hospital at Belem, near Lisbon. The experiences of the sick there and at Figueira, *en route*, were quite horrendous:

The heat of the weather was intense and affected our wounds dreadfully. Doctors were scarce ... maggots were engendered in the sores, and the bandages, when withdrawn, brought away lumps of putrid flesh and maggots. Many men died on board, and others were reduced to the necessity of amputation, but by care, and syringing sweet oil into my wounds, I managed to get rid of the maggots.

With a better standard of care in Belem he soon recovered and remained to convalesce until October, when he left to rejoin his unit at the Lines of Torres Vedras.

Costello fought in numerous skirmishes and minor actions during the course of the year, pursuing the French, seeing the desolation and suffering left in their retreat, and the dreadful vengeance of the guerrillas as bodies of their victims were discovered and smoking villages marked the progress of the army. Costello fought at Fuentes de Oñoro in May 1811 and continued the advance through Spain. Like many of his comrades, he amused himself between marches and combat with wrestling and boxing matches with the peasantry, while the officers went hunting and dancing with village girls, who exchanged lessons in Spanish dance for those of England and Ireland.

At the beginning of 1812 the army laid siege to the border fortress of Ciudad Rodrigo, and when two breaches had been made in the walls Costello volunteered for the forlorn hope which was to be the small party leading in the main assault against the Lesser Breach. A second attacking party would attempt the Greater Breach. He noted that 'many of our men came forward with alacrity for this deadly service. With three officers from my company I had, as I then considered, the good fortune to be chosen. This was a momentous occasion in the life of a soldier, and so we considered it.' Shot and shell roared overheard and each man considered his chances of survival. They shook hands with each other; Costello went so far as to give his father's address to a comrade in the event he did not survive the experience. 'As darkness descended over the city,' Costello relates, 'our imaginations became awake to the horrors of the coming scene.'

'Black Bob' Craufurd, that grim but highly respected commander of the Light Division, came forward to lead the stormers in person. With a clear and distinct voice he addressed the troops:

Soldiers! The eyes of your country are upon you. Be steady, be cool, be firm in the assault. The town must be yours this night. Once masters of the wall, let your first duty be to clear the ramparts, and in doing this keep together.

Costello records that his heart beat powerfully as he and his comrades anxiously watched for the signal, while further to the rear thousands of troops of his division stood in readiness to follow up the storming party. 'We were on the brink of being dashed into eternity,' he recalled, 'and among the men there was a solemnity and silence deeper than I ever witnessed.'

On the appearance of the signal rocket Craufurd cried 'Now lads, for the breach!' and the men raced to the objective. 'As we neared the breach, the shot of the enemy swept our men away fast. Canister, grape, round-shot, and shell, with fireballs to show our ground, and a regular hailstorm of bullets, came pouring in and around us.' Craufurd fell mortally wounded, but the attack never faltered. The men scrambled up ladders placed in the ditch and ascended against a storm of fire. The attackers pushed on undaunted, though when the French sprung a mine many were killed and others scorched by the explosion. Costello himself was nearly killed by a French artillery gunner with whom he grappled until support arrived, but the whole scene was one of bitter hand-to-hand combat. In only half an hour the fight was over. The fortress was in British hands and Costello had again escaped with his life, though there were other 'scrapes' to come.

Costello would go on to participate in the even greater assault on the fortress of Badajoz in April. He again volunteered for the forlorn hope, and said of the two commanders: 'There was never a pair of uglier men, but a brace of better soldiers

never stood before the muzzle of a Frenchman's gun.' Costello was wounded in the breach and 'for the first time for many years, I uttered something like a prayer.' He eventually heard the sound of firing diminish, and above the cries of the wounded he detected cheering from the town. The place had fallen, though Costello was himself wounded in the right leg, while two musket shots had perforated his helmet. Badajoz was not to be his final action, however. He would continue his march with the Light Division and go on to serve at Salamanca, the retreat from Burgos, and at Vitoria, where he took away more than £400 worth of booty from the abandoned wagons. 'All who had the opportunity were employed in reaping some personal advantage from our victory,' he wrote, 'so I determined not to be backward.' There followed the various struggles for the Pyrenees, the action at Tarbes, and finally, the Battle of Toulouse.

Costello also served in the Waterloo campaign, losing his finger to a musket ball at Quatre Bras, and for several years in the occupation of France. He spent many years again fighting in Spain during the Carlist War as part of the British Legion before becoming a yeoman warder at the Tower of London in 1838. He died in 1869, with two of the muskets balls from which he was wounded still inside him. One, which had buried itself in his leg at the Coa in 1810, was, by his request, removed after his death. In addition to his printed recollections, 'Ned' Costello can truly be said to have carried the Peninsular War with him well into the Victorian era.

Recruits of the 95th receiving instruction in the use of the Baker rifle.

George Canning, British Foreign Secretary, 1807–1809

'I hope,' announced George Canning (1770–1827), in a speech he gave near the end of his long political career, 'that I have as friendly a disposition towards the nations of the earth, as anyone who vaunts his philanthropy most highly; but I am contented to confess, that in the conduct of political affairs, the grand object of my contemplation is the interest of England.' This was particularly the case in the realm of foreign affairs and when he became Foreign Secretary in the Duke of Portland's government in March 1807, Canning's principal aims lay in preserving Britain's existing alliances and at the same time seeking to establish others.

Canning assumed office while British fortunes were at one of their lowest points since the start of the Napoleonic Wars four years earlier. His primary responsibility, that of maintaining the Anglo-Russian alliance, proved all but impossible, for Napoleon had already severely checked the Tsar's army at the Battle of Eylau in February, and in June the French victory at Friedland and the peace of Tilsit knocked Russia out of the war altogether, leaving Britain with no allies apart from feeble Sweden and Portugal.

By a secret clause of the treaty Russia agreed that if Denmark should fail to close its ports in accordance with the Continental System, it would support French hostility against Denmark. When Canning learned through covert means of French intentions, he persuaded the cabinet to send a fleet to demand the surrender of the Danish fleet for the duration of the war, thus anticipating Napoleon's plans. As a neutral power, Denmark naturally objected to the British ultimatum. In September Copenhagen was ruthlessly bombarded and occupied and the Danish fleet carried away. The legality of the operation was certainly questionable, but

Canning recognized that with the Danish fleet, together with that of Portugal, in French hands, Napoleon could once again threaten Britain with invasion. Decisive though Trafalgar had been two years before, Britain's security from attack remained foremost in the minds of policy-makers in London.

The following month Canning successfully arranged the hand-over of the Portuguese fleet to the Royal Navy. As has been shown, Admiral Sir Sidney Smith appeared before Lisbon at the end of October, evacuated the royal family and escorted it and the Portuguese fleet to Brazil, just as Junot was approaching the undefended capital. Thus, within the space of a few months, Napoleon had been denied the ships which he would require if he was to threaten Britain directly – thanks in great measure to Canning's foresight and boldness.

Successful as this defensive strategy had proved, it was now time for more active measures. Britain needed a foothold on the Continent – a place from which her albeit limited military resources could be brought to bear in a major and sustained land campaign. That prospect did not arise, as has been shown, until the Spanish rose in spontaneous revolt, and when on 8 June 1808 emissaries from Asturias arrived in London seeking British aid, it was Canning, in his capacity as Foreign Secretary, to whom they applied. When the deputies were soon followed by their counterparts from Galicia and Andalusia, all seeking money and arms, Canning saw a golden opportunity to strike another blow against France, this time through the active resistance of patriots eager to fight.

In Canning's view a war of national resistance had much to recommend itself. As early as 1795 Britain had witnessed with bitterness her monarchical allies detach

George Canning. Working tirelessly to maintain harmonious Anglo-Spanish relations came with its share of obstacles. 'At present,' he wrote in August 1809, 'the Spanish think they are sure of us; and that they have a right to us; and that instead of every assistance that we afford them being another matter of fresh acknowledgement, every point upon which we hesitate is an injury, and a breach of engagement. This tone of theirs is offensive, and becomes irksome to me.' (Roger-Viollet)

He has fought against countries in which the people have been indifferent to his success; he has yet to learn what it is to fight against a country in which the people are animated with one spirit to resist him.

Canning himself declared that the government would furnish whatever practical support it could, notwithstanding the fact that, officially, Britain and Spain remained in a state of war. 'We shall proceed,' he told the House in one of the many masterful speeches of his parliamentary career,

upon the principle that any nation of Europe that starts up with a determination to oppose a Power which, whether professing insidious peace, or declaring open war, is the common enemy of all nations, whatever may be the existing political relations of that nation with Great Britain, becomes instantly our essential ally.

In short, hostilities with Spain would immediately cease and, most significantly, Britain would assist any nation or people prepared to oppose Napoleonic aggression.

Canning backed his words with material assistance: he immediately arranged a treaty of peace between Britain and Spain and appointed a diplomatic representative to the juntas. On 5 August he responded to the practical wants of the same, asking Lord Castlereagh (1769–1822), who went on to serve as an acclaimed Foreign Secretary but was then the Secretary of State for War, for artillery and cavalry on behalf of the Asturian and Galician deputies. He made several requests to Lord Chatham at the Board of Ordnance for supplies of weapons, and by November 160,000 muskets had been

themselves one by one from their respective alliances in violation of treaties which had uniformly prohibited all signatories from concluding a separate peace. Canning had, moreover, seen every attempt to support the minor powers of Europe with troops or aid, such as to Hanover, Denmark, Sweden, Portugal, and Naples, fail dismally. The nature of the conflict in the Peninsula, on the other hand, was singular and unprecedented. A popular rising led by people prepared to die for their country rather than merely a king seemed to offer a much greater hope of success in the long struggle against Napoleonic hegemony.

On 15 June Richard Sheridan, a friend and parliamentary colleague of Canning, brought the question of aid to the House of Commons. In the past, he observed,

Bonaparte has had to contend against princes without dignity and ministers without wisdom.

sent, with 30 to 40,000 more to follow within the next month. Spanish demands for money were considerable and initially exceeded the British government's ability to meet them, but within a month of the deputies' arrival a diplomat had been dispatched to Corunna with £200,000 in Spanish dollars for the Galician junta. By summer's end the five main juntas between them had received over £1,000,000 in silver and more would be available to the Supreme Junta on its formation.

Canning appreciated that his nation's contribution must extend beyond the mere provision of finance and supply: Britain must send an army of its own. Circumstances were more favorable now than ever before, for with the invasion threat relieved by the neutralization of the Danish and Portuguese fleets Britain no longer required a large concentration of troops for home defense. Canning therefore strongly advocated plans to release some of these for service abroad and, as has been shown, in early June Wellesley embarked for the Peninsula with an expedition in support of the Spanish (and Portuguese) which, ironically, had been intended for operations against Spanish America.

The initial results have already been discussed: in August Wellesley landed in Portugal and soon defeated Junot at Vimiero. Sir Arthur might have pursued and destroyed the French entirely, had not his superiors, Generals Dalrymple and Burrard, first prevented him, and then concluded the infamous Convention of Cintra, which arranged for the evacuation of Junot's army back to France in British ships. It took 11 days for official word to arrive in London and on the 16th the terms of Cintra appeared in the newspapers with predictable results. Public opinion, at a pitch of enthusiasm for the war in the Peninsula, began to subside at the news that the hitherto invincible French, having been defeated in the field, would be evacuated home, complete with arms and booty and free to fight again.

Canning was livid, describing the convention to Chatham as 'both disgraceful and disastrous in the highest degree.' To Lord Bathurst he called it 'so utterly, manifestly, shamefully unjust, that I hope and believe the Portuguese people will rise against it.' To allow the French to retain plunder seized from Britain's ally was nothing short of scandalous, and the act would thereafter remain 'as a sort of landmark for the guidance of future commanders, a terror to our allies, and an encouragement to our enemies.' Despite Canning's vehement objections the cabinet reluctantly conceded that the convention must be honored, though the Foreign Secretary did secure the recall of Dalrymple, Burrard, and Wellesley, the first two of whom were denied any further opportunity for active service.

If Cintra were not enough, the second blow to British arms, Sir John Moore's retreat to Corunna, also infuriated Canning, who both condemned the general for 'running away' and blasted the Spanish for failing to support him with provisions and information on French dispositions. Even before Moore had made the decision to retreat to northwest Spain rather than to Portugal, Canning was determined that Spanish authorities not construe this as a general British policy of abandonment. The army would definitely return, he wrote on 9 December to the British representative to the Supreme Junta, but when it was able to do so it must have the supplies and intelligence it rightfully required from Spanish officials. It was not, the Foreign Secretary insisted, to be divided up among the different Spanish armies, but must remain unified under British commanders and left to conduct itself according to plans conceived by officers in the field under orders from the government in London.

The British Army, Canning continued, 'will decline no difficulty, it will shrink from no danger, when through that difficulty and danger the commander is enabled to see his way to some definite purpose.' He rebuked the Spanish for the shortcomings of which Moore had complained in his dispatches. In short, the army must never in future be

Sir John Moore being carried from the field of Corunna. Mortally wounded after being struck by a round shot on the left shoulder, he died later that night, mourned by an army whose respect for him often extended to adoration. Sir George Napier reflected popular sentiment when he described the fallen general as ' … a model for everything that marks the obedient soldier, the persevering, firm and skilful general; the inflexible and the real patriot …' (Ann Ronan Picture Library)

abandoned 'in the heart of Spain without one word of information, except such as they [Moore and Baird] could pick up from common rumour, of the events passing around them.' Before Moore could be expected to return in support of his allies, the Spanish must offer a full explanation of their strategy.

During the closing days of December Canning privately condemned Moore's failed campaign in increasingly stronger terms, but his cabinet colleagues did not share his opinion. With the arrival of news of the successful evacuation of the army and of Sir John's death in action, the Portland ministry chose instead openly to endorse the conduct of an otherwise popular general who had saved the army from certain doom at the cost of his own life.

The time for the government to defend its policy in Parliament was not long in coming, and at the end of February 1809 the Opposition duly moved a motion demanding an enquiry into 'the causes, conduct and events of the last [campaign] in Spain.' Inevitably, they attacked the government for both Cintra and Corunna. Canning, privately exasperated but loyal to Portland, replied, giving what one of his colleagues described to the King as 'one of the best, most eloquent and commanding speeches that was ever heard.' Moore, he declared, had played an instrumental part in disrupting Napoleon's declared object of destroying Spanish opposition in the field once and for all. Indeed, the advance as far as Sahagun, the Foreign Secretary declared, was nothing less than the work of a statesman, not merely that of a soldier.

Canning strenuously maintained that the Spanish will to resist had thus remained intact, and, in the great British tradition of characterizing defeat as victory, insisted that although Moore's army had been pushed out of Spain, his triumph at the Battle of Corunna had left 'fresh laurels blooming upon our brows.' He condemned those who conceded defeat and counseled withdrawal from the Peninsula (British forces still remained in Portugal, of course), and insisted that Napoleon could ultimately be overcome. Closing his oratory, Canning acknowledged that Napoleon's fortunes had doubtless been improved by recent events, 'but still it was fortune, not fate; and therefore not to be considered unchangeable and fixed.'

The discrepancy between Canning's private opinions about Moore's conduct and his public statements on the subject seems hypocritical. However, the situation was complex, for if the ragged troops who disembarked on the south coast of England were to be believed, the Spanish had severely let them down. There were stories of Spanish cowardice in the field – a charge not always justified – as well as indifference to the plight of British troops retreating in the face of overwhelming French forces. To this were added shocking revelations about the Spaniards' failure to provide food and shelter to Moore's desperate men. Thus armed, many on the Opposition benches in Parliament argued that a third attempt to stop the French in the Peninsula was hopeless. Canning disagreed, and while he privately decried the incompetence of Spanish generals and the Supreme Junta, he continued to maintain both in public and private that Britain ought to support the patriotic cause of the Spanish people with all practical means. The government won the debate, public fears were assuaged, and Britain would carry on its commitment to the war in the Peninsula.

In his task of securing and sustaining Spain as a vital ally, Canning had difficulties beyond Parliamentary opposition. Spanish and Portuguese requests for arms and money were incessant, prompting the Foreign Secretary to complain to a friend in July 1809 that in the course of the war with France 'we have supplied by turns almost the whole continent with arms – Russia, Prussia, Sweden, Portugal, Sicily and Spain – while at the same time our own military establishments are sixfold what they formally were ...' When the Portland ministry resigned in September, Canning had not managed to conclude a definitive Anglo-Spanish treaty of alliance establishing mutual responsibilities and benefits. Still, in the end, common hostility to France continued to keep two otherwise traditional enemies on a fairly steady, if at times rocky, course and a formal treaty of alliance shortly followed.

Canning's brief tenure as Foreign Secretary under Portland had – at least respecting the war in the Peninsula – borne considerable fruit. Anglo-Spanish relations had swiftly turned from hostility to friendship under Canning's direction, while Britain's provision of the three elements so essential to the success of the conflict – troops, weapons, and money – owed much to Canning's strong advocacy of the Spanish cause. Although he left office well before the end of the Peninsular War, Canning's connection with foreign affairs generally, and with Spain in particular, was by no means over. In 1822 he returned for a lengthy stay at the Foreign Office, where his attention was devoted to such critical international issues of the day as Spain's political crises, and the problem of French intervention in them, the future of the Congress System and Britain's role in it, the complex issue of Greek independence, and the recognition of, and establishment of trade with, the newly independent states of Latin America. His exceptionally deft handling of these and other thorny issues would eventually establish Canning as one of Britain's greatest foreign secretaries.

Anti-climax: The campaign of 1814

At the opening of the campaign Wellington had 63,000 men, plus his Spanish troops, at his disposal. With these forces he intended to divide the French by drawing Soult away from Bayonne. He would achieve this by maneuvering around the French flanks, a strategy that had succeeded admirably the previous year. Soult had 54,500 men, having been stripped of 10,000 men and 35 guns by the Emperor in the first month of the year. These forces were divided approximately equally between those defending Bayonne, just above the River Adour, and those along the Joyeuse, about 10 miles east of the Nive, in Allied possession since December.

With his 31,000 men Hope began to besiege Bayonne, with orders to pass the Adour as opportunity allowed. While Wellington held back four divisions in reserve at the Nive, Hill moved eastwards with 13,000 men, crossed the Joyeuse on 14 February and three days later reached St Jean-Pied-de-Port. Soult responded by drawing off two divisions from Bayonne, leaving it with only 17,000 men. It was for just such a weakening of defenses that Wellington had hoped. Hope crossed the Adour west of the city on the 23rd by boat and established a lodgement on the opposite bank. Then, having constructed a bridge across the river, by the 26th he had 15,000 men on the other side, leaving Bayonne encircled and cut off from the remainder of Soult's forces.

The French had retreated before Hill's advance with 13,000 men as far as Orthez:

Wellington now opposed them with 31,000 men. At Orthez Soult established his 36,000 men and 48 guns on a ridge west of the city – a strong defensive position. On 27 February Wellington's first assault failed, but his second, now supported from the east by a separate attack by Hill, succeeded, and Soult withdrew in order to save his army from being trapped in the city. A fortnight later, on 12 March, Bordeaux, having declared its support for the Bourbon throne, opened its gates to Beresford. Soult meanwhile continued his withdrawal, his rearguard fighting with spirit at Tarbes on 20 March. Four days later he entered

Lieutenant-General Sir Rowland Hill, 1st Viscount Hill (1772–1842). Arguably Wellington's best subordinate commander, Hill proved himself able in independent command through his victory at Arroyo dos Molinos in 1811, but also in every action in which he served, particularly Vitoria, the Nivelle and the Nive. His scrupulous attention to his own troops' welfare and material needs earned him the nickname 'Daddy Hill'. (Stipple engraving, 1815, Ann Ronan Picture Library)

Major-General William Beresford, Viscount Beresford (1768–1854). He led a division under Wellesley and Moore before his appointment in 1809 as Marshal of the Portuguese army, which was then in a pitiful state. Beresford showed exceptional skill at reorganizing and training the Portuguese, whose language he learned, and through his reforms and the integration of British officers into their ranks he created a respectable fighting force which played an important role in ultimate victory. (Ann Ronan Picture Library)

RIGHT
1. 5.00 am. Hill demonstrates on west bank of Garonne toward suburb of St Cyprien.
2. 5.00 am. Picton, ordered to make feint attack, disobeys and opens all-out assault; repulsed with heavy casualties.
3. Beresford, with two divisions, marches between Calvinet Ridge and River Ers in preparation for main attack against southern section of the ridge. Advance seriously delayed by mud and swampy banks of Ers.
4. Freire, mistakenly believing Beresford in his designated position and attacking, strikes north end of Calvinet Ridge with two Spanish divisions as planned; badly repulsed.
5. Beresford opens attack against Sypière Redoubt; French counterattack of two brigades repulsed. Beresford renews attack against spirited opposition.
6. 2.00 pm. Picton renews his attack, with Spanish support, but with few gains. Beresford attacks again; redoubt taken and retaken five times in savage struggle for possession.
7. 5.00 pm. French begin withdrawal from Calvinet Ridge into city.

with an assault against Toulouse, where Soult had 42,000 men entrenched on a ridge to the east of the city, itself protected by the Garonne to the west and the Ers to the east. Beresford moved with two divisions against the southern end of the ridge, while diversionary attacks were launched from the north and west. After 12 hours of fierce fighting, in which the Spanish, at first repulsed, then returned with success, the French were driven back, and evacuated the city the following day. On the 12th Wellington found the theater decorated with laurel by the residents, who cheered the conqueror's entry as a band played 'God save the King'. The same evening Wellington learned of Napoleon's abdication. Soult thought the report false and was therefore not prepared to capitulate, but accepted Wellington's offer of an armistice.

News of the fall of Napoleon had not yet reached Bayonne, which remained besieged by Sir John Hope. On the night of the 14th General Thouvenot made a desperate sortie from the city in a gamble to break the Allied stranglehold. He failed, and in the attempt each side suffered about 800 casualties. On the 17th Soult, having received confirmation on the 12th that the abdication was genuine, finally surrendered. Bayonne followed suit

Toulouse, where it was possible Suchet might join him by fighting his way north.

Ten days later, on 30 March, the Allied armies to the north captured Paris and on 6 April Napoleon abdicated unconditionally. However, news of this would take some time to reach Soult and Wellington, and in the meantime the latter hoped to prevent the possibility of any junction between Soult and Suchet. He therefore struck first, on 10 April,

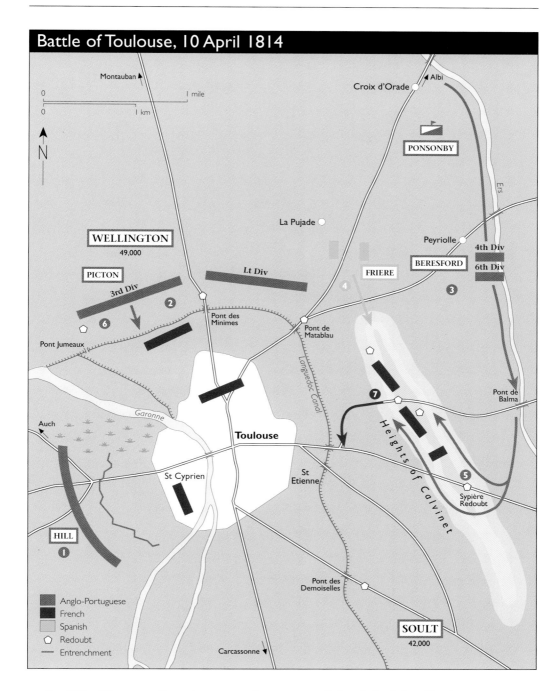

Battle of Toulouse, 10 April 1814

on the 26th. After more than six years, and
for reasons external to the immediate
conflict, the Peninsular War was finally over.

In the immediate aftermath of the
conflict Wellington was appointed British
Ambassador to France. His army was broken
up: some regiments returned home, others

were disbanded, while still others
disembarked at Bordeaux for service against
the United States, with whom Britain had
been at war since June 1812.

However important a role the Peninsular
War played in the defeat of France, it is
important to recognize that the war did not

end as a result of a decisive battle in the style of Austerlitz, Jena or Friedland. On the contrary, when the Allied armies occupied Paris and obliged Napoleon to abdicate, resistance in the south of France, though failing, was still very much under way. Thus, although Wellington's campaign in 1814 did not directly lead to French surrender, it nevertheless contributed to it by occupying Soult in the south.

Battle of Toulouse, 10 April 1814. The last major action of the Peninsular War, it was fought, unbeknownst to both sides, four days after Napoleon had unconditionally abdicated. Driven from most of his outer defenses after bitter fighting, Soult withdrew inside the city walls, only to realize that once Allied artillery was dragged up the heights his occupation would become untenable. The French therefore retreated south on the evening of the 11th. (Engraving by A. Dupray, Philip Haythornthwaite)

Part IV
The fall of the French empire 1813–1815

Napoleon and his forlorn staff lead the army through mud and snow during the campaign of 1814 in France. Despite the immense losses sustained by the *Grande Armée* the previous year, the Emperor steadfastly clung to his conviction that he could ultimately achieve victory, a belief underlined by his apparently callous indifference to losses. 'I grew up upon the field of battle,' Napoleon declared a few months before, 'and a man such as I cares little for the lives of a million men.' (Philip Haythornthwaite)

Origins of Prussian and Russian hostility

Germany in ferment, 1807–1812

Prussia's involvement in the campaigns of 1813–15 may be traced back to the autumn of 1806, when, having remained aloof from the Third Coalition, she foolishly confronted Napoleon with only Saxony at her side and with the Russian armies too far to the east to be of assistance before winter. Prussia had smarted at Napoleon's creation of the Confederation of the Rhine in the heart of Germany, and the French refusal to cede Hanover (formerly a British possession) as promised, convinced King Frederick William III (1770–1840) that the time had come to put into the field his armies, widely acknowledged to be the best in Europe. The twin decisive victories at Jena and Auerstädt on 14 October destroyed the illusion of Prussia's superiority and in a matter of weeks practically the whole of her forces were rounded up or besieged in fortresses and obliged to capitulate.

Seeing the vaunted Prussian ranks broken at Jena and Auerstädt was shocking enough for contemporaries, but to witness the systematic hunting down of the remnants of the army and the pitifully feeble resistance offered by fortresses throughout the kingdom in the weeks that followed was more than the nation could bear. Years of French occupation were to follow. The Treaty of Tilsit, concluded

Meeting at Tilsit, July 1807. While France and Russia settled their differences and established an alliance which recognized Napoleonic mastery of western and central Europe, Prussia was left truncated and humiliated: a new French satellite, the Kingdom of Westphalia, absorbed all Prussian territory west of the Elbe; Prussia was stripped of her Polish possessions to create another satellite, the Grand Duchy of Warsaw; Danzig was created a free city; Prussia was forced to join the Continental System; and, finally, French troops were to remain on her soil until enormous war indemnities were paid in full. (Ann Ronan Picture Library)

in July 1807, imposed subordination and in its wake Napoleon took deliberate and concerted measures to reduce not only Prussia's pride and prestige, but her military and economic power. Her status as a great power was effectively lost as Napoleon raised the status of smaller German states like Saxony, to which he allotted all Prussian territory in her former Polish province, while imposing a series of harsh restrictions on Prussia, including a massive indemnity of several hundred million francs. The much revered Queen Louise (1776–1810), symbol of Prussia's former grandeur and pride, had to endure numerous personal insults under French occupation, including Napoleon's description of her as 'the only real man in Prussia', and the queen's subjects attributed her premature death to such indignities. French troops occupied Prussia's fortresses on the Oder and her ports on the Baltic, while the Continental System destroyed the kingdom's seaborne commerce. Large parts of her territory were ceded to the French puppet state of Westphalia and her army was restricted to 42,000 men for 10 years. By all these measures and others, Prussia was left severely – but not fatally – weakened, and with her pride badly wounded she would remain a potentially dangerous time-bomb in the years after Tilsit.

The result was a movement of reform and growing patriotism, some of it exposed for all to see, though much of it kept secret so as to avoid French detection and suppression. Young Prussians established the anti-French *Tugendbunde* ('League of Virtue'), and other societies which encouraged not simply a narrow form of Prussian patriotism, but a kind of pan-German unity that demanded freedom from foreign domination in general, but French in particular. At official levels reforms were undertaken by men like Baron Stein (1757–1831), who worked in a civilian capacity, and by Gerhard von Scharnhorst (1755–1813) and Augustus von Gneisenau (1760–1831), who introduced new and sometimes radical changes within the army. Though aware of many of these activities, Napoleon did not fear Prussian attempts at

Queen Louise of Prussia. Revered by her subjects as the soul of national virtue, Louise openly advocated war with France in 1806 and regularly referred to Napoleon as 'the Monster'. On taking up the challenge, the Emperor announced in his *Bulletin* to the army, 'A beautiful queen wants to see a battle. So, let us be gallant and march at once ...' The two did not come face to face until the historic meeting at Tilsit in July 1807, by which time Prussia had been comprehensively beaten and occupied. (Ann Ronan Picture Library)

social, economic and military reform, for he believed Frederick William to be too timid to challenge French might. In any event, his kingdom had neither the financial nor the military resources to wage a war of national resistance.

For five years the Prussians suffered under Napoleonic occupation, their passionate hatred of the French and desire for vengeance growing more intense as the years passed. Such sentiments, whether overtly anti-French or simply pro-German, had been fostered and promoted by the philosophies of Immanuel Kant (1724–1804) and Johann Fichte (1762–1814). Before long, Prussians began to channel their discontent into thoughts of patriotism, embracing notions hitherto

Augustus Wilhelm, Count von Gneisenau. A general in the Prussian Army, Gneisenau worked with Scharnhorst in implementing wide-ranging military reforms between 1807 and 1813, including new principles for officer training, the establishment of a general staff, and the introduction of a system of reservists, by which large numbers of men could be trained, released back into civilian life and then called up on short notice to swell the ranks of the army. He performed well as Blücher's Chief of Staff from 1813 to 1815. (Philip Haythornthwaite)

It is only by means of the common characteristic of being German that we can avert the downfall of our nation, which is threatened by its fusion with foreign peoples, and win back again an individuality that is self-supporting and quite incapable of any dependence on others … we alone must help ourselves if help is to come to us … By means of the new [system of] education we want to mould the Germans into a corporate body … The German, if only he makes use of all his advantages, can always be superior to the foreigner … he alone is capable of real and rational love for his nation.

These ideas had an impact on civilians, both among young intellectuals and the nation as a whole, and also profoundly affected the officer corps, including men like Karl von Clausewitz (1780–1831), who would later attain even greater prominence with his magnum opus, *Vom Kriege* ('On War'). Not only did Prussian soldiers adopt the battle cry 'Das Vaterland!' in place of 'Der König!', but they were retrained to employ entirely new methods and tactics introduced by specially convened commissions that scrapped the obsolete system employed by the armies of Frederick the Great (1713–86). These were replaced with drills, organization, tactics, and technology, based on careful studies of Napoleonic innovation. The reformers abolished corporal punishment, much like in the French Revolution, as unworthy of men fighting for the 'nation' or 'fatherland', so that a soldier might follow his officers out of respect rather than fear. Just as in French revolutionary reforms, merit overcame aristocratic privilege as the principal criterion by which eager young men committed to national service acquired a commission and subsequent promotion.

The Prussian Army had been strictly limited to 42,000 men by Napoleonic *dictat*. Prussian military reformers now adopted an ingenious method of circumventing this restriction, enabling them to train more soldiers without exceeding the official size of the army. A system of shrinkage (*Krümpersystem*) was introduced by which men called to the colors received intensive

connected with the French Revolution, particularly the concepts of 'nation' and, in a peculiarly German form, 'fatherland'. Unlike the French, however, the Prussians did not regard such revolutionary principles as entirely incompatible with monarchy.

Wholesale military reforms were introduced in tandem with social reforms, which in turn fostered a growing sense of German nationalism between 1807 and 1813. In his *Addresses to the German Nation*, delivered in the winter of 1807–08 but which provided a model for many others to follow, Fichte defied the French occupiers with a less than subtle appeal for resistance to Napoleonic rule:

training, and joined the ranks for a limited time before being released back to civilian life. These recruits would later be recalled for further periods of training to maintain a reasonable level of fitness and acquaintance with military life, but once demobilized they became a sort of hidden reserve, which by the beginning of 1813 amounted to 80,000 men – in addition to the standing army. Therefore, as the spring campaign season opened, Prussia was reasonably ready – with Russia taking a leading role – to challenge Napoleonic authority, for spiritual and military preparations had been under way for five years. It was clear, moreover, that the winter retreat had inflicted a devastating blow to French arms, and the sight of the shattered remains of the *Grande Armée* shuffling on to Prussian territory emboldened those who were already inclined to resist the occupation.

Resistance emerged elsewhere in Germany during this period. When Austria again opposed France in 1809, Napoleon subdued her yet again, taking Vienna in May, suffering a temporary check at Aspern–Essling, and finally emerging victorious at Wagram on 5 July. By the Treaty of Schönbrunn (14 October), Emperor Francis I (1768–1835) ceded land to the Confederation of the Rhine, to Saxony, and to the Kingdom of Italy. Russia, by then in possession of Swedish Finland, received part of Austria's Polish territories in Galicia. Francis, playing for time in which to recover and reorganize both his army and his shattered finances, offered Napoleon – now divorced from the Empress Josephine (1763–1814) – the hand in marriage of his daughter, the Archduchess Marie-Louise (1791–1847), and the two produced a son, Napoleon II (1811–32), born on 20 April 1811, and known as the 'King of Rome'.

Hereafter, signs of growing German resistance became particularly marked. Not only had Austria risen up, but many individual Germans began to question the legitimacy of French domination of central European affairs. Already in 1806 the French had executed a bookseller from Nuremberg

Emperor Francis I of Austria. Under Francis Austria was a consistent opponent of both Revolutionary and Napoleonic France, fielding armies in numerous unsuccessful campaigns (1792–97, 1800, 1805, 1809) which reduced the vast Habsburg territories in Italy, Poland, and along the Adriatic coastline. After first seeking to appease Napoleon by offering his daughter, Marie-Louise, in marriage, Francis ultimately threw in his lot with the Allies in August 1813, and accompanied his army until the fall of Paris. (Philip Haythornthwaite)

named Johann Palm (1768–1806) for printing and distributing anti-French literature. In 1809 a young Thuringian, bent on assassinating Napoleon and in so doing accelerating the French withdrawal from Germany, was executed. And in the following year Andreas Hofer (1767–1810), who had raised the standard of revolt in the Tyrol just prior to the campaign of 1809, was also executed. The French had also demanded that the Prussian government arrest and hand over their foreign minister, Stein, for alleged conspiracies against France, and only Stein's refuge in Russia prevented a lengthy prison term and possibly death. Such heavy-handed policies against German patriots, accused of treason while merely questioning the French presence in their midst, began to effect a profound change in German attitudes.

Franco–Russian relations, 1805–1812

Russia had been instrumental in forming the Third Coalition in 1805 (including Austria, Britain, Sweden, and Naples) and had contributed substantial military resources to the campaign that ended disastrously for the forces of Tsar Alexander I (1777–1825) and his Austrian allies at Austerlitz, in Moravia, on 2 December of that year. Austria soon abandoned the coalition, while Alexander withdrew his army through Bohemia – his men badly shaken but not crushed.

When Prussia challenged France in the autumn of 1806, Russia prepared to assist her, but military intervention did not become effective until early 1807, by which time Prussia had been thoroughly beaten, and the costly struggle at Eylau on 7 February and, finally, the decisive defeat at Friedland on 14 June, persuaded Alexander to seek terms with Napoleon, in conjunction with the Prussian king. The peace of Tilsit the following month sparked a diplomatic revolution, converting France and Russia from adversaries into allies, with Europe split between them and a chastened Frederick William in control of a much weakened Prussia. By secret clauses in the treaty France promised to assist Russia in 'liberating' most of European Turkey, while in return Russia agreed to open hostilities with Britain and Turkey if Britain refused the Tsar's mediation.

Both sides promised to pressure Sweden, Denmark and Portugal into conforming to the Continental System – Napoleon's ambitious scheme to close the whole European coastline to British commerce in an attempt to strangle the British economy. Russia cooperated, albeit unenthusiastically, and duly declared war on Britain in November (and invaded Swedish territory in 1808), though war with Britain amounted to

Alexander I of Russia. The Tsar's formidable forces opposed the French in 1805 and 1807, before Napoleon finally decided to invade Alexander's vast empire. Despite the occupation of Moscow, Alexander not only refused to negotiate, but pursued the French out of Russia and across Germany in a relentless campaign to reach Paris and overthrow the Bonaparte dynasty. Russia's major contribution to victory and Alexander's considerable influence on affairs at the Congress of Vienna established Russia as the most powerful nation on the Continent until the Crimean War. (Philip Haythornthwaite)

little more than the cessation of trade with her. Napoleon and Alexander renewed their agreement at a conference at Erfurt in September 1808, while French armies were busy in Spain trying to subdue that nation as part of the same scheme to eradicate British trade with the Continent.

That close Franco–Russian relations never fully developed may be divined by Alexander's decision to stand aloof during the 1809 campaign, his armies merely observing on the Austrian frontiers. With victory achieved over Austria for the fourth time since 1792 (1797, 1800 and 1805), Napoleon's new friendship, such as it was, with the Habsburg monarchy caused considerable concern at St Petersburg, and in any event by 1810 Russia was growing tired of the economic hardship caused by her inability to carry on trade with Britain. Pro-British factions in the court of St Petersburg were now once again in the ascendant and there were signs that Napoleon was not fulfilling his side of the Tilsit agreement. He had raised the Electorate of Saxony to the status of a kingdom and had created the Kingdom of Westphalia for his brother Jerome out of Prussian territory, but the Emperor had done nothing to hasten the partition of Turkey, and Russia continued to wage her war against the Ottomans, begun in 1806, without any French aid. Moreover, the territory of the Duke of Oldenburg, a relation of Alexander's, was annexed to France without prior consultation. Russian anxieties grew still deeper when, in 1810, Napoleon not only annexed Holland in order better to enforce the Continental System, but also extended his control along the coastline stretching to the Baltic Sea. Both these actions were clear violations of Tilsit.

For his part, Alexander had also broken his commitments. He faithfully closed his ports to British merchant vessels, yet British and colonial goods still came ashore via ships flying neutral flags and protected by Royal Navy escorts. The fact remained that, by 1810, the exclusion of British commerce had badly injured the Russian economy; by employing this expedient, Alexander could improve his financial situation by collecting import duties on such goods. By the end of the year he had also increased the duty on French imports coming by land – yet another source of grievance. The Tsar also grew increasingly resentful of the French satellite, the Grand Duchy of Warsaw – a Polish state reconstituted from Prussian and Austrian annexations of the partitions of the 1790s – and suspected the French of involvement in the Swedes' nomination of the former Napoleonic marshal, Jean-Baptiste Bernadotte (1763–1844), to their throne, as crown prince. Thus, through a combination of many factors based on mutual mistrust and self-interest, the Franco–Russian alliance established in 1807 had effectively ceased to exist by 1811.

By this time Napoleon, grown tired of Russian refusals to support the ban on British trade, planned his ill-fated invasion, and on 24 February 1812 he enlisted Prussia's nominal support in the form of 20,000 men, augmented by 60,000 Austrians supplied in conformity with a treaty concluded on 12 March. Together with his own *Grande Armée* of genuinely loyal troops – half of whom hailed from outside France herself – the Emperor had 600,000 men ready by the spring. Alexander, for his part, was not idle. Apart from assembling large forces of his own, on 5 April he established an offensive and defensive alliance with Sweden – finding Bernadotte in fact hostile to Napoleon – and on 28 May he ended his six-year war with Turkey, thus releasing much needed troops for the theater of war to the north.

At the end of March, through secret overtures to Frederick William, he learned that Prussia's support for the invasion was nothing more than a demonstration, with an auxiliary corps of 20,000 men under Major-General Yorck von Wartenburg (1759–1830), while the Austrians indicated on 25 April that their army, under Prince von Schwarzenberg (1771–1820), would not take part in serious fighting. In July Britain and Russia happily signed a treaty of peace, ending the quasi-war that Tilsit had created. For the first time since April 1805, during the formation of the Third Coalition, these two peripheral, yet powerful, nations entered into a formal alliance by which Britain promised subsidiary aid and weapons, while Russia prepared to oppose the French invasion with her enormous resources in manpower.

Napoleon's invasion began on 22 June, he fought a costly struggle at Borodino on 7 September and entered Moscow the same month. Weeks passed as he waited for the Tsar to come to terms. Receiving no communication and with most of the city already destroyed by fire, Napoleon began the long winter retreat, with its now well-known and fatal consequences.

Opposing forces

The *Grande Armée*

The catastrophic losses suffered in the Russian campaign had so profound and multi-faceted an effect on the *Grande Armée* as to require virtually its complete reconstitution for the start of the campaign of 1813. Of the approximately 655,000 troops with which Napoleon had crossed the Niemen in June 1812, scarcely 100,000 bedraggled, broken men staggered into East Prussia little more than six months later. Of the 1,300 pieces of field artillery that had accompanied the army into Russia, only about 250 guns remained, most of the others having been simply abandoned due to lack of transport.

Notwithstanding these unprecedented losses, Napoleon immediately set to work to revive his shattered army, demonstrating in the process the organizational genius that had contributed so much to the construction of that institution which had made the empire possible in the first place. Napoleon must be given credit for the almost miraculous effort through which he recreated the *Grande Armée* out of the wreckage of 1812. His vision was ambitious indeed: 656,000 men, and he set about drawing together troops from various sources which ultimately netted him about 400,000, of whom half constituted the field army when hostilities opened in April. A high proportion of the new levies were very young and came to be called the 'Marie-Louises', after the Empress who in 1812 ordered their assembly on behalf of the absent Emperor. With admirable foresight Napoleon had called up the class of 1813 before the Russian campaign. These consisted of about 130,000 conscripts in the process of completing training, 80,000 National Guardsmen placed in the ranks of the regulars, and 100,000 more men who had, for various reasons, not joined the colors between 1809

and 1812. To all these were added troops withdrawn from Spain, from which they could not be spared without adverse effects on that theater of operations. Finally, patient British blockading had trapped naval vessels in ports for years, rendering their crews useless. These underemployed men and others from the coastal garrisons, particularly marines, were sent east where they could be of more immediate use.

As far as equipment and matériel were concerned, feverish efforts were under way on the home front, as the Marquis de Caulaincourt (1773–1827) observed:

France is one vast workshop. The entire French nation overlooked his reverses and vied with one another in displaying zeal and devotion … It was a personal triumph for the Emperor, who with amazing energy directed all the resources of which his genius was capable into organizing the great national endeavour. Things seemed to come into existence as if by magic …

France, with a population of over 30 million, was certainly productive, but one essential commodity could not be manufactured: horses. Shortage of horses was one of the most serious deficiencies suffered by Napoleon's forces at the opening of the spring campaign of 1813. While the ranks of the infantry could, as a result of exceptional efforts, be filled with the young and the old, and while guns could be found in depots or manufactured anew, the complete replacement of lost horseflesh proved impossible.

In all the various arms that required horses in Russia – the artillery, the sundry transport services, and of course the cavalry itself – losses numbered between 160,000 and 200,000. These were not merely woeful, but irreparable losses, depriving Napoleon of the mounted patrols required for proper reconnaissance, in addition to cavalry for ordinary combat and pursuit operations. After the Russian campaign new mounts would never remotely match Napoleon's stated requirements, nor could the numbers or quality of the troopers themselves be replaced, for even where a horse could be provided, it required three times longer to train a cavalryman than a simple foot soldier, and such training could not be provided on the march. Thus, deficiencies in cavalry simply could not be made good in the time available. The same, of course, applied to the artillery, a specialized arm that required time to acquaint officers and their crews with the science of gunnery. Here, too, the guns required horses to pull them, as did the thousands of supply wagons that accompanied the army. An obvious expedient lay in stripping formations posted elsewhere in the empire, and therefore Napoleon issued immediate orders for the transfer of most of his cavalry from Spain. This, however, would take time.

Yet time, like men and horses, was in short supply. The Russians were approaching from the east and the Prussians had yet to commit themselves. There is no doubt that French soldiers would often fight bravely in the campaigns ahead, but their efforts were frequently hamstrung by inadequate training and experience at all levels, and this resulted in a decline in their fighting capabilities. Colonel Raymond de Montesquiou, Duc de Fezensac, attributed the French defeats of 1813 to the decline in the quality of the soldiers.

The Army was composed of young soldiers who had to be taught everything, and of non-commissioned officers who did not know much more themselves. The officers were better, for they were old cadres who had suffered far less destruction in Russia than had the N.C.O. cadres.

But the process had begun even before 1812. As early as 1809, he noted, Napoleon began to complain that his soldiers were not like those of 1805: the men at Wagram were not like those at Austerlitz. By 1813, the new army was not even up to the standards of Wagram. 'No doubt,' de Fezensac continued:

there were moments of élan, and fine examples of gallantry. When the generals marched in the front rank, the troops were inspired by their example, but this enthusiasm was short-lived, and the heroes of one day displayed nothing but despondency and weakness on the morrow. It is not on battlefields that soldiers go through the severest ordeals: French youth has an instinct for bravery. But a soldier must be able to put up with hunger, fatigue, bad weather; he must march day and night in worn-out shoes, must brave the cold and the rain with his uniform in tatters, and do all this without grumbling and while staying in a good humour. We have known men like this; but it was asking too much of young fellows whose constitution was barely formed and who, to start with, could not have the military spirit, the 'religion' of the colours, and that moral energy which doubles a man's strength while doubling his courage.

Nevertheless, no other nation in Europe and no political leader could have accomplished so much with the resources and time available. Napoleon's achievement must be seen in this light.

As for the French allies, they remained loyal at least in name – Denmark, the Confederation of the Rhine, the Italian states – but many of these, particularly the Germans, were disaffected by the experiences of the Russian campaign, where they were often treated as second-class troops, and during the autumn campaign they largely defected, aligning themselves with the Allies. The Polish contingent from the Duchy of Warsaw was effectively destroyed in the previous campaign, and the Russian advance in February 1813 prevented all but a token reconstitution of an armed force.

The Russian Army

The Tsar's forces were impressive both in numbers and doggedness. Major-General Sir

Robert Wilson (1777–1849), British military commissioner attached to Alexander's headquarters, found Russian troops:

… endowed with great bodily strength … with martial countenance and complexion; inured to the extremes of weather and hardship; to the worst and scantiest food; to marches for days and nights, of four hours' repose and six hours' progress; accustomed to laborious toils, and the carriage of heavy burdens; ferocious, but disciplined; obstinately brave, and susceptible to enthusiastic excitements; devoted to their sovereign, their chief, and their country. Religious without being weakened by superstition; patient, docile, and obedient; possessing all the energetic characteristics of a barbaric people, with the advantages engrafted of civilisation …

If such a force appeared unstoppable, it must be observed that the campaign of 1812 had cost the Russian Army a great many experienced officers and men – an estimated 250,000 casualties. Friedrich von Schubert, of German parentage but a senior quartermaster on the Russian General Staff, commented

that by 1812 its quality had markedly declined, largely from losses and from the creation of new, less experienced regiments.

The constant wars had taken away many of the old soldiers, and the young ones did not have the same traditions; nor could they feel the same attachment to their corps as the old ones did.

John Spencer Stanhope, a British civilian traveling with the Russian Army in Germany, considered them impressive soldiers:

I found them a fine and hardy race, almost insensible to pain: they were, indeed, men of

Cossacks. Irregular horsemen with exceptional riding abilities and endurance but lacking discipline, Cossacks generally shied away from direct contact with cohesive units on the battlefield, concentrating instead on harrying their opponents' flanks and rear, raiding, reconnaissance and skirmishing. Cossacks were notorious looters and their presence in Germany was dreaded as much by the local populace as by the French themselves. On the fall of Paris in 1814 the Cossacks established their camp in the Bois de Boulogne, attracting many a curious spectator. (Peter Hofschröer)

iron. I remember seeing one coolly smoking his pipe, whilst the surgeon was cutting and slashing at him, in order to extricate a [musket] ball; and though I witnessed the sufferings of many of their wounded men, I do not think that I heard a single one utter a groan. They really seemed to be made of different stuff from other men: their frames and sinews were, apparently, as hard as their minds ...

Observers seem to agree that the junior officers were appalling, perhaps because, with no opportunity for advancement, there was little incentive to display leadership.

The Cossacks were the most curious element of the army – wild, irregular, extremely adept horsemen from the steppes of the Don and Dniester who specialized in raiding and reconnaissance rather than the massed charges of their regular counterparts in the cavalry. Wilson described them thus:

Mounted on a very little, ill-conditioned, but well-bred horse, which can walk at the rate of five miles an hour with ease, or, in his speed, dispute the race with the swiftest – with a short whip on his wrist (as he wears no spur) – armed with the lance, a pistol in his girdle, and a sword, he never fears a competitor in single combat ... They act in dispersion, and when they do re-unite to charge, it is not with a systematic formation, but en masse, or what in Germany is called the swarm attack ... Dexterous in the management of a horse that is guided only by the snaffle, they can twist and bend their course through the most intricate country at full speed.

The Austrian Army

Like Prussia, Austria had acted as a nominal, but reluctant ally of France during the invasion of Russia, but its army had seen virtually no action and, though it did not participate in the spring campaign, Napoleon had no illusions that Francis was still a friend. When the armistice ended Austria boasted the largest army in Europe, with 429,000 men in uniform, of whom

Prince Schwarzenberg. A veteran of Austria's campaigns against the Turks and the French Revolutionaries, Schwarzenberg managed to avoid falling into French hands when General Mack surrendered his army at Ulm in 1805. In 1812 he led the Austrian corps that reluctantly accompanied the *Grande Armée* into Russia, but deliberately avoided confrontation with the Tsar's forces. When Austria joined the Sixth Coalition in August 1813, Schwarzenberg was appointed C-in-C of the Allied armies and led them to victory during the Leipzig campaign and the invasion of France. (Philip Haythornthwaite)

approximately 300,000 were available for actual operations in the Army of Bohemia, and by the end of the year the army's ranks would swell to over half a million. During the summer British subsidies helped alleviate the deficiencies in equipment and money needed to prepare Habsburg forces for the coming campaign. There were of course veterans of the 1809 campaign in its ranks, but the army had gleaned no combat experience in Russia and over 60 percent of the troops were inexperienced, obliged to complete their training on campaign. Overall, the army was of good quality, and when Sir Charles Stewart watched a review near Prague in mid-August he was suitably impressed, even if such troops would have been specially well-drilled for the occasion:

The composition of this army was magnificent, although I perceived a great many recruits: still the system that reigned throughout, and the military air that marked the soldier…must ever fix it in my recollection as the finest army of the continent ….[T]heir movement was beautifully correct, and the troops seemed formed in the most perfect order.

The cavalry he thought particularly impressive and the artillery, though perhaps not as well-equipped as the Russians', was nevertheless staffed by '…officers and men [who are] scientific and expert, and the artillery is not to be judged of by its appearance.

The Prussian Army

Prussia and her army had learned many lessons since the catastrophic events of 1806–07. The defeats at Jena and Auerstädt were catalysts for fundamental reforms, beginning with the appointment of Graf Lottum and General Scharnhorst to lead the newly created Military Reorganization Commission. In 1807 this body recommended that the nobility lose its monopoly on officer commissions, that universal military service be adopted, and that hitherto draconian methods of military discipline be relaxed. Their recommendations soon bore fruit: by the end of 1808 new regulations put a stop to advancement based solely on seniority, and permitted any man with the requisite educational qualifications to hold a commission in any branch of the army. Corporal punishment was abolished, a new system of organization was adopted for the army as a whole, and the old style of strict linear tactics was replaced with new formations much more in keeping with the effective advances so palpably demonstrated by the French.

Thus, by the time Prussia was ready to fight France again, in 1813, men such as Scharnhorst, Clausewitz and Yorck had made great strides in modernizing the Prussian

Recruitment office for Lützow's *Freikorps* in Breslau, Silesia. In March 1813, Major Adolf Lützow (1782–1834) officially sponsored the formation of a free corps of patriotic Germans eager to liberate German soil. Independent units such as these were employed away from the main battlefields to harass French communications, rear formations, and to foment insurrection in towns occupied by Napoleon's troops. Improvements in discipline, equipment, and combat experience enabled Lützow's unit to become amalgamated into the regular Prussian forces in 1814. (Philip Haythornthwaite)

Army, including the introduction of new tactics for all arms that shook off much of the army's outdated 18th-century practices. Such men introduced new, more democratic regulations on the selection of officers, with regulations issued by the king in 1808 establishing the principle that:

… a claim to officer rank shall in peacetime be warranted only by knowledge and education, in time of war by exceptional bravery and quickness of perception. From the whole nation, therefore, all individuals who possess these qualities can lay title to the highest positions of

honour in the army. All social preference which has hitherto existed ceases completely in the army, and everyone, without regard to his social background, has equal duties and equal rights.

The Prussian Army regulars and militia took on thousands of volunteers in this climate of enthusiasm, and many units were so overwhelmed by young boys wishing to serve as drummers and buglers that many of them had to be rejected. Supply of proper

Crown Prince Bernadotte of Sweden. Commander of the Army of the North, he had previously served Napoleon as a Marshal, particularly distinguishing himself in the Austerlitz and Jena campaigns, before falling foul of the Emperor after Wagram. When elected Crown Prince of Sweden the following year his ties with Napoleon were severed forever. Bernadotte's disinclination to commit his troops against his own countrymen was caustically remarked upon by many at Allied headquarters. (Philip Haythornthwaite)

soldiers, however, could not keep pace with the army's unceasing demands, and resort was made to a comprehensive system of compulsory enlistment.

Conscription provided Prussia with an army very different from that inherited from Frederick the Great which had fought in the campaigns of 1806–1807. Many units in 1813 represented a true cross-section of society, as a battalion commander recorded of his men in the East Prussian *Landwehr* (national militia):

Beside a grey-haired man you might find a boy of seventeen; beside a worthy family-man, who had never conceived the idea of taking up arms while in the quiet circle of his civil profession, might be a gay adventurer; beside an educated young man, who had broken away from the happiest circumstances so as to fight for the Fatherland with high ideas of duty and honour, stood a raw youth.

In terms of size, again the reforms had achieved a great deal, for although the Treaty of Tilsit had strictly limited the army to 42,000 men, this had been cunningly circumvented so as to enable Prussia, by the opening of the campaign season of 1813, to supply 80,000 men. Nevertheless, after years of occupation by French and French-allied troops, Prussia had few funds with which to clothe, equip, and arm her men, and great reliance was placed on shipments of these commodities from Britain, who supplied muskets and uniforms in large quantities. Moreover, while the king issued a decree embodying 110,000 men of the *Landwehr*, enthusiasm for the war could not entirely compensate for fighting efficiency impaired by lack of training and a critical shortage of equipment – and many units resorted to using axes, farm tools, pikes, and obsolete firearms.

Sweden

Sweden provided troops during the autumn campaign of 1813 as part of the Army of the North, which also contained Russian and Prussian contingents. By the time of the

Leipzig campaign the Swedes numbered nearly 65,000 men, the infantry of average quality, their artillery of iron rather than brass, their equipment inferior to their contemporaries, and their cavalry indifferently mounted. Their chief deficiency lay at the most senior level, for their commander-in-chief, Bernadotte, though a former Marshal of the French Empire with considerable battlefield experience, was reluctant to commit his troops to battle. His was a delicate balancing act, for he did not wish to upset his countrymen with the horror of heavy casualties, nor did he particularly wish to inflict them on the soldiers of his native home, which it was often supposed he wished to rule once Napoleon was defeated and deposed.

Britain

Britain, with a population of only 12 million, maintained a small army committed to the ongoing campaign in Spain, where her forces occupied the attention of over 200,000 French troops. Her other major commitment was the Royal Navy's comprehensive blockade of French ports. As in all previous campaigns against Revolutionary and Napoleonic France,

The retreat from Moscow. Setting out in winter conditions, the much-reduced *Grande Armée* not only faced Cossacks and partisans harrying its flanks and rear, but an over-stretched and vulnerable supply system that completely collapsed as temperatures plummeted and snowfall increased. Russian regular forces also pursued, nearly trapping Napoleon's main body at the crossing of the Beresina in late November. Marshal Ney (center) heroically led the rearguard and is reputed to have been the last man to leave Russia. (Philip Haythornthwaite)

Britain would supply massive amounts of arms, ordnance and supplies to the Allies, together with unprecedented subsidies exceeding £26 million for the period 1813–15. From the beginning of the autumn campaign the amount of matériel and other items shipped for the use of the Russian, Prussian, Austrian, and Swedish armies was impressive, including over 200 cannon, complete with transport and ammunition, over 120,000 firearms, over 18 million rounds of ammunition and 23,000 barrels of powder, over 30,000 swords and sabers, 150,000 complete uniforms and 187,000 yards of cloth, over 1.5 million pounds of beef, biscuit, and flour, over 175,000 boots and shoes, 28,000 gallons of brandy and rum, and tens of thousands of other items such as knapsacks, clothing, saddles, and canteens.

A bid for revenge

Although the origins of the War of the Sixth Coalition may be found in the treaty of alliance established between Britain and Russia in June 1812, it was not clear until after the retreat from Moscow that this cooperation between such far-flung allies would develop into a coalition embracing Prussia, and Austrian intentions were far from clear. The immediate origins of the war, therefore, may be found in the snows of Russia, where the catastrophic retreat of the *Grande Armée* – ordered without due regard for historical precedent and against the advice of sounder heads – laid the basis for wider European resistance. Pursued by the Russian Army, local partisans and, of course, the ubiquitous Cossacks, Napoleon's seemingly endless columns withered away under fatigue, hunger, exposure, and constant harassment, culminating in the horrific crossing of the Beresina river at the end of November. Already a shadow of its former self, the army of frost-bitten and starving souls suffered further losses when over 25,000 soldiers and camp-followers were caught on the wrong side of the river, with the bridge unable to bear the traffic. The émigré Comte de Rochechouart related the horrific scene in his memoirs:

Nothing in the world more saddening, more distressing! One saw heaped bodies of men, women and even children; soldiers of all arms, all nations, choked by the fugitives or hit by Russian grapeshot; horses, carriages, guns, ammunition waggons, abandoned carts. One cannot imagine a more terrifying sight than the appearance of the two broken bridges, and the river frozen right to the bottom … Peasants and Cossacks prowled around these piles of dead, removing whatever was most valuable … On the bridge I saw an unfortunate woman sitting; her legs dangled outside the bridge and were caught in the ice. For twenty-four hours she had been clasping a frozen
child to her breast. She begged me to save the child, unaware that she was holding out a corpse to me! She herself was unable to die, despite her sufferings, but a Cossack did her this service by firing a pistol in her ear so as to put an end to her appalling agony.

On 5 December Napoleon mounted a sledge, abandoned what remained of his shattered army and made haste for Paris, there to raise a new army against a vengeful Russia and an almost inevitably resurgent Prussia, which by this stage was Napoleon's unwilling ally.

Back in France, circumstances were also looking grim. General Claude de Malet (1754–1812) had attempted a coup, and the disaster in Russia had been of such a magnitude that even Napoleon's hitherto masterful propaganda could not conceal the fact. In the famous 29th Bulletin, dated 17 December 1812, he reported to his incredulous people the destruction of the *Grande Armée*. The writing was on the wall and the news created shock and disbelief in some and outright terror in the minds of others. Just before midnight on 18 December the cannon at the *Invalides* boomed out, announcing the return of the Emperor to Paris. But the news of the disaster in Russia had preceded him, and Colonel de Fezensac, an aide de camp to Marshal Berthier (1753–1815), on leave in Paris, observed that time was running out:

The Emperor was invincible no longer. While we were dying in Russia, another army was perishing in Spain, and in Paris an obscure conspirator had tried to seize power. The campaign of 1813 was about to open, but in what circumstances! The defection of Prussia was no longer in doubt; the Austrian alliance was at the least very shaky; and the exhaustion of France increased in proportion as the list of her enemies grew longer. The stories told by officers who had survived the retreat contributed to intensify people's fear. Paris, used as she had been to songs of victory during the previous fifteen years, was learning day by day and with pained surprise the details of some fresh public or private calamity … people were shocked to see the Emperor entertaining at the Tuileries. It was an insult to public grief and revealed a cruel insensitivity to the victims. I shall always remember one of those dismal balls, at which I felt as if I were dancing on graves.

The shock was particularly great, not simply because of the scale of the catastrophe, which was revealed by news sent home by the survivors, but because France had long since come to expect victory followed by victory. The Emperor's valet, Wairy Constant (1778–1845), recalled the mortification pervading society, for it was 'the first time that Paris saw him come back from a campaign without bringing with him a fresh peace which the glory of his arms had won.' A deep sense of foreboding pervaded the country, the feeling that, as Talleyrand put it: 'the beginning of the end, and … the end itself could not be far distant.' As a first step to consolidate his support in the empire, Napoleon sought peace with the Pope through a new concordat. Meanwhile, far to the east, the Russians continued their march west, approaching Prussian soil and the Duchy of Warsaw, which they would soon occupy. The French evacuated the Polish capital between 4 and 8 February.

As discussed earlier, during the Russian campaign Prussia had furnished an auxiliary corps under Yorck, subordinate to Marshal Macdonald. But on 30 December Yorck concluded a secret convention with the Russian General Diebitsch at Tauroggen, which then converted Prussian troops under his command from French allies to neutrals, with an implicit part of the agreement being that they would soon join the Russians. Frederick William initially repudiated the agreement, anxious not to confront Napoleon anew, however weakened the Emperor now appeared to be. Yet the king could not hold back the rising tide of nationalism within his country, led predominantly by young Prussians –

Generals Diebitsch and Yorck meet on Christmas Day, 1812. While the French northern flank was busy retreating from Riga, Russian troops under Diebitsch managed to isolate Yorck's contingent of 17,000 disaffected Prussians. Five days of negotiations resulted in the Convention of Tauroggen, by which Yorck rendered his corps neutral, so establishing the precedent for Prussia's *volte face* and active participation against the French occupier. (Philip Haythornthwaite)

though other Germans as well. Hawkish elements within court circles, together with many senior officers, such as Generals Yorck, Blücher, and Bülow, exerted still further pressure on the otherwise feeble-minded and dithering monarch.

With the nation seething with revolt, on 28 February Prussia secretly concluded with Russia the Convention of Kalisch, committing Prussia to join the war in the coming weeks, in return for Russian recognition of Prussia's pre-1806 frontiers. The king was heavily influenced by Baron Stein, the exiled Prussian minister, who had become one of the Tsar's advisers. He frankly told the king, who had maintained a sort of paternalistic relationship with Alexander for over 10 years, not to prevaricate, for the populace of East Prussia, not to mention Yorck's troops, were already in revolt against Napoleon, and that retention of the throne required him to satisfy his own people's expectations and join forces with Alexander. Notwithstanding Frederick William's

continued hesitation and fear of the consequences, Prussia formally declared war on France on 13 March, unleashing feelings of pent-up hatred against her neighbor which were to manifest themselves in future conflicts stretching well into the twentieth century. If the king harbored doubts, the nation did not. The sentiments of one battalion commander summed up the mood when he wrote of this period in his memoirs:

This was a splendid time of noble enthusiasm … In the conviction that individuals as well as whole nations could achieve their destiny by great effort and noble deeds alone, everybody was resolved to do every manly action, [and] was ready for any sacrifice, in order to help liberate the Fatherland.

Austria, for her part, declared her neutrality and quietly withdrew her

ABOVE Staggering out of Russia in January 1813, the remnants of the *Grande Armée* reached safety either in East Prussia (as shown here) or the Duchy of Warsaw. On the 7th, a British liaison officer with the Russian Army reported that 16,000 bodies were left behind in Vilna, only 50 miles (80 km) from the Polish frontier, rendering the streets '… almost impassable, so filled they were with the dead bodies of men, and horses, and broken carriages &c.' (Peter Hofschröer)

RIGHT With the destruction of the *Grande Armée* in Russia, operations shifted to Germany, where by the spring of 1813 Napoleon had raised a new army to oppose the Russians and Prussians. Despite numerous disadvantages Napoleon initially performed fairly well, with victories at Lützen (2 May) and Bautzen (20–21 May), and the capture of Dresden (7–8 May). Nevertheless, after Austria joined the coalition in August, Allied fortunes improved, with a series of reverses inflicted on Napoleon's subordinates at Grossbeeren (23 August), the Katzbach (26 August), Kulm (29–30 August), and Dennewitz (6 September). Napoleon did manage to secure an important victory at Dresden (26–27 August), but his comprehensive defeat at Leipzig (16–18 October) forced him to retreat back to France, drubbing the Bavarians at Hanau (30 October) en route.

Theater of operations in Germany, 1813

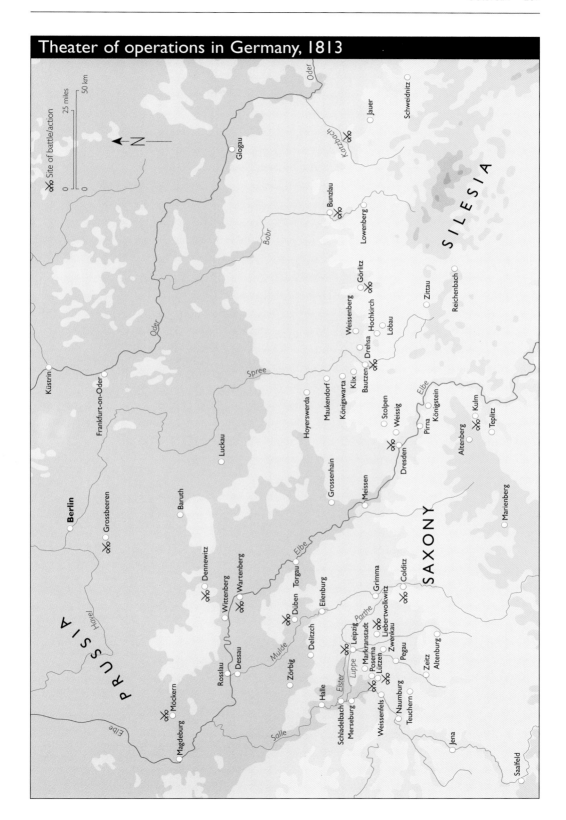

Site of battle/action

50 km
25 miles

N

SILESIA

PRUSSIA

SAXONY

Oder
Oder
Bobr
Katzbach
Spree
Elbe
Mulde
Salle
Elster
Luppe
Parthe
Havel
Elbe

Schweidnitz
Jauer
Glogau
Bunzlau
Lowenberg
Görlitz
Reichenbach
Zittau
Weissenberg
Hochkirch
Drehsa
Löbau
Maukendorf
Königswarta
Klix
Bautzen
Stolpen
Weissig
Königstein
Kulm
Pirna
Altenberg
Teplitz
Hoyerswerda
Küstrin
Frankfurt-on-Oder
Luckau
Grossenhain
Meissen
Dresden
Marienberg
Berlin
Grossbeeren
Baruth
Dennewitz
Wartenberg
Wittenberg
Torgau
Düben
Eilenburg
Grimma
Colditz
Rosslau
Dessau
Zörbig
Delitzch
Halle
Schladelbach
Merseburg
Weissenfels
Naumburg
Teuchern
Leipzig
Markranstadt
Poserna
Lützen
Liebertwolkwitz
Zwenkau
Pegau
Zeitz
Altenburg
Jena
Saalfeld
Möckern
Magdeburg

Frederick William III, King of Prussia. Indecisive and undistinguished, he doomed his country to eventual disaster by declining to join Austria, Russia, and Britain in the War of the Third Coalition in 1805. When he finally confronted France in 1806 he did so before the Russian armies could participate in the opening campaign. Even in the wake of the disastrous retreat from Moscow, Frederick William hesitated to throw in his lot with Russia until domestic political pressure and increasingly strident calls from the army obliged him to join the Sixth Coalition in 1813. (Ann Ronan Picture Library)

contingent, marching it to Bohemia via Warsaw, and thus providing a wide avenue through which the Russians could advance if, as it appeared, they wished to carry the war into the Napoleonic empire itself.

By the Convention of Kalisch, Russia had promised to deploy at least 150,000 men, but had only mustered about 120,000 by April. These were to be led by the veteran of the 1812 campaign, Field Marshal Michael Kutusov (1745–1813), who, in common with most of the other senior generals, was not enthusiastic about pursuing the French and risking the army in Germany. Russian troops had already suffered quite appallingly in the winter campaign of 1812 – almost as badly as the French – and were now operating along lines of communications extending hundreds of miles. Kutusov and other generals were on the whole satisfied with having seen them off Russian soil. Not so the crusading Tsar, who wished to avenge the destruction of Moscow by taking Paris, and to be seen as the liberator of Germany. Kutusov, Alexander insisted, was to assume the offensive and cross the Elbe.

The 'War of German Liberation' and the invasion of France

In grand strategic terms Napoleon understood the seriousness of his predicament at the beginning of 1813, but by no means despaired of his prospects. Austria remained neutral; Prussia, though hostile, could be overthrown again and her capital occupied; Russia, finding herself isolated, would be defeated in turn. The Tsar's army had, for the most part, not offered battle during the advance on Moscow; now that they were looking for a fight, they would have it – and suffer the long-sought blow which had eluded Napoleon at Borodino. Britain, though enjoying increasing success in Spain and continuing her strangling blockade of the European coastline, could be dealt with once the remainder of continental resistance had been subdued and the threat to the empire eliminated.

When the remnant of the *Grande Armée* emerged from Russia in December 1812 it established itself in Poland and East Prussia, under the temporary command of Marshal Joachim Murat (1767–1815). Before departing for Paris Napoleon had issued hopelessly unrealistic orders that Murat, with fewer than 40,000 men, should defend the line of the Vistula. French garrisons remained scattered in the fortresses of Danzig, Stettin, and Glogau-on-the-Oder, but there was little to stop the Russian advance. Kutusov did in fact halt behind that river in order himself to recover from the extreme rigors of the campaign, and to await supplies and reinforcements. But he did not remain stationary for long, and on 16 January 1813 he resumed his march west, occupying Warsaw unopposed on 7 February. Murat withdrew further, toward Posen, leaving 30,000 troops under General Jean Rapp (1772–1821) to hold the port of Danzig, and smaller contingents to occupy Thorn and Modlin. But Murat wanted nothing more to

do with operations, and after command devolved on Eugène de Beauharnais (1781–1824), Napoleon's step-son (the former Empress Josephine's son), Murat returned to Naples, of which he had been king since 1808.

Eugène appreciated that it was hopeless to defend Posen: his troops were exhausted, camped amidst a population seething with revolt, and faced by Russian forces whose advance across the frozen rivers could not be stopped. Fortunately for him, he was not expected to, as new orders arrived, calling on him to hold the River Oder. He therefore withdrew westward to Frankfurt, where he linked forces with a corps under Marshal Gouvion St Cyr (1764–1830). Combined French forces now totaled 30,000, but news that the Russians had already passed the Oder to the north obliged the French to retire west yet again, first in the direction of Berlin and then to Wittenberg, a city on the Elbe. The French arrived on 6 March, but soon discovered that the river was too long to defend. All in all, the Emperor's expectations were too grand, and six days later the French evacuated Hamburg. Eugène was only being realistic, appreciating as he did – and Napoleon did not – that the quality of his men left much to be desired and that popular dissent was growing throughout Germany.

With the assurance of direct Russian assistance as laid down by the Convention of Kalisch the previous month, Frederick William declared war on France on 13 March, and by the end of the month Napoleon, still in Paris, was aware of the fact. Prussia's defection posed an immediate, though not necessarily fatal, danger to the French position in Germany. From Marienwerder, General Wittgenstein (1769–1843) was moving west, soon joined by Generals Yorck and Bülow, with whose forces Wittgenstein now had 40,000 men. Kutusov, with about 30,000 men, stood near Kalisch, while the Russian advance guard under General Winzingerode (1770–1818), numbering 13,000, was considerably forward into Saxony, where it joined forces with 25,000 Prussians under General Gebhard von Blücher (1742–1819). This combined force then moved on Dresden, which it occupied on 27 March. At the same time Bernadotte had mustered a force of 28,000 men in Pomerania, while 9,000 Anglo–Hanoverians were in the vicinity of Stralsund.

The first major action of the campaign occurred at Möckern, where on 3 April Eugène attacked Wittgenstein, whose defeat nevertheless did not prevent the Russian commander from linking up with Blücher, then at Dresden. With Allied efforts at concentration now well under way, Eugène decided to abandon the upper Elbe and withdrew to the river Saale, whose strength would provide Napoleon with the precious time he required to raise sufficient numbers of troops to oppose the Allies with some prospect of success.

Ever since he had returned to Paris in December, Napoleon had been busily employed in trying to raise new armies. Various expedients were resorted to: extending conscription, transferring troops from Spain, and heavy drafts of National Guardsmen into the regular army. Recourse to these drastic measures paid considerable dividends – at least in numerical terms – yielding about 200,000 men by early April, while the Ministry of War continued its efforts of furnishing at least part of the Emperor's further requirements of another 450,000 troops. Napoleon began to deploy approximately 120,000 men at the River Main, consisting of four corps plus the Imperial Guard. Elsewhere, Eugène had 58,000 men at the Saale, Marshal Louis-Nicolas Davout (1770–1823) led 20,000 west of Hamburg and 14,000 cavalry under Horace Sébastiani (1772–1851) were stationed along the lower Elbe. The army was grievously deficient in cavalry, but it nevertheless outnumbered the Allies in the vicinity, who totaled about 110,000 men.

The spring campaign

Napoleon's forces nevertheless fell short of the 300,000 he believed he required, a shortfall partly attributable to the absence of contingents expected from Bavaria and Saxony, which had not yet raised new forces to replace those lost in Russia. In spite of these problems Napoleon decided on an offensive in the direction of Berlin and the besieged cities of Danzig, Thorn, and Modlin. At the same time the Allies began their own offensive from Dresden toward the Saale. Napoleon's plans were therefore temporarily postponed.

Fairly confident that Napoleon was planning to attack the Allies, Blücher and Wittgenstein, exercising caution, had been moving west across and beyond the Elbe, and by 9 April their patrols had reached the area around Saalfeld. Though themselves outnumbered, they placed their confidence in their superior mobility, and planned to attack part of Napoleon's forces before his corps could be concentrated. By the middle of April this strategy, accepted by Alexander and Frederick William, was well under way, and with them on their march to the front were reinforcements which, by 24 April,

1. Lauriston attacks Kleist's bridgehead at Lindenau, crosses the Elster and takes the village. Kleist retreats.

2. 11.30 pm Full-scale Allied attack against Ney. Blücher advances toward Kaja and Grossgörschen. Allies open cannonade with 45 guns. French withdraw first behind Grossgörschen and then Kaja.

3. 1.00 pm–6.30 pm Napoleon orders Ney to hold Kaja and adjacent villages. Support from Macdonald and Latour-Maubourg on his left and Bertrand and Marmont on his right intended to trap Allies in double envelopment. Bitter fighting leaves Ney barely in possession of Kaja, but Allies hold Grossgörschen, Kleingörscher and Rahna. Many villages change hands several times in the course of the day.

4. 6.00 pm Wittgenstein launches his last reserves. Fierce fighting between Russians and Macdonald's division. By 9.00 pm Eugène as far as Eisdorf.

5. 6.30 pm–7.00 pm Young Guard retakes Kaja, but Grossgörschen remains in Prussian hands. Allies abandon field around 10.00pm.

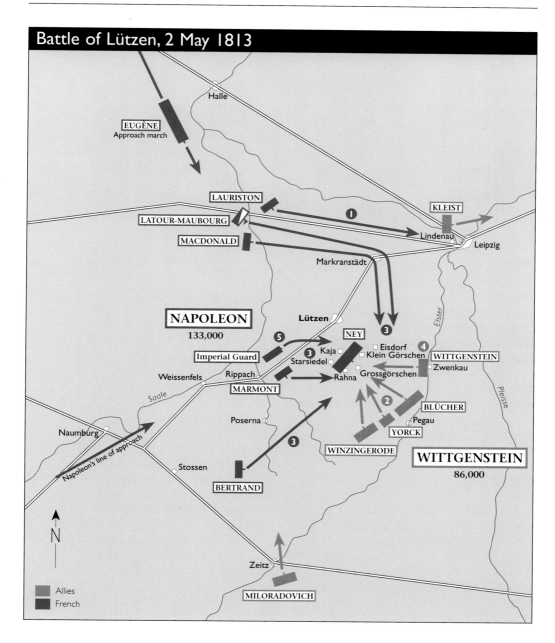

Battle of Lützen, 2 May 1813

Halle

EUGÈNE
Approach march

LAURISTON

LATOUR-MAUBOURG

MACDONALD

KLEIST

①

Lindenau   Leipzig

Markranstädt

NAPOLEON
133,000

Lützen

⑤

Imperial Guard

Weissenfels   Rippach

MARMONT

Poserna

③ Kaja
Starsiedel

Rahna   Grossgörschen

NEY   **③**

Eisdorf
Klein Görschen   **④**

WITTGENSTEIN
Zwenkau

Elster

②

BLÜCHER

Pegau

YORCK

WINZINGERODE

WITTGENSTEIN
86,000

Pleisse

Saale

Naumburg

Napoleon's line of approach

Stossen

③

BERTRAND

N

Zeitz

MILORADOVICH

Allies
French

brought Allied strength near the Saale to 73,000, including 25,000 cavalry and over 500 guns.

Starved of the cavalry requisite for reconnaissance duties, Napoleon developed a two-pronged strategy: to oppose the Russian advance by moving his main army as far as the Saale, with Eugène's army on its left; and to launch a counteroffensive in the direction of Dresden in order to cut Prussian communications with Silesia and Berlin. On 1 May the French armies began their march toward Leipzig by proceeding east over the Saale.

As Eugène made for Schladelbach, Napoleon pushed two columns – one under General Bertrand (1773–1844) and Marshal Oudinot (1767–1847), the other led by Marshals Ney (1769–1815) and Marmont (1774–1852) – toward Naumberg and Lützen.

Prussian infantry advancing up the Kreckwitz Heights at Bautzen. Following the Allied defeat at Lützen earlier in the month, Wittgenstein assumed a new defensive position around Bautzen, 31 miles (50 km) east of the Elbe, deploying 96,000 men against Napoleon's 150,000. The Prussians played a significant part in the fighting alongside their Russian allies and were particularly hard-pressed in the second day's combat when Soult's 20,000 infantry attacked Blücher's fortified positions, seizing the fort at Kreckwitz before stalling due to inadequate artillery support. (Peter Hofschröer)

Meanwhile the Allied commanders were caught up in a dispute over the successor to Kutusov, who had fallen ill from exhaustion in late April and died a few weeks later. News of the French advance obliged them to settle their differences quickly, and command devolved on Wittgenstein, a fairly junior yet competent general officer who ordered forces to concentrate for a thrust against the French right flank near Lützen. The first day's fighting centered around Poserna, where the Allies launched furious attacks, while the second day's fighting focused on Lützen itself, where Ney's corps was hit by strong forces under Wittgenstein. The French emerged victorious but, without adequate cavalry, they could not exploit their success.

Nevertheless, Lützen restored the army's confidence in its chief and reminded the Allies, who retreated east, that Napoleon would not easily be beaten. Not satisfied with an incomplete victory, Napoleon divided his main body in two on 4 May, moving the larger contingent toward Dresden, where intelligence reported the presence of some of Wittgenstein's force, and ordering the remaining troops under Ney to proceed north-east where they were to defend the Elbe crossings at Wittenberg and Torgau. He was also to incorporate the Saxon Army into his forces as soon as the king gave his consent.

At Allied headquarters, meanwhile, new disputes arose – this time on Prussian fears for the safety of their capital, fears exacerbated by Ney's advance. Senior commanders reached a compromise: an unengaged corps under General Friedrich von Bülow (1755–1816) would defend Berlin while the Prussian main body would retire beyond the Elbe to confront the French at Bautzen. Eugène challenged the Prussians at Colditz on 5 May, and the Prussians' failure to destroy the bridges at Dresden behind them three days later enabled Napoleon to establish his men in the suburbs on the same day and to make defensive bridgeheads on the opposite bank of the Elbe on 9 May.

Having established that the Allies were concentrating around Bautzen, Napoleon did the same, recalling Ney's corps from the north and attacking over the course of 20 and 21 May. Again a decisive victory had eluded him because of a shortage of cavalry for pursuit operations and as a result of Ney's having neglected to sever the Allies' lines of retreat. New arguments arose among the Allies as a consequence of their defeat, resulting in Barclay de Tolly (1761–1818) replacing Wittgenstein as commander of Russian forces and the decision to effect a retreat into Silesia toward Schweidnitz, a place well-suited to support Austria in the event that she joined the Allies, or from which to advance to the aid of Prussia.

The next day Napoleon moved his main body east toward the river Katzbach. He ordered Oudinot in the direction of Berlin, while Davout was to advance from the lower Elbe. On 28 May, as Davout entered Hamburg, Prussians under Bülow defeated Oudinot near Luckau. Napoleon's own advance east was slowed up by stiff resistance from the Allied rearguard, and had only reached Breslau by 1 June.

On the following day both sides agreed to a 36-hour ceasefire, extended from 4 June by a general armistice. Napoleon withdrew to Dresden. Although some observers have since identified this decision as the source of Napoleon's ultimate downfall, he had sound reasons for agreeing to an armistice. His army was tired, having assumed the offensive and marched several hundred miles, and it had twice inflicted significant, though not decisive, victories on the Allies, in a continuing effort to deliver a final hammerblow. Lack of cavalry had prevented him from exploiting these successes. Despite many weaknesses Napoleon's army had performed remarkably well, but with his supply lines perilously long, his artillery ammunition nearly exhausted, and his casualties equaling those of his opponents, his army now needed a respite in order to recover and regroup. In the political realm, Napoleon also wished to determine and influence the future course of the Emperor Francis, who had by this time established a sizable army abreast of the French right flank.

Both sides extended the armistice to 16 August, enabling the respective armies to rest from the season's campaigning and the commanders to rebuild the wreck of their formations. The Allies benefited most from this pause in hostilities. By the middle of August Napoleon was able to field approximately 440,000 men for the main theater of operations in Germany, and another quarter of a million were stationed in pockets, such as the Bavarian contingent under General Wrede (1767–1838) on the

river Inn. Moreover, the Emperor had amassed over 1,300 guns, thus replacing the numbers lost in Russia. The Allies, on the other hand, had mustered no fewer than 500,000 men for front-line operations, enjoyed an enormous superiority in cavalry, and would soon muster another 350,000 reserve troops.

On the diplomatic front important developments were under way. At Reichenbach on 24 June the Austrian Foreign Minister, Prince Clemens von Metternich (1773–1859), concluded a treaty with Alexander and Frederick William by which Austria assumed the role of armed mediator between Napoleon and those sovereigns. Four terms would be put to the French emperor, whose failure to agree to them would signal Austrian adherence to the Allied camp. The terms required Napoleon to dissolve the

Field Marshal Gebhardt Leberecht von Blücher. A strident Francophobe, Blücher commanded the Prussian forces in 1813–15, proving himself a man of action rather than of intellect. One fellow officer noted that 'His energy was prodigious, he was always on horseback ... his eye for ground was excellent, his heroic courage inspired the troops, but ... he had little knowledge of strategy, he could not find where he was on a map, and he was incapable of making a plan of campaign or a troop disposition.' (Philip Haythornthwaite)

The battle of Lützen, 2 May 1813. During furious fighting in Ney's sector of the field, General Girard was dismounted and hit twice by musket fire. Spattered in blood, he seized a regimental flag and led his men against massed Prussian artillery, declaring, 'It is here that every brave Frenchman must conquer or die!' On receiving a third bullet wound he passed command to a subordinate, telling him, 'I can do no more.' (AKG, Berlin)

Duchy of Warsaw, permit an enlarged Prussia, restore to Austria her former Illyrian provinces along the Adriatic coast, and re-establish the Hanseatic towns, notably Hamburg, Lübeck, Bremen and Danzig. Napoleon, as was expected, rejected these terms and on 19 July Austria joined the Sixth Coalition, to which Sweden had already been added on 7 July, though the armistice continued in force until the following month.

The autumn campaign

The armistice ended prematurely after 50 days when Austria formally declared war on 12 August. Blücher began to advance from Breslau, in Silesia, on the following day. The truce formally ended on 16 August during which time both sides had been active in raising, training, and shifting troops on a massive scale. Allied forces were organized

into four main armies: Blücher led the Army of Silesia, composed of 95,000 Prussians and Russians, south of Breslau; Bernadotte commanded the Army of the North, consisting of 110,000 Prussians and Swedes at Berlin; Schwarzenberg had 230,000 Austrians in the Army of Bohemia, then massing near the upper Elbe; 60,000 Russians, known as the Army of Poland, were being organized in the rear under General Bennigsen (1745–1826).

All these forces were to fall under the authority of the supreme commander, Schwarzenberg, who soon found his authority undermined and interfered with by the three monarchs accompanying headquarters, together with their staffs, foreign envoys, and others from various countries. Alexander, Francis, and Frederick William had the disconcerting habit of altering Schwarzenberg's orders seemingly by whim:

His Majesty the Tsar of Russia, he wrote to Francis, … *never leaves me alone, not in my headquarters nor on the battlefield … he allows almost every [Russian] general to give advice and suggestions …*

Nevertheless, the Allies formulated a new and promising strategy, called the Trachenberg

Plan, designed to avoid a confrontation with Napoleon's main army and instead concentrate on his subordinates. Results would necessarily be limited, but by these means the Emperor's strength would be gradually diminished. In line with this plan, the Allies decided on 17 August to launch an attack in the direction of Leipzig, conducted from three sides. Meanwhile, news of the victory achieved by the Duke of Wellington (1769–1852) at Vitoria provided a well-timed boost to Allied morale.

Napoleon, with about 400,000 men all told in Germany, did not suffer from the same command and administrative problems facing Schwarzenberg, since he controlled an army which, though it contained foreign contingents, nevertheless was not divided by nationality. Napoleon split his army in two, concentrating about 250,000 men under his personal command along both sides of the Elbe at Dresden, while Oudinot, around Luckau with 120,000 troops, was to make another try against Berlin. Many have criticized Napoleon for his decision to divide his forces and to seek a secondary objective, and this criticism seems largely borne out by

what happened in the course of the next few days, for during that brief period the Emperor would alter his plans several times. First preparing to proceed east for an attack against Blücher, on 18 August he changed direction, moving south toward Zittau in order to threaten Schwarzenberg's rear. Two days later he reverted back to his original march against Blücher, who conformed to the Trachenberg Plan by retreating.

On the following day, 21 August, Napoleon received an appeal from St Cyr at Dresden, calling for assistance against Schwarzenberg, who had switched his main objective from Leipzig to Dresden. Detaching Marshal Macdonald (1765–1840) to keep Blücher in check, Napoleon advanced toward Dresden,

French and Prussian infantry contesting possession of the cemetery at Grossbeeren, 23 August 1813. General Reynier, with a corps of 27,000 men, advanced against the flank of the Prussian main body, seizing the village of Grossbeeren and the heights behind it by late afternoon. The tide soon turned, however, when Bülow arrived with 38,000 troops, smashing through the Saxon contingent to recapture the village and obliging Reynier to withdraw after a failed counterattack. (AKG, Berlin)

only to decide on 23 August that rather than bringing direct support to St Cyr, he must menace the rear of Schwarzenberg's army at Königstein and Pirna. Meanwhile Oudinot had suffered defeat at Grossbeeren on 23 August, and when news of this reached Napoleon's headquarters two days later, together with intelligence reporting that the defense of Dresden was about to collapse, the Emperor again altered his plans, leaving one corps to attack Pirna while pushing the remainder of his forces to the relief of St Cyr.

At Dresden, St Cyr had meanwhile been offering a spirited defense and had ordered several counterattacks, before Napoleon arrived with 70,000 men and threw back the Allied assault on 26 August. At the same time General Vandamme (1770–1830) was in action at Pirna, where he kept Allied reserves occupied while Napoleon concentrated his efforts around Dresden itself. During the night another 50,000 French troops arrived and these, together with Vandamme's diversion, contributed to Napoleon's significant success on the second day of fighting at Dresden. Nevertheless, the victory was tainted when 80,000 men under Macdonald were defeated on the same day at the Katzbach, losing 13,000 killed or drowned, 17,000–20,000 taken prisoner, 150 cannon and two eagles lost. There, in torrential rain, the veteran of Wagram and the Russian campaign had crossed the swollen river and was attacked by the Prussians, who emerged from woods and engaged the French in vicious hand-to-hand fighting, the rain having rendered musket fire impossible. Sword, lance and bayonet accounted for fearful losses and when, together with concentrated artillery fire, Blücher launched 20,000 cavalry, they drove the French down a slope and into the river, where many were drowned and quarter was seldom given to those who survived. French reverses continued elsewhere: Oudinot retreated in the aftermath of Grossbeeren, and the Allies scored a signal triumph at Kulm on 30 August, which not only wiped out Vandamme's command and led to his capture, but enabled Schwarzenberg, then in retreat, to escape. Thus, three of Napoleon's subordinates had lost three battles

in as many days, so canceling out for their emperor the benefits he had accrued at Dresden, where he had defeated an army two and a half times the size of his own.

Pressed on three fronts, French forces also suffered from continuous raids against their communication and supply lines, and morale was falling.

'I have never entertained any hope', wrote a French officer to his wife on 8 September:

that we can withstand so many allied powers, because unfortunately I have noticed among our troops a very feeble degree of enthusiasm, although most of them boast of possessing a great deal of just that quality. Moreover, our soldiers are so small, so weak physically, so young, [and] so inexperienced, that the majority of them give one more cause to fear than to hope.

Lack of training and combat experience and acute shortage of cavalry left Napoleon's army unable either to learn the whereabouts of its enemies or concentrate against them, while the Emperor watched helplessly as his lieutenants were constantly threatened or attacked. Moreover, the mounting pressure imposed by increasing Allied numbers remained a constant source of anxiety for Napoleon, whose decline in health, including depression and lethargy, impaired his effectiveness at a time when the pressure of business most demanded his attention. Napoleon's presence on the battlefield was all the more critical, a fact highlighted in a report to his king by the commander of the Württemberg division of Napoleon's army:

It seems to me that the French generals and officers are sick of the war, and only the Emperor's presence can animate the soldiers … Since the defeats of Macdonald [Katzbach], Vandamme [Kulm], and Ney [Dennewitz] they believe that only the Rhine can afford them any protection against the Cossacks.

With Schwarzenberg beyond his reach over the mountains of Bohemia, Napoleon planned another push toward Berlin beginning on 2 September, and commanded by Ney. Blücher, however, continued his drive against Macdonald, obliging Napoleon on the following day to hold back some of the troops intended for Ney's operations. From Dresden the Emperor proceeded east to reform Macdonald's formations, but Blücher again eluded the main French army by retiring east of Bautzen. In the midst of planning to renew his operations against Berlin, Napoleon had again to divert his attention to a new threat, this time from Schwarzenberg, whose army re-crossed the Elbe and detached a force under Barclay de Tolly toward Dresden. The Emperor had little option but to respond, moving his main body toward Kulm, behind Barclay's rear, but Schwarzenberg refused to give battle and rapidly withdrew back across the Elbe. The French abandoned their pursuit on 10 September, and in the meantime to the north Ney had been forced to retreat from Dennewitz.

A series of threats during the next two weeks continued to rob Napoleon of the initiative. He could not ignore Schwarzenberg's renewed diversionary movements in the direction of Dresden, and he was unable to reinforce Ney's drive on Berlin until that threat had been dealt with. There were further problems to the north: Bernadotte with 80,000 men would soon be at the Elbe, while Blücher once again struck at Macdonald's exhausted men.

By late September the strain on French forces was becoming critical. Their numbers had been reduced by 200,000 men since the middle of August, the shortage of supplies was reaching a state of crisis, and the Allies continued to keep their opponents marching and countermarching in a fruitless attempt to hold back superior numbers threatening from more directions than available numbers could withstand. This critical state of affairs persuaded Napoleon to withdraw all his field forces west of the Elbe, and when the troops began to march on 24 September French garrisons further east were left to fend for themselves as best they could, well aware that all hope for direct relief from their emperor had vanished.

While Napoleon was moving west, in the north Bernadotte was at the Elbe, across which he began to establish bridgeheads. On the following day Blücher began marching to support him, himself relieved by Bennigsen's arrival. Troops under Bernadotte and Blücher combined to form 140,000 men and these, together with 180,000 under Schwarzenberg and Bennigsen, would now march toward Leipzig, a city of great strategic importance as a communications link with the Rhine and France beyond. On his march to reach Bernadotte, Blücher's 60,000 men fought a number of minor clashes before reaching Wartenberg, on the Elbe, on 3 October. Overpowering the weak corps under Bertrand before crossing the river on 4 October, Blücher proceeded to Delitsch, about 20 miles (30 km) north of Leipzig, with Bernadotte marching parallel.

General Dominique Joseph Vandamme. A veteran of the French Revolutionary Wars and every subsequent campaign fought outside Spain, Vandamme was noted for corruption and an eye for loot. Nevertheless, he possessed the aggressiveness and energy required of a successful field commander. During operations in Germany he achieved a minor victory at Pirna before losing more than half his command and falling into Prussian hands at Kulm. During the Waterloo campaign he led a corps at Ligny and Wavre. (Philip Haythornthwaite)

The battle of Kulm, 30 August 1813. Another Allied victory achieved over one of Napoleon's subordinates, as part of the Trachenberg Plan. Despite enjoying a 2-to-1 numerical superiority over Marshal Oudinot, Bernadotte contemplated abandoning Berlin, a course of action roundly condemned by von Bülow, who declared that while the Swedes could do as they pleased, the Prussians would attack. They did so with enthusiasm, capturing Vandamme and thousands of his troops. (AKG, Berlin)

By this time Napoleon had firmly established himself in Leipzig with nearly 250,000 men, and could easily outnumber either of the Allied armies en route to engage him. Napoleon now took the initiative: appointing Murat with 43,000 men to oppose an attack from the south, and corps under Mouton and St Cyr, respectively, to hold Dresden, the Emperor marched north on 7 October with 150,000 men and attacked Blücher at Düben. The attempt at surprise failed, and Blücher managed to retire west to the Saale. Frustrated in his attempts to monitor Allied movements owing to a shortage of cavalry, Napoleon was left to proceed north with caution toward Dresden, where Bernadotte was based.

But if Napoleon was moving slowly in one direction, Schwarzenberg, whose troops after reinforcement numbered 240,000, was advancing even more slowly toward Leipzig. Murat delayed him at Borna on 10 October, and two days later Ney blocked part of Bernadotte's forces from crossing the river Mulde near Dessau. Nevertheless, the various Allied forces were now sufficiently close to one another to cooperate in an attack against Leipzig. The future was looking bleak for the French, prompting one sergeant of dragoons to admit that the war was no longer to defend the Empire, but to keep the Allies away from France herself. 'I'll tell you one thing,' he wrote on 12 October:

in a month we shall be on the banks of the Rhine. The vengeance of the nations we have conquered, trampled upon and plundered, will invade France in order to make a wilderness of the country. To prevent this happening is the only reason a right-minded Frenchman can have for bearing arms.

On 13 October Wittgenstein marched from the south to reconnoiter, while on the

Prussian *Landwehr* cavalry charging at Dennewitz, 6 September 1813. While approaching Berlin, Ney, with 55,000 men, attacked 80,000 Prussians led by von Bülow, while a further 30,000 Swedes remained in reserve under Bernadotte. At a critical point in the fighting, Ney's Saxons deserted, leaving a massive gap in his line through which rode a large body of Prussian cavalry, severing Ney's command and forcing him to retire to Torgau. (AKG, Berlin)

following day Napoleon, aware that he had failed to halt the Allies' approach from the north, ordered all his forces to assemble in defense of Leipzig. His troops were now in a dreadful condition, as a colonel in the Old Guard noted on 15 October:

From the time the regiment left its cantonments on 6 October, the soldiers had not received a single ounce of bread. On this march, made wretched by bad roads and bad weather, the only issue of rations was a little rice and meat. So one can easily picture the state that the army was in and the difference between units which went short of nothing and those which had just enough

food to avoid dying of hunger. To the shortages of food was added the lack of shoes. One saw a great many troops walking barefoot in the mud and water, their feet and legs cut and bleeding. This state of affairs made any officer weep who had not lost all feelings of humanity.

A major cavalry engagement took place at Liebertwolkwitz on 14 October, with no decisive outcome, but the main action took place over three days: 16–18 October. The contest for the village of Möckern exemplifies the bitterness of the fighting. There, Marmont's men struggled against the Prussians, with the village changing hands several times throughout the first day of the fighting. Yorck's men, who contested every house and street, could only be dislodged in dreadful hand-to-hand fighting. By dusk, the Prussians were left in control of the place, albeit choked with the dead and dying. Yorck lost 8,000 of his 21,000 men, and the French about the same number – making this 'battle within a battle' the most costly, as a

Leipzig, 19 October 1813. The battle having been lost, a large French
column (background) attempts to evacuate the city while units of the
beleaguered rearguard (left foreground) defend a barricade against
Prussian *Landwehr*. As ordinary infantry could seldom fire more than
one or two rounds a minute, close-quarter fighting like this sometimes
required use of the bayonet or musket-butt. (Philip Haythornthwaite)

proportion of the numbers engaged, of any combat of the Napoleonic Wars. All the while, Ney, with 15,000 men, had crisscrossed the battlefield, trying to support separate sectors, but in the end failed to reinforce either of them. Savage street-fighting was common during the battle – Möckern was far from unique – with many sections of the city and surrounding villages passing into the possession of one side and then the other, often with no quarter being offered or received. General Langeron, a French émigré fighting for the Russians, retook the village of Schönefeld twice on the third day of the battle:

I believed the position was assured, and went forward of the village to establish a chain of outposts. At this moment Ney ... launched against me so unexpected an attack, and so impetuous and well directed, that I was unable to withstand it. Five columns, advancing at the charge and with fixed bayonets, rushed at the village and at my troops, who were still scattered and whom I was trying to re-form. They were overthrown and forced to retire in a hurry. I was swept along by the fugitives, but I really cannot

blame their sudden retreat because it was impossible to hold out, and I must confess that they moved as fast as I could manage.

... Fortunately I still had considerable reserves, and after letting the regiments which had been expelled from Schönefeld pass through the gaps between them, I soon did to the enemy what he had done to me, because my columns were in good order and his troops were by this time scattered.

Nevertheless, the bitter fighting around Schönefeld carried on for the course of the day until, with their reserves exhausted, the French conceded the place to the Allies. But the suffering did not end there: when fire broke out those who had fallen wounded inside the battered structures or who had crawled into them in search of safety instead found themselves trapped. One anonymous account described this dreadful scene thus:

The struggle for Probstheida, 18 October 1813. On the third day's fighting around Leipzig, Barclay de Tolly halted near this village, doggedly held by Macdonald's troops. By nightfall Probstheida had changed hands several times, leaving the streets and houses clogged with Russian and French casualties, but with Macdonald still in possession. (AKG, Berlin)

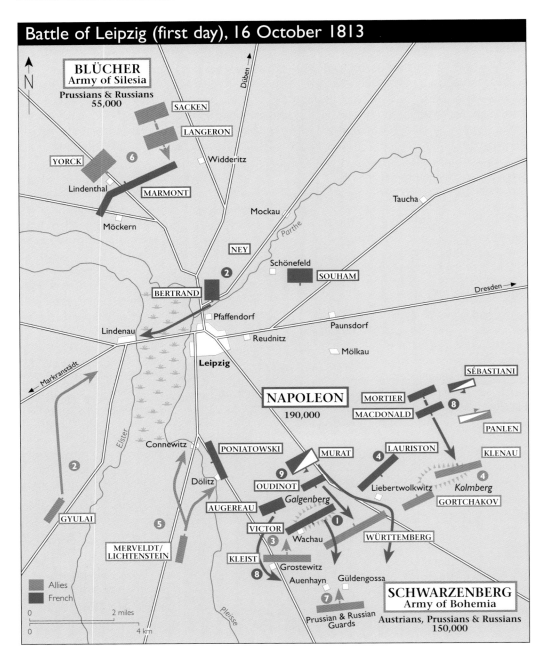

Battle of Leipzig (first day), 16 October 1813

BLÜCHER
Army of Silesia
Prussians & Russians
55,000

N

SACKEN

LANGERON

YORCK   6   Widderitz

Lindenthal

MARMONT

Möckern

Mockau

Parthe

NEY

Schönefeld

SOUHAM

Taucha

Dresden →

BERTRAND   2

Pfaffendorf

Lindenau   Reudnitz   Paunsdorf

Mölkau

Leipzig

Elster

Markranstädt ←

Connewitz

Dölitz

NAPOLEON
190,000

MORTIER

MACDONALD

SÉBASTIANI

8

PANLEN

KLENAU

PONIATOWSKI   MURAT   4   LAURISTON

9

OUDINOT
Galgenberg

Liebertwolkwitz   _Kolmberg_

4

GORTCHAKOV

AUGEREAU

GYULAI   2

5

MERVELDT/
LICHTENSTEIN

VICTOR
3   Wachau

KLEIST

8   Grostewitz

WÜRTTEMBERG

Auenhayn   Güldengossa

7

SCHWARZENBERG
Army of Bohemia
Austrians, Prussians & Russians
150,000

Prussian & Russian
Guards

Pleisse

Allies
French

0 _____ 2 miles
0 _____ 4 km

Many wounded on both sides were burnt to death and in the manor-farm all the cattle perished, even the huge black bull ... Maddened by all the firing and yelling, and by burns, the bull had broken loose ... and run ... against the attacking Russians so irresistibly that on his own he scattered an entire column. The burning church-tower made common cause with the raging bull to defeat the Russians. It collapsed and buried a large number of these soldiers beneath its ruins ... the noise and shouting of the troops, the sound of artillery and small-arms fire, the landing and explosion of shells, the howling, moaning and lowing of human beings and cattle, the whimpering and calls for help from the wounded and those who lay half-buried

LEFT

1. 8.00 am Württemberg attacks Wichau, which changes hands several times in the course of the day.
2. 8.00 am Gyulai advances toward Lindenau in bid to cut French lines of communications and retreat. Bertrand's defense denies Napoleon use of these troops for all-out drive.
3. Kleist advances, but French retain possession of Wachau.
4. 10.00 am Klenau captures the Kolmberg Heights and Liebertwolkwitz. Imperial Guard under Lauriston committed to the fighting.
5. Merveldt and Lichtenstein fail to break through determined French defense.
6. 10.00 am Blücher advances toward Leipzig. Marmont, outnumbered three to one, is now unable to move south to support Napoleon's planned general offensive. Marmont driven back after Möckern and Widdenitz change hands several times.
7. 11.00 am Prussian and Russian Guards called up to stabilize situation.
8. 12.00 pm Macdonald, Mortier, and Sébastiani force Klenau back. Augereau drives Kleist from Grostewitz.
9. 2.00 pm Napoleon shifts to the offensive. Despite bitter fighting involving Oudinot, Murat, and Lauriston, he fails to penetrate Allied line.

alive under the masonry, blazing planks and beams was hideous. The smoke, dust and fumes made the day so dark that nobody could tell what time of day it was.

One of the most dramatic events of the third day was the sudden defection of the Saxons and their guns, followed soon thereafter by the Württemberger cavalry. For the French, retreat was now vital, and on the morning of 19 October Napoleon's troops began to cross the River Elster, protected by a strong rearguard. On seeing this, the Allies, and Blücher in particular, launched a furious attack on the defenders and the city in a determined bid to prevent a French escape. Only one bridge then spanned the river, with a lone sergeant of engineers left with responsibility to ignite the charge on the appearance of opposing forces. The sergeant interpreted his orders literally: when nothing more than a small body of Prussian riflemen appeared on the opposite river bank, he blew the bridge – prematurely – cutting Napoleon's army in two and inflicting more damage on his remaining forces than the previous three days' fighting. Three army corps totaling

37,000 men, including all their artillery, as well as approximately 20,000 walking wounded and others, 30 generals and two marshals, were left stranded on the wrong side of the Elster, there to be captured or killed in the fighting.

Marshal Macdonald barely reached safety: 'I escaped … with a firm resolve not to fall alive into the hands of the enemy, preferring to shoot or drown myself,' he wrote in his memoirs. Encountering a ramshackle 'bridge' originally fashioned from two trees, doors, shutters and planks, but now reduced merely to the trees, Macdonald had no option but to attempt a crossing, as he later recorded in his memoirs:

It was my only chance; I made up my mind and risked it. I got off my horse with great difficulty, owing to the crowd, and there I was, one foot on either trunk, and the abyss below me. A high wind was blowing … I had already made three-quarters of my way across, when some men determined to follow me; their unsteady feet caused the trunks to shake, and I fell into the water. I could fortunately touch the bottom, but the bank was steep, the soil loose and greasy; I vainly struggled to reach the shore.

Practically everyone else was left behind or drowned (including Marshal Poniatowski) in the effort of crossing. Macdonald himself was powerless to assist those left on the opposite bank:

On the other side of the Elster the firing continued; it suddenly ceased. Our unhappy troops were crowded together on the river-bank; whole companies plunged into the water and were carried away; cries of despair rose on all sides. The men perceived me. Despite the noise and tumult, I distinctly heard these words: 'Monsieur le Maréchal, save your men! Save your children!' I could do nothing for them! Overcome by rage, indignation, fury, I wept!

Until the disaster at the Elster the battle had remained a drawn affair. Yet in an instant it had been converted into a great Allied victory. Casualties were enormous, the Allies losing approximately 55,000 killed and wounded, while the French suffered 38,000 casualties between 16 and 18 October, in addition to the more than 50,000 men captured the next day. Another 5,000 German troops had defected during the battle. Practically every piece of French equipment was lost, including over 300 guns. In Leipzig itself, one resident noted how the city had been 'transformed into one vast hospital, 56 edifices being devoted to that purpose alone. The number of sick and wounded amounted to 36,000. Of these a large proportion died, but their places were soon supplied by the many wounded who had been left in the adjacent villages.'

Prince Schwarzenberg at the battle of Leipzig, announcing victory to the Allied sovereigns: Tsar Alexander of Russia, King Frederick William of Prussia, and the Emperor Francis of Austria. Commander-in-Chief of the Allied armies from August 1813 to April 1814, Schwarzenberg found his duties continuously interfered with by these crowned heads and their respective staff officers. 'It is really inhuman what I have to tolerate and bear,' he bitterly complained, 'surrounded as I am by weaklings, fools of all kinds, eccentric project-makers, intriguers, blockheads, gossips and fault-finders.' (AKG, Berlin)

Leipzig was the largest and one of the most decisive battles of the Napoleonic Wars. French political influence in Germany collapsed, and physical control evaporated as the French armies hastily made for the Rhine via the supply lines of Frankfurt and Mainz. Napoleon's German allies had all defected: Bavaria before, and Saxony and Württemberg during, the battle. Saxony, like the Duchy of Warsaw before it, was occupied by Allied troops, with the brief exception of Dresden, whose French garrison finally surrendered on 11 November. The remaining states of the Confederation of the Rhine quickly broke away or were lost to French influence. General van der Gelder, the commander of one of the German brigades of the *Grande Armée*, was not surprised when the troops had finally had enough:

The French were to complain loudly when their allies deserted them during the famous days of Leipzig, but I venture to ask them whether they would tolerate humiliations and bad treatment from allies more powerful than themselves, and whether they would not turn against men who

*devastated their country, burning and plundering
everything, beating and raping without any
redress being made and oblivious to every
complaint. Well! That is what the Saxons and
other Germans had been suffering for years.*

The Allies did not offer a vigorous pursuit
and the French retreat carried on largely
unhindered until it reached Erfurt on
23 October. A week later General Wrede,
with his Bavarian force of 60,000, sought to
block the French march at Hanau. There, on
30 October, he foolishly deployed his men
with their backs to a river with only a single
bridge by which to make their escape if
circumstances so required. By resting one of
his flanks against woods light enough to
permit the passage of artillery, Wrede found
himself under fire from the elite artillery of
the Imperial Guard, which with 50 guns
wrecked havoc in his ranks. Then, Marbot
recalled in his memoirs:

*... just as a puff of wind drove the smoke
away, the Chasseurs [à Cheval] of the Guard
appeared. At the sight of the Chasseurs'
bearskins the Bavarian infantry recoiled in
consternation. Wishing to check the disorder at
any cost, General Wrede made all the cavalry at
his disposal charge our guns, and in a moment
the battery was surrounded by a cloud of
horsemen ... Numbers would, however, have
triumphed but that – at the Emperor's order –
the whole of Sébastiani's cavalry and that of the
[Imperial] Guard ... all dashed furiously on the
enemy, killing a great number and scattering the
rest. Then, flying upon the squares of Bavarian
infantry, they broke them with heavy loss and
the routed Bavarian army fled towards the bridge
and the town of Hanau.*

Wrede's disastrous folly cost him
6,000 men. Napoleon, with approximately
70,000 men and another 40,000 stragglers, was
therefore enabled to reach Frankfurt, only
20 miles (30 km) from the Rhine, on
2 November. Within four days, re-equipped
with new weapons and uniforms from the
magazine at Erfurt, the French crossed the
Rhine at Mainz, and now stood safely – at

least for the time being, on native soil.
However, about 100,000 of their comrades had
been abandoned in Germany – the corps led
by Davout on the lower Elbe, plus many small
forces occupying towns and cities throughout
Germany. Isolated, outnumbered and in most
cases besieged, all of them surrendered, mostly
unconditionally, over the following few weeks
with the exception of the Hamburg garrison,
where Davout steadfastly refused to give in.
With their capture, total French losses in the
autumn campaign had reached about
400,000, and this, combined with the loss of
all German territory beyond the Rhine,
rendered the Leipzig campaign nothing short
of a catastrophe for Napoleon.

The situation may be summed up thus: in
the past two years the Emperor had
commanded forces numbering in excess of
400,000 men. Twice he had ended the
campaigns with fewer than 70,000. Allied
armies numbering 345,000 men were poised
to invade from the east, while another Allied
army of about 125,000 men under
Wellington was already in south-west France,
opposed by 100,000 troops under Marshals
Soult (1769–1851) and Suchet (1770–1826).
With only 80,000 men to defend the east of
the country, and spread across 300 miles
(482 km), France now braced herself for a
crisis not experienced since the early years of
the Revolutionary Wars, two decades before.

The campaign in France, 1814

Following the overwhelming Allied victory
at Leipzig and the retreat of the French to
the Rhine, the main operations in 1814
would shift from Germany to eastern France,
where Napoleon could not even muster
100,000 men to oppose the Allied armies
approaching the Rhine at the end of
1813 with a combined strength of over
300,000 men. French armies on the two
other fronts also faced dire prospects. In
Italy, the Austrian general Bellagarde opened
hostilities against Eugène, and in south-west
France Wellington continued to press French
forces there. In Paris, as well as in the

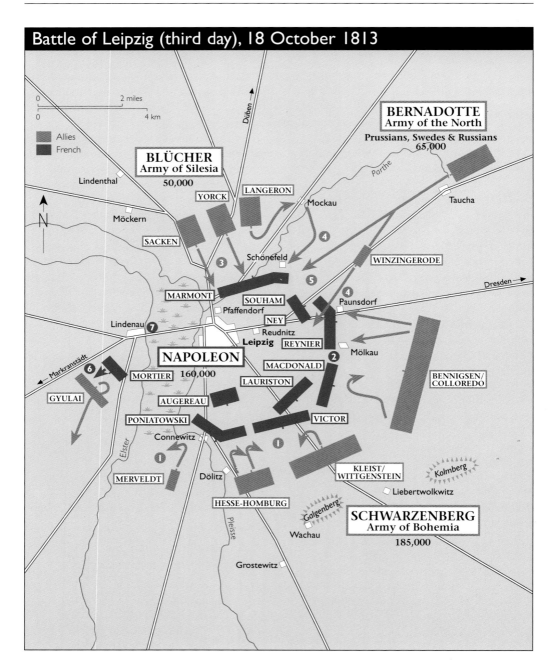

Battle of Leipzig (third day), 18 October 1813

countryside, political uneasiness with the regime and general war-weariness began to exacerbate an increasingly dire military situation.

Napoleon recognized that an acute shortage of men posed his greatest short-term problem. The campaigns of 1812 and 1813 had cost him nearly a million men, and there were no

simple means of replacing even a fraction of these – particularly with the loss (mostly by defection) of his vassal states east of the Rhine. Napoleon wrongly assumed that the Allies on the Rhine would require several months in which to rest and prepare for the next campaign; this would give him time to tap every possible source of manpower to raise new armies. But his target, 900,000 men, was grossly unrealistic. On 5 November, Cambacérès (1753–1824), the Emperor's chief executive, informed the Emperor that the immediate levy of 140,000 men could be met, but not without employing new methods. Nearly 80,000 were already available, but as for the shortfall, he confessed that:

… we can no longer think in terms of unmarried men, since the last available conscript in this category has already been called up. There is little evidence that we can count on the willingness to volunteer of married men, for most of them have only contracted marriage in order not to join up, and the price of substitutes is so high that such a measure as purchasing replacements would be impracticable, unless we recruit married men.

Rather than risk 'certain problems' and 'uncertain results' by calling up earlier classes of men and those married but without children, Cambacérès decided to transfer 100,000 men from the National Guard, with

LEFT
1. 7.00 am General assault by Schwarzenberg. Stiff resistance halts Allied progress. Hesse-Homburg takes Dölitz, while Poniatowski denies Connewitz from Merveldt. Victor repulses Kleist and Wittgenstein.
2. Macdonald keeps Colloredo in check, but reinforcements from Bennigsen enable him to seize Holzhausen. Reynier retains Mölkau and Paunsdorf.
3. Blücher detaches Langeron to assist Bernadotte, then captures Pfaffendorff, before his advance founders. Despite reaching as far as Reudnitz, Prussians are driven out by reinforcements sent by Napoleon.
4. Around mid-day Bernadotte's advance guard links up with Langeron, who attacks Ney at Schönefeld. Winzingerode advances on Paunsdorf, meeting up with Bennigsen, so closing the gap between the Armies of Silesia and Bohemia. Bennigsen resumes attack. Reynier's Saxons and Württembergers defect. Paunsdorf falls to the Allies.
5. Temporarily retaking Paunsdorf, Ney nevertheless is forced back by sheer numbers. Prussians penetrate to Reudnitz. Langeron, in a see-saw action, finally captures Schönefeld.
6. As Allies force French back into Leipzig, Mortier's Young Guard pushes Gyulai back and clears way for westward retreat.
7. Napoleon orders general retreat at 2.00 am on 19 October. Elster bridge at Lindenau prematurely blown, stranding thousands on the wrong side.

BELOW Imperial Guard infantry, 1814. Not only the élite of Napoleon's army, but one of the most famous military bodies in the history of warfare, the Imperial Guard also included cavalry, artillery and engineers. The infantry was traditionally retained as a reserve and rarely saw action on the battlefield until 1814, when desperate circumstances demanded their deployment in the front line. At Waterloo Napoleon was obliged to commit some units of the Guard to defend his vulnerable right flank against the Prussians, while he ordered others against Wellington's wavering center. (Philip Haythornthwaite)

no exemptions for married men. The sources of manpower were rapidly drying up, but if a shortage of men posed insuperable problems, at least Allied indecision and bickering offered Napoleon precious time.

At the same time, Napoleon employed diplomacy to placate his enemies and curry favor with public opinion abroad, particularly in Italy and Spain. He cynically restored Pope Pius VII (1742–1823) to Rome in an attempt to retain the loyalty of Italians, while with Ferdinand VII of Spain (1784–1833) he concluded the Treaty of Valençay, in a feeble attempt to terminate the Franco–Spanish conflict.

It is appropriate here to pause and consider the Allies' political and strategic aims and examine how these affected the conduct of their military operations. Recovery of northern Italy was Austria's prime objective, not the destruction of France, for Marie-Louise, Francis's daughter, remained Empress. Britain wanted to re-establish the balance of power on the Continent, and would not countenance a gravely weakened France. Bernadotte, Crown Prince of Sweden but a Frenchman by birth, was extremely unwilling to attack his native country – a reluctance almost certainly a consequence of his wish to succeed Napoleon on the throne. On the other hand, Alexander wanted vengeance for the invasion of his country, and Frederick William, as Alexander's junior partner, was prepared to support the Tsar – not least because of the vociferous and belligerent attitudes of men like Blücher, who had scores to settle for the humiliations Prussia had suffered in 1806 and for her subsequent partition and occupation.

Allied leaders gathered at Frankfurt in November and on the 16th agreed to offer negotiating terms to the French, with what France considered her 'natural frontiers' (the Rhine, the Alps and the Pyrenees) as the principal basis. In the meantime the three Allied armies poised on the Rhine stood down. With no intention of adhering to these terms, Napoleon first proposed the establishment of an international congress as a forum for negotiation and then, on 30 November,

disingenuously accepted the peace proposals. Allied policy had, however, changed by this time, with the members of the coalition demanding the more restricted borders of 1792, which excluded much of the Rhineland and the whole of the Low Countries. Such terms were deliberately designed to be rejected, and in late December the short hiatus in military activity ceased with a renewed Allied offensive into eastern France conducted from three directions. Just prior to entering France herself, the Allies issued a proclamation explaining that the conflict was directed more specifically against the Emperor:

We do not make war on France, but we are casting off a yoke which your Government imposed on our countries. We had hoped to have found peace before touching your soil: we now go to find it there.

One division of Austrians entered Switzerland unopposed, while the Bavarians under Wrede passed the Rhine on 22 December and began to besiege Hunigen. On the northern front, Prussians under Bülow and a small British force under Sir Thomas Graham (1748–1843) marched into Holland as a prelude to taking Antwerp, occupying the remainder of Belgium and invading France. On the central front, Blücher began crossing the Rhine on 29 December between Koblenz and Mannheim at the head of 100,000 Prussians, with the intention of occupying Napoleon's main army as the other Allied armies approached.

On 1 January the southern wing of the Allied offensive, consisting of 200,000 men under Schwarzenberg, began its march toward Colmar on the upper Rhine, with the intention of threatening Napoleon's right flank and linking up with Allied troops moving north from Spain and Italy. Far to the east, Bernadotte, with a large combined Russo–Swedish army, remained behind in Germany to watch Davout's corps isolated at Hamburg and other smaller French garrisons. Napoleon could only muster around 67,000 men distributed along the whole border stretching from Switzerland to the

Dutch coast. The Imperial Guard was under strength and only about 30,000 partly trained militia stood in reserve. Recruitment yields had fallen drastically short of actual need, and the army was desperately short of weapons, equipment, and experienced NCOs.

Napoleon's diplomatic efforts, meanwhile, failed entirely: Ferdinand of Spain renounced the Treaty of Valençay, ensuring that Wellington would continue operations in south-west France. Murat, as king of Naples, joined the Allies on 11 January, and Denmark followed suit three days later. Even at home the Emperor now began to face opposition and conspiracies were brewing for a Bourbon restoration. No less than the Foreign Minister himself, Talleyrand, had begun secret talks with the exiled Louis XVIII (1755–1824), then in England.

While his forces in the east of the country faced impossible odds against the Allied advance, Napoleon remained in the capital trying to cope with increasingly complex political matters at a time when his troops could not offer adequate resistance without their emperor in the field. To the south, Marshal Victor (1764–1841), defending the border there, abandoned Strasbourg and Nancy without firing a shot, and Marmont with 16,000 men, was pushed back toward Metz, which he reached on 13 January. Within four days both corps, together with Ney's contingent of the Young Guard, had retreated across the Meuse. Although Napoleon shifted Marshal Mortier (1768–1835) and the Imperial Guard to this sector, they were unable to prevent Blücher's Prussians from pushing across the Meuse on 22 January.

On the following day his advance guard crossed the Marne, while at the same time Schwarzenberg, held up for six days by the new proposals, was nearing Bar-sur-Aube, only 25 miles (40 km) to the southwest. Mortier, together with part of the corps under General Gérard (1773–1852), offered a stiff rearguard defense there on 24 January, but were unable to halt the Allies and withdrew west toward Troyes. At the same time, on the distant northern front, Bülow

and Graham were making steady progress against Macdonald's corps of 15,000 men, who were forced out of Liège and obliged to withdraw toward the Meuse.

Apart from their forces in the far north, the Allies had 200,000 men marching on Paris, opposed by only 85,000 French. Although the capital's defenses were badly in need of repair and suspicions abounded that treason was rife, the Emperor was prepared to fight to the end. Having placed his brother Joseph (1768–1844) in charge of the government, Napoleon left the capital on 25 January to resume direct command of the troops at the front.

He arrived in the area south-east of Paris on the following day. This was generally open ground – otherwise ideal terrain over which the Allied advance could proceed – except that it was laced by numerous rivers such as the Meuse and Seine, which offered obstacles to the approach to Paris if the bridges were strongly held or destroyed. Recognizing that his forces could not survive the strain of a major action – whatever the outcome – Napoleon decided to employ a strategy of rapid marches that could take advantage of internal lines of communication without the limitations imposed by supply wagons. Freed from these constraints he could concentrate on and destroy in turn small portions of the Allied armies operating in isolation from their main bodies.

Napoleon first chose to strike at Blücher, who was then moving up in two columns sufficiently distant from one another to be vulnerable. The Emperor failed to make contact at St Dizier on 27 January, and at Brienne, two days later, he achieved only a minor victory. He pursued, but Blücher turned and in a surprise counterattack at La Rothière on 1 February inflicted a sound defeat that seriously damaged French morale. Poor training was now graphically evident. During the action Marmont asked a young infantryman why he was not discharging his weapon, to which the recruit replied: 'I would, sir, if I knew how!' On this, the marshal dismounted and instructed him.

Amazingly, Napoleon still retained the option of concluding a peace which would permit him to retain his throne. The proposal had come from the Allies on 29 January, and on 3 February a conference convened at Châtillon-sur-Seine. At the same time Napoleon's troops stood on the defensive along the Seine near Troyes, while Marmont received orders to retake Arcis-sur-Aube.

BELOW Having rejected a generous Allied peace offer, Napoleon opted to fight under increasingly dire circumstances. Heavily outnumbered and facing opponents on several fronts, he had no real chance of ejecting them from home soil. While he still retained a quarter of a million men under arms, many of these were poorly-trained and recently recruited, while the Allies could deploy more than double this number, including over 100,000 men in the south under Wellington. Bernadotte, approaching from Holland, Blücher, from Lorraine, and Schwarzenberg, from Switzerland, led another 300,000 between them. While the campaign of 1814 demonstrated that Napoleon had not lost his tactical genius, the sheer number of his opponents and the poor quality of his own forces would ultimately tell.

Encouraged by their success at La Rothière, Schwarzenberg and Blücher pushed on up the Seine and the Marne toward Paris, but suffered a succession of minor reverses in the process. Marmont succeeded in recapturing Arcis-sur-Aube on 3 February, cavalry under General Grouchy (1766–1847) blocked a Russian advance near Troyes, and, to the

RIGHT Fighting took place in bitter cold and snow began to fall around 1.00 pm, when Blücher opened his attack. Württemberg (12,000 men) seized wooded high ground around La Giberie, but was then ejected. The main attack took place on the plain in front of La Rothière, where Gyulai (15,000), Sacken (20,000), and Olssufiev (5,000), despite overwhelming numbers, proved unable to break the French line, consisting of Gérard (5,000), Victor (15,000), Marmont (18,000), and Ney (16,000). To the west, Wrede, with 25,000, engaged Marmont at about 5.00 pm, forcing him back, but failing to defeat him. Heavy winds and flurries brought the fighting to an end, narrowly saving Napoleon from disaster. The Emperor had no choice but to withdraw the following day or risk being surrounded as a consequence of massive Allied numerical superiority.

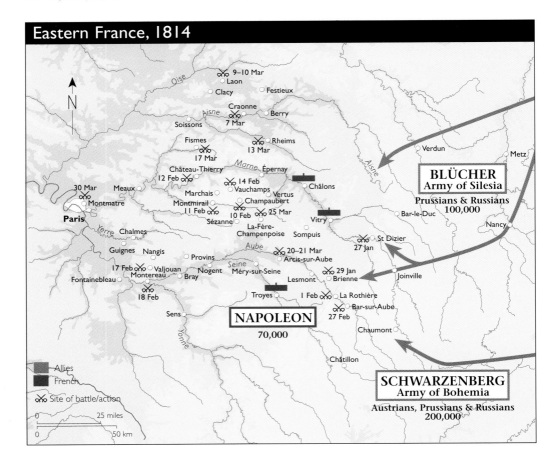

Eastern France, 1814

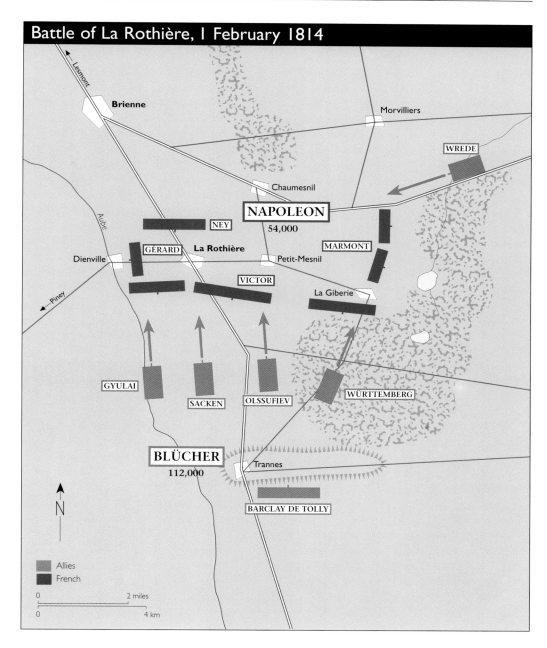

Battle of La Rothière, 1 February 1814

Lesmont

Brienne

Morvilliers

WREDE

Chaumesnil

NAPOLEON
54,000

NEY

Aube

GÉRARD   **La Rothière**   MARMONT

Dienville   Petit-Mesnil

Piney   VICTOR

La Giberie

GYULAI

SACKEN   OLSSUFIEV   WÜRTTEMBERG

BLÜCHER
112,000   Trannes

N

BARCLAY DE TOLLY

Allies
French

| 0 | 2 miles |
| 0 | 4 km |

north, the French held Yorck's advance in check at Vitry. Also, at Sens, on the Yonne, a body of Cossacks were driven off. These minor setbacks persuaded the already cautious Schwarzenberg to slow his advance, concerned as he was about intelligence of a new assembly of French troops at Lyon under Marshal Augereau (1757–1816). Blücher, on the other hand, made all speed up the Marne for Paris,

brushing aside the weak contingents seeking to oppose his progress.

At first Napoleon intended to strike at Schwarzenberg, but when he at last concluded on 5 February that Blücher intended to capture the capital itself and that only Macdonald's under-strength corps blocked his path, he concentrated what forces he could for a rapid march to Nogent. Mortier, in the meantime, launched a sortie from Troyes on 6 February, striking Schwarzenberg's right flank and sending him retreating back to Bar-sur-Aube. When Mortier returned to Nogent on 7 February, French forces there numbered approximately 70,000.

On 6 February Napoleon received reports of widespread panic in Paris, together with word that the Prussians had captured Brussels, and that Allied representatives at Châtillon-sur-Seine would accept no negotiated peace short of limiting France to her pre-1792 borders. Napoleon spent 7 February in solitude to consider his next move: by evening he had determined to carry on the war, concentrating his first efforts against Blücher. On 9 February, intelligence reports indicated the Prussian commander's position to be about 15 miles (25 km) east, near Montmirail. Having left Victor and Oudinot with 34,000 men to defend the bridges on the Seine from Schwarzenberg, and having left Macdonald, positioned north of the Marne near Epernay with 18,000 men, to watch Yorck, Napoleon marched a force of 30,000 eastward to Champaubert.

By 9 February Schwarzenberg had proceeded as far as Troyes, but the Allies failed to coordinate simultaneous movements up the Marne by Blücher, Yorck, and Kleist, all of whom struggled with impaired communications caused by melting snow and the onset of heavy rain. By spreading his force of 50,000 men too widely in an attempt to envelop the French around Sézanne, Blücher and his subordinates fell victim to a series of some of Napoleon's most impressive victories.

The first came at Champaubert on 10 February, where Napoleon's force of 30,000 overwhelmed 5,000 Russians under General Olssufiev whom Blücher had detached to operate in the area. On the following day the Emperor struck at Montmirail, defeating a Prussian corps under Sacken before Blücher could complete his attempts at regrouping his scattered forces. On 12 February the French were victorious again at Château-Thierry, though at the same time Macdonald was unable to prevent the Allies from forcing a passage of the Marne. On 14 February Blücher launched a counterattack at Vauchamps, but was repulsed. All told, what became known as the Six Days' Campaign cost the Allies 20,000 men. Nevertheless, although Napoleon's successes raised French morale, they failed to have a significant effect on the Allies, who brought up 30,000 Russians under Winzingerode to join Blücher's army at Châlons.

To the south, Schwarzenberg was meanwhile pushing west toward Guignes and Chalmes on the river Yerre, driving before him the combined army under Oudinot, Victor and Macdonald. By the middle of the month the Allies were within 20 miles (30 km) of Paris. Panic once again gripped the capital. Schwarzenberg, however, ordered a halt to assess the risks to his flanks. No sooner had he decided to withdraw than Napoleon pounced on and routed his advance guard at Valjouan on 17 February, and on the following day the Emperor defeated Schwarzenberg again at Montereau.

Schwarzenberg's reverse led him to revert back to his cautious strategy, while at the same time it emboldened Napoleon to renew his demand, despite the suspension of peace talks, for the restoration of the 'natural frontiers' as the basis for peace. Circumstances soon obliged him to modify his demand: unable to pursue Schwarzenberg to Troyes because of damage to the bridges across this stretch of the Seine, and aware by 21 February that the main Allied forces were concentrating at Méry-sur-Seine, Napoleon reverted once again to peace terms based on the frontiers of 1792. The offer was rejected, for Francis had already decided to carry on fighting as a result of entreaties from Alexander and Lord Castlereagh, the British Foreign Secretary, not to compromise when total victory appeared to be within reach.

On 22 February the Allies endorsed Schwarzenberg's continued retreat, and despite Blücher's objections, ordered him to withdraw. This denied Napoleon, now reinforced to 74,000 troops near Troyes, the major engagement he had hoped for. The Allies held another summit on 25 February at Bar-sur-Aube, which ordered Schwarzenberg back still further, though he was to advance to Blücher's aid if Napoleon threatened that commander. Blücher's renewed push against Paris had begun the previous day, enabling him to engage Marmont and Mortier near Meaux before proceeding north of the Marne beginning on 1 March. Without bridging equipment Napoleon was unable to pursue the Prussian commander-in-chief, who crossed the Aisne near Soissons with the bulk of his forces in order to link them with those of Winzingerode and Bülow, whose combined strength now exceeded 100,000 men. Quite apart from this overwhelming numerical superiority, Napoleon simply could not be in all places at all times and, taking advantage of this fact, Schwarzenberg resumed his march toward Bar-sur-Aube on 26 February, pushing Macdonald, in temporary command of this sector, toward Nogent, which he reached on 5 March.

Meanwhile, at an historic meeting convened at Chaumont, the Allies belatedly agreed to fight on until final victory, thus ensuring that Austria did not leave the alliance and conclude a separate peace. Castlereagh, fearing that months of careful diplomacy were about to crumble in the face of temporary French successes and bickering and recrimination between Alexander and Francis, had issued an appeal, calling on Austria and Russia to settle their differences for the sake of the common objective. 'I feel it more than ever necessary,' he had written on 18 February:

to conjure you and your colleagues at headquarters not to suffer yourselves to descend from the substance of your peace. You owe it, such as you have announced it, to the enemy, to yourselves, and to Europe, and you will now more than ever make a fatal sacrifice both of moral and political impression, if under the pressure of those slight reverses which are incident to war, and some embarrassments in your council which I should hope are at an end, the great edifice of peace was suffered to be disfigured in its proportions. Recollect what your military position is … If we act with military and political prudence, how can France resist a just peace demanded by 600,000 warriors? Let her, if she dare, and the day

you … declare the fact to the French nation, rest assured Bonaparte is subdued … There can be in good sense but one interest among the [Allied] Powers: namely, to end nobly the great work they have conducted so near to its close.

If the Russians and Austrians were at odds with one another, it was nevertheless clear that the Prussians and French were eager for a fight. Having ordered Marmont to join him from Meaux, Napoleon rapidly crossed the Aisle at Berry-au-Bac on 6 March en route to Laon. Blücher sprung a trap for French forces near Craonne on the same night, leading to fighting on the following day. A few days later, on 9–10 March, another struggle took place, at Laon, from which Napoleon barely managed to withdraw intact.

By now French forces were under great pressure elsewhere. In the south-west, Wellington continued to exert pressure on Soult and Suchet, while in Italy Eugène was faring equally badly. On the north-eastern frontier, Maison had withdrawn to Lille, and French garrisons across eastern France were cut off from all possible relief. Further into the interior, Augereau failed to get clear of Lyons and was forced back on 9 March, while on 12 March the authorities in Bordeaux hoisted the fleur-de-lis. In Paris itself, loyalties were divided and many regarded the restoration as inevitable. Napoleon now had only about 75,000 troops to oppose his numerous adversaries, and these were little more than exhausted conscripts.

Still convinced that he could conclude favorable peace terms, Napoleon marched east with all speed and severely defeated an isolated Prussian corps at Rheims on 13 March. Blücher and Schwarzenberg promptly halted, but Napoleon's troops were too tired to engage them and instead went to the assistance of Macdonald, who had been pushed west to Provins. The Emperor again sought to threaten Schwarzenberg's rear on 17 March, but the Allied commander-in-chief withdrew once more, while on the same day Blücher defeated Marmont at Fismes. Finding the Allies refusing to answer his calls to reopen peace talks, Napoleon planned to march across

The defense of Clichy Gate, Paris. Napoleon left the defense of Paris to his incompetent brother, Joseph, who not only failed to arrest those pro-Bourbon agitators busily sowing dissension, spreading disinformation and Allied propaganda, but also allowed himself to be duped into believing that weapons, funds, and manpower could not be found to mount an adequate defense. He also neglected to order the repair of the city walls or undertake construction of earthworks and ramparts. (Ann Ronan Picture Library)

the Allied rear by moving toward St Dizier and Joinville on the upper Marne, thereby blocking Allied reinforcements for both armies and opening links with French forces holding Metz and Verdun.

Napoleon's only hope of survival lay in defeating his enemies in turn. He therefore planned to assault the garrison at Arcis-sur-Aube under Wrede. Displaying unusual energy, Schwarzenberg foiled this plan on 20 March by moving to Wrede's aid, and after two days' fighting the French were lucky to extricate themselves with only 3,000 casualties. Continuing his advance on the Marne, Napoleon reached St Dizier on 23 March, having first seen off a force of 8,000 cavalry dispatched to obstruct him.

Emboldened by news of Augereau's abandonment of Lyons, the Allies, meeting for a summit at Sommagices on 24 March, decided on a daring step. Winzingerode, with 10,000 men, would create a diversion by marching toward St Dizier, while the two main Allied armies would push directly on the capital, encouraged by the contents of an intercepted report written by the minister of police and intended for the Emperor:

The treasury, arsenals, and powder stores are empty. We have no resources left. The population is discouraged and discontented. It wants peace at any price. Enemies of the imperial government are sustaining and fomenting popular agitation. Still latent, it will become impossible to suppress unless the Emperor succeeds in keeping the Allies away from Paris.

On 25 March Schwarzenberg, en route for Paris, overran positions held by Mortier and Marmont at La-Fère-Champenoise. After waiting four days for reinforcements at St Dizier, Napoleon managed to repulse Winzingerode's advance on 26 March, but on learning of the defeat at La-Fère-Champenoise

he realized that he had failed to halt the Allied offensive. On the advice of senior generals, he therefore abandoned his plans to carry on the campaign on the frontiers and moved toward Paris on 28 March. On the same day, only 25 miles (40 km) from the capital, Schwarzenberg and Blücher combined forces at Meaux.

On 29 March Marie-Louise and the three-year-old king of Rome left Paris, and by the end of the following day so too had Joseph and the remaining government officials. At the same time Napoleon left the army at Troyes and rode rapidly for Paris, whose gates the Allies were now approaching. He was too late: that night French troops on Montmartre surrendered. Despite the presence of nearly 150,000 Allied troops in the capital, Napoleon initially refused to accept defeat. Proceeding south to Fontainebleau, he prepared to resume fighting, only to find his marshals refusing to carry on. Following a parade review on the afternoon of 3 April, Ney, Lefebvre and Moncey angrily interrupted the Emperor and Berthier to declare the futility of continued resistance. Napoleon explained his intention of driving on Paris, to which plan those assembled, now including Macdonald and Oudinot, offered a cold silence. 'We do not intend to expose Paris to

The battle of Montmartre, 30–31 March 1814. During this, the final action of the campaign before Napoleon's first abdication, Marshals Mortier and Marmont could muster fewer than 25,000 dispirited regulars and National Guards for the defense of Paris. Troops on the heights of Montmartre and Romainville offered some resistance, but with 150,000 Allies converging on the capital and Napoleon too far east to be of assistance, Marmont signed an armistice before dawn on the 31st. (AKG, Berlin)

the fate of Moscow,' Macdonald then declared. The Emperor remained steadfast, so prompting Ney to exclaim defiantly, 'The army will not march on Paris.' 'The Army will obey me,' Napoleon angrily replied, only to be disarmed by Ney's coup de grace: 'Sire: The army will obey its generals.' This, and word that Marmont had defected, prompted Napoleon to offer a conditional abdication on 4 April, followed two days later, upon its rejection, by an unconditional abdication. By the Treaty of Fontainebleau concluded 10 days later, Napoleon was granted a residence on the tiny Mediterranean island of Elba, and on 28 April he was conveyed there by a British warship. In Paris, Louis XVIII was restored to the throne and signed the Treaty of Paris on 30 April, bringing a formal end to the war and restoring the borders of his country to their 1792 limits.

Captain Cavalié Mercer, Royal Horse Artillery

Cavalié Mercer was born in 1783, the second son of General Mercer of the Royal Engineers, who had served in the War of American Independence on the staff of General Henry Clinton, and afterwards spent the next two decades as commanding engineer in the west of England. The younger Mercer attended the Military Academy at Woolwich, was commissioned into the Royal Artillery as a second lieutenant at the age of 16, and was posted to Ireland during the rebellion of 1798. He became a captain in December 1806 and in the following year was dispatched to South America with the expeditionary force under General Whitelocke (1757–1833), which suffered ignominious defeat. To his great personal regret Mercer did not see service in the Peninsular War, but was sent abroad during the Waterloo campaign while still a captain, in which capacity he commanded G Troop, Royal Horse Artillery.

Mercer, who related his experiences in his *Journal of the Waterloo Campaign*, was a candid, colorful and accurate observer of the events around him, and unlike many diarists before and since, fully acknowledged the fact that most soldiers have a limited view of the battlefield and seldom know anything of events occurring even a few hundred yards away.

Depend on it, he who pretends to give a general account of a great battle from his own observation deceives you – believe him not. He can see no farther (that is, if he be personally engaged in it) than the length of his nose; and how is he to tell what is passing two or three miles off, with hills and trees and buildings intervening, and all enveloped in smoke?

On the morning of Waterloo (18 June 1815) Mercer's troop was camped in an orchard, where his men busied themselves filling their canteens with rum, preparing oatmeal, cooking soup and digging up potatoes. When firing began he noticed that the bivouacs on the hillside suddenly became deserted, and as the firing grew louder he ordered the troop to be readied for maneuver. The kettles of soup were overturned and the troop was ready to move, but Mercer was entirely without orders.

It appeared to me we had been forgotten. All except only ourselves, were evidently engaged; and laboring under this delusion, I thought we had better get into the affair at once.

Reaching the field of battle, Mercer surveyed attractive open country, covered in fields of corn and dotted with thickets and woods. It was a relatively quiet position, left of the heavily fortified farm of Hougoumont. But as the battle intensified he watched as French cavalry and artillery became more active and round shot began to fall on his position. He briefly exchanged fire with a French battery, in the course of which one of his gunners was struck by a cannon shot:

I shall never forget the scream the poor lad gave when struck. It was one of the last they fired, and shattered his left arm to pieces as he stood between the waggons. That scream went to my very soul, for I accused myself of having caused his misfortune. I was, however, obliged to conceal my emotion from the men, who had turned to look at him; so, bidding them 'stand to their front', I continued my walk up and down, whilst Hitchins [the troop surgeon] ran to his assistance.

Round shot continued to plow into the soft mud around him, one striking a horse from the gun team, depriving it of the whole of its face below the eyes. Yet the beast remained alive and standing, leaving Mercer to order the farrier to end his misery, which he performed with a thrust through the heart with his saber. Shortly thereafter a senior officer, his face blackened from smoke, his sleeve torn open from French fire, galloped up, calling out, 'Left limber up, and as fast as you can.' In moments Mercer's troop was trundling toward the main ridge between Hougoumount and the Charleroi ridge, where the French were massing a large body of heavy cavalry in preparation for a charge.

Wellington's orders, the officer informed Mercer in clear terms, were explicit: if the cavalry were certain to reach the guns, Mercer and his men were to fire for as long as possible before retiring into the safety of the adjacent squares of infantry. As Mercer's troop ascended the reverse slope of the main Anglo–Allied position, the full spectacle and sound of battle burst upon him.

We breathed a new atmosphere, … the air was suffocatingly hot, resembling that issuing from an oven. We were enveloped in thick smoke, and, malgré the incessant roar of cannon and musketry, could distinctly hear around us a mysterious humming noise, like that which one hears of a summer's evening proceeding from myriads of black beetles; cannon-shot, too, ploughed the ground in all directions, and so thick was the hail of balls and bullets that it seemed dangerous to extend the arm lest it should be torn off.

Hitchins, unaccustomed to such a cacophony, watched and listened with utter astonishment, twisting and turning in his saddle, declaring, 'My God, Mercer, what *is* that? What *is* all this noise? How curious! – how very curious!' When a cannon shot came hissing past, Mercer ordered him to withdraw, for the troop would need its surgeon intact.

Still, the troop reached the summit without loss, and the guns were unlimbered between two squares of Brunswick infantry to await the expected onslaught. No sooner had the first of Mercer's guns been maneuvered into position in the interval between the squares than he

perceived through the smoke the leading squadron of the advancing column coming on at a brisk trot. He immediately issued the order 'case shot!' and the guns unlimbered and were ready for action in moments. 'The very first round,' Mercer observed, '… brought down several men and horses. They continued, however, to advance.'

Meanwhile the Brunswickers had begun to issue musket fire, but as the square appeared unsteady he knew that he must remain with the guns and repulse the attackers or watch the infantry dissolve in panic. In this he knew that he must disobey Wellington's explicit order, and face the consequences later,

… a resolve that was strengthened by the effect of the remaining guns as they rapidly succeeded in coming to action, making terrible slaughter, and in an instant covering the ground with men and horses.

The horsemen nevertheless persevered, and though their progress was slowed to a walk they carried on, leading Mercer to the unpleasant conclusion that they would ride over him, though 'the carnage was frightful.'

In a hurried effort to retreat, the cavalry jostled and pushed through the debris, becoming:

a complete mob, into which we kept a steady fire of case-shot from our six pieces. The effect is hardly conceivable, and to paint this scene of slaughter and confusion impossible. Every discharge was followed by the fall of numbers, whilst the survivors struggled with each other, and I actually saw them using the pommels of their swords to fight their way out of the mêlée. Some, rendered desperate at finding themselves thus pent up at the muzzles of our guns, as it were, and others carried away by their horses, maddened with wounds, dashed through our intervals – few thinking of using their swords, but pushing furiously onward, intent only on saving themselves. At last the rear of the column, wheeling about, opened a passage, and the whole swept away at a much more rapid pace than they had advanced … We then ceased firing; but as

French cuirassiers charging Highlanders deployed in square. Hoping to clear the slopes in front of Mont St Jean of its beleaguered defenders, Marshal Ney ordered forward Milhaud's heavy cavalry corps, consisting of two divisions of cuirassiers, which when joined by light cavalry of the Imperial Guard, soon totaled 5,000 horsemen. Wave upon wave of cavalry took temporary possession of the guns but failed to spike them or to break any of the British squares. Ney's failure to destroy the squares with artillery fire, and the squandering of this splendid cavalry, did much to hasten French defeat. (Roger-Viollet)

they were still not far off, for we saw the tops of their caps, having reloaded, we stood ready to receive them should they renew the attack.

One of the first men of Mercer's troop to fall was a gunner named Butterworth, responsible for sponging one of the guns. Having just finished ramming down a shot, he was in the process of stepping back away from the mouth of the cannon when his foot became stuck in the mud, thus pulling him forward just as the gun was fired.

As a man naturally does when falling, he threw out both his arms before him, and they were blown off at the elbows. He raised himself a little on his two stumps, and looked up most piteously in my face. To assist him was impossible – the safety of all, everything, depended upon not slackening our fire, and I was obliged to turn from him.

Eventually Butterworth brought himself to the rear but was discovered dead by the roadside the following day, having bled to death on the way to Waterloo while in search of medical attention.

Meanwhile, the French launched a second determined charge:

None of your furious galloping charges was this, but a deliberate advance, at a deliberate pace, as of men resolved to carry their point. They moved in profound silence, and the only sound that could be heard from them amidst the incessant roar of battle was the low thunder-like reverberation of the ground beneath the simultaneous tread of so many horses. On our part was equal determination. Every man stood steadily at his post, the guns ready, loaded with

a round-shot first and a case over it; the tubes were in the vents; the port-fires glared and sputtered behind the wheels; and my word alone was wanting to hurl destruction on that goodly show of gallant men and noble horses …

I … allowed them to advance unmolested until the head of the column might have been about fifty or sixty yards from us, and then gave the word, 'Fire!' The effect was terrible. Nearly the whole leading rank fell at once; and the round-shot, penetrating the column, carried confusion throughout its extent. The ground, already encumbered with victims of the first struggle, became now almost impassable. Still, however, these devoted warriors struggled on, intent only on reaching us. The thing was impossible …

The discharge of every gun was followed by a fall of men and horses like that of grass before the mower's scythe … until gradually they disappeared over the brow of the hill. We ceased firing, glad to take breath.

Mercer, on seeing yet a third attack on its way, cried: 'There they are again!' But it was a pathetic, or perhaps more appropriately, tragic display.

This time, it was child's play. They could not even approach us in any decent order, and we fired most deliberately; it was folly having attempted the thing. I was sitting on my horse near the right of my battery as they turned and began to retire once more. Intoxicated with success, I was singing out, 'Beautiful! – Beautiful!'

G Troop suffered 18 casualties at Waterloo, three of whom were killed in the battle, two others missing and presumed killed and the rest wounded, among them gunner Philip Hunt, whose left arm was shattered by a round shot. Mercer's troop lost 69 horses, nearly three times as many as

any other troop, and had expended an extraordinary amount of ammunition – about 700 rounds.

After the Napoleonic Wars Mercer was placed on half-pay until 1824, when he briefly served in Canada as a brevet major. In 1837, having attained the rank of lieutenant-colonel, he was again ordered to Canada, where he commanded the artillery in Nova Scotia during the border dispute which nearly led to war between the United States and Britain. He became a colonel in 1846 and major-general in 1854. Afterwards he was commander of the Dover garrison and retired from active service, though continued as colonel-commandant of the 9th Brigade of Royal Artillery. He spent the remainder of his life at his cottage outside Exeter and died in 1868 at the age of 85, immensely proud of having been present at the century's most decisive battle.

Viscount Castlereagh, British Foreign Secretary

Robert Stewart, Viscount Castlereagh (1769–1822), was probably Britain's greatest foreign secretary. Born in Ulster in 1760 to an Anglo–Irish family, he went to Cambridge and entered Parliament in 1790, where he became a close adherent of Pitt and supported the Union of Ireland with the rest of Great Britain. In 1804 he became Secretary of State for War and the Colonies, in which capacity he planned the expedition to Portugal commanded by Sir Arthur Wellesley, later Duke of Wellington, but left office in 1809 as a political scapegoat for the failed Walcheren expedition to Holland. He is best known for his tenure as foreign secretary under the Liverpool government between 1812 and 1822, during which time he was pivotal not only in raising the Sixth Coalition against France, but in planning and implementing the political reconstruction of Europe after Napoleon's fall. The origins of the general European settlement of 1815 may be found in the Treaty of Chaumont, an innovative agreement principally the work of Castlereagh's deft diplomacy, and the subject of this brief review of the Foreign Secretary's varied accomplishments.

Castlereagh, together with the Austrian Foreign Minister, Prince Metternich, played a leading role not only in developing a practical solution to the political upheaval wrought by more than two decades of war, but also in balancing the relative strengths of the Great Powers. He established a system of international cooperation which helped preserve peace on the Continent for several decades after 1815. Castlereagh was regarded as aloof, bordering on the arrogant, being described by one contemporary as 'impenetrably cold'. Unlike his distinguished contemporaries, Pitt, Canning, and Fox, Castlereagh was no skillful public speaker, yet in the realm of foreign affairs he understood the importance of maintaining the balance of power on the Continent, and in upholding British supremacy at sea and in the colonial world.

While seeking to preserve the Sixth Coalition, Castlereagh recognized that while his country could not offer troops for the

Viscount Castlereagh, British Foreign Secretary, 1812–22. A skilled negotiator with a firm grasp of power politics, Castlereagh managed his country's foreign policy during the crucial years 1813–15 through his personal presence at Allied headquarters as well as at the Congress of Vienna which followed the peace. In close collaboration with his Austrian colleague, Prince Metternich, Castlereagh established a new political order in Europe that preserved peace for the next 40 years. (Philip Haythornthwaite)

main theater of operations in Germany, Britain was already playing a vital role in the struggle against Napoleon. While the Treasury supplied tens of millions of pounds in subsidies to Spain, Portugal, Russia, Prussia, and other states, Wellington had close to 100,000 British, Portuguese and Spanish troops operating in northern Spain. The Royal Navy, moreover, had long since kept French ports under close blockade and had swept the seas of French maritime trade. All of these contributions to the struggle gave Castlereagh grounds for believing that Britain was entitled to a voice in continental affairs, and when he set out for Allied headquarters at the end of 1813 he did so with the confident expectation that Britain was not only the equal of the other major European powers, but that his country's status ought to be recognized in the treaty that was to bind them to a series of common objectives.

Nevertheless, defending British interests formed only part of his responsibilities, for Castlereagh would have to draw on considerable powers of discretion and conciliation in order to assuage the suspicions the Allied leaders harbored toward one another, and to ensure that the coalition survived long enough to defeat the common enemy. The precise terms to be offered to Napoleon remained as yet unsettled.

Castlereagh left for Allied headquarters on 20 December 1813, his principal objective being to represent Britain at the peace conference to be convened in the event that Napoleon accepted the Frankfurt proposals. As foreign secretary, negotiating in person, Castlereagh drafted his own instructions, based on Pitt's 1805 plan for the reconstruction of postwar Europe. Particular emphasis was laid on the importance of ensuring an independent Holland, with a secure border, including the strategically vital port of Antwerp. Castlereagh also recognized that an independent Belgium could not hope to defend itself and would probably have to be joined to Holland in order to form a more secure state against a resurgent France. Yet his plans did not call for the destruction of France as a major

power: future European security depended on a balance, and France naturally formed an essential element in this scheme as a counterweight to the pretensions of other possible contenders for continental supremacy, particularly Russia. He was therefore not convinced that France need necessarily be ruled by the Bourbon line: Napoleon and his successors could possibly remain in power.

Castlereagh was also prepared to offer the return of captured French and Dutch colonies in exchange for security on the Continent, but was unwilling to compromise over such strategically important possessions as Malta, Mauritius, and the Cape of Good Hope. Bringing peace to Europe and re-establishing political order was not enough. As he understood from his political mentor, Pitt, some mechanism had to exist to provide for future security. The novel means of maintaining the wartime coaliton after the conclusion of peace would ensure that France did not again threaten her neighbors. Maintaining good relations between the coalition partners was central to Castlereagh's policy, and as Britain had no territorial aspirations on mainland Europe, the Foreign Secretary was in a strong position to keep the Allied powers on good terms.

Castlereagh reached Basle on 18 January 1814, where he met most of the Allied sovereigns and ministers, including Metternich, with whom he struck up an instant friendship, establishing a rapport that would enable the two statesmen to play a decisive role in European diplomacy for the crucial remaining months of the war and in the period of reconstruction afterwards. Indeed, the negotiations of this period involved close contact with diplomats, statesmen, and sovereigns, and much of Castlereagh's success, notwithstanding his reputation among some of his contemporaries, may be attributed to his agreeable manner and charm. Wilhelm von Humboldt, the former Prussian foreign minister, said of him: 'He conducts himself with moderation and firmness, and from the first moment was a conciliating influence here.' The Tsar, too, respected Castlereagh, though Alexander and Castlereagh certainly had their differences, not least the Tsar's wish for Bernadotte to ascend the French throne.

There were other sensitive differences between the Allies, and the British position had to be made clear from the outset. In his first meeting with the Allied foreign ministers Castlereagh argued that future European security depended on the reduction of France to her 'ancient' frontiers:

To suppose that the Allies could rest satisfied with any arrangement substantially short of reducing France within her ancient limits, was to impute to them an abandonment of their most sacred duty, which, if made with a view to peace, must fail of its object, as the public mind of Europe would never remain tranquil under so improvident an arrangement.

When the Allied sovereigns left Switzerland and joined Schwarzenberg's headquarters in France, tensions obliged Castlereagh to play a mediating role between Alexander and Metternich, for the Tsar did not wish to negotiate with Napoleon, but instead to push on to Paris. Largely through Castlereagh's intervention the Allies agreed to extend terms to Napoleon while continuing to prosecute the campaign. In short, France would be offered her prewar frontiers of 1792. Metternich in fact would have conceded more, while Alexander wished to offer nothing at all. Castlereagh's compromise placated them all and preserved intact an alliance whose individual members often pursued conflicting aims, particularly over the issue of territorial compensation for themselves in the postwar settlement.

Castlereagh proved unable to pin down Alexander on the precise form of compensation he sought at war's end. The Foreign Secretary wanted the coalition to state its war aims clearly and comprehensively, so as to avoid disagreements between the various parties that might arise when peace was concluded

and the powers could sit down and redraw the map. Alexander, however, would not commit his aims to paper, though it was well known that he wished to expand into Poland, and this secrecy contributed to Castlereagh's growing closeness with Metternich. Castlereagh wanted 'a just equilibrium or balance of power in Europe,' and he argued that, in a congress to be held after the war, Prussia should receive compensation in Saxony both in return for the losses she had sustained in 1807, and for her participation in the present coalition. Castlereagh offered to assist Bernadotte in his bid for Norway (a possession of Napoleon's ally, Denmark). With regard to Alexander and the Polish question, Castlereagh would offer no firm opinion, reserving that important question to a future congress to be held after the war.

Terms were presented to Napoleon and negotiations for peace began at Châtillon on 5 February. In the meantime, Castlereagh worked hard to establish a formal alliance, binding the Allies by written agreement to a common object. By the Treaty of Chaumont, signed on 1 March, they agreed to prosecute the war until they had achieved the following aims: complete independence for Switzerland and Spain, the latter under the restored King Ferdinand IV; Italy was to be free of French control and the various states of that peninsula were to be restored to their respective legitimate rulers; there was to be an enlarged Holland, to include Belgium as a more secure frontier; Germany was to be reconstituted into a confederation, reducing the number of states and creating larger units in order to provide protection from future French attack. To fund the alliance, Britain would furnish £5 million in subsidies to be equally divided between Russia, Prussia, and Austria over the course of the ensuing year. In return these nations were each to maintain 150,000 men in the field until the conclusion of the war. Finally, no power could sign a separate peace with France without unanimous consent.

The Treaty of Chaumont was in fact revolutionary in diplomatic terms, for it

Prince Metternich, one of the greatest statesmen of the
19th century. As foreign minister he persuaded Francis to
bring Austria into the Sixth Coalition in 1813, at the
same time advocating a negotiated settlement with
Napoleon, including the possibility of his retaining the
throne. Metternich sought the establishment of a balance
of power on the Continent and recognized the necessity
of a stable, intact, and reasonably strong France as a
counterweight to the growing power of Russia and
Prussia. Together with Castlereagh, Metternich shares the
credit as the architect of the successful peace settlement
established after Waterloo. (AKG, Berlin)

established for the first time the principle of
peacetime collective defense by binding the
signatories to support one another with
troops (60,000 in each case) in the event of
attack, extending to a period of 20 years after
the conclusion of the war. Naturally it
contained elements common to great treaties
of the past. It laid down, for instance, the
principle that the Great Powers would,
among themselves, redraw the political map
of postwar Europe as they saw fit, leaving
lesser powers to discuss matters confined to
their immediate region, all, of course, subject
to the veto of the leading nations.

Chaumont was effectively Castlereagh's
personal achievement, and once Napoleon
made the fatal decision to reject the
proposals put to him in February 1814, the
unity Castlereagh had forged remained
unbroken, enabling the Allies, bound by a
mutually agreed set of objectives, to bring to
bear their combined power against a nation
that could not otherwise be beaten. Many
points were naturally reserved for discussion
later in the year, to be held at an
international conference to include all the
nations of Europe – great and small – but the
later success of the celebrated Congress of
Vienna may in great measure be attributed
to Castlereagh's achievements during the
war itself.

Dénouement at Waterloo

On 26 February 1815 Napoleon escaped from exile on the island of Elba, landed in the south of France and marched on Paris, gathering adherents and winning the loyalty of the army as he went. Two Allied forces in the Low Countries were of immediate concern: an Anglo–Dutch army of 90,000 men under the Duke of Wellington, and 120,000 Prussians under Marshal Blücher. Napoleon's plan was to strike at each in turn, thus preventing them from joining forces. On 15 June he crossed the river Sambre with his Army of the North of 125,000 men and moved through Charleroi on the Brussels road. His purpose was to separate the Allies and defeat them in turn. Two battles were fought on the following day, at Ligny and at Quatre Bras. At the former the Prussians were defeated with serious losses but managed to withdraw north to Wavre. A Prussian captain noted the dreadful condition of his men toward the end of the fighting:

The light of the long June day was beginning to fail … The men looked terribly worn out after the fighting. In the great heat, gunpowder smoke, sweat and mud had mixed into a thick crust of dirt, so that their faces looked almost like those of mulattos, and one could hardly distinguish the green collars and facings on their tunics. Everybody had discarded his stock [neck scarf]; grubby shirts or hairy brown chests stuck out from their open tunics; and many who had been unwilling to leave the ranks on account of a slight wound wore a bandage they had put on themselves. In a number of cases blood was soaking through.

As a result of the fighting in the villages for hours on end, and of frequently crawling through hedges, the men's tunics and trousers had got torn, so that they hung in rags and their bare skin showed through.

At Quatre Bras, Wellington, though forced to retire to protect Brussels, had not been crushed, with the result that though both Allied armies had been kept apart, they were capable of fighting another day. On 17 June Wellington marched north and deployed his tired army on a ridge just south of Mont St Jean. Having detached a corps to observe the Prussians at Wavre, 12 miles (19 km) west of Wellington's position, Napoleon established his army, now 72,000 strong, on a ridge just south of the Anglo–Allied position.

Wellington had 68,000 men, comprising mainly mixed Anglo–Hanoverian divisions, and some Dutch–Belgian divisions. Most of these he placed along a two-mile (3 km), crescent-shaped ridge, though 18,000 were detached 5 miles (8 km) west at Tubize, to prevent the French from making a wide sweep around to the west and from threatening his right flank. On Wellington's left stood the villages of Papelotte and La Haye. In his center stood the farm of La Haye Sainte near the crossroads formed by the Ohain and Charleroi–Brussels roads. On his right, and somewhat forward of his main line, lay the chateau of Hougoumont, which included woods, farm buildings, and a garden. Wellington recognized the tactical importance of Hougoumont and La Haye Sainte, and placed strong garrisons in each. These strong-points presented obstacles to a French attack on the Allied right and center, and could offer enfilading fire to any opposing troops that sought to bypass them. Hougoumont was large enough, moreover, to make a sweep round Wellington's right more difficult, though not impossible.

The battle began when, around 11.30 am, a large force of French infantry under Prince Jerome Bonaparte attacked Hougoumont, held by elements of the Foot Guards and a battalion of Nassauers. Fighting would, in fact, rage around Hougoumont all day, but all French attacks were repulsed. At one

point the French actually forced the gate, but the Guards managed to close it and avert disaster. Later, the chateau was set on fire by French howitzers, but with reinforcements the defenders managed to keep possession of the remaining buildings despite unrelenting assaults. While the fighting continued around Hougoumont, at about noon the French massed 80 guns against the British center in preparation for the attack of Lieutenant-General Drouet, Comte d'Erlon (1765–1844). The effect, only 600 yards (549 m) from the Allied line, was horrific, despite Wellington's deployment of his infantry on the reverse side of the slope.

At about 1.30 pm, d'Erlon's corps of four divisions ascended the slope, the troops stretching from Papelotte to La Haye Sainte in one great mass, much of it toward the position held by Lieutenant-General Sir Thomas Picton (1758–1815). Wellington's

Coldstream Guards closing the gate at Hougoumont, a fortified farm which became the focus of some of the bloodiest fighting at Waterloo. This vital strongpoint in the Allied line nearly fell when axe-wielding French infantry broke open the great north door, allowing a handful of men to enter the courtyard. Colonel Macdonnell, sword in hand, along with four other Coldstreamers, just managed to close the gate, an action which Wellington later claimed had been essential to success that day. (Trustees of the National Museum of Scotland)

artillery fired on the advancing columns, inflicting heavy casualties on the front ranks, and when the French reached the top of the ridge they met devastating close-range fire from the red-coated infantry, followed up with a bayonet charge led by Picton, who was shot and killed. At the same time, Lieutenant-General the Earl of Uxbridge (1768–1854), commander of the cavalry, ordered the two heavy brigades behind the Allied center to charge in order to capitalize

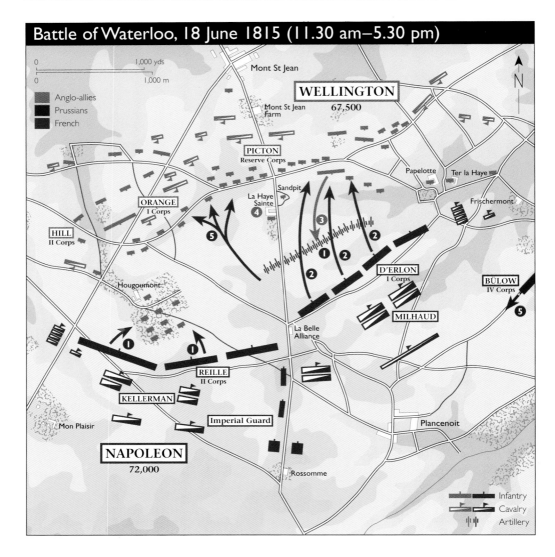

Battle of Waterloo, 18 June 1815 (11.30 am–5.30 pm)

0 _____ 1,000 yds

0 _____ 1,000 m

Anglo-allies
Prussians
French

Mont St Jean

WELLINGTON 67,500

Mont St Jean Farm

PICTON Reserve Corps

Papelotte   Ter la Haye

La Haye Sainte
Sandpit

ORANGE I Corps

Frischermont

HILL II Corps

Hougoumont

D'ERLON I Corps

BÜLOW IV Corps

MILHAUD

La Belle Alliance

REILLE II Corps

KELLERMAN

Imperial Guard

Plancenoit

Mon Plaisir

NAPOLEON 72,000

Rossomme

Infantry
Cavalry
Artillery

1. 11.30 am Massed French guns open fire against Allied center. Reille's corps attacks Hougoumont. Large numbers of French troops bogged down throughout the day in fruitless struggle for possession.
2. 1.30 pm D'Erlon advances against Allied center. Massed ranks lose heavily from concentrated artillery fire, then engage Picton's division.
3. 2.00 pm Somerset and Ponsonby counterattack, routing most of D'Erlon's corps. Cavalry continues to attack the grand battery, but are nearly annihilated while attempting to return to friendly lines.
4. Diminutive King's German Legion garrison at La Haye Sainte defend their fortified position against an entire division, but manage to resist all attempts to break in.
5. About 3.30 pm Bülow's IV Corps approaches from Wavre. Believing Wellington is withdrawing, Ney launches massed cavalry attack. More and more cavalry committed without proper infantry or artillery support in futile attempt to break infantry squares.

on Picton's success. The Household Brigade under Lord Edward Somerset (1776–1842) and the Union Brigade under Sir William Ponsonby (1772–1815), stood to the west and east of the Brussels road, respectively.

The Heavy Brigade defeated opposing heavy cavalry moving in support of d'Erlon's left and struck the left flank and rear of the French division at the western end of the attacking column. The Union Brigade, on the other hand, had to advance through the friendly ranks of Picton's division, thus breaking up the cohesion of both formations. Still, by the time the cavalry descended the slope the French were in

retreat, and the cavalry consequently inflicted huge losses on them. 'The enemy's column,' wrote a British officer present in the charge, 'seemed very helpless, and had very little to fire on us from its front or flanks ... the front and flanks began to turn their backs inwards; the rear of the columns had already begun to run away.' Another officer noted that 'the enemy fled as a flock of sheep across the valley – quite at the mercy of the dragoons.' The charge, however, carried on with a momentum of its own and could not be stopped. The Scots Greys and others managed to penetrate all the way to the French guns, but were virtually destroyed by lancers in a stinging counterattack. Still, by 3.00 pm d'Erlon's attack had been first halted and then thrown back in disarray, while Wellington's line remained stable, if weakened.

The French made a second attempt to break the Allied line around 4.00 pm. In a reckless move, Ney, having provided no proper infantry or artillery support, launched 40 squadrons of cavalry – nearly 5,000 men – at the infantry deployed on the reverse slope of the ridge. The results were as Mercer described them: as the glittering horsemen approached, British batteries inflicted heavy losses before the crews ran for the protection of the infantry, which had formed squares for their own defense. The

Charge of the Scots Greys at Waterloo. In order to counter d'Erlon's massed infantry attack, the Earl of Uxbridge launched two brigades of cavalry, including this distinguished regiment. On catching the French completely by surprise, the Greys inflicted heavy casualties and took 2,000 prisoners and two Eagles. Overcome by their success, oblivious to danger and shouting 'Scotland Forever!', the troopers galloped on, sabering the gunners and drivers of a grand battery before being overwhelmed by French lancers and practically destroyed. (Ann Ronan Picture Library)

squares offered an effective fire of their own and the cavalry, however determined, could not break any of them. Ney repeated the attacks several times, each time with fewer men and at a slower pace. An unnamed British officer noted that the men grew increasingly confident once they saw off the cavalry in the first charge:

The first time a body of cuirassiers approached the square ... the men – all young soldiers – seemed to be alarmed. They fired high, and with little effect; and in one of the angles there was just as much hesitation as made me feel exceedingly uncomfortable; but it did not last long. No actual dash was made upon us ... Our men soon discovered that they had the best of it; and ever afterwards, when they heard the sound of cavalry approaching, appeared to consider the circumstance a pleasant change; for the enemy's guns suspended their fire.

By 5.30 pm the French cavalry, after suffering immense and futile losses, ceased the attack. British casualties were heavy nevertheless, for in the intervals between the cavalry charges the squares were especially vulnerable to French artillery fire. The location of many squares was marked by great piles of the dead lying in formation. Captain Gronow left a graphic description of the scene:

During the battle our squares presented a shocking sight. Inside we were nearly suffocated by the smoke and smell from burnt cartridges. It was impossible to move a yard without treading upon a wounded comrade, or upon the bodies of the dead; and the loud groans of the wounded and dying were most appalling.

At four o'clock our square was a perfect hospital, being full of dead, dying and mutilated soldiers. The charges of cavalry were in appearance very formidable, but in reality a great relief, as the artillery could no longer fire on us.

The fighting around La Haye Sainte was reaching its climax soon after the repulse of Ney's cavalry. As at Hougoumount, La Haye Sainte had been under constant attack all day, and by late afternoon the infantry of the King's German Legion (KGL) inside had been drastically reduced in number, ammunition was nearly expended, and many of the buildings were ablaze. At 6.00 pm the French made a final thrust against the farm, where after desperate hand-to-hand fighting the attackers ejected the 40 survivors of an original garrison of 400. Two battalions of KGL infantry sent to the Germans' support from the ridge were destroyed by opposing cavalry, and French occupation of the place was confirmed. The fall of La Haye Sainte left Wellington's center very vulnerable, obliging him to concentrate every available infantry regiment and battery at this critical point. In addition he placed

Last stand of the Old Guard. As Napoleon's army was routed amid cries of 'Sauve qui peut!', three battalions of the Imperial Guard remained steadfast in square, vainly attempting to stem the Allied onslaught. Surrounded by overwhelming numbers of infantry and artillery, the Guard received concentrated fire at 60 yards, which wrought dreadful carnage. According to 19th century French historians, their commander, General Cambronne, refused the call to surrender with the heroic reply: 'The Guard dies but never surrenders', though eyewitnesses recorded the more prosaic response, 'Merde!' (Roger-Viollet)

two brigades of cavalry in the center rear. Despite the gallant defense shown throughout the day, the prospect of defeat now loomed large for the Allies.

Help was, however, now on its way. From 5.00 pm elements of the Prussian forces in action earlier in the day at Wavre had been arriving piecemeal from that village to the east and were engaging the French right in and around the village of Plancenoit. The Prussians were driven out by the Imperial Guard, but by 6.00 pm, when Wellington's line was at its most critical state, large numbers of Prussians were then arriving to retake Plancenoit and to oppose the French around La Haye and Papelotte, thus aiding Wellington's left as well as striking the French right further south. At last the Allies had managed to concentrate their forces and the French now faced a crisis of their own.

Napoleon believed he had a final opportunity to defeat Wellington before the Prussians could arrive and deploy in sufficient numbers to shift the balance unalterably against him. He ordered up seven battalions of the Imperial Guard from his reserve. These advanced up the slope between Hougoumont and the Ohain crossroads, intending to strike the Allied line, now considerably weakened from the day's fighting, and thus bring about its collapse. The French advanced slightly to the left toward two brigades, one under Sir George Cooke (1768–1837) and the other under Sir Colin Halkett (1774–1856). British guns fired on the advancing infantry but did not halt it; when the Imperial Guard reached the top of the ridge they were suddenly met by the Grenadier Guards, who rose from a prone position and unleashed a series of devastating volleys, causing the French to retire a short distance. The British Guards then charged, obliging the Imperial Guard to retire

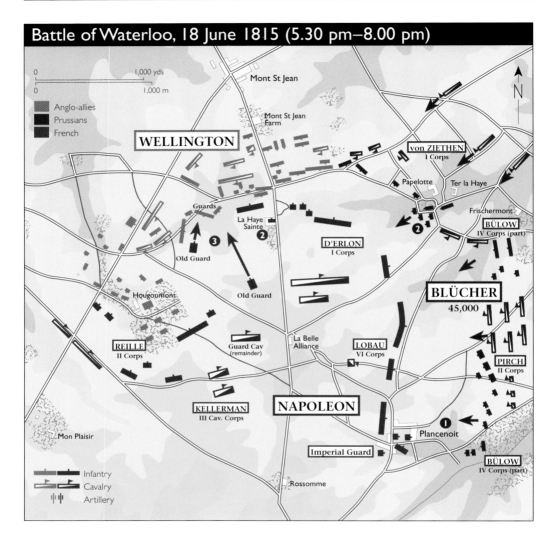

Battle of Waterloo, 18 June 1815 (5.30 pm–8.00 pm)

1. By 5.30 pm the Prussians are heavily engaged at Plancenoit, where Bülow is assisted by Pirch and Blücher himself. Prussians take the village, but are later ejected by Imperial Guard, Napoleon's last reserves.
2. Around 6.00 pm, Ney finally captures La Haye Sainte and brings up artillery to batter Allied center at close range. Wellington's line begins to waver. Perceiving this, Ney sends urgent appeals to Napoleon for attack by the Imperial Guard, but these are already engaged at Plancenoit. Zeithen's corps nears Wellington's left wing.
3. 7.00 pm The Old Guard, recalled from Plancenoit, attacks west of La Haye Sainte to confront Maitland's Guards Brigade and other formations. Fired on from three sides, the attackers recoil. At about the same time, approaching troops from the east recognized as Prussians, contributing to the French rout. Wellington orders a general advance and victory is assured.

again before reforming and returning up the slope. The same procedure was repeated, but on this occasion Napoleon's veterans were faced by a new threat, and failed to reform. From the right of the 1st Division had come a brigade under Major-General Adam (1781–1853) from the division of Sir Henry Clinton (1771–1829), containing the 52nd Foot, which deployed on the left flank of the Imperial Guard and fired enfilade into its wavering ranks. Confronted by deadly fire both to its front and flank, the Imperial Guard retreated, causing a general panic and rout of the entire French army. Wellington signaled a general advance of his entire line and the battle was won.

An artistic perspective

Art in the Empire

The Empire embraced and appropriated a number of artistic influences that had begun before and during the French Revolution. Naturally, the arts often reflected Imperial tastes, which approved of the fascinating and exciting interplay of Neo-classicism and nascent Romanticism.

Painting and music

In the field of painting, artists such as Jacques-Louis David and Antoine-Jean Gros not only reflected the epic glory of the Empire, but also expressed some of its highest sentiments. Music saw the movement from the strict classical style of Franz Joseph Haydn to the more lyrical strains of Romanticism. Ludwig van Beethoven became both the embodiment and the catalyst of this transition. His career would reflect the changes in music better than any other composer. A fervent republican the whole of his life, he composed Symphony No. 3 (the 'Eroica') in Bonaparte's honor, but changed the dedication 'to the memory of a great man' when he heard of Napoleon becoming Emperor.

The court of Napoleon saw a number of composers of whom none but the most scholarly of musicologists would know today – Mehul, LeSueur, Cherubini and Gossec. Napoleon's preference was for Italian-style opera, so that was what was most presented in Paris. This operatic era marked an interregnum period between Mozart and Verdi with little to distinguish it. However, not surprisingly, Napoleon's composers did produce some great martial music. Departing from the preceding fife and drum style, the Napoleonic army bands came close to approaching a modern orchestra. On the day of battle, the sound of 100 drums with accompanying brass would soar over the battlefield and provide an important boost for the morale of the soldiers.

Sculpture and architecture

Other arts flourished as well. Napoleon had opened the Louvre to the public to see the art from the collections of the Bourbon kings and from the spoils of Napoleon's first Italian campaign. Here was the sculpture of antiquity that had graced the palaces of Italian princes and Popes, as well as new masterpieces by contemporary artists such as Antonio Canova. The new public museum was organized by Dominique-Vivant Denon, the father of the modern museum system. Expanding upon ideas being developed in Vienna, Denon perfected the system of organizing the museum into periods of art and styles. Prior to Denon, pictures and sculptures had been presented in a hodgepodge fashion.

The Consulate and Empire saw a building program such had never been seen before in France. Paris witnessed the start of the Arc de Triomphe, the Bourse, the arcades along the Rue de Rivoli, the north wing of the Louvre, the Place Vendôme with its triumphal column, and the reconstruction of the Madeleine church. When you look on modern Paris, much of what you see was the Emperor's inspiration. While the works program in Paris is the most celebrated, Napoleon executed similar programs elsewhere in France.

French society

The society of France was transformed under the Empire. During the Revolution, much of what was considered high society revolved around the private salons, but in the early Empire the places to be were the courts of the Empress Josephine or one of Napoleon's sisters. This allowed Napoleon better to influence the politics and fashions of Paris.

Fashion had become more conservative after the libertine days of the Directory, which Napoleon found in poor taste. Women wore long, high-waisted, 'empire-style' dresses that were meant to hark back to the classical period of Greece. The men wore variants of the topcoat, vest and trousers. These were essentially the beginning of modern styles of men's dress.

It became fashionable to dine out for the first time in history. Restaurants had begun to flourish. France's first great chefs, Brillat-Savarin and Carême, were making their mark. The latter was Talleyrand's chef at the insistence of the Emperor, to employ the culinary as well as the diplomatic arts to enhance French prestige.

Napoleon put his stamp on everything from the theater to furniture, from the law to the Catholic Church. 'The Age of Napoleon' was as much a conquest of style and imagination as it was a military epoch.

Vienna

Vienna was a changing city in 1809. The austere moralism of Emperor Leopold had been replaced with easier virtue and good times. The cafes were teeming with people and there was much more freedom of thought than a generation earlier. One craze that swept Vienna was the waltz. This dance originated at the turn of the century, developed from an Austrian creation, the Ländler. At first the quick whirling around the floor of partners locked in an embrace was thought scandalous, but by 1809 polite society had long since given up their objections and joined the dance floor.

In some ways, though, Vienna was still the product of her great empress, Maria Theresa. The Imperial edifices that adorned the capital were by and large her handiwork. True, the walls that had withstood the two sieges by the Turks, in 1529 and 1683, still encircled the main city, but what lay within exemplified the majesty of the Habsburg dynasty. Vienna was

filled with magnificent churches and palaces. Of equal importance to the Viennese were the theaters and opera houses which nightly were filled with the music of the greatest collection of composers ever assembled. Mozart, Gluck, Haydn, and Beethoven have left a legacy unsurpassed to this day.

Franz Joseph Haydn (1732–1809) was the dominant composer in the years leading up to 1809. He is most famous for developing the classical style. This new style was considered liberating when compared to the older Baroque style. Music was mostly written for wealthy patrons, usually ecclesiastic or aristocratic. In Haydn's case it was the Esterhazy family, for whom he worked from 1761 till his death.

Haydn acted as a bridge in the classical music period. He was a contemporary of Wolfgang A. Mozart (1756–1791), and went on to be an instructor of Ludwig von Beethoven (1770–1827). He was popular throughout his career and died wealthy.

He was one of the few non-Italian or non-French composers that Napoleon greatly admired. This sentiment was not returned by Haydn, however, perhaps wisely for his career in Vienna.

As the French approached Vienna in 1809, Haydn was already dying. Napoleon had a guard put on his home out of admiration for the great composer. Haydn died on 31 May 1809 and his funeral was held at the Schottenkirche, where Mozart's Requiem was performed. His casket was surrounded by French soldiers acting as a guard of honor. His body was transported through the lines, where an Austrian honor guard took over from their French counterparts. He was buried at Hundsturm Churchyard near his home.

Even 18 years after his death, the shadow of Mozart still cast his mark upon Vienna. He had been typical of the composers of the period, working for patrons, but had alienated them in one way or another. Specifically, his flirting with themes that cast the nobility of the time in a less than favorable light and had left him without patronage. Friends supported him and gave him commissions to write for the Opera Buffa. Mozart took to comic opera and wrote such enduring works as *The Marriage of Figaro* and *The Magic Flute*. Twenty years later all society now flocked to the theaters to see this style, and Mozart was much more popular than he had been during his lifetime.

The classical music era was at its height in 1809, and part of the change was the instrumentation of the works being composed. The piano had replaced the harpsichord, and the mark of the new style was a composer's production of music for the piano. The ability to vary the level of sound produced a dynamism that seemed in keeping with the spirit of the new thinking pervasive after the French Revolution.

Personifying this thinking was Beethoven. He was imbued with the ideas of Republicanism, and had renounced his admiration of Napoleon upon hearing of him taking the crown of France. His vibrant works were popular among all classes and he was evolving the medium to a point that a new age called Romanticism would follow, with many of his works being in the vanguard. It is amusing to reflect that his most popular works of that time were rather pedestrian, such as Wellington's Victory, a piece celebrating the British victory at Salamanca in 1812.

The Viennese people were perhaps the most cosmopolitan in the world at the time. While they would nearly bankrupt themselves in trying to defeat the French, they made a distinction when it came to Napoleon. He was, after all, the most famous man alive. Dezydery Chlapowski, an aide to Napoleon, describes the reaction Napoleon received when he first arrived at the gates of the city:

'Here I saw a sight which I would not have believed had I not seen it with my own eyes and heard it with my own ears. The city walls were not crowded, but there were still a good many well-to-do inhabitants on the ramparts. The Emperor rode right up the glacis, so only a ditch 10 meters wide separated him from these people. When they recognized him, they took off their hats and began cheering. I could only explain such behavior by the devotion which a man like the Emperor inspired in all around him.'

It is little wonder that the French soldiers found Vienna a pleasurable place to spend time.

The artistic works of Francisco Goya

When the French occupation began Francisco Goya (1746–1828) was 62 and already established as Spain's foremost artist. His greatest work was yet to come, inspired by the events of the next six years. Ironically this was at a time when the French would commit wholesale looting of Spanish art, from obscure pieces of statuary and painting, to native masterpieces seized from cathedrals, convents, private collections, public buildings and palaces

Francisco José de Goya y Lucientes (1746–1828), c. 1815. One of Spain's greatest artists, he tackled a range of subjects and media and produced many of his most famous works during the Peninsular War. Much of Goya's art involved subtle and not so subtle parody or criticism of the Inquisition and the injustices of the state. His life was nothing if not varied and colorful, and included knife fights, womanizing, the fathering of large numbers of children, and progressive insanity. (Prado Museum/AKG Berlin)

'The Third of May, 1808' (*Tres de Mayo*). One of Goya's most famous works, depicting a French firing squad outside Madrid executing those suspected of having participated in the previous day's uprising. Although the painting is enormous – 9 feet high and 12 feet wide – in order to include both executioners and the condemned Goya placed his subjects at unnaturally close quarters, creating a peculiar perspective. It is a highly emotive, magisterial painting. (Prado, Edimedia)

by French officials, generals, and a host of less exalted thieves.

Even as the crisis was unfolding between Charles IV and his son Ferdinand, in the spring of 1808, Goya was engaged in an equestrian portrait of the prince for the Royal Academy of San Fernando. The picture, which was exhibited in October, was completed after only three sittings of 45 minutes each. Goya was not fond of the Spanish Royal Family and many critics agree that in earlier portraits he caricatured them, portraying them with pompous, idiotic or even cruel expressions and attitudes. The picture of the Crown Prince was to be no exception. Ferdinand had already been deposed and Joseph Bonaparte installed in his stead, even if for the moment he and his army had been temporarily driven from Madrid.

Goya was in the capital during the fateful days of 2 and 3 May 1808 but it is not clear if

he was an eyewitness to the uprising and its suppression. His records of these events, however, were left to artistic posterity in the form of two exceptionally large oils, whose vivid portrayals of the ferocity of feeling in the first instance and brutal vengence in the second are famous around the world. The Second of May (Dos de Mayo) immortalizes one of the great moments in modern Spanish history, when residents of Madrid rose up and attacked the Mamelukes of Napoleon's

French depredations. An engraving from Goya's *Disasters of War*, showing French soldiers abusing Spanish women. Faceless figures cower in the shadows and a baby lies crying on the floor. Rape was an all too common feature of this ghastly conflict. (Museum of Fine Arts, Boston/Roger-Viollet)

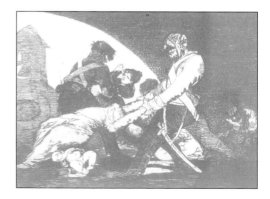

Imperial Guard in the Puerta del Sol. The Mamelukes, men in turbans carrying curved scimitars, evoked for the Madrileños bitter memories of the long past but not forgotten days of Moorish occupation.

The Third of May shows the aftermath of the riot, as faceless French executioners dispatch suspected ringleaders and, as was perhaps inevitable in the chaos of the roundup, many innocents as well on the following evening. Goya's excellent use of color focuses the attention on a white-shirted victim with his arms raised overhead, bearing a moving expression of fatal resignation and foreboding of his imminent demise. Other victims cluster around him, some already lying prostrate and slain, including one of the same figures who appears in the Second of May stabbing a horse. One figure cowers in the background covering his face in horror, another projects a defiant fist, while a monk in the foreground clasps his hands, probably engrossed in final prayer rather than gesturing for mercy. The colors are muted and grim – dark grays, browns, black – as opposed to the orange, red, pink, and brown used in the Dos de Mayo.

At the end of 1808 Goya was summoned to witness the French siege of Saragossa, near his hometown of Fuendetodos. The commander of the garrison, General Palafox, whose portrait Goya would produce in 1814, wished the artist to see the state of the city and record the heroic efforts of its citizens during that epic siege. But his journey did not result in creative work immediately, and he returned to the capital, where throughout the remainder of the war his relationship with the French remained ambiguous. Once the occupiers returned, Goya – along with thousands of other Spaniards in state service – swore allegiance to King Joseph, and resumed his pre-war position as First Court Painter. He even accepted from the usurping king a medal, the Order of Spain, contemptuously referred to by his compatriots as 'the eggplant'.

Goya could not be properly classed a collaborator, but certainly showed no

Atrocities. One of the many eyewitness sketches by Goya in his series *The Disasters of War*. Far from romanticizing war like so many of his predecessors and contemporaries, Goya depicted the more gruesome, barbaric sides of the Franco-Spanish element of the conflict. Here he depicts mutilated corpses suspended from a tree – a not uncommon sight recorded by many other observers. (Museum of Fine Arts, Boston/Roger-Viollet)

inclination towards resistance, either. In the course of the occupation he painted the Allegory of the City of Madrid, which represents the capital as a woman, pointing to a medallion bearing a portrait of Joseph carried aloft by figures representing Fame. Joseph's image was later replaced after his fall with the words Dos de Mayo, which now remain. Goya also painted several portraits of French generals and afrancesados (francophile Spaniards who were French sympathizers), including a fine portrait of Canon Juan Antonio Llorente, a liberal clergyman and former secretary to the Inquisition who now condemned the institution in his writings. Llorente desired social reform and saw French rule as the opportunity in which to carry it through. Goya also produced a series of pen-and-ink drawings, never actually engraved, which by their subjects sharply criticized the old injustices of the medieval Inquisition. Other sketches, which too remained only on paper and were never reproduced as engravings, portrayed thousands of nuns and monks, removed from their religious houses by French edict, engaging in the human pleasures hitherto denied them by their strict vows. His superb portrait of 1810 of Nicholas Guye, a distinguished French general, so impressed the sitter that Guye commissioned a picture of his young nephew as well.

But Goya also painted the liberator as well as the occupiers, and when the French evacuated the Spanish capital in 1812 the grateful Madrileños provided a rapturous welcome to Wellington, who soon commissioned an equestrian portrait of himself, followed later by two other portraits. None of these betray a heroic figure; rather a somewhat wearied one. The equestrian portrait shows him in a blue Spanish cavalry cloak, covering the otherwise striking scarlet uniform of the British Army; he has a somewhat undersized head, and rides alone in a bleak landscape – quite in contrast to David's heroic portrayal of Napoleon crossing the Alps (1800). The half-length portrait of the Duke is recognized as an accurate likeness but is certainly not meant to evoke images of grandeur as was clearly the case in the full-length portrait of him later executed by Sir Thomas Lawrence. He does indeed wear his uniform, replete with his various decorations and medals from Britain, Portugal, and Spain, yet neither his pose nor his expression evoke the kind of passion so common amongst other military portraits of the neoclassical age.

Goya did not confine himself only to the famous; in the course of the war he painted family portraits and pictures of various private individuals. Indeed, the subjects of his wartime work varied greatly. Many of his portraits exude quiet simplicity, gentleness, and even beauty. He painted his son's mother-in-law and father-in-law; his grandson; three children of noted Madrid families; a well-known actress named Antonia Zárate; and the attractive Francisca Sabasa García. In addition to portraits he produced works showing ordinary scenes of life and work in numerous paintings such as *The Water Carrier*, *The Knife Sharpener*, and *The*

Forge, an image of blacksmiths at work.

Goya continued the theme of earlier prewar subjects, like the majas – alluring young women in provocative poses. In contrast, other women appear in *Old Age* and *Celestina and her Daughter*, works which illustrate the irreversible ravages of time on human beauty.

Without doubt Goya's best known work at this time focused on the war. There was the forbidding and inscrutable *Colossus* (c. 1811, Museo del Prado). This naked giant, possibly symbolizing war, strides across the landscape towering above throngs of terrified refugees and their herds as they flee in all directions in a scene of total chaos. The most notable of his wartime work revealed a very different side to the portrayal of the conflict itself and was the antithesis of the glorious battle scenes created by the likes of Jacques-Louis David (1748–1825) and Antoine Gros (1771–1835). Goya's images are patently not about heroes and victories. His series of 82 etchings entitled the *Disasters of War* (*Desastres de la Guerra*), originally drawn in red crayon, which were executed throughout the war though not published until 1863, represent a stark and haunting record of the conflict and his unequivocal views upon it. The modern iconography of war may be traced from them, as can the tradition of the artistic witness to conflict. These powerfully haunting etchings reveal the baseness to which human nature can descend when the extremities of war bring out his more barbarous instincts. Yet they constitute more than a condemnation of the horrors of the war in the Peninsula, for they also record numerous instances of injustice, oppression and hypocrisy on the part of Spanish officials and clergy.

But the brutality of war emerges above others as the dominant theme. Some have allegorical references – some subtle and others flagrantly transparent – drawing the observer's attention to the viciousness of war and its dire influence on society, religion, and human behavior. There is symbolic use of animals: wolves, pigs, eagles, donkeys, and others, each representing something sinister, stupid or ignorant. Most are straightforward in their ghastliness, depicting the worst excesses of conflict: rape, massacre, pillage, torture, homelessness, starvation. Individuals in the *Disasters*, whether the perpetrator of some outrage or its victim, are sometimes rendered almost nonhuman, while in contrast the humanity of others is unquestionable. Goya's art of this period illustrates a living hell: a hell wrought from war and its attendant miseries. Tradition states that when Goya's servant asked him why he produced such dreadful scenes of man's inhumanity to man, the artist replied, 'To tell men forever that they should not be barbarians.'

The *Disasters* remained unpublished for 35 years after Goya's death; they were clearly not meant as propaganda and their publication would certainly have led to his arrest by French authorities. On the other hand, even at the restoration of Ferdinand Goya did not see fit to release them, undoubtedly because of the offence they would have caused to a monarch who, having cravenly first colluded with Napoleon in ousting his father and then abdicated in favor of a Bonaparte king, bore a heavy responsibility for the occupation. Ferdinand had played no part in the war of independence, notwithstanding which its victims focused their hopes on his return from exile.

The *Disasters* may be divided into three main themes, the first of which shows the reaction of rural Spaniards to the invasion. Bodies heaped together, peasants fighting with improvised weapons against the invader, executions and murder all find their place here. A second theme concentrates on urban life, with its squalor and starvation, doubtless inspired by the terrible famine that struck Madrid in 1811–1812. The last theme is more political in tone, revealing how with the close of the war and the restoration of the monarchy under Ferdinand VII, whose reign would continue until 1833, a new phase of cataclysm afflicted the nation.

The first etching in the series depicts a man kneeling, arms outstretched and eyes beckoning the heavens as if desperately seeking an answer for the misfortunes that have befallen him. 'Gloomy presentiments of things to come' reads the caption. Goya did not shrink from scenes of horror; instead, he recorded them bleakly, whether it was mutilated corpses, starving civilians or the wanton excesses of French troops. What emerges is an indictment of man's inhumanity to man, observed by an eyewitness to the atrocities he depicts.

Evidence of such atrocities is supported by the written records of others: Spaniards, French, and British. Simmons of the 95th witnessed the desolation of a Portuguese town in 1811:

... the houses are torn and dilapidated and the few miserable inhabitants moving skeletons; the streets strewn with every description of household furniture, half-burnt and destroyed and many streets quite impassable with filth and rubbish, with an occasional man, mule or donkey rotting and corrupting and filling the air with pestilential vapours ... Two young ladies had been brutally violated in a house that I entered and were unable to rise from a mattress of straw. On the line of march, comparing notes with other officers, I found that they all had some mournful story to relate of the savage French vandals which had come under their immediate observation ... The unfortunate inhabitants that have remained in their villages have the appearance of people who have been kicked out of their graves and reanimated.

Some plates show refugees, huddled together, emaciated, dejected, reduced to begging. Other etchings show dismembered corpses impaled on the branches of trees. Again, such scenes are corroborated by others, no less than Wellington himself: 'I have seen many persons hanging in the trees by the sides of the road,' he wrote, 'executed for no reason that I could learn, excepting that they had not been friendly to the French invasion ... the route of their column on their retreat could be traced by the smoke of the villages to which they set fire.'

Such scenes inspired Goya's *Disasters*. In his twenty-ninth etching, entitled, 'They do not want to', a French soldier clutches the waist of a Spanish woman who in her struggle claws at her assailant's face while an elderly woman, presumably the mother, stands behind the soldier brandishing a dagger to be plunged into his back. Other etchings show naked corpses of civilians grotesquely strewn on the ground, as onlookers cover their faces in horror. Still others show monks dispossessed of their monasteries, and a sinister depiction of a wolf, sitting amongst a group of emaciated and dejected peasants, scribbling in quill pen on a parchment condemning the suffering and misery of the war. 'Wretched humanity,' the caption reads, 'the fault is yours.'

The etchings that comprise the *Disasters of War* together reveal how Goya was revolted by war with its destruction of the nation's spirituality, the brutalization of people driven to reprisal against the invader, ceaseless destruction and bloodshed, and the privations of ordinary noncombatants, victims of a war they neither inspired nor perpetuated. Nevertheless, Goya did not confine his subject to atrocities and privation alone; some of his etchings clearly condemn the betrayal of liberal political reforms instituted by the Cortes during the war. In *Truth is dead*, the artist shows figures representing the return of repressive institutions to Spain standing over the corpse of a young woman representing Truth. Her body emanates light while the clergyman presiding over her funeral appears dark and foreboding. Before the corpse kneels the figure of Justice covering her face with her hands in abject sorrow. Such political themes symbolized a particularly painful expression of hopes unfulfilled in the wake of liberation. Ordinary Spaniards, who had exalted the cause of Ferdinand, casting him as something of a savior, soon lost their fervor when the restoration reestablished the Old Order with a vengeance. No sooner had Ferdinand returned to Spain than he abrogated the Constitution of 1812 and executed the leaders of the Cortes. Such repression ill repaid the Spanish people for the experience of six years of misery and Goya was not loath to record it.

The end of La Gloire

Napoleon at last was defeated and this time the Allies would ensure that there would be no chance of bouncing back again. Now there was an opportunity to negotiate a lasting peace, and to reflect on the course of events that had resulted from one of the most far-reaching revolutions in history and the military and political phenomenon it had spawned - Napoleon Bonaparte.

Russia and Prussia

In the end, the Peace of Tilsit, negotiated in June and July 1807 between France, Russia and Prussia, had failed to hold. Why was this? In essence, the stakes had been too high for a compromise to endure. The conflict had always been, ideologically, a war to the death. The old monarchies of Europe could not bring themselves to accept the principles of the French Revolution that Napoleon so represented to them, nor could they live with his domination of Europe. There were at least three successful imperialist powers, France, Britain, and Russia, each vying for the best position. This created an environment where the powers always looked for an opening to gain the advantage once more. The less successful imperialist powers of Prussia and Austria wished to revive their fortunes, and hoped to gain revenge for the humiliations they had received in 1805 and 1806 from this 'parvenu emperor'. They were potentially available as allies to Napoleon's enemies.

Napoleon strengthened their resentment by instituting his Continental System. While it had come close to driving Britain into bankruptcy, it had also impoverished the mercantile economies that were under Napoleon's control. This had led to widespread smuggling and defections. For

example, as soon as the Treaty of Tilsit had been signed, the Russian merchants had aligned themselves with the established nobility to begin to undermine it. At sea, Britain enjoyed a domination that not only protected her, but gave her direct links to every continental power, and allowed her to strike at any coastline of Napoleon's Empire where an ally supplied an opening.

With an enormous empire to control, Napoleon had had to incorporate more men into his army from outside France, but some new contingents did not have the enthusiasm for Napoleon that had driven his early armies. Furthermore, even the French recruits who had taken up the musket to replace their fallen comrades were now mostly conscripts. The French army no longer fielding volunteers, the rate of desertion had increased. Finally, Napoleon's later armies never achieved the level of training that would have allowed them to perform the most intricate of maneuvers.

In the end, though, it may have been that the allies had caught up with the French techniques for waging war on land. Captain Parquin, in his famous memoirs, tells of having a conversation with a Russian general following a French victory. 'The Russians are today pupils of the French, but they will end up by being the equals of their masters.'

The empires fight back

The campaign of 1813 which had set out to bring Alexander to his senses and close off Russian ports to Great Britain had ended in disaster. Britain, which had been hard-pressed financially in 1810/11, was resurgent and only the war with the United States had prevented her from pouring massive subsidies into the Continent.

Wounded infantry on the field of Lützen, 2 May 1813. A group of fallen French soldiers hail their Emperor as he passes in the background. The grim side of Napoleonic warfare is unmistakably evident around them: the dead sprawled amidst the paraphernalia of war, including drums, muskets, equipment, and broken vehicles. Note the Russian grenadier (right), seated nonchalantly amongst his foes, taking some comfort from a flask doubtless containing rum or vodka. (Philip Haythornthwaite)

Napoleon had started the campaign with 600,000 men and when it had finished, 400,000 had died or never returned to the ranks. The massive loss of horses further compounded the tragedy, crippling the French army in its future campaigns, as they were unable to exploit their victories or transport supplies, artillery, and the wounded.

Russia had lost some 250,000 men and was almost as battered as France, but Alexander, in the grips of a growing messianic complex in which he saw himself as God's deliverer and Napoleon as the Antichrist, had determined to pursue the war, against the wishes of Kutusov.

Another telling moment had been the defection of the Prussian General Yorck, whose entire contingent had changed sides after a private treaty with the Russians. This event had precipitated Prussia's entry into the war against Napoleon. At the same time, Austria had withdrawn from Napoleon's coalition to wait on the sidelines for further developments.

Napoleon had hurried back to France to rebuild his army. He had done a remarkable job but his German allies had become increasingly war-weary and questioning of the benefits of remaining within the French sphere. Sweden, directed by Bernadotte, had been preparing to join in the alliance against France. The story in Spain was no better: things had definitely turned against the French, and Napoleon needed to take troops out rather than send in more.

Europe had become transfixed by the clear vulnerability of the French. The Russian campaign had changed the opinion of the monarchies regarding their ability to stand against Napoleon. Like the circling crows which had followed the Grande Armée during the retreat, waiting for an opening to prey on a carcass, the crowned heads of Europe had seen in the 1812 defeat a chance to destroy the meaning of the French Revolution, and perhaps acquire additional territories into the bargain. The one thing that they did not forget was that Napoleon had not personally lost a single battle during the campaign. Even so, he could not be in all places at once and there were two or three fronts besides the main one where the French could be hit. What this Mars now lacked was able marshals to cover the fronts where he was not. This his enemies knew and this they would exploit.

The Peninsular War

The Peninsular also made an important contribution to the fall of the French Empire. It had not been a mere backwater of the conflict, but a genuine second front which for seven years had continually drained French manpower and matériel with a remarkably small military – though a very large subsidiary – commitment from Britain. The French, on the other hand, had dispatched approximately 600,000 troops to the Peninsula in the course of the war, diverting considerable resources which would otherwise have been available to oppose other adversaries. They had faced the paradox contained in an old saying whose truth was to be borne out yet again: 'In Spain a small army is beaten and a large one starves.'

Napoleon's Continental System had proved personally disastrous, not least because it had alienated his subservient and client states, thus providing Britain not only with moral support, particularly in the

Simón Bolívar (1783–1830), the 'Liberator' of South America. Bolívar fought in the unsuccessful Venezuelan revolt of 1811–1812, and in New Granada (Colombia) in 1813, when his forces retook Caracas from troops loyal to Spain. After three years in exile he returned to fight and eventually won the war of liberation that led to the formation of an expansive Colombia, of which he became dictator until 1825. Thereafter, separatist movements created the independent states of Venezuela, Ecuador, Peru, and Bolivia. (Ann Ronan Picture Library)

Mediterranean, but on a more tangible basis, with ready markets for the illegal trade in British and British colonial goods. Trade was vital to the British economy and by 1808 British merchants had been suffering from the glut created by the French-imposed ban on the importation of British goods. The capture of French colonial possessions had not been enough to alleviate the economic crisis in Britain; manufacturers of cloth and metalware needed regular and reliable foreign markets. The Peninsular War had done much to solve their problems, for it led to the opening of the markets of the Spanish and Portuguese empires to British trade, leading to a rise in British exports from £8 million in 1805 to almost £20 million in 1809. The benefits of this trade were, moreover, to prove long-term, extending well into the twentieth century.

It is no easy matter to quantify precise numbers of casualties in this conflict. Records of battlefield losses and sick lists are generally available, though not always accurate: the war of attrition conducted by the guerrillas considerably complicates accurate tabulation of French and French allied losses. The average daily loss for France has been estimated at 100 men, or a total of nearly 240,000, and this in addition to the unquantifiable financial cost and strain that the war placed on the French treasury. Other estimates place French losses at 300,000. Apart from the cost of paying for and supporting his armies in Spain, Napoleon had also provided huge loans to his brother Joseph, who, by the end of his reign in June 1813, had received a total of 620,000,000 reals. But in spite of such support he owed almost the same amount again to France by the end of the war. One estimate suggests a total cost to the French Empire of four billion reals (or in excess of a billion francs), not including all the cost of weapons and the other sinews of war. Such vast figures in human and financial resources alone demonstrate the important contribution that the Peninsular War played in bringing down Napoleonic rule in Europe. France could sustain a series of major campaigns on a single front; it patently could not on two, and in the wake of the disasters in Russia, Allied pressure ultimately proved too great a strain. The human cost of Britain's effort in the Peninsula is not known, but one aspect of the cost is fairly well documented: the financial support furnished in the form of massive subsidies of cash and huge quantities of arms, ammunition, and uniforms to Spain and Portugal. Between 1808 and 1814 Britain had provided no less than £18 million in cash alone.

Ingredients of Allied success

The Peninsular War had seen the rise of Britain's greatest general and, arguably, its greatest army. The high professional standards which the army had achieved in Spain and Portugal were a testament to Wellington's abilities not only as a superb commander, but also as a highly skilled administrator. What qualities did he possess and how did they translate into success on the battlefield?

Wellington possessed remarkable stamina. He rose at 6.00 am and worked until midnight, writing large numbers of orders and dispatches, and riding between 30 and 50 miles (48 and 80 km) a day. In the six years he spent in the Peninsula he never once went on leave. His supreme self-confidence about his plans and his abilities was tempered by an understanding of his limitations based on clear-sighted forward planning and good use of intelligence. Wellington began the war with a clear and effective long-term strategy in mind and he adapted his tactics – usually but not always, defensive – to suit the ground, his opponents' strengths and

weaknesses, and the capabilities of his men. He possessed the sort of intelligent mind that could quickly understand and assess a situation, whether at the strategic or tactical level. He laid his plans carefully and often anticipated those of his enemy. He had a good grasp of logistics and understood that an effective army required regular supplies of food, equipment, and ammunition. As such, he recognized the importance of an efficiently-run Commissariat.

Wellington seldom delegated authority to his subordinates in order to maintain personal control of affairs wherever possible, particularly on the battlefield. His orders were clear and he saw to it they were carried out precisely. While his failure to delegate may be seen as a fault, his consistent battlefield successes owed much to his presence on the scene, where by exposing himself to fire he encouraged his men and could see at first hand where action needed to be taken: sending reinforcements, exploiting a success, withdrawing, and so on. Proof of his constant presence in the thick of things is shown by his narrow escape from

Sir Arthur Wellesley, First Duke of Wellington. Having risen to military greatness as C-in-C of Allied forces during the Peninsular War, his first and last encounter with Napoleon took place at Waterloo, where he deployed a mixed force of British, Hanoverians, Dutch, Belgians, Brunswickers, and Nassauers, most of whom were not the hardened veterans he had led to victory only a year before. Thus, without the timely intervention of Blücher's Prussians in the afternoon, history's most famous battle might well have ended inconclusively. (Philip Haythornthwaite)

capture on three occasions and the three times when he was hit by musket balls – though without receiving serious injury. At Busaco Schaumann noted Wellington's conduct under fire: 'As usual, of course, Lord Wellington displayed extraordinary circumspection, calm, coolness and presence of mind. His orders were communicated in a loud voice and were short and precise.'

Wellington recognized – and acknowledged early in the war – that with only one army, and a small one at that, he could not afford to be defeated: he simply could not enjoy that luxury. Criticisms leveled against him as a strategically 'defensive' general should be analyzed in this light. He spent three years in a largely defensive posture and seldom took risks, fighting only when circumstances were favorable and then with positive results. By preventing the French from concentrating their massive numbers against him, he could fight their armies separately on reasonable terms and wait for the time to switch to the offensive. Thus, though the French had several hundred thousand men in the Peninsula at any given time, Wellington normally fought battles with about 50,000 men on each side. Napoleon's invasion of Russia in 1812 enabled him to do so, since that campaign not only required some French troops to transfer east, but would later deny to French commanders in the Peninsula much-needed reinforcements. From then on the French were obliged to fight a two-front war, thereby emboldening Wellington to move to the offensive. While it is true that at the tactical level he largely fought on the defensive, this was by no means always the case, as demonstrated at Oporto, Salamanca, Vitoria, and elsewhere.

Wellington also understood that the war would be long, and where other commanders might have regarded the odds as hopeless, he persisted. If his campaigns failed, he would accept responsibility, and he understood his dependence on the goodwill and cooperation of his hosts. 'I am convinced,' he declared to his superiors in London in October 1810,

that the honour and the interest of the country require us to remain here to the latest possible moment ... I shall not seek to relieve myself of the burden of responsibility by causing the burden of defeat to rest upon the shoulders of ministers. I will not ask from them resources which they cannot spare ... If the Portuguese do their duty, I can maintain myself here; if not, no effort in the power of Great Britain to make [war] will suffice to save Portugal.

He never gave in to what he called 'the croakers', officers in his own army who suggested, often behind the scenes, that the war was a lost cause, particularly in the period between Talavera and the withdrawal of Masséna from the Lines of Torres Vedras. Wellington inherited an army that, though it had undergone reforms under competent men like Abercromby and Moore, had a poor military record. Yet in the course of a few years he organized and trained the finest army of its size in Europe. And, whatever one may say about the contribution made by the Spanish soldiers and guerrillas, the balance of Allied victory or defeat in the Peninsula ultimately hung on the ability of Wellington's army to defeat the French in the field. This he did consistently with small numbers that usually varied between 30,000 and 60,000 men, of mixed nationality, but men of exceptionally high caliber, training, and leadership.

In short, Wellington's consistent victories owed much to his careful planning, his personal supervision of the fighting and his ability to react appropriately as circumstances changed. He anticipated the actions of his adversaries, who were often experienced generals, and so could plan accordingly. Finally, he commanded an army composed, in the main, of competent general officers and well-trained men, probably the best Britain has ever produced.

The setbacks at the Coa and at Burgos, though not battles in the usual sense of the word, show that British troops were not universally successful. In addition, operations in eastern Spain in 1813 led by Murray and Lord William Bentinck

(1774–1839) met with lackluster results. Nor can it be said that the troops always conducted themselves with honor: their conduct after the fall of Badajoz and, to a lesser extent, San Sebastian, was nothing short of disgraceful, tarnishing what would otherwise have been a war waged by the British mostly on civilized terms. The fact that the government failed to provide Wellington with an adequate siege train only contributed to the huge losses and consequent desire of the men to run wild in the aftermath.

Wellington, who keenly appreciated the vital part played by logistics in war, wisely disrupted French supply lines wherever and whenever possible, while protecting his own. He also operated an extensive intelligence network, considerably facilitated by campaigning in friendly country, whereas, conversely, the French had virtually nothing in the way of reliable intelligence.

While the French were continuously dogged by severe problems of supply and communication, the British operated in friendly country and were, for the most part, well supplied by sea. Thus, while by its nature the war could only be won by operations conducted on land, the contribution made by the Royal Navy was absolutely vital to the success of its terrestrial arm by maintaining unrestricted communication and supply links with Britain. The French could only communicate via the Pyrenees and could neither supply their troops nor transport them by sea either in the Bay of Biscay or in the Mediterranean. The British, conversely, could operate with complete freedom at sea, and it was this extraordinary flexibility that enabled them not only to land an expeditionary force in Portugal in 1808, but also to be able, when circumstances demanded it, to withdraw it from Corunna in January 1809 and then to send another back to Portugal again in April. The relationship between sea power and the success of armies on land is often overlooked; the Peninsular War provides an excellent example of how sea power is not simply confined to great fleet actions.

Having said this, only a great naval power like Britain could enjoy such flexibility and it was won as a result of a great naval action, the victory of Trafalgar in 1805.

Allied success had owed much, but not all, to Wellington. One can also trace it to Portugal and Spain's contribution to the war effort and to French mistakes and shortcomings. Beresford's reconstitution and reconstruction of the Portuguese army had also made a significant contribution to Allied victory. So also had the extremely formidable system of strongpoints established to protect Lisbon. The Lines of Torres Vedras enabled Wellington to sit in complete security behind a defensive cordon, so protecting at least central and southern Portugal, and wait for the opportune time to project his forces into Spain.

One may easily dismiss the regular Spanish armies of 1808–1809 on the grounds of their poor performance, but if French losses at Bailén were easily replaceable, the reputation lost there could not be. The very existence of these armies, however easily they were shattered in 1808–1809, gave heart to many Spaniards, especially the guerrillas. In short, the Spanish armies, though consistently defeated and unreliable, were persistent and could never be completely discounted by the French. Their mere existence tied down large numbers of troops who otherwise would have concentrated against the much smaller British and Portuguese forces, who never numbered more than 60,000 men. Given the utterly inadequate transport and equipment, appalling training and acute shortage of cavalry horses, combined with a penurious rabble led by fools or worse, it is little wonder that the Spanish armies would consistently meet disaster in the field. Yet back they would come with a determination not seen elsewhere in Europe. It must be acknowledged, moreover, that toward the end of the war, after Wellington had assumed supreme command over the Spanish armies, the regular forces managed to raise their standards and acquitted themselves well at such actions as Vitoria and the siege of San Sebastian.

Although impossible to quantify by their very nature, and whether one condemns the combatants as savage brutes and murderers or brave patriot heroes (or perhaps a combination of the two), the impact of guerrilla operations must not be underestimated. These largely anonymous characters had harried French communications throughout Portugal and Spain and had tied down large numbers of men sent in usually fruitless attempts to exterminate them. In effect, the French had been forced to fight on two fronts: against the regular Allied armies in the field and against the Spanish, and, to a lesser degree, the Portuguese guerrillas along their flanks and in their rear. Communications and supply lines could be severed sometimes at will and the geography of the countryside proved ideal for guerrilla operations. Apart from the actual combatants, unarmed civilians often paid the price, marking the Peninsular War out from all other conflicts since the seventeenth century as the most vicious and comprehensive in its impact on civilian life. The military consequences were significant: unremitting guerrilla operations had not only sapped French strength, but the cost to morale had been very great as well. In short, without the support and contributions to the war effort made by Spain and Portugal, as he himself acknowledged after 1814, Wellington could not have won the war.

The contributions of Spain and Portugal, combined with the ever-present guerrillas, and, of course, the British Army itself, had rendered the French strategy of concentrating superior forces against a critical point in search of a decisive result much less feasible. True, the French had enjoyed overall numerical superiority, but they had seldom been able to profit from this advantage. To concentrate they had had to abandon large areas to their enemy, only to have to seize them back later. Their numbers had been dissipated in a hopeless attempt to keep the population under control, supply lines open and to garrison towns and cities. Perhaps the greatest

miscalculation made by France had been her failure to recognize the hostility felt by the Iberian people. Trying to subjugate a hostile civilian population while simultaneously taking on the Allied army had proved too much. As Wellington himself stated:

It is true that [the French defeat in Spain] may in part be attributed to the operations of the allied armies in the Peninsula; but a great proportion of it must be ascribed to the enmity of the people of Spain. I have known of not less than 380,000 men of the French army in Spain at one moment & yet with no authority beyond the spot where they stood.

The French themselves admitted there was no military solution to civilian animosity. Recalling his days as provincial Governor-General of Catalonia 1810–1811, Marshal Macdonald described the problem with telling succinctness: 'The enemy were ubiquitous, and yet I could find them nowhere, though I travelled the length and breadth of the province.'

Traditional French methods of supply failed completely in the Peninsula. Campaigning in the rich and fertile Po and Danube Valleys was not the same as in East Prussia and Poland, as Napoleon had discovered in 1807, and Spain and Portugal were even worse, exacerbated by 'scorched earth'. Here, 'living off the land' alone proved impossible, making supply at best tenuous and at worst an insupportable problem in an intensely hostile and geographically inhospitable land. In compelling subservient peoples to support them, the French opened a Pandora's box.

In contrast to Wellington's exceptional leadership qualities, French commanders, though often excellent men, such as Junot, Victor, Masséna, Marmont, and Soult, were at times their own worst enemies, acting out of motives of jealousy, mistrust, and professional rivalry in competition for independent success. The net result was painfully predictable: consistent and sometimes disastrous failure to cooperate with one another in a war where their combined

numerical superiority could have been tapped with success and in a country where communication was already nearly impossible owing to the ubiquitous guerrilla presence.

Much credit is due to Wellington for persuading his government to continue the war even after the disastrous evacuation of Moore's army from Spain. Not only did Wellington recognize that he could hold Portugal with a relatively small force in conjunction with a reorganized Portuguese army, he appreciated the tenuous nature of France's occupation of Spain. Its sheer size and the scale of popular hostility to the occupier meant that France could probably never completely subjugate the country. In a land where the population already lived at subsistence levels, it was hopeless, despite the most draconian methods, to try to supply armies that totaled hundreds of thousands. To cope with this intractable problem, French lines of communication had necessarily to become overstretched, leaving them extremely vulnerable to guerrilla attacks. Those who claim that the war was unwinnable from the outset can do so only

ABOVE The captive Napoleon on the deck of HMS *Northumberland*, bound for St Helena. 'I desire to live in England, a free man, protected by and subject to its laws …', he had written in a bid for amnesty. With no desire for a repetition of the escape from Elba, British authorities refused and, accompanied by a suite of 15, Napoleon was interned on one of the world's most inaccessible islands, garrisoned by 3,000 British troops and patrolled by four Royal Navy frigates. (Ann Ronan Picture Library)

RIGHT The Vienna Settlement graphically demonstrates the extent to which the triumphant Great Powers benefited territorially, and sought to create a buffer around a possibly resurgent France, whose borders were restored to those of prewar 1791. In general, frontiers shifted westward: Russia kept Finland (taken from Sweden in 1809) and most Polish territory; Sweden received Norway from France's ally Denmark; Prussia, in addition to a third of Saxony, received substantial Rhenish territories that greatly increased her presence in the north-west. Austria made gains in northern Italy: two thirds of the Po Valley, including the return of Milan and Mantua and the annexation of Venice. Florence and Parma passed to minor Habsburg rulers, thus rendering Austria the clearly dominant power in Italy. Britain desired only off-shore possessions: Heligoland in the North Sea and Malta and the Ionian Islands in the Mediterranean. Belgium, too weak to defend itself against France, was merged with Hollland to create a more viable power. Similarly, the various German states were loosely joined in a confederation to ensure greater security.

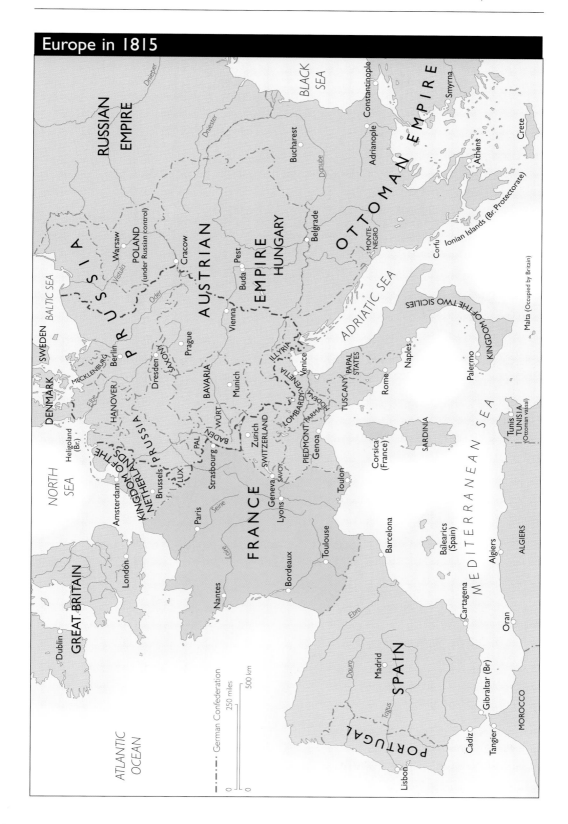

Europe in 1815

with the safety of hindsight, but it is clear that the French faced daunting obstacles from the moment the Spanish people rose up – and still more when Wellesley arrived in Portugal a few months later.

However daunting the obstacles appeared at the outset of the war – poor supply, uneven leadership at senior levels, varied and often times harsh climate and terrain, and great distances – Napoleon remained largely oblivious to the challenge that loomed ahead. Perhaps he had good reason for viewing his prospects optimistically: after all, when Junot marched into Portugal in 1807, France had no other active fronts competing for men and the veterans of the campaigns of 1805–1807 were not even required for the occupation; they could remain in the cantonments on the Rhine, the Elbe, and the Oder. Neither the scale nor the determination of Spanish resistance were initially clear, and even after all these obstacles became obvious, including Britain's inevitable intervention, Napoleon continued to prosecute the war, and his ardor never faded. Of course it may be argued with some justice that it was precisely this miscalculation and his self-deluding bravado that cost Napoleon the war, yet only with hindsight does the victory won by the Allies seem a foregone conclusion. It could easily have been different for, even when Britain did intervene, there were many, not just the 'croakers' in Wellington's army but also those on the Opposition benches in Parliament, who, in the wake of Corunna and at various other critical moments in the war, advocated withdrawal from the Peninsula.

It must also be stressed that, even when Britain continued her efforts, it was not until 1812, with the diversion of French troops to the Russian front, that Wellington could hope to undertake a full-scale invasion of Spain. Any time before that period a major battlefield defeat might have spelled the end of Britain's commitment to her Iberian allies. This was the reality of a country with only one army to lose and governments that depended on parliamentary support for

survival. This was never the case with Napoleonic France, which, in spite of consistent setbacks and the realization that Spain could never be subjugated, stubbornly continued to maintain her hold on Spain until forcibly driven out.

The War in the Peninsula enabled the British Army to share in the overall Allied effort against Napoleonic France, not simply to be left to diversionary operations as in the past. For the first time in a century a major British force, much larger than in the wars of the mid-eighteenth century, could operate on the European mainland. The army won a series of unbroken victories in the field and, apart from Burgos, succeeded in every assault on a fortified position. Almost every regiment in the army earned some share of glory in the Peninsula, as is shown by the battle honors which adorn their regimental colors even today.

Thus, when the Allied powers sat down to conclude the Treaty of Paris in 1814, Britain's major contribution to the defeat of France was more than acknowledged by the other Great Powers. Had Britain confined her war effort to the supply (large though it was) of subsidies and naval operations alone, her influence at the peace conferences which followed Napoleon's first and second abdications would never have been so considerable as it ultimately proved to be. Whether his empire and dynasty would have survived had Napoleon never embarked on his Iberian adventure is open to debate, but clearly his decision to do so, and Britain's determination to press on for final victory, contributed materially to his ultimate downfall.

The Vienna Settlement

Between November 1814 and June 1815 the leaders of Europe gathered in the Austrian capital for an international conference, later known as the Congress of Vienna, to fix the borders of European states in the aftermath of more than two decades of war. Although Napoleon had been overthrown and France defeated, the leaders of the victorious powers understood that neither the threat of war nor the future outbreak of revolution had been eradicated. The settlement which they sought at Vienna was, therefore, to a considerable degree intended to maintain peace and stability. Some leaders, like the arch counter-revolutionary Prince Metternich of Austria, wanted a league of sovereigns designed not only to preserve the settlement reached between them, but to enforce it as circumstances required anywhere on the Continent. This aim was theoretically possible, but in practice it would require at least basic cooperation between not only the victorious powers, but France as well.

To the leaders who gathered in Vienna, the French Revolution and the generation of war that arose out of it offered a stark lesson: radical political change, once begun, could not be controlled. Recent history had demonstrated that revolution brought with it political turmoil, civil war, regicide, military dictatorship, and years of war with the renegade power. If the French Revolution and Napoleon were indeed precedents of what Europe might face in the future, it was necessary for national leaders to take whatever steps were necessary to avoid future catastrophe.

Metternich firmly believed that rather than tame movements for economic, political or social reform as some advocated, it was better to smother the movement for change altogether before it gathered momentum. Stability was all-important to Metternich, who believed revolutions resulted from an international conspiracy of agitators. Austria, an empire of numerous nationalities, was particularly vulnerable to the nationalistic strain of revolution and the instability that war could bring. In effect, maintaining the integrity of that empire became for him synonymous with the maintenance of peace on the Continent in general.

Metternich believed that two leading principles ought to be applied to the prevention of revolution and the problem of

The Congress of Vienna. After Napoleon's downfall the principal victors convened an international conference which met between November 1814 and June 1815. In addition to implementing the terms of the first Treaty of Paris and dismantling the Napoleonic Empire, the Congress's principal function was to re-draw the political map of Europe, restore the numerous dynasties to their respective thrones, provide territorial compensation to the victorious Great Powers, and to create a system for the preservation of peace and security on the Continent. (AKG, Berlin)

maintaining European peace and stability. According to the principle of legitimacy, nations should be monarchies with their rulers established on the basis of a strong claim, such as hereditary right. The relative effectiveness of a sovereign was secondary to his right to rule. Secondly, Metternich believed in the principle of intervention, which meant that in combating the spread of revolution across international borders, states that perceived a threat to themselves reserved the right to interfere in the internal affairs of other countries or to send troops to crush the movement, either unilaterally or in conjunction with other states.

The two men most responsible for the final reconstruction of the European states system were Metternich and Castlereagh. However, neither they nor the other politicians and sovereigns arrived at the Congress to begin with a clean slate. Many agreements between individual states already existed, some dating from 1813. Any product of their collective work would necessarily have to form a compromise of such deals and the conflicting views of the participants. Notwithstanding these complications, the various problems under discussion in Vienna could be settled by the application of three main principles.

First, rulers and states would be restored according to the principle of legitimacy. Metternich and Talleyrand were the main proponents of this principle, which provided dispossessed individual rulers or their dynastic successors with a restored throne on the basis of hereditary right. The powers gathered together in Vienna applied this principle to France, Spain, Piedmont, Tuscany, Modena, and the Papal States. After the First Treaty of Paris King Murat of Naples was permitted to retain his throne, though this was taken from him when, on Napoleon's return from Elba, he changed sides during the Hundred Days, only to be defeated by the Austrians at Tolentino on 2–3 May and executed shortly thereafter.

The fact remained, however, that radically changed circumstances since 1792 rendered impossible the uniform application of this principle. This was particularly so in the case of Germany, where such fundamental political changes had taken place since the French Revolution that it was simply impossible to restore the more than 300 states that had previously existed. These were instead rationalized into 39 states and formed into the new German Confederation, administered by a diet at which each state was represented by a specified number of delegates. With her delegates acting as presidents of both chambers of the diet, Austria would exercise the leading influence. The principle of legitimacy could not be applied where it was deemed inconsistent with a particular state's security or self-interest.

The second principle applied at Vienna concerned territorial compensation. In short, the victorious states were to be rewarded at the expense of the defeated. The victorious powers not only expected to be rewarded for their contribution to Napoleon's defeat, but were determined that France and her allies should be penalized for their aggression. By the terms of the First Treaty of Paris, signed on 30 April 1814, France, largely at the behest of Castlereagh, was to face only moderate terms. France was to be restored to her frontiers of 1792; this still left her Savoy and the Saar, which between them provided an additional 500,000 inhabitants over her prewar population. Britain agreed to return all her captured French colonies except Mauritius, Tobago, and St Lucia. The victors imposed no indemnity on France and no army of occupation would remain on her soil. Nor would France have to return the thousands of pieces of looted art and treasures seized from Germany, Italy, Spain, and elsewhere over the past two decades. Britain retained the Cape of Good Hope from Holland in return for £2 million in compensation, but returned the valuable Dutch East Indies.

After the Hundred Days the Allies were far less forgiving, and the Second Treaty of Paris, signed on 20 November 1815, was much more punitive in nature. The French frontiers were reduced to those of 1790, the nation was to pay an indemnity of 700 million francs and an army of occupation would remain for three to five years to ensure that the indemnity was paid. But this is partly to anticipate the story, for the Congress had already concluded that France's allies were also to be punished, and it was largely at their expense that the four victorious Great Powers received territorial compensation.

Austria forswore all right to the Netherlands, which she had lost during the French Revolutionary Wars, but in exchange she received the northern Italian states of Lombardy and Venetia. To this was added the Tyrol from Bavaria and Illyria and Dalmatia on the eastern coast of the Adriatic.

Britain had no desire to acquire territory on the European continent. In satisfaction of her naval and maritime requirements she received Malta, the Ionian Islands in the Adriatic Sea, Heligoland in the North Sea, Cape Colony, and Ceylon.

Russia was to retain Finland, which she had seized from Sweden in 1808, together with the province of Bessarabia, which she had wrested from Turkey in the war of 1806–12. Sweden would in turn be compensated with Norway, itself taken from France's ally, Denmark. Most importantly, Russia received from Prussia most of her Polish provinces which she combined with her own to form a new Kingdom of Poland, with the Tsar at its head. It would not re-emerge as an independent state again until after the First World War.

Prussia, as noted above, gave up most of the territories she had taken from Poland during the partitions of 1772, 1793, and 1795. In exchange she received substantial compensation in the form of the Kingdom of Westphalia, Swedish Pomerania, most of the newly reconstituted Rhineland, and, above all, about 40 percent of the Kingdom of Saxony.

None of the Great Powers could be said to be completely contented with these arrangements, but by and large they were satisfied with the compromise.

Finally, the victorious Great Powers would make provision for the maintenance of peace in Europe. Two methods would be implemented to achieve this. First, France was to be ringed with buffer states forming a barrier between herself and her neighbors. To the north, as it was well recognized that Belgium could not defend herself unaided, she was amalgamated with Holland to produce a larger, more powerful state. In the south-east, Piedmont was augmented with Nice and Genoa in order to bolster the frontier with Italy. On France's eastern frontiers, Switzerland, known as the Swiss Confederation, was enlarged to 22 cantons, while the Rhineland became a Prussian possession.

Maintaining peace in Europe depended to a great extent on the balance of power. It was not sufficient to erect barriers to prevent France from committing future aggression without ensuring that the other Great Powers were themselves generally satisfied with the gains they themselves received. The fact remained that another state could threaten peace in the future, particularly Russia, who now possessed the greatest army in Europe. As Russia's acquisition of extensive Polish territory had greatly increased her power and influence, a balance was struck which granted Prussia much of Saxony. The Tsar had promised Prussia the whole of Saxony, but grave objections from Austria had nearly led to war and a compromise was finally agreed. The crisis had in fact reached such a point of contention that Britain, France, and Austria had secretly arranged an alliance should hostilities ensue with Prussia and Russia.

Assessing the Vienna Settlement

The relative success of the Vienna Settlement may be gauged by the fact that no general European war broke out for another 40 years, a circumstance generally attributed to the fact that it left no significant grievances outstanding. However, it had its share of flaws. The extensive territorial adjustments made at Vienna took virtually no account of language, culture or nationality. Any national aspirations that the Belgians may have had had to be subordinated to the perceived reality that their tiny country could not stand alone against a resurgent France. That the Belgians spoke French and Flemish and were almost entirely Catholic did not overly concern the men tasked to redraw the map of Europe, who saw amalgamation with a Protestant Dutch-speaking Holland as the only option. Much the same principle applied in northern Italy, where French rule was for the most part replaced with Austrian rule. On the other hand, drastically reducing the number of states in order to create the new German Confederation paved the way for eventual unification – for good or ill. The settlement also stipulated that all the individual rulers were to establish constitutions – an important precedent on the path toward political liberalization.

If the war had been won through the cooperation of the Great Powers it seemed reasonable to attempt to maintain peace and stability through some sort of 'concert' in the postwar era. Each power had differing ideas of how this could be accomplished, and in the case of Metternich, Great Power cooperation could also serve to combat revolution wherever it might arise. What has become known as the 'Congress System' was embodied in three documents: the Quadruple Alliance, Article VI of the Second Treaty of Paris of November 1815, and the Act of the Holy Alliance issued by Tsar Alexander in May of the same year.

Castlereagh in particular recognized that safeguarding the settlement required some sort of permanent arrangement, particularly with regard to the government of France. By the terms of the Quadruple Alliance, Russia, Austria, Prussia, and Britain agreed to cooperate for the next 20 years to prevent the accession of a Bonaparte dynasty to the throne of France. Article VI of the Treaty of Paris stipulated that future congresses would be convened in order for the Great Powers to discuss important issues of mutual concern and where necessary to take action in order to preserve European peace and stability.

A document with rather vaguely defined aims, the Holy Alliance, was drawn up by Alexander under the influence of Baroness von Krudener, a German religious mystic. This pseudo-religious document was intended to draw the sovereigns of Europe together on a personal and religious basis, whereby leaders and their peoples were to work together as one Christian body. Its wording was sufficiently obscure that practically every ruler agreed to it, apart from the Pope, the Sultan, and the Prince Regent. If it did not serve much practical use it was at least a basis for cooperation between Russia, Austria, and Prussia.

As a result of the Vienna agreement, four international conferences were held between 1815 and 1822 to discuss issues of mutual concern, particularly the outbreak of revolutions in Europe and the ongoing independence movements in South America. The period of congress diplomacy was short-lived, as it soon became apparent that the powers could not reach a consensus on a number of major issues, but the foundation of congress diplomacy at Vienna provided Europe with peace until the outbreak of the Crimean War in 1854 – even then a conflict with limited objectives and confined to Russia, France, Britain, and Turkey.

The Napoleonic legacy

Having abdicated a second time, Napoleon was sent a captive to the remote South Atlantic island of St Helena, from where he never again emerged to threaten European peace, and died there in 1821. Yet his influence scarcely ended with his death, for, despite only a decade in power, his legacy was far-reaching, both within France and throughout Europe as a whole.

It is important to consider what precisely accounted for Napoleon's extraordinary achievements. It is not to exaggerate the point to say that he was a genius, possessed of immensely wide knowledge and extraordinary powers of memory, for issues great and small. Natural intelligence accounted for his meteoric rise from a mere captain of artillery one year to brigadier-general the next, at the age of 23. He was a major-general at 26, he seized political power five years later and became Emperor at 35. By the time he was 40 he controlled most of the Continent. Apart from his unparalleled understanding of military affairs, he possessed considerable knowledge of civil administration, law, education, and science, to the point where many Napoleonic reforms remain in place today. Few historical figures, like Napoleon, leave their name and achievements to posterity, but he even has an era named for him.

He effected important religious reforms through his famous concordat with the Pope; sweeping civil and administrative reforms within France and throughout large parts of the empire reined in the excesses of the Revolution and gave order to inefficiency. Internally, France had well-functioning departments, newly re-opened primary schools and colleges of higher education. An antiquated legal system, based on French and German feudal principles, along with over 10,000 decrees issued under the Revolution, had been abolished, replaced in their turn by a new system – the Code Napoléon, or Civil Code. He went far in furthering the process of Italian and German unification, particularly in the latter's case, where he consolidated hundreds of petty principalities, free and ecclesiastical cities into a more rational entity – the Confederation of the Rhine.

Napoleon viewed himself as a consolidator rather than a promoter of the Revolution, and as early as December 1799, when he became First Consul, his government declared: 'Citizens, the Revolution is stabilized on the principles which began it.' His formulation of the Civil Code was an exceptional innovation, but apart from that he largely confined himself to preserving the reforms of the Revolution, which had ended so many of the laws and institutions of the ancien régime. Politically, he preserved a limited form of manhood suffrage and a constitution. Economically, he maintained the system that had abolished internal customs. In education, he established a national system. He preserved the revolutionary principle of equality before the law, the form of its administration and the principle of meritocracy – careers open to talent. Nevertheless, he did not, like the various revolutionary governments, permit much freedom to representative institutions; after all, the empire represented an autocracy.

Napoleon's remarkable military qualities enabled him to export the principles of the Revolution, and he styled himself a 'soldier of the Revolution'. Reforms made in France during the Revolution, Consulate and Empire were duly introduced, or sometimes imposed, in conquered territories, such as Holland, where Louis Bonaparte introduced the Napoleonic Code at his brother's behest. The Code became ensconced as far east as the Duchy of Warsaw, where the liberal-minded Alexander saw fit to allow retention of its central precepts, including equality before the law, even after the war. In some places, like in reactionary Spain, political and social reforms introduced in the wake of French armies had virtually no impact, notwithstanding the short-lived constitution established by Spanish liberals, but elsewhere, such as in Italy, Napoleonic reforms had a widespread and lasting – sometimes profound – impact.

As the Revolution had abolished serfdom in France, so too did Napoleon in many parts of Europe, particularly in western and southern Germany, and in Italy. Even in Naples, the poorest and politically most backward of Italian states, the restored King Ferdinand did not replace the Civil Code or re-establish the feudal system. Reactionaries generally succeeded in re-establishing some form of royal authority, but they simply could not reverse the myriad social and economic changes that had taken place during an absence from power which in some cases extended back a decade or more.

Napoleon's political legacy in Germany was particularly great, but the form it took in Prussia was not his work. It was a prime example of how a vanquished state endeavored to reform itself as a result of defeat – in this case a comprehensive one. As has been shown, in Prussia men like Yorck,

Blücher, Scharnhorst, and Gneisenau utterly transformed not only the army, but society in general, to an extent that would lay the foundations of eventual German unification and the ascendancy of her army to the first rank on the Continent. The seeds of German nationalism were laid in the years 1807–15, and when wedded to militarism they would become a potent force that the French, invaded three times by Germany between 1870 and 1945, would bitterly regret.

Most of Napoleon's reforms were intended for the middle class, who benefited substantially from his regime. Legal rights were vastly extended, as were economic opportunities, and the stimulation to industry specifically raised the standard of living for millions of French citizens. The natural by-product of this was, of course, a growth in political consciousness and a desire for further political concessions whose full manifestations would emerge during the revolution of 1830. The bourgeoisie in many occupied or conquered lands often saw Napoleon as a positive force for change, politically as well as economically. The Civil Code provided equality across class lines, administrative reforms abolished feudalism and ancient proprietary rights, and the aristocracy's powers, notwithstanding the technical victory of monarchy, dwindled as those of the middle classes rose. To be sure, improved legal rights outside France did not always bring immediate benefits to the peasants, and there was no remarkable improvement in their standard of living, but new principles of equality implanted some opportunities for social advancement and

Longwood House, St Helena, the residence assigned to Napoleon. The approach was guarded by a company of infantry which established a ring of sentries at night. The governor of the island warned his sole captive that 'the orderly officer <u>must</u> see him daily, come what may, and may use any means he sees fit to surmount any obstacles or opposition … and that if the officer has not seen Napoleon by 10 o'clock in the morning he is to enter the hall and force his way to Napoleon's room.' (Philip Haythornthwaite)

laid the groundwork for future economic developments.

In the field of arts and culture, it was natural that Napoleon should regard Paris – as indeed did so many Europeans – as the cultural center of Europe. He justified the looting of European art treasures on a massive scale in order to establish the ascendancy of the Louvre as the preeminent repository of paintings and sculpture. While his methods were extreme, the vast collection he assembled remains intact and continues to be appreciated by millions yearly. Napoleon had a particular interest in architecture, and the buildings he commissioned, inspired like so much else at the time by classical forms, generally assumed impressive proportions and continue to be admired today.

In the realm of military affairs, Napoleon's reputed quip on St Helena, while not entirely accurate, has much to be said for it: 'I have fought sixty battles, and I have learned nothing which I did not know in the beginning.' How then can we assess his military legacy? This question alone accounts for countless volumes on the subject, but a few brief observations may be offered here.

Ironically, though he remained the central military figure for a generation, Napoleon did not emerge as a great military reformer, like Gustavus Adolphus or Frederick the Great, however much he may have inspired reforms in countries outside France. To the development of weapons and tactics he made some contributions, it is true, such as the use of massed artillery, but many of the changes that occurred had developed in the eighteenth century, particularly during the wars of the Revolution – such as the growth of mass armies.

Nevertheless, Napoleon rightly holds a place among the pantheon of great military commanders and it is important to understand both why this is so and why, notwithstanding this fact, he ultimately failed. First, Napoleon was extremely industrious – a key element in a successful commander. Marshal Marmont noted that:

Whenever the moves of his headquarters allowed it, he went to bed at six or seven o'clock in the evening, and got up again at midnight or one o'clock. In this way he was ready to read reports as they came in and to give out his orders accordingly.

He was assiduous in keeping abreast of his enemies' movements and dispositions, and knowing the composition of his own forces. He placed great importance on accurate maps. During the 1813 campaign a Saxon officer serving as a topographical adviser on Napoleon's staff, noted that General Caulaincourt accompanied Napoleon everywhere with 'the necessary map fastened to his chest, because he always rode next to Napoleon so as to be able to hand it to him when he said, 'La carte …'' He was also a brilliant organizer, and it was a testament to Napoleon's genius and efficiency that he, supported of course by a nation nourished by past victories, was able to rebuild his armies twice in 1813 and again in 1814.

It must be stressed that he enjoyed the advantage of having inherited from the Revolution massive armies of men well motivated by the freedoms provided by

merit. Capitalizing on this, Napoleon possessed the extraordinary ability to manage armies of hitherto unheard-of size – exceeding at times 200,000 men – and to move them across vast distances at rates never before conceived or achieved. Once his army reached the theater of campaign, Napoleon showed a masterful ability to maneuver this great mass of men, horses, and ordnance into a position from which he could exploit his enemies' generally consistent failure to concentrate their forces. In so doing, he could oppose and destroy forces in turn, or divide them if they had already combined. With respect to his own forces, he understood the vital importance of achieving – at the critical time – a local superiority of force and so wielding it to decisive advantage on such battlefields as Austerlitz and Jena. Even as late as the Waterloo campaign this strategy lay at the heart of his genius.

Yet where Napoleon failed to implement this strategy, or where his enemies denied him the opportunity to do so, he failed. Despite employing the largest army in history for the Russian campaign, Napoleon failed in part because he simply could not exercise the degree of personal control over his massive forces that was necessary for military success – much less to maintain political control over France. He failed to appreciate that the sheer size of his forces, combined with the primitive state of communications and agriculture in the area of operations, could not supply his vast needs, or enable him either to execute rapid marches or live off the land. Finally, the Russians, though they stood to oppose the French at Borodino, withdrew beyond the reach of the Grande Armée. To win, Napoleon needed to inflict a decisive blow on the opposing army. Alexander, however, denied him this satisfaction: he not only declined to fight, but went so far as to yield ground, including his capital, all territory that Napoleon could not ultimately retain. Through indecision and the mistaken belief that the Russians would come to terms, he postponed the retreat from Moscow until it

338   The Napoleonic Wars

was too late to avoid the coming winter. In a greater geostrategic sense, he made the fatal mistakes later to be repeated by Hitler: leaving an undefeated enemy in his rear (Britain in the Peninsula) while trying to defeat a new opponent whose country was so vast and whose weather was so forbidding, as to swallow up even massive armies unprepared for winter conditions.

If Napoleon's personal form of leadership – his insistence on handling substantial bodies of troops largely on his own – often led to victory, it nevertheless served him ill where he could not be present to manage affairs. In planning and conducting a campaign largely by himself, he underlined his lack of confidence in his subordinates, the consequence of which was that he formulated no permanent staff system and

therefore left no legacy on which to build one. This, instead, was taken up by the Prussians, who with their development of a permanent staff organization were ultimately to replace the French later in the century as the Continent's premier power.

In the end, excessive ambition and territorial overextension robbed Napoleon of permanent rule, both over Europe, as well as over France herself. Yet his legacy – the product of a mere decade in power – remains profound and enduring even today. Tens of thousands of books have been devoted to the Emperor's life and campaigns, and there is perhaps no greater testament to his enduring fascination than that this ever expanding body of literature continues to inspire and inform new generations of soldiers and civilians alike.

Further reading and bibliography

Alexander, Don, *Rod of Iron: French Counterinsurgency Policy in Aragon during the Peninsular War* (Wilmington, Del., Scholarly Resources, 1985).

Arnold, James, *Crisis on the Danube: Napoleon's Austrian Campaign of 1809* (Paragon House, 1990).

Bond, Gordon, *The Great Expedition*

Boutflower, Charles, *The Journal of an Army Surgeon during the Peninsular War* (New York, De Capo Press, 1997).

Bowden, Scott, *Armies on the Danube 1809* (Emperor's Press, 1989).

Bowden, Scott, *The Glory Years: Napoleon and Austerlitz* (Emperor's Press, 1997).

Brett-James, Anthony, *Life in Wellington's Army* (London, Allen and Unwin, 1972).

Bragge, William, *Peninsular Portrait, 1811–1814: The Letters of Capt. W. Bragge, Third (King's Own) Dragoons*, ed., S. A. Cassels (London, Oxford University Press, 1963).

Chalfont, Lord, ed., *Waterloo: Battle of Three Armies* (New York, Alfred Knopf, 1980).

Chandler, David, *The Campaigns of Napoleon* (London, Macmillan, 1966).

Chartrand, René, *Bussaco 1810* (Oxford, Osprey Publishing, 2001).

– *Vimeiro 1808* (Oxford, Osprey Publishing, 2001).

Chlapowski, Dezydery, *Memoirs of A Polish Lancer* (Emperor's Press, 1992).

Clausewitz, Carl von, *The Campaign of 1812 in Russia* (Greenhill Books, 1992).

Costello, Edward, *Adventures of a Soldier: The Peninsular and Waterloo Campaigns*, ed., Antony Brett-James (London, Longmans, 1967).

Dallas, Gregor, *The Final Act: The Roads to Waterloo* (New York, Henry Holt, 1996).

Davies, David, *Sir John Moore's Peninsular Campaign, 1808–1809* (The Hague, M. Nijhoff, 1974).

Delderfield, R. F., *Imperial Sunset: The Fall of Napoleon, 1813–14* (New York, Stein and Day, 1980).

Duffy, Christopher, *Austerlitz 1805* (Cassell, London, 1999).

Duffy, Christopher, *Borodino* (Cassell & Co., 1999).

Elting, J. R., *Swords Around a Throne: Napoleon's Grande Armée* (London, Weidenfeld & Nicolson, 1988).

Epstein, Robert, *Prince Eugene at War* (Empire Press, 1984)

Epstein, Robert M., *Napoleon's Last Victory and the Emergence of Modern War* (University Press of Kansas, 1994).

Esdaile, Charles, *The Spanish Army in the Peninsular War* (Manchester, Manchester University Press, 1988).

– *The Duke of Wellington and the Command of the Spanish Army, 1812–14* (Houndmills, Basingstoke, Hampshire, Macmillan, 1990).

Esposito, Vincent J., and Elting, John R., *Military History & Atlas of the Napoleonic Wars* (Greenhill Books, 1999).

Fletcher, Ian, et. al., *Aspects of the Struggle for the Iberian Peninsula* (Staplehurst, Kent, Spellmount Publishing, 1998).

Fletcher, Ian, *Badajoz 1812* (Oxford, Osprey Publishing, 1999).

– *Bloody Albuera: The 1811 Campaign in the Peninsula* (Crowood Press, 2001).

– *Galloping at Everything: The British Cavalry in the Peninsular War and at Waterloo, 1808–15* (Staplehurst, Kent, Spellmount Publishing, 2001).

– *Salamanca 1812* (Oxford, Osprey Publishing, 1997).

– *Vittoria 1813* (Oxford, Osprey Publishing, 1998).

Fletcher, Ian, ed., *Voices from the Peninsula: Eyewitness Accounts by Soldiers of Wellington's Army, 1808–1814* (London, Greenhill Books, 2001).

Fortescue, Sir John, *History of the British Army*, 13 vols. (London, Macmillan, 1910–1930).

Gates, David, *The Spanish Ulcer: A History of the Peninsular War* (London, W. W. Norton & Co., 1986; repr. 2001).

Gill, John H., *With Eagles to Glory: Napoleon and his German Allies in the 1809 Campaign* (Greenhill Books, 1992)

Glover, Michael, *Legacy of Glory: The Bonaparte Kingdom of Spain* (New York, Charles Scribner, 1971).

– *The Peninsular War, 1807–14: A Concise Military History* (Newton Abbot, David & Charles, 1974).

– *Wellington's Army in the Peninsula, 1808–1814* (New York, Hippocrene Books, 1977).

– *Wellington as Military Commander* (London, Batsford, 1968).

– *Wellington's Peninsular Victories* (London, Batsford,1963).

Grehan, John, *The Lines of Torres Vedras: The Cornerstone of Wellington's Strategy in the Peninsular War, 1809–1812* (Staplehurst, Spellmount Press, 2000).

Griffith, Paddy, ed., *A History of the Peninsular War: Modern Studies of the War in Spain and Portugal, 1808–1814* (London, Greenhill Books, 1999).

Griffith, Paddy, *Wellington Commander* (Chichester, Sussex, Anthony Bird, 1985).

Guedalla, Philip, *The Duke* (London, Hodder & Stoughton,1931).

Hamilton-Williams, David, *The Fall of Napoleon: The Final Betrayal* (London, Arms and Armour Press, 1994).

Harris, John, *Recollections of Rifleman Harris* (London, 1848.; repr. Hamden,Conn, Archon Books, 1970).

Haythornthwaite, Philip, *The Napoleonic Sourcebook* (London, Arms and Armour Press, 1990).

Haythornthwaite, Philip, *The Armies of Wellington* (London, Arms and Armour Press, 1994).

– *Corunna 1809* (Oxford, Osprey Publishing, 2001).

– *Uniforms of the Peninsular War* (Blandford Press, Poole, Dorset, 1978).

Henderson, E. F., *Blucher and the Uprising against Napoleon* (New York, G. P. Putnam's Sons, 1911).

Hibbert, Christopher, *Corunna* (New York, Macmillan, 1961).

Hofschröer, Peter, *Leipzig 1813* (Oxford, Osprey Publishing, 1993, repr. 2000).

— *Lützen and Bautzen 1813* (Oxford, Osprey Publishing, 2001).

Hourtoulle, F.-G., *Jena, Auerstadt, the Triumph of the Eagle*

Howarth, David, *Waterloo: Day of Battle* (New York, Athaneum, 1968).

Humble, Richard, *Napoleon's Peninsular Marshals*, London, Purcell Book Services, 1973.

Jones, Proctor Patterson, *Napoleon: An Intimate Account of the Years of Supremacy:1800–1814*, Random House, USA, 1992

Josselson, Michael, *The Commander: A Life of Barclay de Tolly*, Oxford University Press, 1980

Lachouque, Henri, Tranié, Jean and Carmigniani, J-C., *Napoleon's War in Spain* (London, Arms and Armour Press, 1982).

Larpent, F. Seymour, *Private Journal of F. Seymour Larpent, Judge-AdvocateGeneral* (London, R. Bentley, 1853; repr. 2001).

Lawford, James, *Napoleon: The Last Campaigns, 1813–15* (New York, Crown Publishers, 1977).

Longford, Elizabeth, *Wellington: The Years of the Sword* (New York, Harper & Row, 1969; repr. 1985).

Lovett, Gabriel, *Napoleon and the Birth of Modern Spain*, 2 vols (New York, NYU Press, 1965).

Mercer, Cavalié, *Journal of the Waterloo Campaign* (London, Blackwood, 1870, repr. New York, Da Capo Press, 1995).

Murray, Venetia, *High Society in the Regency Period, 1788–1830* (London, Penguin, 1998).

Myatt, Frederick, *British Sieges in the Peninsular War* (Tunbridge Wells, Spellmount Press, 1987).

Oman, Sir Charles, *A History of the Peninsular War*, 7 vols. (Oxford, Oxford University Press, 1902–30; repr. 1996).

Nafziger, George, *Lützen and Bautzen: Napoleon's Spring Campaign of 1813* (Chicago, 1992).

— *Napoleon at Dresden: The Battles of August 1813* (Rosemont, IL, Emperor's Headquarters, 1991).

— *Napoleon at Leipzig: The Battle of the Nations 1813* (Rosemont, IL, Emperor's Headquarters, 1997).

Nafziger, George, *Napoleon's Invasion of Russia* (Presidio Press, 1988)

Napier, William, *A History of the War in the Peninsula and the South of France, 1807–1814*, 6 vols. (London, T & W Boone, 1832–40; repr. 1993).

Nicholson, Harold, *The Congress of Vienna: A Study in Allied Unity, 1812–1822* (London, Constable, 1948, repr. New York, Harvest Books, 1974).

Paget, Julian, *Wellington's Peninsular War* (London, Leo Cooper, 1990).

Parkinson, Roger, *The Peninsular War* (London, Granada, 1973; repr. 2000).

Palmer, Alan, *Napoleon in Russia: The 1812 Campaign* (Simon & Schuster, 1967)

Palmer, Alan, *Metternich* (New York, Harper & Row, 1972).

Paret, Peter, *Yorck and the Era of Prussian Reform* (Princeton, Princeton University Press, 1966).

Pelet, Jean Jacques, *The French Campaign in Portugal, 1810–1811: An Account*, ed. and trans., Donald Horward (Minneapolis, University of Minnesota Press, 1973).

Petre, F. Lorraine, *Napoleon and the Archduke Charles* (Greenhill Books, 1991)

Petre, F. Loraine, *Napoleon's Conquest of Prussia 1806* (Greenhill Books, 1993)

Petre, F. Loraine, *Napoleon's Campaign in Poland 1806-1807* (Greenhill Books, forthcoming)

Petre, F. Loraine, *Napoleon at Bay, 1814* (London, John Lane, 1914, repr. London, Arms & Armour Press, 1977).

— *Napoleon's Last Campaign in Germany, 1813* (London, John Lane, 1912, repr. London, Arms & Armour Press, 1977).

Rathbone, Julian, *Wellington's War: Peninsular Dispatches presented by Julian Rathbone* (London, Michael Joseph, 1984).

Rudorff, R., *War to the Death: the Sieges of Saragossa* (London, Hamish Hamilton, 1974).

Schaumann, A. L. F., *On the Road with Wellington: The Diary of a War Commissary* (London, Greenhill Books, 1999).

Shanahan, W. O., *Prussian Military Reforms, 1786–1813* (New York, Columbia University Press, 1945).

Simmons, George, *A British Rifleman: The Journals and Correspondence of Major George Simmons, Rifle Brigade* (London, A & C Black, 1899).

Smith, Digby, *1813 Leipzig: Napoleon and the Battle of the Nations* (London, Greenhill Publishing, 2001).

Suchet, Louis-Gabriel, *Memoirs of the War in Spain* (London, H. Colburn, 1829).

Thiers, Louis, *A History of the Consulate and Empire under Napoleon*

Tomkinson, Lt.-Col. William, *The Diary of a Cavalry Officer in the Peninsular and Waterloo Campaigns, 1809–1815* (London, S. Sonnenschein & Co, 1894; repr. 2000).

Tone, John, *The Fatal Knot: The Guerrilla War in Navarre and the Defeat of Napoleon in Spain* (Chapel Hill, University of North Carolina Press, 1994).

Vachee, Colonel, *Napoleon at Work*

von Brandt, Heinrich, *In the Legions of Napoleon: The Memoirs of a Polish Officer in Spain and Russia, 1808–1813, trans. and ed., Jonathan North* (London, Greenhill Books, 1999).

Walter, Jakob, (trans. Marc Raiff), *The Diary of a Napoleonic Foot Soldier* (Doubleday, 1991)

Weller, Jac, *Wellington in the Peninsula* (London, N. Vane, 1962, repr. 1992).

Wheatley, Edmund, *The Wheatley Diary, ed., Christopher Hibbert* (London, Longmans, 1964).

Wheeler, W., *The Letters of Private Wheeler, 1809–28*, ed., B. H. Liddell-Hart (Boston, Houghton Mifflin, 1951).

Webster, Sir Charles, *The Congress of Vienna, 1814–1815* (New York, Barnes & Noble, 1963).

Webster, Sir Charles, *The Foreign Policy of Castlereagh, 1812–1815: Britain and the Reconstruction of Europe* (London, G. Bell and Sons, 1931).

Wellington, Duke of, *Supplementary Dispatches and Memoranda*, 15 vols., ed., his son, (London, John Murray, 1858-72).

–Dispatches of Field Marshal the Duke of Wellington, ed., Col. J. Gurwood, 8 vols. (London, Parker, Furnivall & Parker, 1844; repr. Millwood NY, Kraus Reprint Co., 1973).

Wooten, Geoffrey, *Waterloo 1815* (Oxford, Osprey Publishing, 1999)

Index

References to illustrations are shown in **bold**.